The
Guitar
& rock equipment

The Guitar

& rock equipment

Nick Freeth

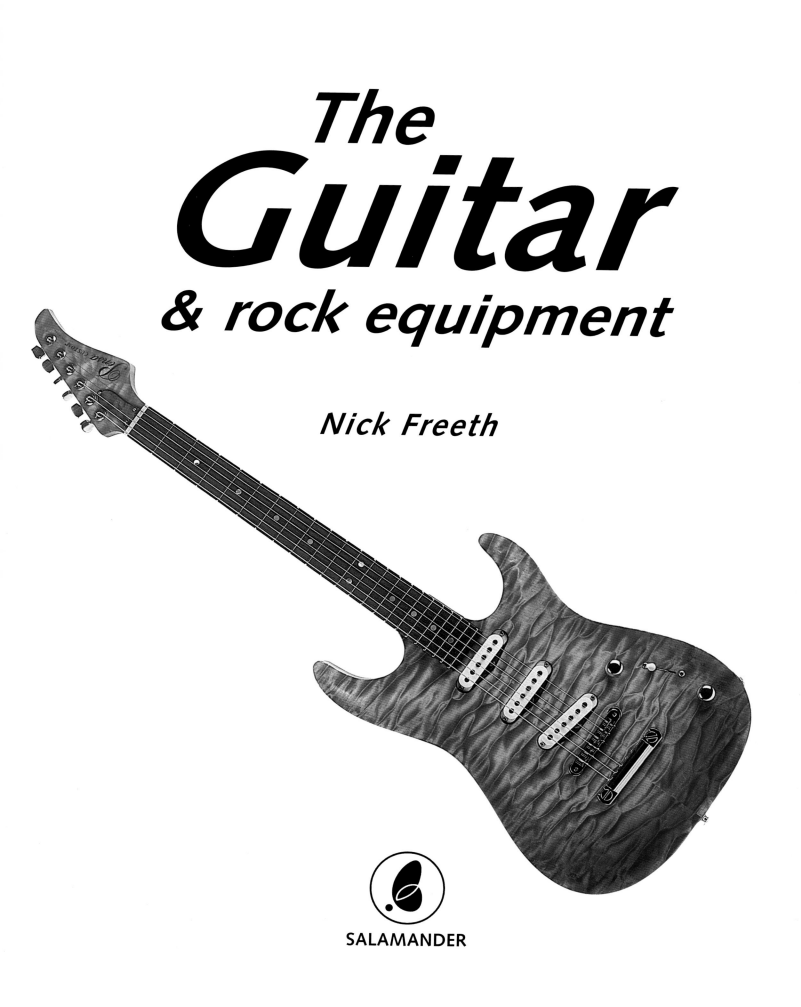

SALAMANDER

A SALAMANDER BOOK

Published by Salamander Books Limited
8 Blenheim Court, Brewery Road, London N7 9NY

A member of **Chrysalis** Books plc

9 8 7 6 5 4 3 2 1

ISBN 1 84065 395 7

CREDITS

Editorial Directors: Charlotte Davies, Will Steeds
Editor: Phil Hunt
Designers: Heather Moore, John Heritage, Cara Hamilton
Production: Phillip Chamberlain
Indexer: Chris Bernstein
Reproduction: Media Print (UK) Ltd.

Printed in China

ACKNOWLEDGEMENTS

The author would like to express his gratitude the many luthiers, dealers, collectors and musicians who allowed their instruments and equipment to be included in this book. Especial thanks to the manager of the Acoustic Centre and Bass Centre in Wapping, London; Tom Anfield; Jez Ayscough of John Henry's, London; Max Brittain; Mitch Dalton; the manager of Guitar Village, Farnham; Martin Taylor and Mike Vanden, who gave permission for us to photograph their guitars and amplifiers.

The quotation from Chet Atkins on page 23 is taken from *The Gretsch Book* by Tony Bacon & Paul Day (© 1996 Tony Bacon & Paul Day), and is reproduced by kind permission of the copyright holders, and the publishers, Balafon Books.

The quotations from Hank Garland on page 24 are taken from his interview in the January 1981 issue of *Guitar Player* magazine (© 1981 Guitar Player), and are reproduced by kind permission of the copyright holder.

The quotations on pages 67 and 70 are taken from Richard R. Smith's book *Fender: The Sound Heard 'Round The World* (© 1995 Richard R. Smith), and are reproduced by kind permission of the copyright holder, and the publishers, Garfish Publishing Co.

The quotation from Ted McCarty on page 85 is taken from *The Gibson* (© 1996 Rittor Music Europe Ltd./International Music Publications Ltd.) and is reproduced by kind permission of the copyright holders and publishers.

The quotation from George Fullerton on page 98 is taken from his interview with Willie G. Moseley in the October, November and December 1991 issues of *Vintage Guitar* magazine, as reprinted in *Stellas & Stratocasters* by Willie G. Moseley (© 1994 Willie G. Moseley), and is reproduced by kind permission of the copyright holder, and the publishers, Vintage Guitar Books.

The quotation from Robert Lane on page 108 is taken from his website, www.jacksoncharvelworld.com, and is reproduced by his kind permission.

The quotation from Geoff Lawson on page 174 is taken from an interview with *Guitarist* magazine, and is reproduced by kind permission of the copyright holder.

The 1890 guitar patent, displayed and described on pages 310-11 and preserved in the Rickenbacker archives, was drawn to the author's attention by Mr. John C. Hall, Chairman & CEO of Rickenbacker International Corporation.

The quotation from Jim Marshall on pages 326-7 is taken from an interview with *Vintage Guitar* magazine, and is reproduced by kind permission of the copyright holder.

CONTENTS

THE GUITARS

Guitars first appeared in sixteenth-century Spain, soon spread throughout Europe, and eventually made their way to the New World, where they were in widespread use by the mid-1700s. The next century saw the emergence of larger, louder instruments; by the early 1900s, the modern, steel-strung acoustic was taking shape, and several of today's most famous lutherie companies, including Martin and Gibson, were already established. These firms were crucial to the subsequent, rapid development of the guitar, and some of their most famous and successful acoustic and electric designs are featured on the following pages – alongside the work of later innovators like Rickenbacker and Fender, and guitars by a range of other leading craftsmen from the USA and beyond.

Introduction

Orville Gibson (1856–1918), who set up the company that bears his name in 1902, was one of the first luthiers to build large-bodied guitars with carved, arched tops and steel strings. These features gave his instruments a uniquely rich, powerful tone, and after his death, Gibson staffer Lloyd Loar took the archtop concept to new heights with the L-5 acoustic (1922), which boasted violin-style f-holes. A series of similar models followed, and most of the company's early electric guitars – produced in the 1930s – were essentially acoustic archtops with added pickups, rather than radically new designs.

After an enforced shutdown during the War years, Gibson resumed instrument production in 1946. However, there were important differences in the postwar specifications of some of its classic models. Guitars such as the groundbreaking ES-150 (closely associated with pioneering jazzman Charlie Christian) had originally been made from solid, premium quality

LEFT: *1940 Gibson ES-300. (courtesy Elderly Instruments: photo by Dave Matchette)*

RIGHT: *1937 Gibson ES-150. (courtesy Lloyd Chiate, Voltage Guitars, Hollywood)*

tonewoods, just like their acoustic cousins; but after 1946, this and other models were built using laminated timbers, and their tops were no longer carved, but pressed into shape. There were a number of reasons for these changes: carving instrument tops was slow and labor-intensive; guitar-making materials were scarcer and more expensive than they had been before the War; and, significantly, some designers had come to the conclusion that solid wood was not necessary for a good electric sound. Gibson went on to use laminates for the majority of its subsequent archtop designs.

Among other postwar innovations was a new Gibson pickup (the P-90); this was fitted to the ES-150 and also to the company's latest models – including the ES-175, which was to become the company's longest surviving and bestselling archtop, and is profiled on the next two pages.

Gibson ES-175

Gibson's ES-175 – the ES ("Electric Spanish") prefix was used to differentiate between standard and "Electric Hawaiian" (EH) guitars – made its debut in Fall 1949. It took its name from its retail price ($175), and was conceived as a midrange, workhorse jazz guitar. Built with plywoods (a laminated spruce top and laminated maple back and sides), it boasted few of the rich inlays and other decorations found on Gibson's more expensive archtops. Nevertheless, traditionally minded players immediately felt at home with its deep body and elegant curves, although the sharp "Florentine" cutaway was still a novelty; the company had produced its first-ever electric cutaway model, the ES-350P, only two years previously. Fitted with a single P-90 pickup in the neck position (later replaced by a humbucker), the 175 produced a rich, warm sound that quickly endeared it to leading jazz guitarists such as Kenny Burrell, Herb Ellis, and Joe Pass.

LEFT: *1961 Gibson ES-175D. (courtesy Guitar Showcase, San Jose)*

RIGHT: *1995 Gibson ES-175. (courtesy Mitch Dalton)*

Thanks in part to these players' endorsements, the ES-175 became a bestseller, and although it has undergone a number of significant changes over the years, it has remained in continuous production since it was introduced. Our main photograph shows a 1979 version of the 1949 design, with its simple trapeze-style tailpiece, and a single "Charlie Christian" pickup in place of the original P-90. Its owner, leading British session musician Mitch Dalton, uses it primarily for big-band work, and has fitted it with tape-wound strings, which further enhance its naturally mellow tone. In 1953, Gibson launched the double-pickup ES-175D; and three years later, the guitar was given a new "zigzag" tailpiece – as seen on the other model illustrated here. This also boasts humbucking pickups, which were introduced on the 175 in 1957. In its newer form, the guitar was to become popular not only with jazzmen, but pop and rock musicians: its famous users include Steve Howe of Yes, The Edge of U2, and Mark Knopfler.

The Gibson ES-5 and L5CES

The ES-175 was not the only Gibson archtop unveiled in 1949. The same year, the company introduced its ES-5 model, a "supreme electronic" version of its classic L-5 acoustic, fitted with no fewer than three P-90 pickups. The ES-5 was clearly intended as a true electric guitar, not an acoustic with pickups: mounting a trio of bulky transducers onto its laminated top did no favors for its "unplugged" tone, but certainly provided a remarkable range of amplified sounds. And, as each pickup had its own individual volume knob, there was almost no limit to the subtle gradations of timbre that could be obtained. Gibson's publicity proclaimed the ES-5 an "instrument of a thousand voices," although some musicians found the lack of straightforward pickup selector controls inconvenient for onstage work. The designers responded to these concerns six years later with the ES-5 Switchmaster, which included a four-way selector switch.

LEFT: *Gibson ES-5. (courtesy Mark Knopfler)*

RIGHT: *1961 Gibson L5-CES. (courtesy Lloyd Chiate, Voltage Guitars, Hollywood)*

For lovers of the L-5 who required less elaborate electronics, Gibson produced the L-5CES (the C stands for "cutaway" – the rounded type found on the L-5CES and ES-5 is in what Gibson call their "Venetian" style) in 1951. This guitar, one of the two "flagships" of the Electric Spanish range (together with the Super 400CES – see overleaf) was among the few postwar Gibson electric archtops to retain a carved, solid spruce top; its back and sides were maple, and it also boasted an ebony fingerboard with mother-of-pearl inlays, as well as a gold-plated tailpiece. When the instrument first appeared, it was fitted with two P-90 pickups. They were later replaced by new, higher-performance Alnico V units (their name comes from the constituent materials of their magnets: aluminum, nickel, and cobalt); these can be seen on the instrument here, which dates from 1961. The L-5CES has had many devotees among famous jazzmen, among them Wes Montgomery, Oscar Moore (guitarist with the Nat King Cole Trio), and Mundell Lowe.

Gibson Super 400CES

The Super 400 acoustic had been a landmark model for Gibson when it appeared in 1934. At $400, it was the most expensive guitar the company had ever produced, and it received an appropriately opulent finish, including gold-plated tuning machines and fine pearl inlays. It was also the largest archtop of its time, with a lower body width of 18 inches (45.7cm) subsequently exceeded only by the Epiphone Emperor (see next two pages) and Elmer Stromberg's 19-inch (48.3-cm) Master 400. In 1951, Gibson launched the Super 400CES, a cutaway, amplified version of its prewar classic, designed (as the company's publicity put it) to offer "the tonal quality of an acoustic guitar with the advantages of an electric instrument." Like the L-5CES, which was introduced at the same time, it had a solid wood, hand-carved body; and, with a retail price of $470, it once again became the highest-priced guitar in Gibson's catalog.

LEFT: *1961 Gibson Super 400CES. (courtesy Lloyd Chiate, Voltage Guitars, Hollywood)*

RIGHT: *1953 Gibson Super 400CES. (courtesy Mark Knopfler)*

In common with most other Gibson electrics of this period, the Super 400CES was originally given P-90 pickups. However, by 1953, when the instrument in our main photograph was made, these were being replaced with Alnico V transducers, and in 1958, the Super 400 acquired humbucking pickups. These can be seen on the other guitar shown here, which dates from 1961, and also features a sharper, "Florentine" cutaway.

Like its famous acoustic predecessor, the Super 400CES is associated with a string of distinguished musicians. Elvis Presley's original guitarist, Scotty Moore, frequently used a 400, and other great names who performed with it include country music instrumentalist, songwriter, and singer Merle Travis (who had several customized 400s specially made for him), in addition to jazzmen George Benson, Kenny Burrell and Larry Coryell.

The Epiphone Emperor

While Gibson was undoubtedly the market leader in archtop guitar production, it had a number of important rivals. The most significant of these was Epiphone, which began making guitars in the 1930s under the leadership of Epaminondas ("Epi") Stathopoulo, son of the business's Greek founder, Anastasios. Epiphone constantly sought to outdo Gibson's archtop innovations: it challenged the dominant position of the L-5 with the launch of its "Masterbilt" range in 1931. When Gibson increased the body sizes on its guitars, Epiphone made its products a little larger still, and the company's flagship instrument, the Emperor (1936), was conceived as a direct rival to its Gibson counterpart, the Super 400. In 1952, Epiphone produced an electric cutaway version of the Emperor, fitted with three pickups – a fine instrument that sadly failed to halt the financial difficulties that the firm had been suffering since the 1940s. These eventually led to its takeover by Gibson in 1957.

LEFT: *1961 Epiphone Emperor. (courtesy Lloyd Chiate, Voltage Guitars, Hollywood)*

RIGHT: *1941 Epiphone Emperor. (courtesy Chandler Guitars, Kew)*

After acquiring its old competitor, Gibson made a number of changes to the Emperor's specifications. The original model had been a full-depth, carved top instrument constructed from solid maple. However, the Emperors made at the Gibson factory in Kalamazoo, Michigan, from 1958 onwards had much thinner bodies. And, by 1961 (when the electric Emperor shown here was produced) the Epiphone "New York"-style pickups had been replaced by smaller humbucking transducers designed by Gibson's Seth Lover, and also used on several other "Gibson-Epiphones." The Emperor retained its distinctive "wandering vine"-decorated headstock and 1930s-style double-trapeze "Frequensator" bridge, which was designed to "equalize" treble and bass response by shortening the top three strings' path from bridge to tailpiece (though it is doubtful whether this made much difference to the sound). By the mid-1960s, the Emperor was only available to special order. It was discontinued in 1969, shortly before manufacture of the entire Epiphone range was switched from the USA to the Far East.

Gretsch

Like Epiphone, Gretsch was founded by European émigrés in the nineteenth century. Friedrich Gretsch came to New York from Mannheim, Germany, in 1872, and established a flourishing drum- and banjo-manufacturing business in his new home. After his early death in 1895, the company was taken over by his son, Fred Sr., who later branched out into lutherie. In the 1930s Gretsch began producing acoustic archtop and flat-top guitars, and the firm's first amplified model, the "Electromatic Spanish" guitar, appeared in 1940. By the early 1950s, Gretsch (now run by Fred Jr., Friedrich's grandson) had introduced a number of other well-received, if rather conservative-looking electric archtops. Fred Jr., like other influential music industry figures, was skeptical to the point of derision about some of the more radical developments in instrument design; when Gibson introduced its solid-bodied Les Paul, he complained that "[now] anybody with a band-saw and a router can make a guitar."

LEFT & INSET: *1966 Gretsch White Falcon. (courtesy Lloyd Chiate, Voltage Guitars, Hollywood)*

RIGHT: *1961 Gretsch Double Anniversary. (courtesy San Diego Guitars)*

Despite this reaction, market forces soon obliged Gretsch to take a bolder, more contemporary approach to guitar design – and the company quickly developed a flair for colorful finishes and extra gadgetry. This altered outlook was manifested on Gretsch's top-of-the-line White Falcon model, which made its first appearance in 1955. An unashamedly ostentatious guitar, with a retail price of $600, it boasted gold sparkle decoration, gold-plated metalwork, and bird-and-feather engravings on its pickguard and fingerboard position markers. Its later versions incorporated stereo circuitry and an ingenious mechanical string "muffler" mounted between the back pickup and the bridge.

In 1958, Gretsch celebrated 75 years of instrument-making by launching a pair of new electric archtops, the Anniversary (single pickup) and the twin pickup Double Anniversary, both fitted with the company's new "Filter'Tron" humbuckers. At under $200 each, they were comparatively inexpensive guitars, but are now desirable collectors' items.

Gretsch and Chet Atkins

In 1954, Gretsch signed an endorsement deal with star Nashville guitarist Chet Atkins (1924–2001), a top session musician with a high profile thanks to his solo work and TV appearances, who was later to become Chief of RCA's Country Division. By the mid-1950s he had already played on, arranged, and produced a string of hit records.

The earliest versions of the first Gretsch Chet Atkins guitar, the 6120, were not entirely to the endorsee's liking. As he explained in The Gretsch Book *by Tony Bacon and Paul Day: "The [pickup] magnets pulled so strong on the strings that there was no sustain there, especially in the bass." Nevertheless, he started using the new model for recordings and live work; it carried his signature on the pickguard, and, as he acknowledged to Bacon and Day, "I was thrilled to have my name on a guitar like Les Paul had his name on a Gibson."*

LEFT: *1959 Gretsch Chet Atkins hollow-body. (courtesy Guitar Showcase, San Jose)*

RIGHT: *1965 Gretsch Chet Atkins Country Gentleman. (courtesy Lloyd Chiate, Voltage Guitars, Hollywood)*

Gretsch was equally happy to have a major star like Chet Atkins on board, and the company quickly acted on his comments and criticisms. The 6120's single-coil pickups were eventually replaced by "Filter'Tron" humbuckers, and changes were also made to its finish – which had originally incorporated a longhorn headstock logo and "Western" fret markers! Atkins' endorsement had an impressive effect on the instrument's sales, and in 1957 a second Chet Atkins guitar, the Country Gentleman, was launched. It had one highly unusual feature for an electric archtop: no soundholes. Atkins and Gretsch found that sealing the instrument's top helped to minimize acoustic feedback, and the f-holes on most models (including the one shown here) are simply painted on as a *trompe l'oeil* effect.

The Country Gentleman was followed a year later by a lower-price design, the Tennessean, which was originally fitted with a single pickup; all three instruments remained in production until the 1980s.

The First Gibson "Thinlines"

"What would you like in a guitar that we don't already have?" This intriguing question was posed by a Gibson staffer to Hank Garland and Billy Byrd, two of Nashville's leading 1950s session musicians, at a disc jockey convention held in Music City in 1955. During a later interview with Guitar Player *magazine, Garland recalled that he and Byrd "sat down [with the Gibson executive] and said we'd like an instrument like the L-5, but with a thin body and a bunch of other stuff. He wrote it all down on a piece of paper, and after he went back to... the Gibson factory, they made the guitar and sent us one."*

The model Garland and Byrd inspired, named the Byrdland in their honor, was announced only a few months after their first discussions with Gibson. It went on sale in 1955, and represented an important new direction for the company's archtop line.

LEFT: *1958 Gibson ES-350T. (courtesy Mark Knopfler)*

RIGHT: *1964 Gibson Byrdland. (courtesy Lloyd Chiate, Voltage Guitars, Hollywood)*

While it retained the L-5's carved spruce top and outline, the Byrdland's reduced depth – 2¼ inches (5.7cm) as opposed to the L-5 and Super 400's 3⅜ inches (8.6cm) – gave it a much less bulky feel, particularly for guitarists who preferred to play standing up. The original 1956 model had Alnico V pickups and a rounded "Venetian" cutaway. Two years later, the Alnicos were replaced by humbuckers, while the cutaway shape was changed to the sharper Florentine style in 1960.

The Byrdland was an immediate success, and has proved popular with a wide range of performers, from jazzman Barry Galbraith (with whom Hank Garland subsequently worked and studied in New York) to hard rocker Ted Nugent. Gibson's commitment to this new design was confirmed by the rapid introduction of another thinline, the ES-350T; based on the 1947 ES-350, but more than an inch (2.5cm) shallower than the original, it also sold well, remaining in the catalog until the 1980s.

Birth of the Gibson 335

Early "reduced depth" archtops like the Byrdland and ES-350T paved the way for an even more radical Gibson design: the ES-335 "semi-solid," introduced in 1958. While the 335 looked similar to its thinline predecessors, its smooth, laminated top concealed a number of internal innovations. The two outer sections of the guitar's body were hollow, but at its center was a strip of maple, with glued-in pieces of spruce above and below. These were cut to the shape of the instrument's top and back, sealing off its side chambers. Two humbucking pickups, a "Tune-O-Matic" bridge, and a "stud" or "stop" tailpiece were all mounted on this central section. Their positioning contributed to the 335's highly distinctive sound, which was modified and enriched by the arched top and the side cavities, but had almost as much sustain and freedom from feedback as a solid-bodied instrument's.

LEFT: *1959 Gibson ES-335TD.* (courtesy Real Guitars, San Francisco)

RIGHT: *1958 Gibson ES-335TD.* (courtesy Mark Knopfler)

The 335 was a major landmark in electric guitar technology. Its innovative body design was complemented by a slim, comfortable neck with unrivaled access to the top of the scale; all 22 frets could be reached with ease, and the action was as fast and light as a Les Paul's. At a basic price of $267.50 for a sunburst model (natural finish 335s were $15 more), it quickly became a bestseller, and has subsequently been used by a host of leading names in jazz, blues, and rock, including Lee Ritenour, John Scofield, Hubert Sumlin (guitarist with Howlin' Wolf), Bob Weir of the Grateful Dead, and Johnny Marr.

Although it has been in continuous production since 1958, many musicians and collectors believe that the earliest 335s are superior to later models. The two examples shown here are so-called "dot" 335s, made before 1962, when Gibson replaced the original fingerboard dot position markers with block inlays.

More Recent 335s

Early ES-335s, like all Gibson guitars until the 1970s, were made at the company's factory in Kalamazoo, Michigan. Production of most electric Gibsons was shifted to a new plant in Nashville, Tennessee, in 1974, and the firm (which was acquired by a management partnership led by its current President, Henry Juszkiewicz, in 1986) now has its headquarters there. In Nashville, Gibson manufactures a superb range of modern electrics, but it also continues to produce many of its earlier, classic designs like these recently built 335s, which are closely based on the model's original specifications. The brand-new six-string 335 shown here is finished in tobacco sunburst (the guitar is also available in a variety of other colors, including cherry and natural), and has the same maple body, rosewood fingerboard with "dot" markers, and pickups as the highly collectible 1950s examples of the instrument illustrated on the previous two pages.

LEFT: *2000 Gibson ES-335. (courtesy Guitar Village, Farnham)*

RIGHT: *1989 Gibson ES-335-12. (courtesy Guitar Village, Farnham)*

The ES-335-12 *(right)* dates from 1989, and is based on the 12-string version of the 335 first introduced in 1965. Gibson launched the guitar as a competitor to Rickenbacker's 360/12 electric *(see pages 36–37)*, which had been used by Jim (now Roger) McGuinn on the Byrds' classic 1965 singles "Mr. Tambourine Man" and "Turn, Turn, Turn." The resultant craze for electric 12-strings was relatively short-lived, but the ES-335-12 sold well, remaining in Gibson's catalog until 1971. Our 335-12 (a prototype model) has a conventional trapeze tailpiece instead of the "stud" or "stop" unit seen on the other 335s in this book: this was needed to cope with the extra tension exerted by the additional strings. Most of its other features are identical to those of its six-string cousin.

29

Gibson "Artist" Guitars

The approach to Billy Byrd and Hank Garland that led to the creation of Gibson's "Byrdland" archtop was not an isolated occurrence. During the early 1960s, the company's President, Ted McCarty (1909–2001), went on to commission a number of other "Artist" hollowbodies bearing the names of leading performers. One of the first of these was the "Johnny Smith" model, launched in 1961. Smith (b.1922) had helped to define the "cool jazz" movement with his 1952 album Moonlight in Vermont, *and was greatly admired as a player and bandleader. A meticulous man, he gave Gibson precise instructions about the design of his instrument, insisting that its acoustic tone should not be compromised by fitting any pickups or controls directly onto the top. Instead, the Johnny Smith had a "floating" humbucker attached to the end of the guitar's neck, and a volume control built into its pickguard.*

LEFT: *1964 Gibson Tal Farlow. (courtesy Lloyd Chiate, Voltage Guitars, Hollywood)*

RIGHT: *1963 Gibson Johnny Smith. (courtesy Paul Leader)*

Following the success of the Smith guitar and the Gibson "Barney Kessel" archtop that appeared at the same time, Ted McCarty introduced a third "Artist" model in 1962. Developed in collaboration with virtuoso bebop musician Tal Farlow (1921–98), who had made his early reputation with vibes player Red Norvo's trio in the late 1940s and early 50s, and was now leading his own jazz groups, this was a 17-inch (43.2-cm), two-pickup instrument. It had a laminated maple top, back, and sides, a rosewood fingerboard, and a Venetian cutaway inlaid to resemble a scroll. Like the Johnny Smith and Barney Kessel, it featured a "personalized" tailpiece displaying the endorsee's name. Despite its elegant looks and Tal Farlow's active association with it, the guitar was not very successful, and was withdrawn in the late 1960s.

Gibson B.B. King Lucille

Over the years, there has been no shortage of major players willing to give their names to Gibson guitars – and even to collaborate in their design. One of the company's most distinguished endorsees is the great bluesman B.B. King (b.1925), who was sometimes photographed with a Fender Telecaster in his early days, but has been a faithful Gibson user since the mid-1950s.

King's first Gibsons were ES-5s (see pages 14–15), but from the early 1960s onwards, he has used a succession of ES-355s, all of which have had the same famous nickname, "Lucille." In 1980, Gibson introduced a production "B.B. King" model, and since 1982, King has officially endorsed the instrument, which was later renamed "B.B. King Lucille."

LEFT & RIGHT: *1998 Gibson B.B. King Lucille. (courtesy Gibson Guitar Corporation)*

"Lucille" is part of the line of Gibson semi-solids that began with the ES-335 in 1958. A year later, the company brought out the ES-345 – similar in many respects to the 335, but with stereo circuitry (allowing the output from each pickup to be sent to a separate channel or amplifier) and a six-position rotary "Varitone" switch, which provides a selection of pre-set sounds. The ES-355 followed soon afterwards; its differences from the 345 were largely cosmetic, although it featured a vibrato as standard.

B.B. King's "Lucille" is essentially an adapted 355 with no f-holes or vibrato; the sealed top helps to avoid feedback at high playing volumes. The instrument's pickups are both Alnico humbuckers; its body is laminated maple, with a solid center block like its 335/345 predecessors, and the fingerboard inlays are pearl. The "Lucille" shown here is finished in ebony, but Gibson also makes a cherry-colored version.

Rickenbacker Archtops

In 1931, a wealthy Los Angeles-based engineer, Adolph Rickenbacker (1892–1976), co-founded what later became the Rickenbacker Corporation to produce the first-ever mass-produced electric guitar – a Hawaiian model nicknamed the "Frying Pan." The company maintained its impressive record of innovation over the following decades, and by the mid-1950s, its new owner, F.C. Hall, was nurturing ambitious plans for a line of electric archtops. Initially known as the Capri series, and later as the 300 series, these instruments were soon to bring Rickenbacker international recognition – and some very famous customers from the world of pop and rock. The Capri/300s were designed by Roger Rossmeisl, a German émigré who had previously worked, like his father, at Gibson. Rossmeisl took charge of the wood shop at Rickenbacker's Los Angeles factory, where he developed a variety of single- and double-cutaway, thin- and full-bodied models in an integrated "house style" that made them instantly recognizable.

LEFT: *1960 Rickenbacker 375F. (courtesy Rickenbacker International Corporation)*

RIGHT: *pre-1958 Rickenbacker Capri Deluxe. (courtesy Rickenbacker International Corporation)*

The range divides into a number of distinct types and classifications, though all Capri/300s share the characteristic sloping Rickenbacker headstock, and are made from maple with rosewood fingerboards. The earliest guitar illustrated here is a natural-finish pre-1958 Deluxe. "Deluxe" Rickenbackers, whether they are single-cutaway "full-body" instruments such as this one, or thinner double cutaway designs, all have triangular fingerboard inlays and bound bodies.

Guitars like the Deluxe and the other Rickenbacker shown here, a 1960 three-pickup 375F "thin full body," were well received, and a few years later, the 300 series instruments enjoyed a major boost in sales when they became associated with The Beatles. John Lennon acquired his trademark Model 325 while the group was working in Hamburg during 1960, and subsequently, George Harrison was often seen and heard with a 12-string 360.

The Rickenbacker 330 and 360

The six-string Rickenbacker Capri 330 seen here, finished in two-tone sunburst and dating from the late 1950s, boasts the distinctive double cutaway body shape that has become the brand's best-known feature. By the early 1960s, Rickenbackers were being widely used by jazz, country, and pop musicians; but it was The Beatles' adoption of them that finally established these strikingly elegant guitars as mainstream instruments. Large numbers of young UK and American players bought models like the ones associated with the Fab Four, and in 1964, a folk-inspired singer-guitarist from Chicago, Jim (Roger) McGuinn, acquired a Rickenbacker 360/12 as a result of seeing George Harrison with one in the movie A Hard Day's Night. *The following year, McGuinn co-founded The Byrds, and used the new guitar on many of the group's classic recordings. This historic 12-string, currently owned by Lloyd Chiate of Vintage Guitars in Hollywood, is shown opposite and described below.*

LEFT: *c.1959 Rickenbacker Capri 330. (courtesy Rickenbacker International Corporation)*

RIGHT: *1964 Rickenbacker 360/12. (courtesy Lloyd Chiate, Voltage Guitars, Hollywood)*

McGuinn's guitar has undergone considerable modifications. It was originally a two-pickup model, but in 1966 he returned it to the Rickenbacker factory in Santa Ana, California, where it was fitted with a third pickup, a new nut, and what the instrument's surviving documentation describes as a "pickguard with special wiring." The following year, a Vox treble booster was added to the instrument, but this has now been removed.

McGuinn was photographed using his 360/12 onstage before and after these changes; he subsequently bought several other Rickenbackers, but this model was the first and most famous of his 12-strings. It has triangular fret markers and a bound body, and – like all Rickenbacker 12-strings – features an ingenious "compact" headstock design, which disguises the six extra tuning machines by mounting them with their tuner buttons facing downwards.

Rickenbacker's John Lennon and Tom Petty models

Both the Rickenbackers on these pages are special, limited edition guitars named for distinguished rock musicians who have especially close associations with the company and its instruments: John Lennon and Tom Petty.

The Lennon guitar is a 355 12-string, with a 15¼-inch (38.7-cm) body width and three pickups. It was one of three limited edition models bearing the former Beatle's name (the others were a six-string 355, and a 325 with a three-quarter size neck) and produced by Rickenbacker in 1990. Only 2,000 Lennon instruments were made: the first one to come off the production line was presented to John's widow, Yoko Ono, and the others were quickly sold to collectors and fans; the example shown here was photographed at the firm's California headquarters. The cartoon on the scratchplate is a reproduction of a drawing by John Lennon himself.

LEFT: *1991 Rickenbacker 660/12 Tom Petty model. (courtesy Guitar Village, Farnham)*

RIGHT: *1990 Rickenbacker 355/12 John Lennon model. (courtesy Rickenbacker International Corporation)*

Tom Petty, famous for his work with The Heartbreakers and the Traveling Wilburys, has been using Rickenbackers since the start of his career in the mid-1960s. This limited edition 12-string (number 966 of 1000) was produced in 1991 to honor his long connection with the company and its guitars. It is a model 660 with a "fireglo" finish, made from solid maple, and featuring a wider-than-normal neck built to Petty's personal specifications, as well as "vintage"-style knobs and pickups.

Like the Lennon models, the Petty guitars are now sold out. Other recent Rickenbacker limited editions have included instruments endorsed by Susanna Hoffs of the Bangles, the Eagles' Glenn Frey, and, most recently, Lemmy Kilminster from Motorhead.

Fender Hollow-Bodies

The Fender company, founded in Fullerton, California in 1946, is most famous for its solid-bodied guitars, but in the 1960s, it began to produce a number of acoustic and semi-acoustic guitars. Many of them were designed by Roger Rossmeisl, creator of Rickenbacker's classic Capri/300 series models, who had joined Fender in 1962.

Rossmeisl's output included the Coronado range of hollow-bodies, which debuted in 1966. These were available for a time either in standard finishes or in five shades of "Wildwood" – a type of beechwood injected, while still growing, with special dyes that created distinctive colorings. Wildwood (not itself a Fender product; it had been developed in Scandanavia) was also used on several of the company's other models, but was perhaps most effective on designs such as the Coronado II shown here, which boasts a "Wildwood II" (green, gold, and brown) finish.

LEFT: *c.1976 Fender Starcaster.*
(courtesy John Firth)

RIGHT: *1968 Fender Coronado II Wildwood II.*
(courtesy Rod & Hank's, Memphis)

The Coronados had considerable merits, but the guitar-purchasing public identified Fender too closely with solid electrics such as the Telecaster and Stratocaster to accept them. Sadly, the same fate was to befall Fender's most attractive and underrated hollow-body, the Starcaster, which dates from 1975. A thinline model, fitted, unusually for Fender, with humbucking pickups (the "Fender sound" is invariably associated with single-coil units, although humbuckers were available on a number of its later guitars) and a master volume control, the Starcaster might have provided an effective challenge to rival models by Gibson and Gretsch. However, it never sold in large numbers, and was withdrawn in 1982. There have been few subsequent hollow-body Fenders, though the company has continued to make budget-priced flat-top acoustics.

D'Angelico and D'Aquisto

While Gibson, Rickenbacker, and other large companies produced high volumes of factory-made guitars, individual makers, many of them Italian-Americans steeped in the traditions of European lutherie, were creating unique, handcrafted instruments, often to special commission. Among the greatest of these artisans was John D'Angelico (1905–64), who rarely completed more than 30 guitars a year, and is best known for his New Yorker model – an exquisite 18-inch (45.7-cm) archtop whose exact specifications could be precisely tailored to his customers' requirements.

D'Angelico worked with two assistants, the first of whom, Jimmy DiSerio, left his firm in 1959. For the last five years of his life, D'Angelico's only regular employee was his apprentice Jimmy D'Aquisto (1935–95), and most of the guitars produced during this final period were built by D'Aquisto under his master's guidance.

LEFT: *c.1980 D'Aquisto New Yorker. (courtesy Dale Rabiner)*

RIGHT: *1953 D'Angelico New Yorker. (courtesy Mandolin Brothers, New York)*

Following D'Angelico's death, D'Aquisto quickly established himself as a distinguished luthier in his own right. However, he also continued making D'Angelico's classic archtop guitar designs under his own name, often investing them with variations of his own. His New Yorkers (like the 1980 model shown here) featured reshaped f-holes and pickguards, as well as adjustable ebony tailpieces in place of the "stairstep" design favored by D'Angelico. D'Aquisto's friend and fellow-luthier John Monteleone describes the motivation behind these and other changes as the desire to break away from convention, "to carry the instruments on from where they've left off," and this process continued with D'Aquisto's later guitars, which are strikingly original and effective re-interpretations of the "traditional" archtop. Two versions of his remarkable "Solo" model are pictured and described on the next two pages: one dating from 1993, the other unfinished at the time of D'Aquisto's death and later completed by John Monteleone.

The "Solo"

Jimmy D'Aquisto's "Solo" archtop model is fittingly summarized by his friend and colleague John Monteleone as "playable art." It has a body made from spruce and Tyrolean maple, and dramatically reshaped soundholes intended to increase the guitar's projection. Among its many other striking features are the carved-out headstock and tailpiece, the massive ebony bridge, and the cutaway fingerboard. D'Aquisto made Solos in 17-inch (43.2-cm) and 18-inch (45.7-cm) sizes (this is a 17-inch), and there is some variation between individual models – particularly in the positioning of the soundholes, which are sometimes placed nearer the edges of the body. D'Aquisto made only nine Solos before his sudden death in April 1995, and among the advance orders he left unfulfilled was one from composer and guitarist Craig Snyder, who subsequently asked John Monteleone to build a version of the Solo for him. The remarkable outcome of this request is shown here alongside D'Aquisto's original.

LEFT: *1996 D'Aquisto/Monteleone Solo. (courtesy Craig Snyder/John Monteleone)*

RIGHT: *1993 D'Aquisto Solo. (courtesy Dale Rabiner)*

To make his Solo, Monteleone selected materials from D'Aquisto's own workshop, including wood, lacquer, and a partially completed neck and set of sides. He also had access to a number of earlier D'Aquisto Solos, taking tracings from them and examining their construction carefully. He explains that "out of respect for Jimmy, I felt it was a good idea to stay as close to the original design as possible. I knew that I could never duplicate the sound, and that wasn't my intention. Someone's sound and their tone is their thumbprint – and realizing that, when I got to building the inside of the guitar, I knew that I'd have to rely on my own instincts and experience to get the best tone I could for this particular guitar. I stayed pretty close to the concept, but yet I went my own way a little bit, just to conduct it as I thought would be best." The outcome – a magnificent creation nicknamed the "Montequisto" by John's wife – is a superb tribute to D'Aquisto, as well as a fine example of John Monteleone's skill and artistry. Two more of his guitars can be seen on pages 54–55.

44

Robert Benedetto

Robert Benedetto, born in the Bronx, New York, in 1946, is another distinguished heir to the grand Italian-American tradition of instrument-building. In a 30-year career, he has completed over 400 guitars, and is generally regarded as the leading archtop maker of his generation.

Benedetto's approach to archtop guitar creation is based on years of practical experience as a player and luthier. He has moved away from the large, heavy body construction favored by some of his predecessors; Benedetto archtops are lighter and more responsive, with distinctively shaped tailpieces made from ebony, not the more massive brass seen on other instruments in this chapter. Bob comments that "big isn't necessarily better or louder," and says the most popular body size for his archtops is 17 inches (43.2cm), although he also builds 16-inch (40.6-cm) and 18-inch (45.7-cm) guitars.

Left: *Benedetto Manhattan. (courtesy Gina Benedetto)*

Right: *Benedetto seven-string, custom-made for Jimmy Bruno. (courtesy Jimmy Bruno)*

Bob Benedetto has been responsible for a number of significant developments in archtop design. In 1982, he constructed a guitar without inlays or bindings for the late Chuck Wayne, setting a trend for simplicity and purity that was followed by many other luthiers. Bob has also been influential in developing the seven-string guitar, which features an extra bass string tuned a fifth below the existing low E, and was first used in a jazz context by the great George Van Eps (1913–98). Benedetto seven-strings are owned by a growing number of leading players, such as Howard Alden, Bucky and John Pizzarelli, Ron Eschete, and Jimmy Bruno, whose instrument is shown here. Benedetto's many other distinguished customers include Kenny Burrell, Cal Collins, Frank Vignola, and British guitarists Martin Taylor, Andy Summers, Andy MacKenzie, and Adrian Ingram.

The Guild/Benedetto Range

Robert Benedetto continues to accept personal commissions for one-of-a-kind instruments, but since 1999, production of all his regular models has been taken over by Guild Guitars. The Benedetto line is currently hand-built at the company's Custom Shop in Nashville, Tennessee. Bob himself has provided the craftspeople there with exact specifications and detailed training to ensure that the highest standards of construction are maintained on the guitars that bear his name.

The "Guild-Benedetto" range features long-established models such as the Manhattan and Fratello, as well as more recent designs like the Bambino, created in collaboration with guitarist Howard Alden, and intended for players who prefer an instrument somewhat smaller than the typical, 16-inch-plus (40.6-cm-plus) archtop. The Bambino measures just 14¼ inches (36.19cm) across its lower bout, but has a big, powerful sound, and is currently being used by a number of leading performers, including Alden and Jeff Linsky.

LEFT: *Guild/Benedetto Bambino.*
(courtesy Guild Guitars)

RIGHT: *Guild Artist Award.*
(courtesy Guild Guitars)

As well as supervising the production of his standard models at Guild, Bob Benedetto has made modifications and refinements to two of the company's existing electric archtops, the Stuart and Artist Award models. His new version of the Artist Award is shown opposite. It is a full-depth, 17-inch (43.2-cm) acoustic-electric, with a spruce top and maple back, sides, and neck, and is fitted with a "floating" humbucking pickup, attached to the end of the fingerboard so as not to affect the instrument's "unplugged" sound (the volume control can just be seen on the scratchplate).

At $10,000, the Artist Award is Guild's flagship archtop model, and only 50 are produced each year. However, its outstanding quality demonstrates the success of the company's collaboration with Bob Benedetto, which seems certain to yield many more outstanding instruments over the following years.

Martin Taylor's Yamaha Electro-Acoustics

The dividing line between "acoustic" and "electric" instruments is not easy to draw. Almost all steel-strung acoustic guitarists now use some form of amplification onstage, while a number of electric archtop players like to mix the signal from their magnetic pickups with natural, acoustic tones. One musician who can easily combine or alternate between these two sounds, thanks to the Yamaha guitar he helped to design, is distinguished British jazzman Martin Taylor.

In 1989, Yamaha approached Martin with an idea for a guitar with two pickups: a conventional humbucker in the neck position, and a piezo device to capture the acoustic sound. He worked on plans for the instrument with Martyn Booth of Yamaha-Kemble UK, and these were eventually submitted to the company's Design Department in Hamamatsu, Japan. There, luthier Jackie Minacuchi built a prototype, which Martin used on his Artistry *CD (1992) and during subsequent tours.*

LEFT: *Yamaha Martin Taylor AEX 1500 prototype. (courtesy Martin Taylor)*

RIGHT: *Yamaha Martin Taylor AEX 1500 production model. (courtesy Martin Taylor)*

After trying his new guitar out in the studio and on the road, Martin sent a list of suggested modifications back to Minacuchi, who responded with a second prototype; Martin has never used this for live dates or recordings, although he has frequently played it at home. After some further changes, Yamaha completed the final, production version of the design, the Martin Taylor AEX 1500. It can be seen opposite, together with the first prototype.

The Yamaha has since become one of Martin Taylor's main working instruments, providing him with the range of tone-colors he needs for both solo and group work. He has used it on many TV appearances, videos, and CDs, including the *Portraits* album, recorded in Nashville with the late, great country music guitarist and producer Chet Atkins. During the sessions, Chet paid tribute to Martin by signing his guitar with the simple inscription: "Your the best." [sic]

Heritage

Heritage is a young company, but paradoxically, it draws on a long and distinguished tradition of guitar-making. Its factory is located in Kalamazoo, Michigan, home of Gibson until 1984, and many of its employees – including its founders, Jim Deurloo, Marv Lamb, J.P. Moats and Bill Paige – are ex-Gibson staffers who decided to remain in town rather than make the 500-mile (800-km) move to their old firm's new headquarters in Nashville.

Heritage was formed in April 1985, and produces mandolins and banjos as well as electric and acoustic guitars. The company is steeped in the Gibson/Kalamazoo tradition. It uses premises and machinery formerly owned by its predecessor; its headstock logo, "The Heritage," is an echo of "The Gibson," a trademark used on many pre-war Kalamazoo-made instruments. In addition, a number of its models are strongly influenced by classic Gibson designs, although Heritage's guitars often include new innovations and refinements.

LEFT: *1998 Hertiage Sweet 16.*
(courtesy Barnes & Mullins Ltd.)

RIGHT: *1998 Heritage Prospect Standard.*
(courtesy Barnes & Mullins Ltd.)

The firm's "Alvin Lee" model (named for the Ten Years After lead guitarist) has an ES-335-like body combined with a special three-pickup system featuring two humbuckers and a single-coil transducer. The "Johnny Smith," a reworking of the jazzman's classic "floating-pickup" electric/acoustic *(see pages 30–31)*, has delighted its creator, who personally signs every example. All Heritage's full-body archtops, including the "Sweet 16" illustrated opposite, are fitted with solid wood tops (most postwar Gibson semi-acoustics are made with laminates); and a wide variety of custom options is available across the company's entire range, from personalized inlays and special finishes to alternative pickups by EMG or Seymour Duncan. This combination of expert craftsmanship and extensive customer choice – at highly competitive prices – has already brought Heritage considerable prestige, and after less than two decades in business, it seems likely to succeed in its stated aim of creating "the collectible guitar of tomorrow."

John Monteleone

In the 1970s, British guitarist Ivor Mairants commented that the archtop guitar's days seemed to be numbered: "Development of it has almost stopped, and until it again increases in popularity, very few makers will concentrate on its improvement." Thankfully, things have changed considerably since then, and a wide range of first-class archtops is now being built and played. This healthy situation is at least partly due to the influence of luthiers like Bob Benedetto, John Monteleone, and the late Jimmy D'Aquisto, who have inspired younger guitar-builders to turn their attention to archtop construction.

We saw Monteleone's "Montequisto" on pages 44–45; here now are two original instruments of his: the striking "Radio City" archtop, whose handsome "Art Deco" look was inspired by the appearance of New York's Radio City Music Hall; and the electric/acoustic "Electric Flyer", with a carved-out headstock and reshaped f-holes that are slightly reminiscent of Jimmy D'Aquisto's work.

LEFT: *1997 Monteleone Radio Flyer.* (courtesy John Monteleone)

RIGHT: *Monteleone Radio City.* (courtesy John Monteleone)

Monteleone's designs (he builds flat-top guitars and mandolins as well as acoustic and electric archtops) are highly sought-after by leading players. His close knowledge of the work of Jimmy D'Aquisto, John D'Angelico, and other distinguished luthiers, as well as his extensive experience as a guitar restorer, give him a special insight into the technical aspects of instrument construction. But he also draws inspiration from key figures in other areas of design, notably Raymond Loewy, who created the Lucky Strike cigarette packet, the Studebaker Avanti motorcar, and other classic American artifacts. Like Loewy and other commercial designers, Monteleone stresses the importance of simplicity and functionality in his work: "The first requirement is that [the instrument] has to play up to expectations. Once you've achieved that, then you can begin to look at how to make the parts harmonious in their appearance. It's another kind of vibration. The guitar has a sound – but it also has a look that moves."

John Buscarino and Mark Campellone

John Buscarino is a former apprentice of Robert Benedetto, and has also studied with the leading classical guitar-maker Augustine LoPrinzi. Buscarino is now based in Florida, where he builds archtops, flat-tops, and nylon-strung guitars. His instruments are hand-made from American and European woods, and are in strong demand from players and collectors. The Buscarino model shown here was made to commission for millionaire music-lover Scott Chinery (1960–2000), who created a unique collection of 22 custom-built "Blue Guitars" (all 18-inch (45.7-cm) archtops) as a tribute to Jimmy D'Aquisto, one of whose last completed guitars was a blue Centura Deluxe (also owned by Chinery). The Blue Guitars were displayed in public at the Smithsonian Institution in Washington DC in 1998. Among the other luthiers who contributed to the collection were Benedetto, Monteleone, Linda Manzer (see pages 194–197), and Mark Campellone.

LEFT: *Campellone Special 17-inch. (left-hand model) (courtesy Dale Rabiner)*

RIGHT: *Buscarino "Blue Guitar." (courtesy John Buscarino)*

Campellone was born in Providence, Rhode Island, and studied at the famous Berklee College of Music in Boston, Massachusetts. He began his lutherie career in the mid-1970s after several years' experience as a professional musician, and built his first archtop in 1988. His instruments are strongly influenced by the work of Gibson and other classic archtop-makers; he works largely alone, and is entirely self-taught. He currently produces about 30 guitars a year, offering three models: the Standard, Deluxe, and Special *(illustrated opposite)*. This model is a thinline design, with a slimmer profile than most standard archtops. Its top is spruce, its back and sides maple, and its fingerboard ebony. The pickup, built by Ibanez in Japan, is a replica of the Gibson "Johnny Smith" transducer.

Introduction

The first solid-bodied electrics were pre-war Hawaiian (or "lap steel") models; a few experimental "Spanish-style" solids were produced in the 1930s and early 40s, but it was not until a few years later that their development began in earnest. One of the key pioneers of this process was Ted McCarty, who became Gibson's General Manager in 1948, and was later appointed its President. In the immediate postwar years, Gibson's output was still dominated by labor- and cost-intensive acoustic archtops – but McCarty, a shrewd judge of musical trends, quickly realized that demand for amplified instruments was beginning to outstrip sales of these older-style models. He responded by scaling up electric guitar production, modernizing and expanding Gibson's manufacturing facilities, and presiding over the introduction of its most famous solid, the Les Paul, in 1952. It was to be the first of many successful Gibson electrics, several of which are illustrated in this section.

LEFT: *1960 Gibson Les Paul Standard. (courtesy Real Guitars, San Francisco)*

RIGHT: *1965 Fender Telecaster. (courtesy Lloyd Chiate, Voltage Guitars, Hollywood)*

By contrast, former radio repair man Leo Fender (1909–91) and his small, California-based company, were relative newcomers to guitar manufacture. Leo himself was not a traditional luthier, but a skilled engineer with a firm grounding in practical electronics. His basic, functional instruments were easy to mass-produce and maintain, with pickup assemblies that simply slotted into place, and necks that could be removed by unscrewing just four bolts. The Fender Telecaster (1950) and Stratocaster (1954) rapidly became accepted as classics, and are perhaps the most profoundly influential of all solid guitar designs.

While Fender and Gibson set the pace for the industry throughout the 1950s and 60s, a considerable number of other makers were also catering for the electric boom. We will be featuring some of their models (from the elegant Rickenbacker "Tulips" to the inexpensive but brilliant designs of Nathan Daniel) before going on to look at a cross-section of more recent instruments.

Birth of the Fender Telecaster

Unlike previous solid "electric Spanish" models, the guitar that Fender began to develop in 1949 was specifically conceived as a factory-made instrument, and intended to be as cheap and easy as possible to manufacture and repair. It had a basic, single-cutaway body shape and a bolted-on, detachable neck, as well as two important innovations: a new pickup with individual pole-pieces for each string, and an adjustable bridge to ensure better intonation.

By the end of 1949 two prototypes of the "Electric Standard," as the instrument was initially known, had been made; it was only on the second of these that Leo Fender introduced his soon-to-be famous headstock with all six tuning machines on one side. In Spring 1950, the new model was formally announced by the company; it was renamed the Esquire, and displayed for the first time at that year's National Association of Music Merchants (NAMM) show in Chicago.

LEFT: *1951 Fender "No-Caster."* (courtesy Lloyd Chiate, Voltage Guitars, Hollywood)

RIGHT: *c.1950 Fender Broadcaster.* (courtesy David Gilmour)

Many of the earliest Esquires shown to dealers during the following weeks had warped necks, and Don Randall, one of Leo Fender's colleagues, urged him to remedy this defect by installing metal truss-rods on the instruments. Meanwhile, Leo himself was planning a more fundamental change: the addition of a second pickup, fitted in the neck position. This caused some concern among his sales force, which had been promoting a single-pickup instrument. The solution was to rename the modified two-pickup guitar the Broadcaster (although a number of two-pickup Esquires were also sold) and to delay the introduction of the single-pickup Esquire until the following year. Another snag also befell the new model. In February 1951, the New York-based Fred Gretsch Company complained that the "Broadcaster" name infringed the "Broadkaster" trademark used on Gretsch's drumkits and banjos. Fender's initial response was to remove the word "Broadcaster" from its headstocks, but soon afterwards, yet another name was found for its two-pickup electric Spanish guitar: the Telecaster.

The "Pre-CBS" Telecaster

The original 1950-style Telecaster offered three basic sounds, selected by the switch on the right of the strings: a "rhythm guitar" tone from the neck (or front) pickup; a bassy timbre created by passing the front pickup signal through a special pre-set circuit; and a harder, more cutting "lead" tone from the bridge (or back) pickup, which could be blended with the front pickup by adjusting the lower of the instrument's two knobs. A 1952 modification removed the "blend" function, substituting a conventional tone control. This meant that players could no longer combine the front and back pickups, and it was not until 1967 that the instrument was reconfigured in its "modern" form, offering a choice of front, back, or front and back pickups. At this time, the "bassy" circuit was finally abandoned; thanks to the popularity of the bass guitar (another Fender invention), it had become an anachronism.

Left: *1959 Fender Telecaster.*
(courtesy San Diego Guitars)

Right: *1958 Fender Telecaster.*
(courtesy Guitar Village, Farnham)

Between 1951 and 1965, when Leo Fender sold his company to the broadcasting and entertainment conglomerate CBS (Columbia Broadcasting System), several alterations were made to the Telecaster's neck shape, and in 1959 the original all-maple neck was replaced by one with a rosewood fingerboard. There were also cosmetic changes to the instrument; a white pickguard was introduced in 1954, and soon afterwards, alternative body finishes began to be offered (at a five percent surcharge) – at first in any color of the player's choice, and later, in a range of specified "custom colors." A mahogany-bodied Telecaster was introduced in 1963, but discontinued two years later.

After the CBS takeover, Leo Fender took no further part in running his old business. However, a bewildering variety of new and "reissued" versions of the Telecaster and his other classic instruments continued to emerge from Fender's Fullerton headquarters – and, later, from other, overseas factories operated by the company. Some of these are shown on the next two pages.

Fender and the Telecaster – 1965 to the Present

Telecasters and other Fender guitars made immediately after the CBS takeover in January 1965 look and sound little different from their pre-1965 counterparts, and it was not until several years later that any significant modifications to the company's classic designs were introduced. The first of these occurred in 1967, when the Telecaster was rewired to remove its bass boost circuit and allow two-pickup operation (see previous pages). The following year, a new variant model, the Thinline, was launched. This combined a half hollowed-out body with the standard Tele pickup configuration, neck, and body shape, and remained in production until the late 1970s.

Gradually, though, changes did occur at Fender, as CBS's "big business" style of management began to have an adverse effect on workmanship and quality control. During the 1970s, these difficulties were compounded by the increasing availability of cheap, imported guitars, and the bleak overall economic climate.

LEFT & INSET: *2000 Fender "relic" Telecaster. (courtesy Guitar Village, Farnham)*

RIGHT: *1971 Fender Telecaster Thinline. (courtesy Dave Peabody)*

In the early 1980s, CBS made a serious effort to solve Fender's problems: bringing in a new management team, replacing worn-out plant at the Fullerton factory, and launching new models. These included a range of lower-priced Japanese-made Fender guitars, which gave many impecunious young players their first chance to own a "real" Tele or Strat.

Despite these achievements, however, CBS eventually decided to withdraw from the guitar industry. In 1985, it sold Fender to a consortium headed by Bill Schultz, and over the last 15 years, he and his colleagues have succeeded in restoring the company's fortunes. The proof of Fender's renaissance lies in the range of excellent instruments it now produces – from the fine guitars made at its new factory and Custom Shop in Corona, California, to the cheaper models (including a variety of Telecasters in different configurations and finishes) manufactured in Mexico and Asia.

Birth of the Fender Stratocaster

After introducing the Telecaster in 1950, Leo Fender quickly turned his attention to new projects. His groundbreaking Precision Bass Guitar appeared in 1951, and his next "electric Spanish" design, the Fender Stratocaster, has proved to be one of the most innovative (and widely copied) instruments of all time.

The "Stratocaster" name, with its image of high-flying modernity, was probably coined by Don Randall, president of Fender's sales division. As Randall explains in Richard R. Smith's book, Fender: The Sound Heard 'Round the World, *"The Stratocaster's introduction was market driven. And without minimizing Leo's invention, it was a composite of ideas from many players." Customer feedback from Telecaster owners had revealed some areas of dissatisfaction, especially with the instrument's body, which some of them found bulky and awkward. Meanwhile, other manufacturers were busily introducing rival solid guitars, and Fender needed an innovative new model of its own.*

LEFT: *1954 Fender Stratocaster.*
(courtesy Mark Knopfler)

RIGHT: *1961 Fender Stratocaster.*
(courtesy Mark Knopfler)

The response from Leo and his team was to create a radically different double cutaway shape for the Stratocaster, with "comfort contouring" on the back and at the point where the player rests his or her picking arm. The "Strat" would also have three pickups, and a patented vibrato system ("tremolo" in Fender nomenclature) combined with an innovative bridge setup allowing all six strings to be adjusted separately for length and height. Among the Fender staffers who contributed to the design were Freddie Tavares, a skilled musician and craftsman who joined Fender in 1953, and George Fullerton, who had worked with Leo since 1948, and subsequently became his business partner and one of his closest friends.

The Stratocaster was introduced in 1954 with a fanfare of publicity, proclaiming it "years ahead in design – unequalled in performance." This judgment would quickly be echoed by its first players, including leading names from country music, blues and, a little later, rock and roll.

The "Pre-CBS" Stratocaster

The first Stratocasters were sold for $249.50 (with tremolo) and $229.50 (without it). Like the Telecaster, the original Strat had an ash body and an all-maple neck; this was replaced in 1959 by a maple model with a rosewood fingerboard. The guitar was given a sunburst finish as standard, with custom colors, and eventually a range of Fender's "standardized" optional finishes, available at extra cost.

Fender's "years ahead in design" claim for the Strat was certainly justified. In fact, some of the instrument's features were not fully exploited until over a decade after its appearance. These included its innovative tremolo/bridge unit, which, unlike some other vibratos, was able to keep the strings fairly well in tune after being used, and could produce much more dramatic effects than the gentle pitch fluctuations favored by most early Strat players. As Jimi Hendrix and his successors were later to demonstrate.

LEFT: *1962 Fender Stratocaster.* (courtesy Real Guitars, San Francisco)

RIGHT: *1958/60 Fender Stratocaster.* (courtesy Room 335, Rose-Morris, London)

There was also more to the Strat's electronics than may have been intended by its designer. The pickups were selected by a three-position switch, below which were three knobs: an overall volume control, and individual tone controls for the neck and middle pickup. (The bridge pickup was wired straight to the volume knob.) When the switch was used in its three standard settings, only one pickup at a time could be activated; but guitarists soon learned how to balance it between these positions to give combinations of neck-and-middle and middle-and-bridge pickups, creating unexpected and distinctive tone-colors. Surprisingly, it was many years before Fender fitted a five-position switch to make these sounds easier to obtain.

Stratocaster sales took a brief downturn in the early 1960s, but the instrument's longer-term popularity was unaffected, and today its only serious rival as the most sought-after of all solid electric guitars is the Gibson Les Paul.

Fender and the Stratocaster – 1965 to the Present

By 1966, CBS-Fender had a new 120,000ft^2 (1,115m^2) factory, built adjacent to its original premises in Fullerton, California, and soon the Stratocasters coming off its production line were displaying small but significant design changes. Within a year of the CBS takeover, the Strat's distinctive headstock had been slightly enlarged – an apparently minor modification that is felt by many players and collectors to spoil the instrument's looks. As many of them have commented, it was possibly done to permit the use of a larger name/model decal, which, from 1967, displayed a ® symbol for the first time. (Leo Fender had never bothered to register his company's "Fender" and "letter F" trademarks, but this was quickly remedied by the firm's new owners.) Another cosmetic change took place after 1968, when Fender abandoned the use of three-coat nitro-cellulose finishes on its instrument bodies, substituting polyester, which is easier to apply during mass production.

LEFT & INSET: *1994 Fender 40th Anniversary Stratocaster. (courtesy Amanda's Texas Underground, Nashville)*

RIGHT: *1966 Fender Stratocaster. (courtesy Amanda's Texas Undergorund, Nashville)*

Like the Telecaster, the Strat underwent various restylings and modifications in the 1970s, but many guitarists retained a (perhaps exaggerated) reverence for vintage, "pre-CBS" models. Such attitudes may not always have been fair, but it was a fact of life that while

"an older [Fender] guitar was not necessarily better, most of the better guitars were old," as Richard R. Smith comments in his book, *Fender: The Sound Heard 'Round the World.*

The changes in Fender management in the 1980s have led to a significant improvement in quality and design; and while the trade in earlier instruments remains as strong as ever, more and more players are now buying newer Fenders. An impressive variety of Strats is currently available, from replica axes offering the features and finishes of "classic" 1957 and 1962 guitars, to "hot-rods" with high-output, humbucking pickups, and "Artist" models named for famous Stratocaster players like Eric Clapton, Jeff Beck, and the late Stevie Ray Vaughan.

Les Paul and Gibson

Les Paul, born in 1916 in Waukesha, Wisconsin, was already a skilled guitarist by his teens. After achieving early fame as an acoustic player, he became attracted to the possibilities of the electric guitar during the 1930s. His musical abilities were paralleled by a strong interest in electronics and instrument design, and in 1941, he constructed an experimental instrument that would later become famous as "The Log." After cutting up an old Epiphone archtop body, he reassembled it with a slab of solid pine at its center. This block of wood carried two home-made pickups, a bridge, and a vibrato tailpiece, and the guitar was completed with an old Gibson neck and fingerboard. "The Log" proved to have remarkable sustain, and was also impervious to the acoustic feedback that dogged many hollow-body electrics. But despite Les Paul's efforts in the following years, he was unable to persuade anyone to manufacture it commercially.

LEFT: *1952 Gibson Les Paul. (courtesy Guitar Showcase, San Jose)*

RIGHT: *1989 Gibson Les Paul Standard. (courtesy Mark Knopfler)*

By the early 1950s, however, the musical instrument industry was more receptive to the idea of solid guitars. Foremost among the leading companies eagerly developing rivals to the Fender Telecaster was Gibson, with a carved-top prototype solid that the company's President, Ted McCarty, showed to Les Paul – then at the height of his fame as a recording artist – in about 1951. The exact role that Les played in the guitar's evolution is a matter of debate (he has always maintained that it was entirely his brainchild), although he was certainly responsible for the original tailpiece, and had some input into later modifications. He also agreed to endorse the guitar, and the Gibson Les Paul went on sale in 1952, priced at $210. In its original incarnation (as shown here) it had a maple top with a gold finish, a mahogany neck fronted with a rosewood fingerboard, and two Gibson P-90 pickups – often nicknamed "soapbars" because of their characteristic shape.

The Evolving Les Paul

Unlike the Fender Telecaster and Stratocaster, the Gibson Les Paul underwent substantial changes to its hardware and electronics throughout the 1950s. Ironically, the first of these was the removal of the trapeze bridge/tailpiece that had been Les Paul's major contribution to the design. In 1953, it was replaced with a simpler "stud" or "stop" bridge/tailpiece attached directly to the top of the guitar. The following year, Gibson introduced its "Tune-O-Matic" bridge, invented and patented by Ted McCarty, and allowing individual string adjustment. This was incorporated onto a new model, the all-black Les Paul Custom, and subsequently fitted to the original instrument (which was later named the Les Paul Standard).

Gibson then launched another pair of Les Pauls; in contrast to their predecessors, the "Junior" (1954) and "Special" (1955) had flat, uncarved tops, but retained the simple "stop" bridge/tailpiece. The Junior had a single pickup, while the Special featured two.

LEFT: *1956 Gibson Les Paul Special. (courtesy San Diego Guitars)*

RIGHT: *1959 Gibson Les Paul Custom. (courtesy Lloyd Chiate, Voltage Guitars, Hollywood)*

The next and most important alteration was to the pickups on the two top-of-the-line models. The Les Paul's P-90s, like all previous guitar pickups, had single coils, which can be affected by interference from nearby electrical equipment. In 1954, Gibson engineer Seth Lover (1910–97) began developing a guitar pickup containing two adjacent coils, wired out-of-phase with each other. This design canceled out ("bucked") stray electrical fields, while producing a richer tone and more powerful output from the strings.

In 1955, Lover submitted a patent application for his "humbucking" twin-coil pickup (it was granted four years later), and from 1957 onwards, humbuckers were fitted to Standard and Custom Les Pauls. While some players still favor the single-coil P-90s, it is Seth Lover's humbuckers that are responsible for the distinctive "Les Paul sound," familiar from countless rock and blues records. Replicas of both transducers are currently made by several specialist pickup manufacturers.

From Les Paul to SG

In the late 1950s, Gibson decided to make radical alterations to its Les Paul guitars. The Junior and TV models were relaunched with double cutaways in 1958; the Special followed suit a year later. These modified instruments retained the 1¾-inch (4.4-cm) thickness of the original design, and also continued to carry Les Paul's endorsement – at least for a while. The musician's contract with Gibson was drawing to a close; over the next few years, his name gradually disappeared from the company's headstocks and catalogs, and the "Les Paul" range was eventually given a new classification: "SG" (for "solid guitar").

The thick-bodied double cutaway design proved to be only an intermediate stage. In 1960, the Les Paul Standard adopted what became known as the "classic" SG shape, with its much thinner profile and sharp-horned cutaways. The following year, this slimline style was introduced on the other models, and the old, single cutaway Les Paul went into (temporary) retirement.

LEFT: *1961 Gibson Les Paul/SG Standard. (courtesy Lloyd Chiate, Voltage Guitars, Hollywood)*

RIGHT: *1961 Gibson SG Special. (courtesy Mark Knopfler)*

SGs were intended to satisfy Gibson players who found the 1950s-style Les Pauls too heavy, but the instruments' mass had been crucial to their distinctive sustain, and the thin-bodied SGs had a very different sound. Another significant change was the inclusion of a vibrato unit on some SG models. The earliest type (seen on the 1961 Les Paul/SG Standard opposite) had a hinged arm that was pulled from side to side; this was replaced by a Vibrola unit with an up-and-down action. SG pickup configurations corresponded to those on the Les Pauls; humbuckers were used on the Standard and Custom SGs, and single-coil P-90s on the Specials and Juniors.

The SG was Gibson's first attempt at a slim, streamlined solid body design, and it has retained its popularity for over 40 years. Leading players who have used it include Angus Young of AC/DC, Tony Iommi of Black Sabbath, and the late Frank Zappa.

The SG and the Melody Maker

Gibson's promotional literature was upbeat about the prospects for the "ultra-thin, hand contoured double cutaway" SG design. One advertisement described the new, distinctive shape as "an exciting new approach to the solid body guitar" and quipped that it was "a solid success with players."

In fact, SGs were only fairly modest sellers, due in part to the overall shift in public tastes towards folk-style music in the first years of the decade. This was not a matter of great concern to Gibson; as a highly acclaimed manufacturer of both acoustic guitars and of electric instruments, its diversity – and sheer size – seemed to be a guarantee of its continuing success. By 1966, the company was the largest guitar-maker in the world, and its output had expanded to include not only its own instruments, but also the less-expensive Epiphone and Kalamazoo lines.

LEFT: *1964 Gibson Melody Maker.*
(courtesy Guitar Showcase, San Jose)

RIGHT: *1965 Gibson SG Special.*
(courtesy Room 335, Rose-Morris, London)

Gibson understood the importance of keeping its more basic models within the reach of beginners and younger players. In 1959, it launched the Melody Maker solid-body guitar, priced at only $99.50 for a single pickup version in full or ¾ sizes (a twin pickup instrument was also available). In its original form, the Melody Maker bore a close resemblance to the Les Paul Junior *(see pages 74–75)*, but the example shown here dates from 1964 – two years after the introduction of a double cutaway. In 1967, the Melody Maker underwent some more substantial changes, acquiring an "SG" shape and also appearing in three-pickup and 12-string configurations.

Like the Melody Maker, Gibson's SG Junior, launched in 1963, was a direct descendant of the Les Paul Junior; it had the same single P-90 pickup as its predecessor, but was fitted with a vibrato in as a standard feature in 1965. The model remained in production until 1971.

The Return of the Les Paul

In 1967, Les Paul renewed his endorsement deal with Gibson, and over the following years there was a rash of new and reissued instruments bearing his name, and reviving the classic single-cutaway body shape that the company had abandoned a few years earlier. These ranged from gold-top models like the Les Paul Deluxe shown here (fitted with "mini-humbucking" pickups) to more elaborate guitars with special on-board electronics. In 1973, Gibson also produced a short-lived Les Paul Signature thin-line archtop that bore only a passing resemblance to its solid-body cousins.

The 1970s were as uncertain for Gibson as they were for Fender, and the sound, feel, and appearance of the instruments made by the company during this period has often been criticised by players and connoisseurs. However, following its change of management, Gibson is again at the forefront of quality guitar production – and some of its recent Les Pauls are undoubtedly among the finest it has ever produced.

LEFT & INSET: *1998 Gibson Jimmy Page Les Paul. (courtesy Gibson Guitar Corporation)*

RIGHT: *1971 Gibson Les Paul Deluxe. (courtesy San Diego Guitars)*

Perhaps the most outstanding of these newer guitars is the Signature Model designed in collaboration with Led Zeppelin axeman Jimmy Page. He has been one of the key figures behind the popularity of the Les Paul over the last 30 years, and is a virtuoso player with precise and demanding requirements for his instruments. The Page Signature guitar, which is based on the musician's own customized 1959 LP Standard, incorporates a number of special features. Gibson's Quality Control Supervisor, Francis Johns, explains that Page "wanted to try and achieve a guitar that felt like it had [already] been played, and was 'broken in.' The neck is unique: it's actually thinner in the center than it is at the top – Jimmy Page shaves his own guitars down to get this feel." The electronics are also unusual, with control circuitry offering coil-tapping, phasing, and series/parallel switching. The Jimmy Page Les Paul is currently Gibson's most expensive production model; Page has given permission for only 2,200 instruments to be built.

Gibson Firebirds

The Les Paul had been a major design breakthrough for Gibson in the early 1950s, but by the start of the following decade, the company's boss, Ted McCarty, was eager to develop a new, contemporary-looking solid-body guitar. He decided to seek inspiration from Ray Dietrich, an automobile designer famous for his work with Chrysler and Packard. Dietrich submitted sketches for a new-style guitar body, and his ideas were eventually realized as the Gibson Firebird. The original Firebirds featured a reverse body shape, with its treble "horn" larger than the one on its opposite (bass) side, and a "six-tuners-in-a-row" headstock, oriented the "wrong" way round. The new models had a "neck-through-body" construction (in which a single piece of wood is used for the entire center section of the instrument from headstock to tail), and their pickups were mini-humbuckers designed by Seth Lover. Four Firebirds were launched in 1963; the name was suggested by Dietrich, who also contributed the bird sketch visible on the pickguards of the guitars.

LEFT: *1966 Gibson Firebird VII (non-reverse body). (courtesy Lloyd Chiate, Voltage Guitars, Hollywood)*

RIGHT: *1965 Gibson Firebird VII (reverse body). (courtesy Lloyd Chiate, Voltage Guitars, Hollywood)*

The Firebirds were competitively priced (from $189.50 to $445 for a top-of-the-line Firebird VII like the one illustrated here), and certainly lived up to the claims of Gibson's publicity, which described them as "revolutionary in shape, sound, and colors." However, they provoked a complaint from Fender, who claimed that the design infringed their patents. This was denied by Gibson, and no action was ever taken, but the dispute was probably a factor in Ted McCarty's decision, made during 1965, to modify the Firebirds' appearance and construction, and drop the reverse body shape.

The line survived only four more years before being discontinued, but like several other "radical" Gibson solid-body models, Firebirds have grown in popularity since their initial appearance, and the company has produced numerous reissues and replicas of them in recent years.

Gretsch and Epiphone Solid-Bodies

The runaway success of the solid-bodied guitar meant that even traditional archtop manufacturers such as Gretsch (whose President, Fred Gretsch Jr., had previously expresssed his contempt for the new design) were obliged to produce them in order to survive. Accordingly, Gretsch launched its Duo-Jet in 1953. Like other Gretsch electrics of the period, it was fitted with pickups made by DeArmond, which had made its early reputation with removable "floating" transducers for acoustic archtops. The Duo-Jet had some superficial similarities to the Gibson Les Paul, but was not completely solid – its mahogany body contained a substantial cavity. Over the following years, the Duo-Jet went through a number of design changes, eventually acquiring a double cutaway body and a pair of Gretsch's own twin-coil "Filter-'Tron" pickups. The company also produced several other closely related "Jet" models.

LEFT: *1965 Gretsch Jet Fire Bird. (courtesy Eric Schoenberg)*

RIGHT: *1962 Epiphone Crestwood. (courtesy Lloyd Chiate, Voltage Guitars, Hollywood)*

Epiphone, like Gretsch, had been a major name in archtop manufacture; but following Epi's takeover by Gibson in 1957, it too introduced a range of solid guitars, built at its new parent's headquarters in Kalamazoo, Michigan. As former Gibson President Ted McCarty explained in an interview for *The Gibson*, published in 1996, "Epiphone... was a useful marketing tool as we could sell the Epiphone line to the newer dealers and keep selling Gibson guitars to loyal Gibson dealers... they were a companion line for Gibson but not an exact copy, and fitted perfectly with our plans."

Some Epiphones were deliberately produced as budget-price alternatives to more upmarket Gibson designs. However, other models had no direct Gibson counterpart, and among these was the Crestwood – the first of the Kalamazoo-designed Epi solids. The example shown here dates from 1962, and was probably aimed at would-be SG owners whose finances could not stretch to the more expensive instrument.

85

The Fender Esquire and Jazzmaster

In 1950, the single-pickup Esquire had been announced as Fender's first "electric Spanish" guitar (see pages 60–61); but after the company decided to launch the dual-pickup Broadcaster/Telecaster instead, the Esquire's debut was delayed until the following year. One curious result of the company's indecision over the specifications for the Esquire and Broadcaster is the presence of a routed-out space for the "missing" neck pickup on production Esquires. This cavity is concealed beneath the guitar's pickguard.

In most other respects, the Esquire's design and finish are identical to the Telecaster's. It has a simplified version of the Tele tone-circuitry, with a three-position switch that can provide a preset "bassy" sound, and allow the instrument's rotary tone control to be used or bypassed. The original version of the Esquire continued in production until 1970. The model illustrated here dates from 1957.

LEFT: *1960 Fender Jazzmaster. (courtesy San Diego Guitars)*

RIGHT: *1957 Fender Esquire. (courtesy Lloyd Chiate, Voltage Guitars, Hollywood)*

Fender's next premier model was the Jazzmaster, which appeared in 1958. It featured new pickups, a shape designed to fit the contours of the player's body even more snugly than the Stratocaster, and a "floating" vibrato system that could be disabled with a "trem-lok" to allow easy restringing and minimize tuning problems caused by string breakages. There were initial doubts about the Jazzmaster's look and feel. Leo Fender's friend and colleague Forrest White said that at first sight, it reminded him of "a pregnant duck," and other players were put off by its considerable weight. However, the guitar proved highly successful with 1950s and 1960s pop groups, and later with punk and New Wave artists such as Elvis Costello.

Fender's follow-up to the Jazzmaster was its 1962 Jaguar model. It had many similarities to its predecessor, but was given a 22-fret neck, and newly designed pickups incorporating metal screening as protection against electrical interference.

The Fender Mustang and Jag-Stang

The Fender Mustang, introduced in 1964, was designed as a student model. It had a 24-inch (61-cm) scale length, but was also available with a 22½-inch (57.15-cm) scale, like Fender's other beginners' instruments, the Musicmaster and Duo-Sonic. Compared to them, however, the Mustang had a much more sophisticated range of features, including a new vibrato unit (patented by Leo Fender in 1966) with a floating bridge that moves backwards and forwards when the unit is activated. Its two single-coil pickups are angled for optimum bass and treble response.

While the Musicmaster and Duo-Sonic are rarely used by serious performers, the Mustang has developed something of a cult following over the years. One of its more recent high-profile devotees was Kurt Cobain of Nirvana, who made it the basis for his "Jag-Stang" – the custom model that he played from 1993 until his death.

LEFT: *1997 Fender Jag-Stang (left-hand model). (courtesy Amanda's Texas Underground, Nashville)*

RIGHT: *1965 Fender Mustang. (courtesy Lloyd Chiate, Voltage Guitars, Hollywood)*

As its name suggests, the "Jag-Stang" (designed by Cobain in association with Fender Custom Shop luthier Larry Brooks) also incorporated elements of the Fender Jaguar; the new instrument was conceived by combining cut-up photographs of Mustang and Jaguar bodies to create a hybrid. Cobain used the first, prototype version on Nirvana's 1993 tour dates; as he explained in Fender's *Frontline* magazine, the Jag-Stang represents his attempt "to find the perfect mix of everything I was looking for." A second example was completed shortly before his suicide in 1994, and Fender subsequently obtained the agreement of his estate to manufacture the instrument. The 1997 left-hand example shown here, made by Fender in Japan, is finished in sonic blue (like the second of the two Custom Shop Jag-Stangs made for Cobain himself – the other was red). It has a humbucking pickup at the bridge, and a single-coil unit in the neck position. The vibrato tailpiece and bridge are very similar to the Mustang's; the Jaguar influence can be seen in the shape of the bass (right) side of the body.

Sears and Danelectro

Leo Fender's designs stimulated demand for the electric guitar at all levels. His "flagship" models, including the Telecaster and Stratocaster, attracted professionals and serious players, while his student instruments were priced within reach of reasonably well-heeled beginners – or their parents! But by the mid-1950s, considerably cheaper electric guitars and amplifiers were readily available, thanks to the buying power and marketing muscle of America's premier sales catalog company: Sears, Roebuck, and Company.

Sears had been selling musical instruments since well before World War I, and in 1954 it launched its first electric Spanish solid-bodied guitars. These carried the Sears "Silvertone" label, but were actually made by a variety of outside contractors, including Harmony, Kay, and Nathan Daniel, an innovative New Jersey-based designer. Daniel (1912–94) had been Sears' exclusive amp manufacturer since 1948, and his company, Danelectro, also supplied equipment to a number of other leading wholesalers.

LEFT: *Early 1960s Danelectro Convertible.*
(courtesy Guitar Showcase, San Jose)

RIGHT: *c.1965 Danelectro Pro 1.*
(courtesy Real Guitars, San Francisco)

The earliest Silvertone solids had poplar bodies; Daniel made them in single and double pickup versions, and soon began selling similar models under his own Danelectro trademark. The second generation of Silvertone/ Danelectros, introduced in 1956, still had poplar or pine sides, necks, and bridge blocks, but for their tops and backs, Daniel started using Masonite – a cheap hardboard material containing wood chips and fiber, mixed with resin. The guitars' finish and hardware were also highly unconventional; their sides were coated with Naugahide (a durable plastic often used on chair seats), and the metal pickup covers were made from surplus chrome-plated lipstick tubes.

Daniel fashioned these odd ingredients into strikingly effective designs. One of his Silvertone guitar outfits featured an amp and speaker built into the instrument's case, and he also produced six-string basses, and even a hybrid sitar guitar. His company shut down in 1969; but since the mid-1980s, Jerry Jones *(see pages 116–117)* has been making high-quality Danelectro-style electrics.

Rickenbacker and Electro Solids

In 1953, work began at Rickenbacker's factory in Santa Ana, California, on a new line of Rickenbacker solid-bodies, named the "Combo" range. The first Combo guitar emerged a year later, and the instrument below, the distinctively tulip-shaped Combo 450, made its debut in 1957. The 450, and its single-pickup version, the 400, quickly found favor with distinguished jazz musician Toots Thielemans (b.1922), who used them while working with the quintet led by British-born pianist George Shearing. The instruments also attracted the attention of the young John Lennon; according to John C. Hall, Chairman and CEO of Rickenbacker, it was the sound of Thielemans playing a "Tulip" that prompted Lennon to buy a Rickenbacker of his own. The 400 and 450 were the first Rickenbackers to use neck-through-body construction (the company abandoned the technique when designing its Capri hollowbodies – see pages 34–35). This 450 is finished in jet black; brown and green were also available.

LEFT: *1968 Electro ES-17. (courtesy Rickenbacker International Corporation)*

RIGHT: *1957 Rickenbacker Combo 450. (courtesy Rickenbacker International Corporation)*

The other guitar shown here dates from 1968, and its "cresting wave" double cutaway, single pickup, overall shape, and finish are identical to those on a Rickenbacker Combo 425. However, it carries the Electro label. Electro String was the name of Rickenbacker's original manufacturing company, and for some years, the Electro marque was retained for instruments sold directly to teaching studios, usually as part of a beginner's "outfit" that also included an amplifier and case. As John C. Hall explains: "Electro guitars were made in the same factory as Rickenbackers, and a lot of the models are the same [as] Rickenbacker models – except that they were not buffed out and polished to the same degree, in order to keep the cost down." Occasionally, though, an Electro instrument would be out-of-stock when required. Then an equivalent, finely polished Rickenbacker, like the one opposite, would have its original logo replaced, and be sent out as an Electro.

Guitars by National and Martin

National Reso-Phonic, of San Luis Obispo, California, specializes in the design and construction of resonator guitars. Resonator instruments, which use one or more internally mounted diaphragms to produce a distinctively powerful acoustic tone, were originally developed by John Dopyera (1893–1988) in the days before amplification, and National's Reso-lectric is an ingenious combination of old and new technologies.

The sound from the single, 9½-inch (24-cm) resonator cone recessed into its solid alder body is captured by a Highlander piezo pickup mounted inside its "biscuit" bridge. The output from this transducer can be mixed with the signal from the Seymour Duncan P90 "soapbar" pickup positioned near the neck. The Reso-lectric, which has a top made of maple veneer, and a hardrock maple neck and rosewood fingerboard, is also effective when played acoustically. (See pages 166–69 for more examples of National resonator guitars.)

LEFT: *1997 National Reso-Lectric. (courtesy National Reso-Phonic)*

RIGHT: *c.1980 CFM EM-18. (courtesy Amanda's Texas Underground, Nashville)*

C.F. Martin & Company, of Nazareth, Pennsylvania, is justly famous for its fine flat-top acoustic guitars *(see pages 138–41)*. However, the firm's strong association with these instruments has meant that its occasional forays into archtop, electric, and bass production have never been especially successful. The Martin EM-18 illustrated opposite was part of a range of solid-body guitars introduced in 1979, which remained in the catalog for only four years. Significantly, its headstock (whose scrolled shape is reminiscent of the earliest nineteenth century Martin acoustics) bears the company's initials (CFM) rather than its full name.

The EM-18 is an attractive and versatile instrument, with two humbucking pickups (bought in from other manufacturers), coil selector and phase switches, a "Badass" bridge (designed to improve sustain), and a maple body with walnut laminates. The short-lived E series also featured some models with active electronics, as well as a pair of basses.

Guitars by Fisher and Kapa

This custom-built "Saturn V" left-hand guitar, with its rocket-style, NASA-inspired body, was commissioned by Memphis-based blues guitarist Eric Gales from luthier Charles Fisher. The guitar, which dates from 1994, has two humbucking pickups and a specially designed vibrato bridge/tailpiece incorporating tuners for each string. Fisher, based in Coalport, Pennsylvania, currently runs The Point Technologies, a company specializing in vibrato unit design.

Eric Gales, who is now in his mid-twenties, signed his first recording contract at the age of only 15, winning the "Best New Talent" category in Guitar World *magazine's Readers' Poll only a year later. Nicknamed "Raw Dawg," and influenced by Jimi Hendrix, Stevie Ray Vaughan, and John Lee Hooker, Gales has recently released his third album,* That's What I Am. *His two brothers, Eugene and Manuel, are also talented players.*

LEFT: *late 1960s Kapa Continental. (courtesy Amanda's Texas Undergroud, Nashville)*

RIGHT: *c.1994 Fisher Saturn V (left-hand model). (courtesy Rod & Hank's, Memphis)*

The second guitar on these pages, a Kapa Continental, is something of a collector's item, as Kapas were only in production for about four years (1966–70). They were made by a Dutch luthier, Kope Veneman, whose father had run the Amka instrument company in Holland. Kope immigrated to the USA, and eventually settled in Hyattsville, Maryland, where the Continental range (including both six- and 12-string electrics) was manufactured.

Their body shapes, sliding switches, and vibrato units are all strongly reminiscent of the Fender Jazzmaster and Jaguar, although there are several important differences. These include the zero frets found on some Continentals, their three control knobs (one volume and two tones), and strikingly unusual finishes. They are described by one devotee as having "really nice necks... and a raunchy retro sound."

Leo Fender at Music Man and G & L

Leo Fender's departure, in 1965, from the company that bore his name did little to dampen his subsequent creativity. However, legal restrictions prevented him from doing guitar design work on his own until 1970, and it was two more years before he launched his next business venture, Tri-Sonics, later renamed Music Man. Leo's partners, Forrest White and Tom Walker, were both ex-Fender employees, and another Fender "old-timer," George Fullerton, joined in 1974. Leo could probably have had great success by turning out replicas of his classic Telecasters and Stratocasters, but he had no intention of retreading old ground. As George Fullerton explained in a 1991 Vintage Guitar interview, "what Leo tried to do... was to make [guitars] that didn't look like the legendary instruments he'd designed at Fender. He wanted these newer brands to be improvements on his earlier designs."

LEFT: *1998 G & L ASAT Junior.*
(courtesy G & L Musical Instruments)

RIGHT: *late 1970s Music Man Sabre I.*
(courtesy Rod & Hank's, Memphis)

New features on Music Man guitars included Leo's first humbucking pickups (fitted to the Sabre model illustrated here), a redesigned bass headstock with one tuning machine positioned opposite the other three, and active electronics similar to those pioneered by Alembic a few years earlier. But despite the high quality of Music Man's instruments, the company's success was limited, due, in part, to growing disagreements between the three principal shareholders. In 1980, Fender and Fullerton left to set up another company, G & L (the initials stand for "George and Leo"). They were joined by Dale Hyatt, whose association with Leo dated back to 1946; he became G & L's Director of Marketing and Distribution.

This new venture saw the last flowering of Leo Fender's genius for instrument design. He worked at G & L until his death in 1991, and the firm remains one of America's most innovative and highly respected guitar manufacturers.

G & L Today

G & L maintains Leo Fender's far-sighted approach to guitar design, as well as the hands-on production methods he always favored. Johnny McLaren, the current Plant Manager, explains that Leo "was fascinated by the mechanics of the manufacturing side," and always keen to purchase the finest and most advanced equipment for guitar-making. Since the company's formation in 1980, as many of its components as possible have been produced at its own factory in Fullerton, California; those that have to be bought in come from manufacturers with established traditions of excellence. For example, the cloth-wrapped wire used in some instruments is made by Gavitt Wire & Cable of Massachusetts, which once supplied pioneering automobile builder Henry Ford. G & L also draws more direct inspiration from its founders. George Fullerton, Leo Fender's partner in the company, lives nearby, and continues to work as a consultant, while Leo's many surviving drawings and notes still provide Johnny McLaren with valuable guidance.

LEFT: *1998 G & L Legacy. (courtesy G & L Musical Instruments)*

RIGHT: *1998 G & L S.500 (courtesy G & L Musical Instruments)*

George and Leo's approaches to guitar-making were complementary. Leo could not play the instrument, although he loved music; while George, an accomplished performer, often contributed to the more artistic aspects of a design. Leo excelled at the mechanical and engineering sides, and never lost his enthusiasm for developing fresh ideas. John C. McLaren, Johnny McLaren's father, whose company, BBE Sound, now owns G & L, paints a vivid picture of Leo on holiday with his second wife, Phyllis: "To please [her] he went on these cruises. They'd be invited to sit at the captain's table... and Leo'd be sitting there drawing new pickups. Then, at the next port, he'd fax them back to George Fullerton!"

One of the last guitar components designed by Leo Fender, the Dual Fulcrum tremolo, is fitted to both the instruments shown here, the S500 and the Legacy. The latter was produced posthumously as a tribute to Leo's life and achievements, and is largely based on his own ideas and sketches.

PRS Guitars

Rock and jazz are radical forms of music, but the guitarists who play them often have strongly conservative views about instrument design. After more than 40 years, the classic Fender and Gibson solid-bodies are as popular as ever, and many musicians still believe them to be unsurpassed in terms of sound and feel. Significantly, a number of successful contemporary guitar-makers share their customers' reverence for the past, and seek to develop, perfect, and even combine key aspects of the old "favorites" in their current models. Maryland-based luthier Paul Reed Smith has used this approach brilliantly. His guitars are elegant, versatile, and full of new ideas, while incorporating two familiar basic features: a Gibson Les Paul-style carved top and glued-in neck, and a Strat-like double cutaway and vibrato unit.

LEFT: *1998 PRS McCarty Soapbar.* (courtesy Room 335, Rose-Morris, London)

RIGHT: *mid-1980s PRS solid.* (courtesy Mitch Dalton)

Paul Reed Smith's designs have evolved through years of experimentation and "field-testing" in live performance. As a struggling young craftsman in Annapolis, he would obtain backstage passes to concert venues and offer his instruments to star players on the understanding that "if [they] didn't love the guitars they didn't have to pay me even when I knew I couldn't make my rent the next day." His efforts eventually paid off, and today his instruments are in demand all over the world.

One of Reed Smith's many satisfied customers is top UK session guitarist Mitch Dalton, who describes his PRS (the blue model shown opposite, which dates from the mid-1980s) as "a great rock guitar – it really does produce a very nice, sustained sound." He is also full of praise for the guitar's somewhat unconventional controls (the lower knob is a five-position selector providing a range of tones from mellow to hard and brittle), which he finds quick and convenient for studio and live use.

Alembic

An "alembic" is defined in the dictionary as "anything that refines or purifies;" more specifically, it was the vessel in which medieval and Renaissance alchemists combined base metals as they sought to transmute them into gold. A different kind of alchemy is practiced at Alembic, Inc., of Santa Rosa, California, which produces fine instruments for some of the world's most outstanding performers. Its General Manager, Mica Wickersham, explains that the company name "has become for us a symbol of purity – and one of our primary goals is purity of sound."

Alembic was founded in 1969 by Mica's parents, Ron and Susan, who are still at the helm of the business. Their company shared premises near San Francisco with the city's legendary rock group, the Grateful Dead, and Ron, a skilled engineer, was responsible for much of the band's sound technology – including its PA system, and the "active" pickups used by bassist Phil Lesh and guitarists Jerry Garcia and Bob Weir.

LEFT: *1978 Alembic Series I 12-string.* (courtesy Alembic, Inc.)

RIGHT: *1971 Alembic prototype.* (courtesy Real Guitars, San Francisco)

In 1974, after several years combining electronics and instrument design with studio management and live recording work, Alembic decided to focus solely on making guitars, basses, and pickups. From the start, its instruments were strikingly different from those of more mainstream manufacturers. While standard electric guitar pickups are "voiced" to create a distinctive tone-color that cannot be substantially modified, Alembic transducers deliver a clean, high fidelity response that musicians then tailor to their needs by the use of active on-board filters, whose roll-off characteristics are carefully chosen to sound "natural" and musical. The resultant range of sonic possibilities gives players a uniquely versatile tool with which to realize their ideas. As Ron Wickersham puts it: "Rather than handing a musician something and saying, 'We have this great inspiration, and if you take our instrument, you'll be famous just like somebody else,' we do the opposite; the musician is free to come to us, and we don't try to talk him out of his dream."

Hugh Manson

The southwest of England's peaceful rural environment has attracted a number of leading British luthiers. One of the most distinguished of these, Hugh Manson, has lived and worked in the village of Sandford, near Exeter, for the last 12 years. He makes a wide variety of guitars, from the "Classic" range of Tele- and Strat-style six-strings (sold at his music stores in Exeter and Plymouth) to custom models for famous players such as Martin Barre from Jethro Tull and Led Zeppelin's John Paul Jones.

Hugh built his first guitar at the age of 14, and has been a professional luthier for the last two decades. His success did not come overnight. As he explains, "first you have to get a foot in the door, and until you get a name it's very difficult." One guitar design that helped to establish his reputation, the Kestrel electric, originally sold for under $400, but currently fetches well over double that amount on the second-hand market.

LEFT: *1998 Hugh Manson 7-string archtop. electric (courtesy Hugh Manson)*

RIGHT: *1998 Hugh Manson Classic S. (courtesy Hugh Manson)*

Hugh now produces about 35 handmade instruments a year, with a delivery time of 12 to 15 weeks, and has a preference for more unusual commissions; his output includes "mandolas, mandolins – everything with frets or without frets on. I don't like to make the same guitar day in, day out." One of the advantages of Hugh Manson's rural location is its proximity to high quality, sustainable sources of timber, and he chooses and matches the woods for his instruments with as much care as any acoustic luthier, commenting that "the art of making electric guitars is tailoring the wood to the sound." The two instruments seen here – a standard solid-body, and a hollow-chambered archtop seven-string – display very different approaches to this crucial task, but share the striking visual appearance and superior playability that are hallmarks of all Manson electrics. Some of Hugh's more exotic guitars are featured on pages 184–185.

Charvel and Jackson

During the late 1970s, a new generation of virtuoso American guitarists was beginning to emerge. It included Eddie Van Halen (b.1957), born in Holland but brought up in California, who gave his surname to the powerful rock band he formed with his brother Alex while still a teenager. Van Halen's debut LP appeared in 1978, and Eddie quickly gained a reputation as a lightning-fast, intensely dramatic soloist who demanded the utmost from his instrument. Unsurprisingly, he and artists like him found basic, off-the-shelf guitars inadequate for their high-octane playing, and were obliged to turn to custom shops and individual craftsmen to obtain "axes" that answered their needs. By the end of the decade, Eddie Van Halen was using stripped-down, single-pickup models with Strat-shaped bodies and powerful vibratos. One source for these hybrids was Charvel Manufacturing – named after Wayne Charvel, who had run a repair and customizing business in Azusa, California, but had sold it in 1978 to his former employee, Grover Jackson.

LEFT: *1998 Jackson Soloist SL1. (courtesy Akai/EMI Guitar Division)*

RIGHT: *1998 Jackson KV1. (courtesy Akai/EMI Guitar Division)*

The company's mission to provide musicians with instruments that exactly matched their requirements was enshrined in one of its early catalogs, which stated that "Charvel Mfg. believes very strongly in individual tastes... [there are] absolutely no color or design limitations." However, in 1980, Jackson was approached by another leading Californian rock player, Randy Rhoads (1957–82), to build a hot-rodded, V-bodied guitar, and was, according to Jackson/Charvel expert Robert Lane, "hesitant to use the Charvel logo on [it] because of its wild shape and contours." The problem was quickly solved: "Grover simply signed his last name on the headstock, and the first Jackson was born!" Rhoads had recently become lead guitarist for British heavy rocker Ozzy Osbourne, and his use of the new solid led to substantial demand for Grover Jackson's instruments. The following year, Jackson launched a hugely successful new model, the Soloist. It combined a so-called "Superstrat" shape with the neck-through-body design used on the custom Rhoads guitars. More Jacksons are featured on pages 180–181.

Guitars by
Steve Klein and Ken Parker

Californian luthier Steve Klein's electric guitars look strikingly unconventional, but their appearance is no visual gimmick. These headless instruments are designed to provide optimum balance and ease of playing, and are favored by a long list of famous musicians, including Bill Frisell, Andy Summers, Henry Kaiser, Kenny Wessel (guitarist with Ornette Coleman), and Lou Reed.

Klein, who started making guitars while still in high school in 1967, is based in Sonoma, about 30 miles (50km) north of San Francisco. He is also renowned for his acoustic instruments, and the bodies of his electrics are shaped to support the player's right (or striking) arm in the same way that the upper bout of an acoustic does. This design also benefits the left (or fretting) arm, which is given easier access to the higher reaches of the neck by the gently sloping body shape that replaces a conventional cutaway.

LEFT: *1997 Klein DT-96. (courtesy Klein Electric Guitars)*

RIGHT: *1998 Parker Fly Deluxe. (courtesy Room 335, Rose-Morris, London)*

Also featured on these pages is another innovative guitar from a contemporary American luthier: the Fly by Ken Parker, which got its name because of its remarkably light weight – less than 5lb (2.3kg). The instrument incorporates piezo-electric pickups as well as humbuckers, offering players a wide palette of "acoustic" and electric tones. Beneath its carbon- and glass-fiber outer shell (or "exoskeleton") is a core of resonant wood, and Parker, who started out as an archtop maker, has likened his design to the construction of Renaissance lutes, whose sound was similarly enhanced by the use of softwoods covered in ebony veneers. The Fly's many other unusual features include stainless steel frets set directly onto the fingerboard; they have no tangs (pointed undersides slotted into grooves at the fret positions) and withstand wear better than conventional fret wire. Since its introduction in 1993, the Fly has attracted a number of high-profile users, among them David Bowie's guitarist Reeves Gabrels.

111

Rick Turner's Pretzel and Model I Guitars

Rick Turner, one of America's most creative and respected luthiers, designs and builds his guitars in the Monterey Bay-side city of Santa Cruz. He came to California in 1968, having previously worked as a musician and instrument repairer on the East Coast – where he played guitar in Boston coffee houses, and backed the leading Canadian folk duo Ian and Sylvia. Rick continued his musical career as a guitarist and bassist after moving west, but by 1969 he had decided that his ambitions lay in electric instrument-making.

He constructed his earliest guitars, including the "Pretzel" shown opposite, entirely by hand. As he explains, the Pretzel was "the first instrument where I ran the neck all the way through the body, and added wings onto the side. It was an easy way to attach the neck, and ideally suited to hand building. I think the only electric tool I had at that time was maybe an electric drill."

LEFT: *1998 Rick Turner Model I.*
(courtesy Rick Turner)

RIGHT: *1969 Rick Turner "Pretzel."*
(courtesy Rick Turner)

During this period, Rick became one of a group of highly talented engineers and craftspeople associated with the Grateful Dead. This team eventually coalesced into Alembic, Inc. *(see pages 104–05)*, of which he was a co-founder and stockholder. Rick left the company in 1978 to start his own guitar-making business, and his first post-Alembic guitar, the Model 1, caught the attention of Fleetwood Mac's Lindsey Buckingham while it was still on the drawing board. Buckingham ordered one of the new instruments, and Rick delivered an early prototype to him in 1979, during Fleetwod Mac's rehearsals for their Tusk tour. He recalls that "after [Lindsey] had been playing the guitar for about two hours, he yelled to his guitar tech, 'You can leave the Strats and the Les Pauls and the Ovations at home – this is all I need!'" Buckingham has used the Model 1 ever since, and it has been featured on many Fleetwood Mac videos and recordings.

Rick Turner's Renaissance and "Model T" Guitars

Rick Turner is especially interested in what he calls "the big fuzzy grey area between pure acoustic and pure electric. That's where most of what I do is done." Good "acoustic" sound is notoriously hard to obtain from amplified instruments, and even the finest acoustic guitars will give disappointing results when used with unsuitable added-on pickups. Rick's solution is his "Renaissance" model, which is conceived as a fully integrated system – with instrument, transducer, and electronics all designed to operate together effectively.

The Renaissance has a solid, Gibson 335-type center body section with hollow cavities on either side, a bolt-on neck, a slim, fast-playing fingerboard, and a deep cutaway. But other aspects of its construction – the braced, solid wood top, the overall shape, and light weight – are typical of an acoustic instrument. Rick Turner designates it an "ampli-coustic."

LEFT: *1998 Rick Turner Model T.*
(courtesy Rick Turner)

RIGHT: *1998 Rick Turner Renaissance.*
(courtesy Rick Turner)

Rick has a refreshingly straightforward attitude to the complex process of creating a new instrument. He describes it as "being like a slot machine – but instead of three or four windows there may be 20 or 30, and each one of those represents something important in the design. And what happens is that ideas pile up in the wheels behind the windows, and every now and then I can pull the lever, and the windows will all come up cherries – and I've got a new guitar design!" Rick certainly hit the jackpot with his Model T *(shown opposite)*, which won the "Best of Show" prize for "retro" guitars at the 1996 NAMM (National Association of Music Merchants) show. Its appearance was inspired by the oddly shaped range of guitars and mandolins manufactured by the Chicago-based Kay company from the late 1920s until the mid-1930s, although these did not have the Model T's Formica covering. Rick says the instrument epitomizes "taste carried to its absolute extreme!"

Jerry Jones Guitars

Nashville-based luthier Jerry Jones is dedicated to recreating the classic Danelectro, Silvertone, and Coral electric guitar designs of Nathan Daniel (see pages 90–91). Jerry, who was born in Jackson, Mississippi, has been making guitars in Music City since the early 1980s. He started out by producing a line of self-designed custom models, but a visit from a customer with a damaged Silvertone soon led to a change in direction. Jerry had always been interested in Nathan Daniel's instruments, and as he explains, "this was the first time I ever really got to have one in my shop for repairs. I sat down and thought, 'This is more like the kind of guitar that I would build for myself – rather than one of the custom guitars I was building for other people.' So I [decided] I'd just make myself one."

LEFT: *1998 Jerry Jones Longhorn six-string bass. (courtesy Jerry Jones Guitars)*

RIGHT: *1998 Jerry Jones Shorthorn. (courtesy Jerry Jones Guitars)*

Like Nathan Daniel, Jerry constructs his guitar tops and backs from Masonite, and covers their sides with vinyl. However, he has made various upgrades and improvements to their design, and now makes their necks out of maple, not poplar. He also uses high-technology CNC (computer numeric control) systems to carve out bodies and necks – this speeds up production, enabling him and his four employees to complete 16 guitars a week.

Jerry relishes the simplicity and unpretentiousness of Nathan Daniel's instruments, and remembers their creator with admiration. In 1991, he visited Daniel in Hawaii, and recalls the fascination of "being able to sit down and talk to him about all this stuff – it was just incredible." He is uncertain about the origins of the Danelectro's distinctive shape, but comments that "if that design had been drawn out on a napkin in some diner back in the 1950s, I'd love to have that napkin!"

Patrick Eggle Guitars

In 1990, a young guitar-maker from the English Midlands, Patrick Eggle, was displaying his wares at a local trade fair. He had only a small number of instruments on show, but one of the visitors to his booth, Andrew Selby, was so impressed with their quality and originality that he decided to set up a company to manufacture them.

Just a year later, the new firm, Patrick Eggle Guitars, launched a production version of the model Selby had seen at the fair. This instrument, the Berlin, quickly established itself as a modern classic, and it is currently used by a string of major players, including Tony Iommi of Black Sabbath, Big Country's Bruce Watson, Bill Nelson, Midge Ure, and Ali and Robin Campbell of UB40. By the mid-1990s, the company was producing up to 2,000 electrics, acoustics, and basses a year.

LEFT: *1998 Patrick Eggle Custom Berlin Pro. (courtesy Patrick Eggle Guitars)*

RIGHT: *1998 Patrick Eggle Berlin Legend. (courtesy Patrick Eggle Guitars)*

Recently, however, Eggle has undergone a fundamental reorganization, moving from its original home in Coventry to smaller, newly converted premises in Birmingham. It has also rationalized its range of models, and now makes only electric guitars, which are built using tools and equipment taken from the firm's old Coventry plant – including a neck profiler converted from a machine for making rifle butts!

Sales Director Peter Goalby welcomes the changes, while acknowledging that Patrick Eggle Guitars has had to face "a lot of tears and a lot of heartache" to reach its present, impressive level of success. Patrick Eggle himself left the business in 1994, although he remains on excellent terms with his former colleagues. Peter Goalby explains that "Pat never wanted to be involved in a manufacturing situation. He's a designer, and he designed what became a world-class guitar – and you don't do that every day."

Eggle "Fret King" Esprit Range

*Among Patrick Eggle Guitars' recent additions to its range are the "Fret King"
Esprit models, a trio of strikingly shaped solid-bodies launched in late 1998.
They were designed by the company's Creative Director, Trevor Wilkinson, an
influential figure in the electric guitar world, famous for the widely used vibrato
unit that bears his name. He explains that the Esprits, his first project for Eggle,
are aimed at "people who are wanting something a little different from a Strat,"
and there is certainly nothing run-of-the-mill about these distinctive and
reasonably priced new instruments.*

*The Esprits' shape suggests a cross between a Fender Jazzmaster and a Gibson
Firebird: all three models have reversed headstocks, with six-in-line tuning
machines facing away from the player, but non-reverse bodies. The instruments
are made from korina (sometimes known as limba) wood, a mahogany-like
African timber first used for lutherie by Gibson in the early 1950s.*

LEFT: *1998 Patrick Eggle Esprit 5.*
(courtesy Patrick Eggle Guitars)

RIGHT: *1998 Patrick Eggle Esprit 3.*
(courtesy Patrick Eggle Guitars)

The new guitars offer a variety of pickup configurations.
The Fret King Esprit 1 (not illustrated here) and Esprit 3
are fitted with Gotoh-made replicas of the classic Gibson
single-coil P-90 "soapbar" pickup. (This vintage transducer,
originally fitted to a wide range of classic Gibson models,
from the ES-5 and ES-175 to the Les Paul and the Firebird,
is as popular as ever; another version of it can be seen on the
Paul Reed Smith "McCarty Soapbar" model featured on
pages 102–103.) By contrast, the top-of-the-range Esprit 5
has two humbucking pickups, wired to a three-way coil-
tapping switch. This arrangement allows a wide range of
tonal variation, including useful approximations of Strat-type
single-coil sounds.

The three Fret King Esprits are an ingenious combination
of "retro" features and contemporary design, and were
awarded the "Best Guitar of the Show" accolade when they
were displayed at the 1998 Frankfurt Music Fair. The range
has now been augmented by two new models, the Corona
and the Country Squire.

Two Unusual Instruments

Acoustic "harp guitars", with up to 12 unfretted extra bass strings, were produced by a number of leading American companies, including Gibson, Martin, and the Larson Brothers (who marketed their harp guitars under the Dyer label) from the early 1900s onwards. The Dyer design proved to be the most manageable and successful of these instruments, and in the 1980s, the brilliant young American guitarist/composer Michael Hedges (1953–97) regularly played a 1920s Dyer model onstage and in the studio. A little later, Hedges switched to a new, electric harp guitar specially made for him by Californian luthier Steve Klein. This was fitted with two EMG pickups, and also had a Steinberger "TransTrem" bridge – a highly sophisticated transposing tremolo unit that allows the player to lock the six main strings into higher or lower tunings with its controlling arm. The Klein harp guitar shown opposite is almost identical to Hedges' instrument, but does not include the TransTrem.

LEFT: *1998 Jerry Jones Electric Sitar.*
(courtesy Jerry Jones Guitars)

RIGHT: *1997 Klein Harp Guitar.*
(courtesy Klein Electric Guitars)

Emmett Chapman and the "Stick"

The Stick® is an ingenious and versatile electric stringed instrument with a substantial, steadily widening base of players throughout the world. Its inventor, Emmett Chapman, started out as a jazz guitarist; in 1964, he built himself a nine-string electric, and used it to develop his own highly original fingering techniques. As he explains, "I was playing complex chords in the style of jazz pianists while trying to free my melody lines in the style of Jimi Hendrix. Under Hendrix's influence I had the urge to play standing up, sliding my left hand around on the fingerboard, and doing one handed hammer-ons and hammer-offs in his style." Chapman eventually began repositioning his right hand perpendicular to the fingerboard (see photo), and using both hands to hammer the strings. This breakthrough revolutionized his playing style: "I threw out 10 years of jazz guitar playing and started over".

LEFT: *1998 Chapman Grand Stick. (courtesy Emmett Chapman)*

RIGHT: *Emmett Chapman, inventor of the "Stick." (courtesy Emmett Chapman)*

Using Emmett Chapman's basic "two-handed tapping," players can, in his words, "do the common scalar fingering techniques with both hands equally, either independently or interdependently," combining chords and melodies in a rich, varied range of textures. Emmett modified his home-made guitar to take full advantage of these possibilities, changing its tuning, lowering the action, raising the pickups, incorporating a string damper, and creating a double strap system to position the instrument more vertically. In 1970, he built a bodiless version of the newly evolved instrument out of an ebony board, naming it "The Electric Stick." This ten-string model went into commercial production four years later, and Emmett and his staff now produce about 50 instruments at a time over two and three month periods from their headquarters in Woodland Hills near Los Angeles. These include the original standard Stick and the 12-string Grand Stick® introduced in 1990 (each encompassing a range of over five octaves), as well as their newest model, an eight-string Stick Bass®.

Betty Boop and the Guitar Harp

The earliest electric guitars were conceived as working tools rather than props or art objects, but performers quickly recognized the instrument's visual and theatrical possibilities. Onstage, it could be posed with as well as played, used suggestively or aggressively, and even smashed up to excite an audience. It was also comparatively simple to make solid-bodied electrics in unusual shapes and finishes. One of the first artists to feature such instruments was rhythm and blues star Bo Diddley (b.1928), who commissioned the Gretsch company to build him several guitars with oblong bodies, and at least one covered in fur!

However, the "Betty Boop" guitar shown here takes the concept of decorative bodywork several stages further. It was made in about 1984 by Johnson of Los Angeles for Earl Slick, best known as the guitarist on David Bowie's "Young Americans" and "Station To Station."

LEFT: *c.1985 Johnson "Betty Boop" guitar.*
(courtesy Gary Brawer)

RIGHT: *1993 Gibson Guitar Harp.*
(courtesy San Diego Guitars)

Betty herself probably has rather different tastes in music – her cartoon films, originally made by animator Max Fleischer, sometimes featured guests like Louis Armstrong, Cab Calloway, and Rudy Vallee – but she seems to have survived her transformation from celluloid into wood and metal remarkably well. Other Johnson creations include guitars shaped like spaceships and machine-guns.

The other, equally bizarre instrument on these pages is a Gibson guitar harp dating from 1993. It was designed by Roger Giffin, an English luthier who was in charge of Gibson's Los Angeles-based Custom Shop for five years, and later worked for its Research and Development department. Giffin now runs his own successful lutherie business in California's San Fernando Valley. This strange hybrid has 18 strings, attached to a headstock that is almost two feet (61cm) wide. There is no fingerboard, and the instrument is much closer to a harp than a guitar. It is fitted with a specially extended Seymour Duncan Zebra pickup.

Introduction

The electric guitar is a wholly American creation – but the acoustic instrument from which it evolved has its roots in European lutherie, and even contemporary US designs like the Taylor and Laskin flat-tops seen here have clear links to the work of Old World craftsmen. The father of the flat-top, Christian Friedrich Martin, who, in 1839, founded the famous Pennsylvania-based guitar company that bears his name, was himself an émigré from Saxony. He had learned his trade as an apprentice to a Viennese luthier, Johann Georg Stauffer, and many of his instruments' features, from their shape to the type of internal bracing they use, are derived from Austrian, German, and Spanish models. Soon, however, Martin's guitars took on a new, distinctively American form, and when his successors began fitting their instruments with steel strings, the modern acoustic was born; in this section of the book, we shall trace its subsequent development.

LEFT: *Taylor "Pallet Guitar."*
(courtesy Taylor Guitars)

RIGHT: *1991 Laskin "Grand Auditorium."*
(courtesy Mandolin Brothers, New York)

But first, we focus on some recent trends in the construction of the traditional gut- (or nylon) strung "classical" guitar. Its 16th century ancestors had small bodies, and four or five "courses" (pairs) of strings; but over the next 200 years, such instruments gradually gave way to bigger, richer-toned six-string models. The classical guitar we know today was largely the creation of Antonio de Torres (1817–92), whose designs were popularized by the leading Spanish players of his day, and strongly influenced later craftsmen such as José Ramírez I (1858–1923) and his brother Manuel (1864–1916). It was Manuel Ramírez who provided a guitar for the 1912 Madrid debut of Andrés Segovia (1893–1987). Segovia continued to use his Ramírez for the next two decades, but by the mid-1930s he had replaced it with an instrument by German luthier Hermann Hauser. On the next two pages, we look at some of the great virtuoso's other favored makers.

Classical Guitars by José Ramírez III & Ignacio Fleta

For much of the latter part of his career, Segovia played instruments by two Spanish luthiers, José Ramírez III (1922–95), and Ignacio Fleta (1897–1977). Ramírez's first assignment for Segovia was the repair of the maestro's treasured 1936 Hauser. He then began the lengthy process of developing his own designs to Segovia's satisfaction; his patience was rewarded in the early 1960s, when the guitarist started using Ramírez instruments regularly.

Ramírez was innovative in his designs and choice of materials, using different types of tonewoods on some of his later guitars, extending the string length for extra projection, and creating special lacquer finishes to enrich their sound. He also developed a method of production that enabled his craftsmen to turn out thousands of instruments without sacrificing quality. His achievements have ensured him an important place in classical guitar history.

LEFT: *1960 Ignacio Fleta. (courtesy Shel Urlik)*

RIGHT: *1979 José Ramírez III. (courtesy Mandolin Brothers, New York)*

Ignacio Fleta was born at Huesa del Común, in the north-eastern Spanish region of Catalonia, in 1897. Trained as a violin- and cello-builder as well as a luthier, he made a variety of stringed instruments throughout the earlier part of his career, only focusing full-time on the guitar in 1955, after having heard a radio broadcast of Andrés Segovia playing a Bach transcription. Segovia was the first major player to use a Fleta (he acquired one in 1957, and subsequently bought two others), and since then, many other distinguished players, most notably John Williams, have been associated with his instruments. The Fleta guitar shown here dates from 1960. It has a spruce top and a rosewood back and sides; the neck and the headstock (which is veneered with rosewood) are cedar, and the fingerboard is ebony.

Fleta's two sons, Francisco and Gabriel, have continued building guitars using the "Ignacio Fleta e hijos" ("and sons") label since their father's death in 1977.

Classical Guitars by David Rubio and Philip Woodfield

David Rubio (1934–2000) was probably the most internationally famous of UK-based classical guitar-makers. His Spanish-sounding name is misleading: he was a Londoner, born David Joseph Spinks, who renamed himself (taking his new surname from a village in Spain) while studying and performing flamenco as a young man. Fascinated by this music and by all things Spanish, Rubio spent a number of years during the late 1950s at the workshops of leading luthiers in Seville and Madrid. After learning the principles of guitar-building from them, he moved to New York in 1961, eventually setting up a lutherie and instrument repair business of his own in Greenwich Village. David Rubio returned to Britain in 1967, and for the next two years he worked closely with the great English guitarist and lutenist Julian Bream, producing instruments for him and other leading players.

Left: *1998 Philip Woodfield. (courtesy Ray Ursell)*

Right: *1969 David Rubio. (courtesy Ray Ursell)*

During the 1970s, Rubio branched out into harpsichord design and construction, but in his later years he focused once again on guitar- and violin-making. The example of his work shown here dates from 1969.

Philip Woodfield lives and works in rural Cornwall, an area of England that holds a particular attraction for instrument builders; the distinguished British-based luthier and writer, José Romanillos, once described it jokingly as "the graveyard for guitar-makers." Woodfield, however, is prospering there, and has produced over 130 instruments to date, including lutes, violins, and vihuelas as well as guitars. His designs are strongly influenced by the great nineteenth century Spanish luthier, Antonio de Torres, and he prefers to work using traditional methods, avoiding the use of technology wherever possible. He has recently sold guitars to players throughout Europe, Japan, and the USA.

Classical Guitars by Thomas Humphrey and Robert Ruck

For many years, the main source for high-quality classical guitars was the instrument's birthplace – Spain. More recently, though, Spanish luthiers have faced growing competition from elsewhere in Europe, Japan, Australia, and, increasingly, the USA. The two American luthiers whose instruments are featured on these pages, Thomas Humphrey and Robert Ruck, are especially highly regarded by leading players and experts throughout the world.

Humphrey was born in Minnesota in 1948, but now lives and works in New York. He began his career there during the early 1970s in the workshop of American classical and flat-top guitar-builder Michael Gurian, and started producing his own designs in the early 1980s. The most famous of these is the "Millennium," which features an unconventionally braced, steeply angled top; this increases power and improves access to the upper fingerboard positions.

LEFT: *1986 Robert Ruck.*
(courtesy Shel Urlik)

RIGHT: *1990 Thomas Humphrey.*
(courtesy Shel Urlik)

Humphrey's somewhat controversial designs are favored by leading guitarists such as Sharon Isbin, Carlos Barbosa-Lima, and Eliot Fisk; in 1997 he began a joint venture with the Martin Guitar Company to produce two classical models that will be built to his specifications.

Robert Ruck (b.1945) is based in Hansville, Washington. A largely self-taught luthier, he has completed over 600 guitars. His work is in great demand, and at one point there was an eight-year waiting list for his instruments. He currently offers three basic styles of guitar (available as standard or special, limited production models). The one seen here dates from 1986, and has a cedar top, and a back and sides made from Brazilian rosewood – a material Ruck has now stopped using due to its acute shortage. Robert Ruck's instruments are the choice of a number of distinguished guitar players, including Cuban virtuoso Manuel Barrueco.

Classical "Hybrids" by Benedetto and Buscarino

The two guitars shown here, though borrowing from traditional "classical" models, are the work of luthiers best-known for their work in other fields. Robert Benedetto's "Il Fiorentino" is a nylon-strung archtop guitar with strong echoes of violin design. This is the first instrument in Benedetto's "Renaissance" series, which also includes a similar steel-strung archtop, "Il Palissandro" (The Rosewood). Il Fiorentino's 16-inch (40.6-cm) top is made from aged European spruce, and the back and sides from European curly maple, with a centerpiece of American birdseye maple. Solid ebony tuning pegs are used instead of conventional tuning machines, and the guitar features a violin-style bridge, hand-carved from curly maple, and an ebony tailpiece (with abalone inlay), which is attached to the body using cello tailgut. Il Fiorentino dates from 1994.

LEFT: *Buscarino Cabaret.* (courtesy John Buscarino)

RIGHT: *1994 Benedetto Il Fiorentino.* (courtesy Robert Benedetto)

Our second instrument is a jazz/classic hybrid. Its creator, John Buscarino, christened it the "Cabaret," and intended it to provide what he describes as "the perfect blend of a traditional classical guitar and an acoustic archtop guitar." The Cabaret's body is based on the designs of the great German luthier Hermann Hauser, but its cutaway and built-in pickup make it especially suitable for fingerstyle jazz performers. One leading British jazz musician, Adrian Ingram, has described it as "the best amplified nylon-string guitar I have ever played."

Buscarino also offers a slightly larger "Grand Cabaret" electric classic in a similar style to the acoustic, based on a José Ramirez III model.

Martin – From 00 to OM

The Martin company, based in Nazareth, Pennsylvania, makes fine steel-strung, flat-top instruments whose design is strongly influenced by the ideas of its founder, C.F. Martin Sr. (1786–1873). In the 1850s, he began to reinforce the tops of his gut-strung, classical-style guitars with a special system of X-shaped struts. These not only strengthened the guitars, but improved their tonal characteristics. By the 1920s, when "X-braces" were being applied to Martin's steel-strung guitars, they helped to create the company's "trademark" sound – a rich, singing tone very different from the more cutting, less sustained quality of most archtop models.

From the early 1900s, Martin (like Gibson and other rivals) was also enlarging the bodies of its guitars to boost their sound and projection. At the turn of the century, the firm's widest guitar body was "size 00," which measured 14⅛ inches (35.9cm). In 1902, the 15-inch (38-cm) 000 was introduced, and models in these sizes have remained in production ever since.

LEFT: *1995 Martin 000-42EC. (courtesy Martin Guitar Company)*

RIGHT: *1928 Martin OM-28. (courtesy Eric Schoenberg)*

The 000 flat-top was to be the starting point for a significant design modification. This was inspired by Perry Bechtel, a leading American banjoist planning to make the transition to the guitar, who approached Martin with a request for a flat-top that he would find more manageable to play. In particular, he wanted a narrower neck, and easier access to the higher reaches of the fingerboard. Martin responded by squaring off the top of the 000's body to accommodate a reshaped and repositioned neck, which joined the body at the 14th fret. (Previous Martins followed classical guitar design, and had necks with only 12 frets easily accessible.) The new instrument, named the OM (Orchestra Model), was launched in 1930.

Illustrated here are a Style 42 000 limited edition (only 461 were made) produced in 1995 and endorsed by Eric Clapton, whose inlaid signature can be seen on the fingerboard; and a vintage OM-28 dating from 1931.

The Martin Dreadnought

Martin's next major innovation, the large "Dreadnought"-size acoustic, was introduced in 1931 and is one of the most influential of all flat-top models. Derived from a design the company had previously manufactured for the Boston-based Ditson retail chain, its bulky shape led to its being named after a class of battleship! Dreadnoughts quickly became the instruments of choice among players who needed the extra power they provided. Among the select group of star names who have given their name to "limited editions" of the guitar is singer-songwriter Don McLean, whose classic song American Pie has been a worldwide bestseller, and who has used Martins throughout his performing career. In 1999, the company brought out a special Style 40 Dreadnought in McLean's honor; only 71 were produced (the number marks the year of American Pie's release, 1971) and the guitar, illustrated here, is now a collectors' item.

LEFT: 1999 Martin D-40DM "American Pie." (courtesy Ritz Music, London)

RIGHT: Martin HD-28 (500,000th completed), 1990. (courtesy Martin Guitar Company)

Each "American Pie" Dreadnought (this is number 35) is signed by Don McLean and C.F. Martin IV, current CEO of Martin Guitars and the great-great-great-grandson of the company's founder. The instrument's other unique features include fingerboard markers inlaid with key words from the lyrics of American Pie.

The model has an Engelmann spruce top, East Indian rosewood back and sides, and an ebony fingerboard; part of its $5,750 retail price will be donated by Martin to a children's charity, the Don McLean Foundation.

A very small number of Martin guitars are "one-of-a-kind" custom creations kept on permanent display at the firm's factory in Nazareth. These include the other Dreadnought shown here – an HD-28 that was the 500,000th instrument to be produced by the company since its foundation in 1839. This guitar carries the signatures of the entire workforce; the "H" prefix refers to the herringbone trim – a favorite Martin feature dropped after World War II, but reintroduced in 1976.

Gibson's First Flat-Tops

It took some time for Gibson to approach Martin's level of commitment to the flat-top. The first Kalamazoo-made instrument to present a serious challenge to the 00s and 000s was the "Nick Lucas" model, launched in 1928, and named for the American vaudeville and cabaret performer who was later to compose the multimillion-selling hit, "Tiptoe Through the Tulips." Six years earlier, Lucas (1897–1982) had recorded some of the first jazz-influenced guitar solos, including the classic "Teasin' The Frets." His guitar, which had a spruce top, maple back and sides, and a neck with 12 frets clear of its body (later examples were given a 14-fret neck, like the one in our photograph) was highly successful, despite its $125 price tag. Over the next few years, Gibson's flat-top range was to receive growing acclaim, as the company responded to Martin's OMs and Dreadnoughts with some innovations of its own.

LEFT: *1934 Gibson Jumbo. (courtesy Mandolin Brothers, New York)*

RIGHT: *1998 Gibson Nick Lucas. (courtesy Mandolin Brothers, New York)*

In 1934, Gibson launched a large-bodied flat-top, the "Jumbo." The original model (illustrated opposite) was described in the company's catalog as "[producing] a heavy, booming tone so popular with many players who do vocal or small combination accompaniment." It was superseded in 1936 by two new guitars, the "Advanced Jumbo" and the "Jumbo 35." All three instruments were 16 inches (40.6cm) wide; like Martin's Dreadnoughts, they featured X-braced tops, but were slightly shallower-bodied and more "round-shouldered" than their rivals. They were also competitively priced: the Advanced Jumbo sold for $80 and the J-35 for only $35. (Martin's D-28 Dreadnought cost $100 in 1935, while Gibson's own top-of-the-line archtop guitar was priced at $400.) The Gibson Jumbo range (the name would eventually be taken up by many other manufacturers of larger flat-tops) was soon expanded further, as the Advanced Jumbo gave way to the Super Jumbo (SJ), a model which is still available today.

The Gibson SJ-200 and Country-Western Jumbo

Gibson's "Super Jumbo" line evolved from a collaboration with "cowboy" singing star Ray Whitley. Whitley, a major name in radio and films, visited Gibson's Kalamazoo headquarters to help develop the design, and the SJ-200 was launched in 1937. It was named, like many Gibsons, after its price ($200), and its lavishly decorated body, originally 16⅞ inches (42.9cm) wide, was later enlarged to 17 inches (43.2cm). It had a more pronounced waist than Gibson's previous jumbos, a distinctive, pearl-inlaid "mustache" bridge, and a large pickguard engraved with flowers and vines. The guitar stayed in limited production throughout the War years, and in 1947 was renamed the J-200. It is one of the most instantly recognizable and respected of all Gibson flat-tops; the many artists associated with it include Elvis Presley, Emmylou Harris, Rick Nelson, and blues/gospel performer Rev. Gary Davis, who used to refer to his J-200 as "Miss Gibson."

LEFT: *1998 Gibson SJ-200.*
(courtesy Hank's, London)

RIGHT: *1959 Gibson Country-Western.*
(courtesy Derrick Weskin)

Among the SJ-200's many striking features are its elaborate bridge, with four rectangular pearl inlays above and below the string-pins, the "crest" fingerboard markers (similar to the "cloud" inlays first used in the 1930s by Gibson's competitors, Epiphone), and the beautiful hand-carved pickguard.

In 1942, another Gibson "SJ" instrument appeared. Confusingly, its initials stood not for "Super Jumbo" but "Southerner Jumbo;" the name is rumored to have been the result of a sales campaign targeting the Southern states of the USA. The Southerner was a 16-inch (40.6-cm), mahogany-bodied flat-top (although the first few production models had backs and sides made from rosewood) which remained in the catalog, with minor alterations, for over 30 years. Among its devotees were the Everly Brothers, who featured it on several of their hit records, including "Wake Up, Little Susie." In 1954, Gibson introduced a natural-color version; this was renamed the "Country-Western" two years later, and is shown opposite.

Santa Cruz: Californian Craftsmanship

One of the most important developments in the recent history of flat-top guitar-building has been the emergence of a number of small, dedicated companies committed to the highest standards of workmanship and design. Richard Hoover, of Santa Cruz, California, was one of the first American luthiers to set up such a firm. He began making guitars during the early 1970s, working alone in his garage, and explains that "in building on my own, I saw an impossible learning-curve ahead of me – years and years of experimenting to come up with the perfect guitar." Richard decided to take on two partners, and together they formed the Santa Cruz Guitar Company. "My intent was to have each of us specialize in a certain aspect of guitar-building, so that we could accelerate the learning process and make more guitars, while keeping to the principle of the individual luthier having control over each aspect of building."

Left: *1998 Santa Cruz OM.*   **Right:** *1998 Santa Cruz Tony Rice.*
(courtesy Santa Cruz Guitar Company)   *(courtesy Santa Cruz Guitar Company)*

This philosophy has created a thriving business. Richard Hoover now runs the Santa Cruz Guitar Company himself, employing 11 guitar-makers and six other staff. There is no assembly line; the builders work closely together on what Richard describes as "a logical series of processes that contribute to the whole; they can understand what they've done and how it affects the guitar." Santa Cruz produces 15 basic models, and its instruments have been associated with leading players such as Eric Clapton and bluegrass guitarist Doc Watson.

The company's close relationship with a second major name in bluegrass, Tony Rice, led to the creation of the Santa Cruz Tony Rice Model *(shown opposite)*. This is based on the classic Martin Dreadnought, but offers a more balanced response than the original 1930s D-28, which had a powerful bass but less treble and mid-range presence. Also shown here is another Santa Cruz guitar derived from a prewar Martin design: its OM (Orchestra Model).

Santa Cruz: Anatomy of a Flat-Top

Santa Cruz's first reworkings of vintage Martin styles were one-off custom orders for individual clients. But their guitars attracted so much interest that Richard Hoover eventually added them to the company's regular catalog. "Not only were these guitars in demand, but they were also really nice designs. At the time, Martin wasn't making them, so there was a lot of pent-up demand." Richard acknowledges the importance of Martin's influence on his own development as a player and luthier, and is proud that the appearance of Santa Cruz 000s and OMs has played a part in encouraging Martin itself to restart production of these classic models.

The two Santa Cruz guitars shown here are a 000 with a 12-fret neck, and a "Model F" 12-string; both instruments were built in 1997, and were photographed at the company's headquarters.

LEFT: *1998 Santa Cruz 000. (courtesy Santa Cruz Guitar Company)*

RIGHT: *1998 Santa Cruz Model F 12-string. (courtesy Santa Cruz Guitar Company)*

Like nearly all serious producers of flat-top guitars, Santa Cruz uses X-bracing on its instruments. The tops themselves are made from sitka or German spruce, which is carefully selected and evaluated; more flexible wood tends to accentuate the guitar's bass response, while greater rigidity will boost the mid-range and treble. The positioning of the braces helps to "tailor" the sound of the instrument by stiffening some areas of the top, making them more responsive to higher frequencies, and the completed structure is lined with basswood to isolate it from the guitar's sides and back.

Santa Cruz instruments are a blend of tradition and innovation, and the company's pioneering approach to the business of guitar-making has since been followed by several other firms. Richard Hoover observes that "for the most part, there used to be nothing between the single builder and the factory. That's the niche we want to fill – to be a small company that is building superior instruments and really responsive to the players' needs."

Bob Taylor: High Technology and Fine Design

In 1974, a young Californian luthier, Bob Taylor, started a guitar-making business with a colleague, Kurt Listug, in a small shop in Lemon Grove, near San Diego. The company they created, Taylor Guitars, has developed a unique, innovative approach to instrument-building, combining traditional craftsmanship with high technology. Today, it is a major force in the industry, with almost 70,000ft² (6,500m²) of factory space in El Cajon, California, a daily output of 100 guitars, and an enviable reputation among leading players throughout the world.

Among the many major performers associated with Taylor's instruments are Nanci Griffith, Kenny Loggins, Jewel, Kathy Mattea, Iris DeMent, Bonnie Raitt, Neil Young, and the late John Denver. Former US President Bill Clinton also has a Taylor; in 1997, the company presented him with a commemorative guitar (bearing his Inaugural Seal on the headstock) to mark his re-election.

LEFT: *1998 Taylor PS-14. (courtesy Taylor Guitars)*

RIGHT: *1994 Taylor XX-MC 20th Anniversary. (courtesy Taylor Guitars)*

Bob Taylor's own innovative approach to lutherie lies at the heart of the company's success. To manufacture his guitars, he makes use of Computer Numeric Control (CNC) systems, which drive machinery capable of cutting, carving, and planing at speeds and tolerances no human craftsman could match. CNC's precision removes the inevitable inconsistencies that occur when working by hand, allowing Bob and his staff to "get closer to actually producing what it is we had in mind." It also enables them to make even intricately carved or decorated parts quickly and in considerable numbers. However, as Bob emphasizes, this impressive technology is simply a means to an end: "We're guitar-builders first. Choice of tools [comes] second, and we're very comfortable with high-technology tools to make a low-technology product. [CNC] makes us more consistent and more efficient, so that we can deliver more guitars to people at reasonable prices that really give them what they're hoping to have when they play that guitar."

Taylor's "Cujo" and Leo Kottke Models

Taylor's limited edition "Cujo" guitar is the product of two years' painstaking preparation and design. The instrument takes its name from Stephen King's 1981 novel, in which Cujo, a St. Bernard dog, is bitten by a rabid bat and becomes a crazed predator. The story was filmed in 1983 on a Californian ranch, and wood from a black walnut tree that grew there and was seen in the movie has been used to make 250 special guitars, each signed by Stephen King himself. The elaborate fingerboard decorations on these instruments, showing images related to the story, were all inlaid using computer numeric control. The fine detail achieved by the automated system would be difficult enough for a skilled engraver to match on a single custom guitar, let alone a production run of 250.

LEFT: *1998 Taylor Leo Kottke Signature Model 12-string. (courtesy Taylor Guitars)*

RIGHT: *1998 Taylor "Cujo." (courtesy Taylor Guitars)*

The CNC process turns out a series of perfect realizations of an original design; Bob Taylor points out that "every one's a master – none of them is a copy." In the development of that design, however, the emphasis is on traditional methods: experience, experimentation, and consultation with players – the creation of Leo Kottke's Signature Model 12-string (shown here) involved about four years of discussion with the artist. Such processes remain central to Taylor's approach to guitar-building, and can never be replaced by technology.

The company's future plans focus on further refinements and improvements to the design and production of their instruments. Bob Taylor explains that "what we'll be doing over the next five or ten years is redesigning the way a guitar goes together to really exploit the precision that we have at our disposal. I've been trying to do this for 20 years, and it's only now that I have the equipment to do it with."

Guitars by Goodall and Breedlove

James Goodall, whose 12-string Rosewood Standard is shown below, is a self-taught luthier who grew up in California. A former seascape artist, he built his first guitar in 1972, bartering one of his paintings to acquire the wood he needed. (Coincidentally, his source for supplies was the shop in Lemon Grove, California, later acquired by Bob Taylor and Kurt Listug of Taylor Guitars.) That instrument took him more than three months to complete, but over the next few years, Goodall painstakingly acquired further knowledge, and in 1978, he became a full-time guitar-maker. Since 1992, he has been based in Hawaii, where he produces about five guitars per week with the help of a small team of employees. Goodall's Rosewood Standard 12-string is shown opposite: similar in size to a Martin-style Dreadnought, it has a spruce top, a rosewood body, and an ebony fingerboard.

LEFT: *1998 Breedlove C1. (courtesy Mandolin Brothers, New York)*

RIGHT: *1998 Goodall Rosewood Standard 12-string. (courtesy McCabe's, Santa Monica)*

James Goodall's mother was an art teacher in Southern California; one of her pupils, a teenager called Larry Breedlove, subsequently became production manager at Taylor Guitars. Larry Breedlove and another Taylor employee, Steve Henderson, soon became close friends; in 1990, they decided to set up their own guitar-building business, and the Breedlove Guitar Company was born. The company's headquarters is just outside Bend, in the mountains of central Oregon, and since 1994 (when Breedlove left the firm), Steve Henderson has been in charge of instrument production there.

Breedlove guitars are immediately recognizable, with their distinctively shaped headstocks and bridges, tight waists, and smaller-than-average soundholes. The company makes approximately 12 instruments per week, and in 1995 its CM "Asymmetrical Concert" model won the American Guitar Players Association's coveted "Guitar of the Year" award.

154

Guitars by Eric Schoenberg

Eric Schoenberg brings a player's perspective to the art of guitar design. Since the 1960s, he has been searching for an instrument that would measure up to his own musical and technical needs, and the Schoenberg Soloist and its successors are the results of this quest.

As a distinguished performer of ragtime transcriptions and other elaborate fingerstyle arrangements, Eric Schoenberg's first requirement was for a guitar that would respond sympathetically to the subtleties of his technique. His initial choice, a Martin 000-45 with a 12-fret neck, could not provide the unrestricted access to the higher frets that he needed. He changed to a 14-fret 000-45, but found its scale length unsuitable. His next instrument solved the problem: "I ended up playing a Martin OM, and never found anything like it."

LEFT: *c.1993 Schoenberg Soloist. (courtesy Eric Schoenberg)*

RIGHT: *1996 Schoenberg Standard (prototype). (courtesy Eric Schoenberg)*

Eventually, though, he began to consider the possibility of creating a new guitar, combining the features of the original OM with a cutaway to make the top frets even easier to reach. The Schoenberg Soloist, designed with luthier Dana Bourgeois, was the embodiment of these ideas, and it first appeared in 1986. For the next seven years, Soloists were built at the Martin factory in Nazareth, Pennsylvania, with Eric and Dana supplying the wood, the tops and bracing, the bridges, and the binding for the bodies.

Eric Schoenberg's subsequent design projects have been undertaken in partnership with Massachusetts guitar-maker Julius Borges. Their first production model was a replica of a 1923-style Martin 000-28, made in Hawaiian koa wood. More recently, they have realized what Eric describes as "one of my goals for years:" the creation of the Schoenberg Standard, a 12-fret 000 with a cutaway, offering an ideal combination of neck dimensions and fret access.

Guitars by Bill Collings and Jean Larrivée

Bill Collings, whose D3 flat-top is illustrated opposite, makes his guitars in Austin, Texas. He began his career in another Texan city, Houston, working as a instrument repairman while establishing himself as a luthier in the mid-1970s. During this period, he made contact with a number of leading musicians on the local scene, including singer-songwriter Lyle Lovett, and his reputation spread rapidly. Collings moved to Austin in 1980, and in 1988 he received a major commission from fretted-instrument dealer and expert George Gruhn – an order for 24 guitars to be sold in Gruhn's Nashville music store. Collings guitars are now available worldwide; they are sought after by a wide range of players, and the larger-bodied models are especially popular with bluegrass performers. The D3 is Collings' top-of-the-line Dreadnought. This instrument, made in 1991, has a spruce top, and sides and back of Brazilian rosewood.

LEFT: *1998 Larrivée OM-10. (courtesy Mandolin Brothers, New York)*

RIGHT: *1991 Collings D3. (courtesy Dale Rabiner)*

Jean Larrivée is another specialist in traditional flat-top design. A Canadian whose instruments have a worldwide reputation, he has recently celebrated 30 years as a luthier. He started out as a maker of nylon-strung classical guitars, but began to build flat-tops in the early 1970s, in response to the folk music boom then sweeping Canada.

Since then, his company has produced over 20,000 instruments; the Larrivée factory in Vancouver, British Columbia, uses some of the same computer technologies as Taylor Guitars, and Bob Taylor describes Jean as "one of my best guitar-building buddies." The beautiful headstock inlays found on many Larrivées are created by Jean's wife, Wendy. The model shown here (an OM-10 with a spruce top, mahogany neck, and ebony fingerboard) features a mother-of-pearl, abalone, ivoroid and silver "Mucha Lady;" other instruments are decorated with dragons, jesters, angels, and djinns.

British Acoustics

For many years, top quality UK-made flat-tops were few and far between, and most serious British players would usually be seen with a Martin, a Gibson, or some other "high-end" American instrument. However, thanks to the work of a handful of skilled and enterprising luthiers, British designs are now competing with the finest US guitars, and a growing number of musicians – not just in the UK, but throughout the world – are making them their first choice.

Our first British instrument is a Fylde Oberon. Fylde was set up in 1973 by Roger Bucknall, a British luthier with extensive experience of small-scale instrument production, and the company's guitars quickly gained a high reputation among leading UK folk performers such as Martin Carthy. Fylde's distinctive designs, now manufactured in Penrith, Cumbria, and often named after characters in Shakespeare plays, have subsequently attained much broader popularity; recent customers include Sting, Pat Metheny, and Martin Simpson.

LEFT: *1995 Fylde Oberon. (courtesy Hank's, London)*

RIGHT: *1998 Lowden LSE-1. (courtesy Chandler Guitars, Kew)*

George Lowden is another long-established name in British lutherie. His Ulster-based company produces four basic models (with a wide variety of optional features), as well as a number of "Premiere Range" instruments made to special order from exotic tonewoods such as koa, black cedar, and Brazilian rosewood. Lowdens are played by singer-songwriter Richard Thompson, French fingerstylist Pierre Bensusan, and other leading guitarists on both sides of the Atlantic. The Lowden shown here, an LSE 1 cutaway acoustic, features a sitka spruce top and mahogany back and sides. It is fitted with a built-in pickup, making it easy to amplify onstage; the volume control for this can be seen on the guitar's left shoulder.

Fine custom-made acoustic and electro-acoustic instruments by other UK-based luthiers, including Mike Vanden, Alan Timmins and Gary Southwell, can be seen in this book's Custom Guitars section (see pages 172–207).

Ovation Guitars

Contemporary luthiers have introduced many major changes in guitar construction, but they nearly all continue to use wood as the basis for their designs. Companies experimenting with other materials, particularly man-made ones, have often had to face considerable resistance and criticism; and so far, only one large-scale American manufacturer, Kaman, has succeeded in overcoming this by achieving mass-market success for its "Lyrachord"-backed Ovation guitars.

Kaman was originally an aerospace engineering company, although its Chairman, Charlie Kaman, has always been a keen guitarist. In 1964, he and a team of technicians began analyzing the ways in which various guitars absorbed and reflected sound. Having found that instruments with rounded backs were more acoustically efficient than traditional flat-back shapes, they used their discoveries to create a radical new guitar design – the Ovation Balladeer, which appeared in 1969.

LEFT & INSET: *1997 Ovation Standard Balladeer. (courtesy Chandler Guitars, Kew)*

RIGHT: *1998 Ovation Custom Legend. (courtesy Hank's, London)*

The Balladeer has a spruce top, but its novel "bowl-back" is manufactured from Lyrachord, a specially developed fiberglass formulation that is strong, sonically reflective, and impervious to climate change. The instrument's construction drew directly on Kaman's experience in helicopter design. He explained recently that "in helicopters, [you] spend all [your] time trying to figure out how to remove vibration. To build a guitar you spend your time trying to figure out how to put vibration in. But vibration is vibration."

Kaman's earliest models were entirely acoustic, but in the early 1970s, his company pioneered the development of high-quality, feedback-resistant piezo-electric pickup systems for its guitars. As a result, Ovations have become especially popular for stage work. Although opinion remains divided about the instruments, a number of eminent players use them regularly. These include Glen Campbell (Ovation's first endorsee), solo guitarists Adrian Legg and Al Di Meola, and singer-songwriter Joan Armatrading.

Mario Maccaferri and the "Gypsy Guitar"

While leading American luthiers were developing their archtop and flat-top guitars during the pre-World War II years, a visionary European musician and designer was following a slightly different path. Mario Maccaferri (1900–93) was born in Bologna, Italy, and made his early reputation as a virtuoso classical guitarist. He was also a skilled luthier, and in 1930 he accepted an invitation to collaborate with the Paris-based Selmer company on a range of four new guitars bearing his name. Selmer insisted that one of these should be a steel-strung instrument aimed at jazz players, and Maccaferri sought to give this model an especially powerful, cutting tone by using a slightly bent top to boost the sound (an idea borrowed from mandolin construction). His "Selmer-Maccaferri" also featured a distinctive D-shaped soundhole (changed on later models to an oval), and, on some early Maccaferris, a wooden resonator fitted inside the body.

LEFT: *Early 1930s Selmer-Maccaferri. (courtesy Fapy Lapertin)*

RIGHT: *1990 Dupont Selmer-Maccaferri replica. (courtesy Dave Kelbie)*

The guitar, when it appeared, was highly successful throughout Europe, and became closely identified with the brilliant gypsy musician Django Reinhardt (1910–53), whose recordings and performances as a soloist and with the Quintet of the Hot Club of France had a key influence in the development of the jazz guitar. Despite the success of his instrument, however, Mario Maccaferri's relationship with Selmer proved to be short-lived; he severed his relationship with the company in 1933 after a disagreement, and eventually left France to settle in the USA.

Selmer continued to manufacture Maccaferri's designs until the outbreak of war, and since 1945 several other luthiers have created replicas and reinterpretations of his instruments. Among them is Maurice Dupont, whose 1990 Selmer-Maccaferri style model is shown here alongside a 1930s Maccaferri original. Apart from the lighter color of the top on the newer guitar, and the increased distance between the edge of its fingerboard and its soundhole, there are few discernable differences between them.

The Dopyera Brothers and National Resonator Guitars

The need to boost the acoustic guitar's relatively quiet sound has been addressed in many different ways, but perhaps the most radical solution was devised by John Dopyera (1893–1988). He filed a patent in 1927 for a guitar fitted with three aluminum resonators, and went on to manufacture his invention through the National String Instrument Corporation. John and his four brothers, Rudy, Louis, Emil (Ed), and Robert, were émigrés from Austro-Hungary who had settled in California with their parents, and by the mid-1920s John and Rudy were running a thriving banjo-manufacturing business. John had already come up with a number of ingenious devices to improve the sound and playability of various stringed instruments. In 1926, a commission from a local vaudeville musician, George Beauchamp, for an acoustic guitar loud enough to carry clearly in large theaters, led to the development of the "resonator" concept set out in his patent application.

LEFT: *1928 National Triolian wood-body. (courtesy Mark Makin)*

RIGHT: *1929 National Style 2. (courtesy Mark Makin)*

John Dopyera's prototype "tri-cone" guitar was fitted with an aluminum, T-shaped bridge, topped with wood where the strings made contact with it, and mounted over a set of three aluminum diaphragms. The bridge carried vibrations from the strings to the three diaphragms, and the extra resonance they provided gave the instrument a powerful and distinctive tone. After Dopyera filed his patent for the tri-cone, the new guitars went into production under the auspices of a company set up in 1928 by George Beauchamp and the Dopyeras: the National String Instrument Corporation.

Only a year later, an acrimonious parting of the ways with Beauchamp led to the Dopyeras launching a rival resonator-making business, Dobro. However, after Beauchamp's departure from National in 1933, the two firms merged, and National-Dobro continued building its resonator instruments until 1941, when it was forced to cease production in the wake of the United States' entry into World War II.

National Reso-Phonic – Continuing the Dopyera Tradition

National never resumed production of metal-body resonator guitars after the War, but the Dopyera brothers revived the Dobro line in the 1950s, and eventually set up the O.M.I. (Original Musical Instrument) Company to manufacture Dobros in wood and metal. Among its employees in the early 1970s was Don Young, a luthier who had been fascinated by resonator guitars since childhood. Don subsequently left the company, gaining other experience in instrument-building and repair, but returned in 1984 as plant supervisor.

During his absence, he had met McGregor Gaines, a graphic designer and skilled woodworker; they became friends, and McGregor soon joined Don at O.M.I., where he became shop foreman. The two craftsmen were keen to make improvements to guitar production, but in 1988, after several suggestions were rejected by the management, they resigned and began building National-type designs by themselves.

LEFT: *1998 National Reso-Phonic Radiotone Bendaway. (courtesy National Reso-Phonic)*

RIGHT: *1998 National Reso-Phonic Style O. (courtesy National Reso-Phonic)*

For three years, Don and McGregor worked together to establish their new business, National Reso-Phonic Guitars, which is based in San Luis Obispo, about 200 miles (320km) north of Los Angeles. They were initially restricted to wooden models; the tooling for metal guitars was too expensive, and, as McGregor observes, "we were definitely lacking in capital. Good ideas don't impress banks!" However, by 1992 they could finally afford to begin production of the two classic metal-bodied designs that are currently their biggest sellers: the Style O and the Delphi. National Reso-Phonic now employs 17 people, and makes 80 guitars a month. Don describes their instruments as "pretty close, structurally, look-wise and tonally, to the 1920s- and 1930s-type Nationals. We have definitely made some improvements, but that's not to snub the old stuff – our hats are always off to the old makers, and we're directly linked to the Dopyera brothers."

Travel Guitars

Acoustic guitars can be demanding traveling companions. Their dimensions make them unsuitable as in-flight hand luggage, and many musicians are unhappy about exposing their delicate instruments to the rigors of aircraft holds and baggage carousels. Other means of transport can be equally hazardous; yet keen players hate to be parted from their guitars on vacations or business trips.

Recently, several American companies have offered a solution to this dilemma by developing smaller instruments that retain the feel – and some of the sound – of full-size models. Two examples are shown here – the Baby Taylor and the Martin Backpacker. Their growing success is reflected in the fact that they are both currently finding favor with professional musicians for onstage and studio use.

LEFT: *1998 Baby Taylor. (courtesy Taylor Guitars)*

RIGHT: *c.1995 Martin Backpacker. (courtesy Martin Taylor)*

The Baby Taylor, introduced in 1996, is a remarkable piece of design, offering a deep, Dreadnought-style body and a standard-width neck on an instrument that measures only 34 inches (86.4cm) from headstock to endpin. It has many of the features found on full-size Taylors, including an X-braced sitka spruce top and ebony fingerboard, and unlike some travel guitars, it is designed to be played at standard pitch.

Martin's Backpacker has a more unconventional look and feel. Its small, exceptionally light body is combined with a heavier, full-size neck, and a strap is needed to keep the instrument in the correct playing position. The guitar shown here is a steel-strung model; Martin also produces a nylon-strung Backpacker with a slightly wider and longer body. Both instruments can be amplified using built-in pickup systems. They provide excellent access to the upper positions on the fingerboard, and have a pleasing, slightly banjo-like sound.

Introduction

Before the days of production lines and standardized specifications, every guitar was, to some extent, a custom instrument. When placing their orders with a company or individual craftsman, clients would frequently ask for small modifications to "regular" models (special finishes, different pickups), and could also commission wholly original, one-off designs – though this was expensive, time-consuming, and undertaken relatively rarely. Due to today's more streamlined manufacturing practices, this personalizing and customizing can no longer be handled on the factory floor, as it once was. Instead, most companies have "custom shops" staffed by experts who hand-build "no-compromise" versions of their firms' classic instruments, and can also collaborate with players to create the guitar of their dreams. Some of their finest work is featured on the following pages, together with a selection of the special guitars made by leading independent luthiers such as Linda Manzer, Rudy Pensa, and Mike Vanden.

LEFT & RIGHT: *Gibson SG Standard with handpainted artwork (replica of model formerly owned by Eric Clapton). (courtesy Guitar Village, Farnham)*

Most musicians order custom instruments because they provide extra performance and sonic refinement, but there are sometimes other motivations behind the production and purchase of "non-standard" guitars. The Gibson SG pictured here is a regular factory model with a hand-painted finish by World Class Guitars of New Fairfield, Connecticut; it is an exact replica of former Beatle George Harrison's famous "Fool" SG. The original, named for the Dutch art collective hired by Harrison to paint his SG in about 1964, was later given to Eric Clapton, who used it extensively during his time with Cream; it is now owned by Todd Rundgren. Ed Roman of World Class Guitars began making a version of it in 1983; his earliest "replica Fools" sold for $2,500, but he now produces so many of them that the price has been considerably reduced: a new "Fool" like the one shown here can cost as little as $895.

The Fender Custom Jaguar Stratocaster

The Jaguar company, based in Coventry, England, has been producing classic sports cars since the 1930s. The limited edition Fender Custom Jaguar Stratocaster shown here was the brainchild of Ivor Arbiter, a Jaguar enthusiast whose family firm is Fender's UK distributor. After detailed discussions with designers at Jaguar, blueprints for a specially decorated Strat, plus some of the materials needed to make it (including walnut burl for the fingerboard, headstock, and scratchplate, and the white seat leather used for its gig bag) were sent from the UK to Fender's Custom Shop in Corona, California in 1996. By the following year, the craftspeople there had completed the first prototype of the guitar, but the 25 production models (no more have ever been produced) were not issued until 1999; most of them went straight to Jaguar, and only about five instruments were available for retail sale. The Jaguar Strat shown here (No. 25 of 25) is one of these.

LEFT, RIGHT, & INSET: *1999 Fender Custom Jaguar Stratocaster. (courtesy Guitar Village, Farnham)*

Appropriately, the guitar is finished in racing green, and the celebrated Jaguar logo is inlaid on its fingerboard and displayed on its headstock. The instrument's hardware is gold plated, and it is fitted with three Lace Sensor pickups – a high-output "red" unit at the bridge, and "gold" transducers for the neck and middle positions.

One of key figures behind the development of the Jaguar Stratocaster was the car manufacturer's former Head of Design, Geoff Lawson, who sadly died before the guitar went into production. However, he was able to see the project through to its final stages, commenting to the UK's *Guitarist* magazine that "I can't think of two more appropriate companies [than Fender and Jaguar] for this collaboration. Both are world renowned for aesthetics, style, and quality and I hope that anyone who loves the practicalities of design as much as I do will appreciate our very British take on the world's most famous guitar."

Mark Knopfler's Pensa Guitars

Custom-designed guitars by Rudy Pensa are played by an impressive list of world-famous performers, including Mark Knopfler, Eric Clapton, and Lou Reed. His instruments, created in the workshop of his music store on West 48th Street in Manhattan (his base since the 1980s), originally carried the Pensa-Suhr label, and it was John Suhr, described as Rudy's "repair guru," who was responsible for building the model that first brought the two men international attention. This guitar – Pensa-Suhr No. 001 – was commissioned by Mark Knopfler, and its design evolved from a drawing made on a napkin while he and Rudy were having lunch! It made its debut in 1988 during Dire Straits' appearance at Nelson Mandela's 70th birthday concert (broadcast live throughout the world at a time when the future President of South Africa was still in prison) and Mark Knopfler has gone on to use it for many other major performances and recordings.

LEFT: *1996 Pensa Custom.*
(courtesy Mark Knopfler)

RIGHT: *c.1997 Pensa-Suhr.*
(courtesy Mark Knopfler)

Pensa-Suhr No. 001 *(illustrated opposite)* features EMG pickups, a Floyd-Rose bridge, and a beautiful one-piece top made from quilted maple. Mark, who possesses a wide range of vintage electrics, confirms that the Pensa-Suhr is something special: "[It] enables me to play with a lot more power than a Strat, and it's more flexible. I've got more range on it than most other guitars."

In 1990, John Suhr and Rudy Pensa parted company; Suhr spent the next few years working for Fender's Custom Shop, and has recently started his own lutherie business. Meanwhile, Rudy Pensa has continued to design superb electric instruments for Mark Knopfler and other distinguished customers. In 1993, Knopfler took delivery of a new Pensa solid-body with a flamed koa top and three single-coil pickups made by Lindy Fralin. Mark's most recent Pensa, dating from 1996 and shown here, also uses Fralin pickups, but this model features active circuitry, as well as a shorter, Gibson-style scale length.

Guitars by Tom Anfield

Tom Anfield, the resident consultant luthier at the Guitar Tree Luthiery in Putney, South London, has been a keen guitar player since childhood, and began making instruments in 1985 after first becoming expert in restoration work. He is self-taught, and developed his skills through necessity: "When I was a boy, I couldn't afford to get other people to set my guitars up, so I learned to do it myself." His ambitions were spurred by a bad experience with a careless guitar repairer during his teenage years; dissatisfied with the shoddy work that had been done on his instrument, Anfield remembers "banging the desk" and telling the offending craftsman that "one day, I'll be your nemesis!" He has made good on his promise; many leading performers now bring their treasured guitars to him for adjustment, maintenance, and modification, and his own custom designs are also highly sought after.

LEFT: *Tom Anfield blue mirrored Telecaster-type solid. (courtesy Tom Anfield)*

RIGHT: *Tom Anfield blue mirrored Stratocaster-type solid. (courtesy Tom Anfield)*

Most of Tom's guitars appear under his own logo, but the two Fender-style models shown here carry the Guitar Tree name, and represent his first attempt at building "economy price" instruments. Made within a few weeks of each other in early 2000, they have necks and bodies bought in from WD Components in the USA. Their perspex scratchplates give them an especially striking appearance, and thanks to their Kent Armstrong pickups, and Tom's innovative electronics, they play as well as they look. Both guitars incorporate "coil tap fade" controls, which act more subtly than the usual switches. As Tom explains, "If you set up your onstage sound so that you're just about to feed back on one coil, you can literally dial on and off your feedback with the knob!" The instruments also boast top quality hardware (including Gotoh bridges and Spertzel machine heads), and despite their sophistication, they sell for less than $900 each.

Custom Guitars by Jackson

Randy Rhoads, who commissioned the first-ever guitar to carry the Jackson logo (see pages 108–109), died in a flying accident while on tour with the Ozzy Osbourne Band in 1982. However, his advocacy of Grover Jackson's instruments encouraged many other hard rock and heavy metal players to adopt them, and the Rhoads guitar remains in Jackson's catalog in a variety of configurations and finishes.

In 1995, it received a startling "makeover" when the radically reshaped Roswell Rhoads made its debut. As its name and space age appearance suggest, this instrument was inspired by events in Roswell, New Mexico, where a UFO and its crew of aliens are alleged to have crashed in 1947. Its fingerboard inlays are modeled on another mysterious manifestation – the "crop circles" that sometimes appear in English cornfields. The custom version illustrated here, made from aircraft-grade aluminum alloy, dates from 1996.

LEFT: *1996 Jackson Roswell Rhoads.*
(courtesy Akai/EMI Guitar Division)

RIGHT: *Jackson Custom Shop FB.*
(courtesy Akai/EMI Guitar Division)

Although its founder is no longer directly associated with the firm (he left in 1989), Jackson maintains the tradition of offering an extensive range of choices on made-to-order instruments. The custom "FB" shown opposite is a reworking of a standard model; but Jackson undertakes to build its clients "almost anything they can dream up," and can provide flamboyant graphic finishes, special inlays, and other exotic extras.

Jackson guitars have a bold, outrageous quality that makes them ideal and highly sought-after instruments for rock playing. The company acknowledges that its designs are not for everyone, but remains strongly committed to the original and daring approach it has pioneered over the last two decades. As it states in its current catalog, "our goal is not to try and appeal to every last guitar player on earth, but rather to offer the most unique and individually styled instruments in the world."

Two Custom Models from Alembic

The Alembic Series II illustrated here was custom-made in 1972 for English rock musician Greg Lake (b.1948), best known as a bassist, but also an accomplished six-string player. Lake first came to fame with King Crimson in 1969, before becoming a member of the hugely successful progressive rock trio Emerson, Lake and Palmer (ELP).

When this guitar was built, model names had only just been introduced at Alembic, and there was considerable variation between individual instruments. Lake's Series II is slightly thicker than more recent examples, and its electronic circuitry is mounted on the right of its body (later Alembics have their electronics split between both body halves). It has an African zebrawood top and back with a maple core; the front and back veneers on the headstock are coco bolo, and the "through" neck is made from layers of maple, purpleheart, and cherry wood.

LEFT: *1972 Alembic Series II. (courtesy Alembic, Inc.)*

RIGHT & INSET: *1997 Alembic 25th Anniversary Sterling bass. (courtesy Alembic, Inc.)*

Alembic is also renowned for its bass guitars; distinguished users include the great jazz-rock player Stanley Clarke, who bought his first Alembic model in 1972. The limited edition instrument shown opposite (only 25 were made) dates from 1997, and commemorates 25 years of bass-building at Alembic.

The company's co-founder, Susan Wickersham (who designs the body shapes of all Alembic instruments), was responsible for the selection of woods and other materials for the bass. Its metal parts are sterling silver, while its top and back are made from 15-year-old Brazilian burl rosewood (highly prized by luthiers for its sound, and now a protected species), and the neck is maple and ebony. It was photographed at Alembic's headquarters in Santa Rosa, California.

Hugh Manson's Multi-Neck guitars

Many players and music fans associate double-neck guitars with the progressive and jazz-rock scenes of the 1970s, when stars like Jimmy Page and John McLaughlin frequently used axes such as the Gibson ES-1275, which combined six- and 12-string necks and pickups. Elaborate instruments such as these have retained their appeal for some virtuoso players, many of whom now prefer to have custom models made to their own exacting specifications.

Hugh Manson (see pages 106–107) is the UK's leading maker of electric guitars of this type. His creations seem to arouse keen anticipation in his customers; one leading rock guitarist was so eager to see the blueprints for his new Manson that the plans for it had to be redrawn to fit into the fax machine!

LEFT: *c.1980 Hugh Manson custom triple-neck. (courtesy Paul Evans)*

RIGHT: *c.1996 Manson double-neck. (courtesy Paul Evans)*

The two examples of Hugh Manson's work shown here, both commissioned by musician Paul Evans, clearly demonstrate his ability to create double- and triple-neck guitars that are musically and aesthetically unique. His blue-bodied double-neck was made in 1996, and is a combined six-string guitar and six-string bass. Both its necks are headless; the strings are tuned using the adjusters on each tailpiece, and the standard guitar section is fitted with a vibrato and a locking nut. The instrument has a maple body, and its two 22-fret fingerboards are ebony.

The triple-neck model dates from 16 years earlier, and provides two six-string necks and one 12-string neck. Like a number of Manson instruments, it incorporates illuminating LED (light-emitting diode) fret markers, connected to a power supply via a network of wires that run through tiny holes drilled through the body, which is made from mahogany and maple.

Custom Resonator Guitars from National Reso-Phonic

In order to build spectacular custom resonator guitars like the "Liberty" and "Coy Koi" shown here, Don Young and McGregor Gaines of National Reso-Phonic Guitars in San Luis Obispo, California (whose work is also featured on pages 168–169) use both hand-crafting and high technology. Nearly all the company's necks – which used to take more than six hours to carve manually – are now made using high-precision Computer Numeric Control equipment. This completes the carving and fretting in only 12½ minutes, and can mill, slot, and radius fretboards in seven minutes. Since acquiring CNC, National's production has increased by 80 percent; McGregor describes it as "a godsend – and it doesn't have mood swings or get cranky in the afternoon!"

LEFT: *National Reso-Phonic "Coy Koi" custom. (courtesy National Reso-Phonic)*

RIGHT: *National "Liberty" custom. (courtesy National Reso-Phonic)*

However, when it comes to tasks like nickel-plating the brass bodies on the Coy Koi and other National Reso-Phonic guitars, Don and McGregor prefer to use the traditional techniques developed in the late 1920s and 30s by the Dopyera brothers, founders of the original National company. Discovering and implementing such procedures has not been easy, as few surviving plans or blueprints survive from the prewar period. Nevertheless, Don and McGregor have succeeded in mastering their predecessors' methods, while also developing new approaches to production and design, and their synthesis of old and new has satisfied the demands of established resonator players, many of whom now play modern Nationals in preference to their fragile prewar instruments. And by raising the profile of the resonator guitar, the company is also helping to introduce it to younger performers, who, as Don Young observes, "are coming along, seeing this strange metal guitar with the hubcap on the front of it – and they go 'Wow!'"

Alan Timmins' Resonator Guitars

Alan Timmins, from Nottingham, was almost certainly the first luthier in Britain to build resonator guitars, and his unusual, carbon-fiber instruments are favored by Mike Cooper, Dave Peabody, Michael Messer, and several other leading players.

Alan received his first-ever guitar commission from a friend, resonator expert and collector Mark Makin. It was for a traditional, metal-bodied National Style 97-type model; Alan completed it in 1989, and was soon working on others, similar instruments. "I built half-a-dozen, maybe ten of them... but there were 16 bits of metal in each guitar, and it was a struggle, all the soldering, warping and lining up – a nightmare of a job." He decided to make molds, and use these to construct his guitar bodies from carbon-fiber. This simplified the production process, which required only two moldings: one for the back and sides, and one for the front.

LEFT: *Alan Timmins F1 carbon-fiber resonator model. (courtesy Alan Timmins)*

RIGHT: *Alan Timmins Style-97 type resonator model. (courtesy Mark Makin)*

The outcome of Alan's experiments was his F1 model. The strength and durability of its body's carbon-fiber formulation provides remarkable stability. Alan guarantees his instruments "airport baggage-handler-proof," and unlike metal-bodied guitars, they do not expand and go out of tune when exposed to heat. Wood is still used for the neck, and the cover-plates are made from laser-cut brass.

The crucial question of how the carbon-fiber bodies sound is best answered by one of Alan Timmins' customers, blues guitarist Dave Peabody, who summarized his reactions – and those of his audience – in a recent edition of *Blueprint* magazine. "Apart from looking wonderful, being black and silver, it's got the tone to me. It's very loud and it projects brilliantly into a microphone... I picked [my instrument] up on my way to the Edinburgh Blues Festival, where it had its inauguration. And it got a round of applause on its own."

Mario Maccaferri and John Monteleone

After emigrating to America in 1939, Mario Maccaferri, creator of the "Selmer-Maccaferri" acoustic made famous by gypsy guitarist Django Reinhardt (see pages 164–165), became involved in a wide range of design projects. These included working on the production of violins, saxophone reeds, guitars, and ukuleles, all made from plastic. He also remained active in more traditional methods of instrument-building, and developed a close relationship with one of today's leading American luthiers, John Monteleone, who recalls him as "a beautiful, incredible man. When I went up to his place, we'd sit down with his wife, Maria, have lunch together and tell stories, and then Mario would pick up the guitar after coffee and play for half an hour – beautiful classical arrangements. I was very fortunate to have had the opportunity to be a friend of his, and learn how to make a Maccaferri from Maccaferri himself."

LEFT: *1993 Monteleone Hot Club. (courtesy John Monteleone)*   RIGHT: *1987 Monteleone/Maccaferri Django. (courtesy John Monteleone)*

During one visit to the Maccaferris, John Monteleone discovered a badly damaged Selmer-Maccaferri that had been given by Django Reinhardt's widow to the great American guitarist Les Paul. John successfully restored it, and went on to work with Mario on a number of instruments, including the "Django" model shown here. This experience led to the creation of his "Hot Club" model, which combines the Maccaferri-Selmer influence with John's own approach to body design. Unlike the original "bent-top" Selmers, the "Hot Club" has a flat top, and the oval soundhole is enlarged and reshaped to boost the bass and projection. Another departure from tradition on this and many other Monteleone guitars is the use of butcher bone instead of ivory for the nut and saddle. As John explains, he entrusts this material to an assistant: his dog, Sasha. "My dog is actually a participant – she is a luthier apprentice, and she has the benefit of preparation of the bone!"

190

Classical Guitars by Gary Southwell

British luthier Gary Southwell draws inspiration from a range of different classical guitar-making traditions, and also creates his own strikingly original designs, which reflect his detailed knowledge of the past while offering ingenious new approaches.

Illustrated here is a Southwell replica of an instrument by the French luthier René Lacôte (1785–1855). Guitars from this period were smaller than the Torres designs that later became the accepted standard for makers and players, but their well-focused sound provides sufficient volume for many modern concert halls, as Gary explains. "Although they don't have the warmth and depth of a post-Torres guitar, they do have a very clear, ringing tone which tends to penetrate and cut through very well." The Lacôte replicas are used by a number of distinguished players, including early music expert Nigel North, and David Starobin, who has also worked closely with Gary on the development of his "Series A" range.

LEFT: *Southwell series "A" classic. (courtesy Gary Southwell)*

RIGHT: *Southwell replica Lacôte classic. (courtesy Gary Southwell)*

The "A" on these models stands for "adjustable," and the instruments feature a refined version of the moveable neck system invented by Johann Georg Stauffer (1778–1853) and used on early guitars by his pupil C.F. Martin. A key in the heel of the neck allows the string action to be raised or lowered swiftly, even in mid-concert; and the "floating" fingerboard is free from contact with the top, increasing the overall vibrating area. The instrument's intricately inlaid rosette is based on a Neolithic rock carving seen by Gary in Northumberland.

Gary aims to provide musicians with instruments that are inspiring, practical, and versatile. As he says, "to me the most important thing about a guitar is that it responds to what the player wants to do to it. A lot of guitars dictate to the player. I want to make an instrument that's full of character, but has the ability to be directed and enjoyed by the player."

Linda Manzer I

Toronto-based luthier Linda Manzer began making stringed instruments in the late 1960s. She then spent four years as an apprentice to Jean Larrivée (see pages 158–159), before going on to study archtop construction with the great Jimmy D'Aquisto (see pages 42–45). Linda is now recognized as one of the most imaginative guitar-builders of her generation, and she has undertaken commissions for several famous clients, including Carlos Santana, singer-songwriter Bruce Cockburn, and jazzman Pat Metheny, who approached to her in 1984 with a request for a guitar with "as many strings as possible." The result was the 42-stringed Pikasso seen here: it boasts four necks, two sound holes, and a custom-made Mark Herbert pickup system. The instrument, which took two years to complete, is designed not only to sound and look superb, but also to withstand an awesome degree of string tension, approaching 1000 lbs. when the Pikasso is fully tuned up!

RIGHT: *Linda Manzer Absynthe archtop. (courtesy Linda Manzer)*

ABOVE: *1984 Linda Manzer "Pikasso." (courtesy Linda Manzer*

Linda Manzer calls her Absynthe archtop acoustic "a museum quality instrument"; the late Scott Chinery, who commissioned a "Blue Absynthe" guitar from her as part of his famous "Blue Guitars" collection, described it simply as "a phenomenon." Among its special features is a sliding panel in the upper bout, which acts as an adjustable sound port, projecting some of the instrument's tone towards the player. An 18-inch (45.7-cm) model, the Absynthe is made from seasoned European timbers; its body and inlays are all hand-carved, and each piece of wood is carefully matched to achieve the best possible tone. Linda's designs are all built to order, and there is currently an 18-month waiting list for them: she comments that "because I work largely alone and give each guitar the careful attention required to create a customized instrument, I can only make about 15 instruments a year." Prices begin at $6,500; the Absynthe costs $22,000.

Linda Manzer II

All Linda Manzer's instruments are special, but The Bear (shown on the left) has a particularly significant place in her output. The design was created in 1998 to mark her 25th anniversary as a luthier, and takes its name from its "bear claw" spruce top. In her catalog, Linda explains that "'bear claw' refers to a distinctive feature, found in a few spruce trees, which makes the wood look as if it has been gouged by the massive claws of a bear." The guitar's beautiful headstock inlay depicts a spirit bear, a species native to northern British Columbia, while its heel incorporates a carving of the animal's paw reaching for berries. (The fine heel embellishment, designed by Linda, was carved, under her guidance, by her part-time assistant Tony Duggan-Smith.) Curly maple is used for The Bear's back and sides, and its neck is carved from a single piece of the same wood. The guitar dates from 2001, and is one of a trio of custom Manzer archtops (also including the 17-inch (43-cm), steel-strung Paradiso and Wildwood models), known collectively as the "Power of Three."

LEFT & INSET: *Manzer "The Bear."*
(courtesy Linda Manzer)

RIGHT: *Manzer "Classic 7."*
(courtesy Linda Manzer)

Linda Manzer builds all types of guitars, from classical models and flat-tops to exotic creations like the Pikasso *(seen on the previous pages)*, and the South American-style charango – sometimes called "the mandolin of the Argentine cowboy" – that she recently made for Bruce Cockburn. Since all her instruments are precisely tailored to her clients' requirements, even unusual features like customized pickups or extra strings can easily be accommodated. Her Classic 7 (right) is a special, seven-string version of her top-of-the-line "Au Naturel" 17-inch (43-cm) archtop. Like the regular model, it has a hand-carved European spruce top, curly maple back and sides, and an ebony fingerboard, pickguard, and tailpiece. Unusually for a Manzer, inlays and other decorations are kept to a minimum (hence the "Au Natural" appellation); but the quality of the woods and the guitar's striking shape ensure that its superlative sound is matched by its looks.

Rosendean Guitars

Trevor Dean, whose one-man company, Rosendean, is based in the southern English town of Woking, has been building custom guitars professionally since 1989. His best-known client is the distinguished British jazzman John Etheridge, who commissioned the six-string Black Ruby model seen here.

Etheridge is a hard-working player with a vigorous playing style, and the Black Ruby is designed to withstand a good deal of wear and tear. Its back and sides are made from black-eyed Persian larch, giving exceptional lightness and strength, and Trevor has protected the edges of the body with plastic binding. The instrument also offers an impressive range of tones, and its six-way control circuit and special high-pass filters ensure that, in Trevor's own words, there is always "treble to burn."

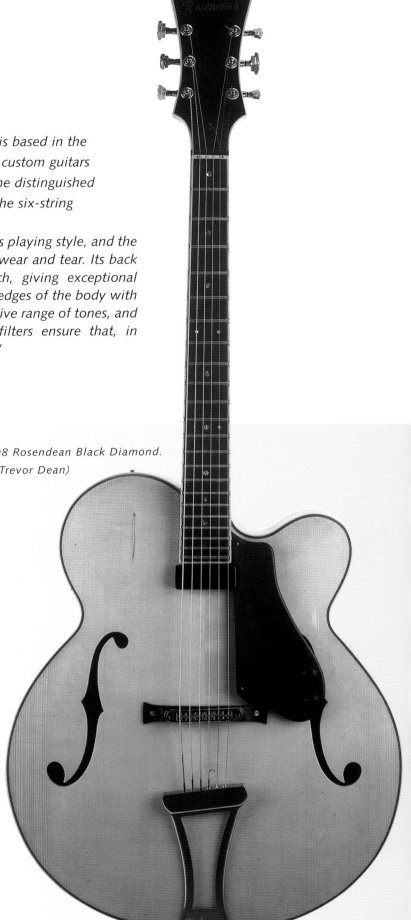

LEFT: *1996 Rosendean Black Ruby John Etheridge Signature Model. (courtesy Trevor Dean)*

RIGHT: *1998 Rosendean Black Diamond. (courtesy Trevor Dean)*

The second Rosendean model on these pages is a Black Diamond archtop with a pine top, maple back and sides, and maple, ebony, and satinwood bindings. It was made for musician Stewart Cockett, who recalls how, while the instrument was being built, he would call at Trevor's workshop every week to check on its development. "From November 1997 the guitar progressed quickly. Eventually the neck was fitted and I could sit [it] on my knee and get a sense of its size and balance. I was impatient to hear it, but weeks of finishing and polishing were still to come before strings went on and we heard how it would sound." The completed instrument proved to be well worth the wait. Stewart describes it as "quite fantastic," and characterizes its tone as "full, smooth, evenly balanced and totally inspiring... [it] will stimulate a whole new musical direction for me."

199

Mike Vanden I

Mike Vanden designs and builds guitars, mandolins, and other stringed instruments and electronics at his home in a remote rural area of Argyll, western Scotland. An expert in archtop making, he used the classic, 17-inch (43-cm)-bodied Gibson L-5 as a basis for many of his earlier models. However, in the last few years, he has slightly reduced the size and depth of his guitars – though his unique system of internal bracing (using four struts instead of the more usual X-pattern) and other special features ensure that they lack nothing in power and tone quality. Vanden archtops retain the projection and clarity of their more traditional predecessors, but also possess exceptional warmth and sustain; and Mike takes great pains to optimize their "plugged-in" performance. He explains that "It's important to me not just to get things to work well acoustically, but for the amplified sound to be good without needing to use masses of EQ."

LEFT & RIGHT: *Vanden custom archtop. (courtesy Max Brittain)*

The Mike Vanden archtop seen here was custom made for jazz guitarist Max Brittain, who commissioned it in 1994 and took delivery of it three years later. Max had previously used a Gibson L-7 as his main working instrument, but comments that "as soon as I got [the Vanden] I put the L-7 away – and I haven't used it since!" At 16 inches (40.6cm), it is an inch smaller than his Gibson, and it also boasts a slightly shallower body, making it exceptionally comfortable to play. The guitar has a top made from Canadian sitka spruce, and back, sides and neck of Scottish sycamore. Equally effective as an acoustic or electric, it is fitted with a Kent Armstrong pickup controlled by a single volume knob mounted on its ebony pickguard. A similar finish is used on the headstock, which bears Max Brittain's name, as well as the date of the instrument's completion.

Mike Vanden II

Mike Vanden and top British jazz guitarist Martin Taylor have been friends for over 20 years. Both now live in Scotland, and have recently collaborated on the development of two custom instruments, the Martin Taylor "Artistry" archtop, and the "Gypsy," a flat-top model intended (in Mike's words) to be "versatile enough to use for Django [Reinhardt]-type swing as well as fingerstyle Celtic or blues."

The "Artistry" is an inch narrower than the Max Brittain guitar seen on the previous pages, and features a more sophisticated pickup system, using a Vanden-designed Mimesis humbucker, and a modified Fishman piezo unit installed in the bridge. Their signals can be blended (via a preamp mounted underneath the pickguard and powered by two small lithium batteries) to produce a wide range of tones, from traditional jazz guitar timbres to acoustic sounds. The instrument has a sitka spruce top, and its back and sides are Scottish sycamore.

LEFT: *Vanden Martin Taylor Gypsy.*
(courtesy Mike Vanden/Martin Taylor)

RIGHT: *Vanden Martin Taylor Artistry.*
(courtesy Mike Vanden/Martin Taylor)

Martin Taylor observes that "what sets Mike apart is that, apart from being a great guitar builder, he sees [his instruments'] electronics as part of the overall design." This approach is clearly demonstrated by the "Gypsy" flat-top, used by Martin on his 2000 "Spirit of Django" tour, and described by him as "a very, very complete instrument – everything is there for a reason." It includes a detachable pickup unit that combines magnetic and piezo transducers and a high-quality condenser microphone; as the mic has its own output, its signal can be fed to a PA system, but excluded from the onstage monitors to prevent feedback. The "Gypsy" also performs outstandingly as an acoustic; like the "Artistry," it has a 15-inch (38-cm) body and a sitka spruce top, but its back and sides are mahogany, and ebony is used for the fingerboard and bridge. It is available to special order for approximately $2,700.

Custom Guitars by Robert Benedetto

In the last 30 years, Robert Benedetto has designed instruments for many leading players, from Johnny Smith and Chuck Wayne to Andy Summers and Earl Klugh, and a recent commission from the great American jazz guitarist Kenny Burrell (b.1931) has given him particular pleasure. As Bob explains, "in 1966, I bought my very first jazz guitar album, [Kenny Burrell's] Man at Work. He instantly became a great inspiration, [and] I felt strongly that someday I would make him a guitar. Imagine my excitement when I received a phone call from Kenny 30 years later: 'Bob, I'd like to talk with you about making me a guitar.' Wow, I'm living my dream!" The original plan was for Benedetto to build a single, custom instrument for Burrell, but it was subsequently decided to produce a limited edition "Kenny Burrell" model, incorporating a number of special features developed by its two creators.

LEFT: *1995 Benedetto "Il Colibri." (courtesy Carl Trollinger)*

RIGHT: *Benedetto "Kenny Burrell" model (prototype). (courtesy Robert Benedetto; photo by John Bender)*

The Burrell guitar has a tapered body depth (widening from neck to tailpiece) which, in Kenny Burrell's words, makes it "the most comfortable [instrument] you'll ever play," and is fitted with a single Benedetto B-6 pickup. Kenny first used the prototype in public at The Chinery Collection and Smithsonian Institution's "Blue Guitar" concert in June 1998. His response to Bob Benedetto's craftsmanship is simple and heartfelt: "You made my dreams come true."

The other custom Benedetto electric shown here is "Il Colibri" (The Dove), built for guitarist Carl Trollinger in 1995. Bob has been at pains to maximize the acoustic tone on this beautiful instrument, using an arched construction for the top and back, and leaving openings around the two pickups for the sound to escape. The guitar's body and neck are made from American bird's-eye maple, and it also boasts fine mother-of-pearl and abalone inlays on its headstock, fingerboard, and tailpiece.

The "Bird" and the "Pizzar"

Some of Steve Klein's recent electric guitars were featured on pages 110–111, but the instrument illustrated here, an earlier, custom model known as "The Bird," offers a sharp contrast to the ergonomic perfection of his current work. Described by his friend and colleague Lorenzo German as "the Anti-Klein guitar," it is heavy, not so comfortable to play, but, as he says, "an amazing art-piece." "The Bird" was commissioned in the early 1970s by W.G. "Snuffy" Walden, who had met Steve Klein in Colorado, but left for England with his band, the Stray Dogs, before the instrument was completed. The two men subsequently lost touch, but a few years ago, Steve discovered that Snuffy Walden had returned from overseas and had become a leading Los Angeles-based musical director, providing music for major TV shows such as Roseanne, Thirtysomething, *and* The West Wing. *Snuffy has now seen the guitar, but has yet to take delivery of it!*

LEFT: *1999 Benedetto "Pizzar." (courtesy Robert Benedetto; photo by John Bender)*

RIGHT: *Klein "Bird." (courtesy Klein Electric Guitars)*

The other custom instrument featured on these pages is a tongue-in-cheek Robert Benedetto solid-body creation, the "Pizzar." It dates from 1999, and was displayed at that year's National Association of Music Merchants (NAMM) show in Los Angeles. Shaped like a slice of New York-style pizza, with oregano, garlic, and other herbs and spices sealed into its finish, it was recently sold at auction in the USA. Sadly, Bob has no plans to make another "Pizzar," but has promised us some more "unexpected designs" in the near future!

PLAYERS A-Z

*T*his section is an encyclopedia of great guitarists: it profiles a cross-section of contemporary rock, blues, country, and jazz players, provides an outline of their careers, and lists some of the finest recordings on which they appear (including CD compilations and recent reissues of classic older albums and singles). Distinguished performers who are closely associated with particular bands are listed under their respective group names, while soloists, sidemen and session musicians have their own dedicated entries. There are also longer, more detailed biographies of especially influential axemen such as Jimi Hendrix, B.B. King, Eric Clapton, Edward Van Halen and Steve Vai.

AC/DC

Australian group formed 1974

Original line-up: Malcolm Young, guitar; Angus Young, Gibson SG guitar; Phil Rudd, drums; Mark Evans, bass; Bon Scott, vocals.

Career: Malcolm and Angus Young formed band in Sydney, Australia, but moved to Melbourne where original line-up evolved. Malcolm and Angus are younger brothers of George Young of 60s pop outfit Easybeats. This connection proved invaluable to AC/DC in terms of experience and production. However, there is no trace of the Easybeats' pop melodies in the sonic, full-frontal assaults of AC/DC, dominated by Angus' raunchy, visceral lead guitar.

The band developed a strong home following via release of two 1975 albums: **High Voltage** and **TNT**. Then came low-budget, hard-working tour of UK, which earned enough favorable response for UK album release. (Entitled **High Voltage**, UK LP is actually **TNT** minus two tracks, with two added from the Australian release **High Voltage**.)

Making every performance an athletic endurance contest for both band and audience, AC/DC gained notoriety in US. Everything else took second place to Scott's rivet-driving vocals and Angus' head-bobbing gyrotechnics. (Change in bass players in 1977 from Mark Evans to Cliff Williams almost went unnoticed.) Bon Scott's death from alcohol abuse in April 1980 occurred when AC/DC was on fringe of super-group status. In a fortunate twist of fate, AC/DC hired Scott-soundalike Brian Johnson (from band Geordie).

Following classic 1980 **Back In Black** LP, band maintained set formula with little original spark. Rudd quit AC/DC in 1983, with Simon Wright taking drum chair. Period of relative inactivity ended in 1987, when **Heatseeker** single earned UK Top 20 placing. Further personnel upheavals occurred when an "indisposed" Malcolm Young was temporarily replaced by cousin Stevie Young, and former Gary Moore and Firm drummer Chris Slade stepped in for Wright.

ABOVE: *Angus Young of AC/DC.*

1990 set **The Razor's Edge** returned group to both Top 10 UK/US album charts, and prompted major US tour, with Paul Greg ousting Williams for bass spot. In January 1991, AC/DC suffered traumatic concert date at Salt Lake City, when three fans were killed during frenetic crowd scenes. The group was later cleared of any responsibility for the tragedy.

Cliff Williams subsequently returned to the band, and original drummer Phil Rudd rejoined in 1995. They, Johnson, and the Young brothers remain tirelessly committed to AC/DC's distinctive brand of heavy rock, playing sellout shows throughout the world, and releasing massively successful recent albums such as **Ballbreaker** (1995) and **Stiff Upper Lip** (2000).

Recommended listening

High Voltage (Atco/Atlantic), 1976
Dirty Deeds Done Dirt Cheap
  (Atlantic), 1976
Let There Be Rock (Atlantic), 1977
Powerage (Atlantic), 1978
If You Want Blood (Atlantic), 1978
Highway to Hell (Atlantic), 1979
Back In Black (Atlantic), 1980
For Those About To Rock (Atlantic),
  1981
Fly On The Wall (Atlantic), 1985
Blow Up Your Video (Atlantic), 1988
The Razor's Edge (Atco), 1990
Ballbreaker (Electra), 1995
Stiff Upper Lip (Electra), 2000

AEROSMITH

US group formed 1970

Original line-up: Steve Tyler, vocals; Joe Perry, Gibson Les Paul guitar; Tom Hamilton, bass; Joey Kramer, drums; Brad Whitford, guitar.

Career: The band formed in Sunapee, New Hampshire, during summer 1970. Lots of local gigging in Boston led to dates at Max's Kansas City, where they were seen and signed by Clive Davis for CBS in late 1972. Despite emphasis on group participation, Aerosmith's undoubted stars were Jagger look-alike Tyler and guitarist Perry – also the band's main songwriters.

Long-term liaison with producer Jack Douglas began with second album **Get Your Wings** (1974). The following year, extensive touring finally paid off with success in American singles and album charts. **Toys In The Attic** (1975) went platinum within months of release and stayed in charts for two years. This sparked interest in first two albums which went platinum by the release of **Rocks** in 1976. 1976 saw re-issue of **Dream On**, which earned gold record three years after first appearance.

A well-deserved rest from touring may have caused 1977's **Draw The Line** to miss the fire of earlier albums, and in 1979, Perry quit, having devoted more time to solo projects than the band. His replacement was New Yorker Jimmy Crespo. Brad Whitford became the second original member to depart; Rick Dufay took his place, and this new aggregate cut just one album, **Rock In A Hard Place** (1982), the release of which was delayed by Tyler's motorcycle injury.

Unhappy with new line-up, Tyler approached Perry and Whitford to rejoin. They agreed and reformed band soon put a tour together and returned to the studios.

In 1986 Tyler and Perry forged an alliance between heavy metal and hip hop when they joined forces with Run DMC in remake of the Aerosmith hit **Walk This Way**.

In Spring 1987, Aerosmith recorded new album **Permanent Vacation** in Vancouver, Canada, produced by Bruce Fairburn and released in October. It sold out its first pressing and yielded a major hit single **Dude (Looks Like A Lady)**.

Pump album (1989) spawned UK Top 20/US Top 5 single **Love In An Elevator**, and led to first European tour for over a decade.

Aerosmith continues to make multi-million selling albums, and, in 1994, was the first-ever group to have a song (**Head First**) released exclusively on the Internet. Two years later, Gibson Guitars launched a limited edition Joe Perry Les Paul model, based on Perry's favorite, 1960 instrument, and now in regular production.

Recommended listening
Aerosmith (Columbia), 1973
Get Your Wings (Columbia), 1974
Toys In The Attic (Columbia), 1975
Rocks (Columbia), 1976
Draw The Line (Columbia), 1977
Night In The Ruts (Columbia), 1979
Greatest Hits (Columbia), 1980
Rock In A Hard Place (Columbia), 1982
Done With Mirrors (Geffen), 1985
Permanent Vacation (Geffen), 1987
Pump (Geffen), 1989
Get a Grip (Geffen), 1993
Big Ones (Geffen), 1994
Just Push Play (Columbia), 2001

DUANE ALLMAN

US guitarist, songwriter
Born Nashville, Tennessee, November 20, 1946
Died Macon, Georgia, October 29, 1971

Career: Duane Allman was raised in Daytona Beach, Florida; moved to Los Angeles in 60s. Formed Hour Glass with brother Gregg (born December 8, 1947) on keyboards, guitar, vocals; debut album, on Liberty Records, was cut at label's own LA studio. Band recorded follow-up at Rick Hall's Fame studio in Muscle Shoals, Alabama. Tapes for second album were rejected by Liberty, and band broke up.

Allman returned to Muscle Shoals for session work with Percy Sledge, Wilson Pickett, and others, before signing to Phil Walden's Capricorn label (based in nearby Macon, Georgia). Walden had previously managed the late Otis Redding, and helped Allman put together what became Allman Brothers Band.

New band gigged around Southern States building big following. Debut album **The Allman Brothers Band** (1969) was exciting mixture of progressive rock and R&B/blues roots. Interplay between Duane Allman's potent slide work and forceful technique of Dickie Betts was focal point of band's attractive new sound. From **Idlewild South** album (1970), single **Midnight Rider** was smash.

While band's reputation grew ever stronger, Duane Allman continued session work, both at Muscle Shoals and elsewhere. Allman's trading-off of licks with Clapton on the Derek And The Dominos' **Layla** album (1970) was among his finest work.

Tragedy hit band when Duane Allman died in motorcycle crash on October 29, 1971; he was just 24 years old. Last testament was superlative **The Allman Brothers Band At Fillmore East** album, recorded shortly before. Contained superb versions of blues standards **Statesboro' Blues** and **Stormy Monday** plus a 22-minute 40-second workout on **Whipping Post**.

Unbelievably, on November 11, 1972, Allman Brothers bassist Berry Oakley was killed in another motorcycle accident close to where Duane Allman had met his death the previous year. Band subsequently added Chuck Leavill, keyboards, and Lamar Williams, bass, and produced **Brothers and Sisters** album (1973), dedicated to Oakley. From this, instrumental hit **Jessica** proved to be Betts' tour-de-force; revealed depth of talent that had previously been somewhat overshadowed by Duane Allman.

Group has survived subsequent splits and internal disputes, and was inducted into the Rock and Roll Hall of Fame in 1995.

Recommended listening
The Allman Brothers Band (Capricorn), 1969
Idlewild South (Capricorn), 1970
At Fillmore East (Capricorn), 1971
Eat a Peach (Capricorn), 1972
An Anthology (Mercury), 1972
An Anthology Vol.2 (Mercury), 1974
Best of Duane Allman (Mercury), 1979
Fillmore Concerts (Mercury), 1992
With Derek and the Dominos:
Layla and Other Assorted Love Songs (Atco), 1970
Later Allman Brothers albums:
Brothers and Sisters (Capricorn), 1973
Win, Lose or Draw (Capricorn), 1975
Reach for the Sky (Arista), 1980
Brothers of the Road (Arista), 1981
Seven Turns (Epic), 1990
Peakin' at the Beacon (550), 2000

CHET ATKINS

US guitarist, record producer
Born Luttrell, Tennessee, June 20, 1924
Died Nashville, Tennessee, June 30, 2001

Career: The son of a piano teacher, Atkins made an early reputation as both fiddle player and guitarist, appearing on leading country music station WNOX, in Knoxville, Tennessee, while still a teenager. His guitar style was strongly influenced by Merle Travis (1917–83), whose technique of picking with thumb and forefinger was widely copied – although Atkins had his own variant of "Travis picking," and usually played with thumb and two or three fingers.

Atkins, soon in demand as a backing musician and solo performer, moved to Nashville in 1950. The following year, he released his first LP, **Chet Atkins Plays Guitar**. This (like earlier singles such as **Galloping On The Guitar**) was released on RCA Records, where Atkins became a senior A&R (Artists and Repertoire) man, supervising and playing on many major recordings, including sessions for Elvis Presley's 1956 classics **Heartbreak Hotel**, **Hound Dog**, and **Don't Be Cruel**. In 1957, he was appointed Chief of the label's Country Division, combining his managerial and production duties with a highly successful guitar-playing career.

Frequently credited (or blamed) for the development of the lush, string-laden "Nashville Sound," which helped to sell millions of country records, but was felt by purists to have diluted the music's essence, Atkins often brought new sounds and techniques to his own solo efforts. He was an early adopter of electronic effects like wah-wah and tremolo, and later developed an innovative nylon-strung electric classical guitar in association with Gibson.

By 1968, Atkins was a Vice-President at RCA, and he spent much of the next 10 years seeking out, signing, and developing the careers of some of the label's major stars. He resigned from the company in the late 1970s, but remained active as a player, recording and

performing prolifically for much of the next two decades. His studio projects included highly acclaimed duet CDs with Mark Knopfler and jazzman Martin Taylor, and he also guested on albums by Nanci Griffith, Emmylou Harris, and other Nashville luminaries. His final solo disc, **Almost Alone**, appeared in 1996.

During his 60-year career, Atkins was awarded no less than 13 Grammys, and in 1973 he was inducted into the Country Music Hall of Fame. At the ceremony, he was described as "A musician's musician, a gentleman's gentleman... [with a] distinctive [guitar] style, much copied but unduplicated."

Recommended listening

Finger Style Guitar (RCA), 1956
Mister Guitar (RCA,) 1959
The Guitar Genius (RCA), 1963
The Best of Chet Atkins (RCA), 1964
Fingerpickin' Good (RCA), 1965
Me And Jerry (w/Jerry Reed) (RCA), 1970
Nashville Gold (RCA), 1972
Chester & Lester (w/Les Paul) (RCA), 1975
Neck and Neck (w/Mark Knopfler) (Columbia), 1990
Almost Alone (Columbia), 1996

THE BAND

Canadian group formed late 50s

Original line-up: Jamie "Robbie" Robertson, Fender Telecaster and Stratocaster guitar; Garth Hudson, organ, saxophone; Richard Manuel, piano, vocals; Rick Danko, bass, vocals; Levon Helm, drums, vocals, mandolin.

Career: Levon Helm came from Arkansas, the rest from Canada. Group started out as backing band for Toronto-based rock 'n' roller Ronnie Hawkins; billed first as Canadian Squires, then as Levon And The Hawks, they quickly found fame in their own right, and toured Canada and US. Recorded classic single **The Stones I Throw** while in New York, where they met white blues singer John Hammond Jr, whose father was A&R boss of Columbia. Through the Hammond connection,

The Band encountered and began working with Bob Dylan, who was then moving more heavily into electric music. First collaboration was 1965 single **Can You Please Crawl Out Your Window**, and some members played on **Blonde On Blonde** album (1966). With Mickey Jones playing drums instead of Helm, The Band accompanied Dylan on 1965–66 US/European tour. Following Dylan's motorcycle accident in July 1966, The Band settled in Woodstock, New York, rehearsing and recording with him while he recovered. The results were heard on **The Basement Tapes**, originally a bootleg, but officially released in 1975.

The crossfertilization between Dylan and The Band can be heard on Dylan's **John Wesley Harding** album and The Band's own **Music From Big Pink** (1968), from which **The Weight** remains true classic.

Robertson's songs for second LP, **The Band** (1969), included **Up On Cripple Creek** and **The Night They Drove Old Dixie Down**, both subtle yet powerfully evocative traditional-style, truly American songs.

Undertaking lengthy tours on their own led to **Stage Fright** LP (1970). **Cahoots**, released the following year, included track cut in collaboration with Van Morrison.

There followed four-year hiatus before Robertson came up with new material; their next LP, **Moondog Matinee** (1973) was a tribute to their rock 'n' roll roots.

Before The Flood encapsulated live work with Dylan on 1974 tour; they provided back-up work on his **Planet Waves** (1974) album, and issued their own **Northern Lights, Southern Cross** the following year.

In late 1976 came shock announcement – their current tour was to be The Band's last, and would climax with a special Thanksgiving Day concert at San Francisco's Winterland, to be dubbed **The Last Waltz**. It was a triumphant occasion with such friends and collaborators as Bob Dylan, Ronnie Hawkins, Neil Young, Van Morrison, Joni Mitchell, Eric Clapton, and Muddy Waters turning out.

Islands (1977), a very laid-back effort, completed group's contractual obligations to their record label, Capitol, and they embarked on solo projects leaving the album and movie of **The Last Waltz** as their testament.

Recommended listening

Music From Big Pink (Capitol), 1968
The Band (Capitol), 1969
Stage Fright (Capitol), 1970
Cahoots (Capitol), 1971
Rock Of Ages (Capitol), 1972
Moondog Matinee (Capitol), 1973
Northern Lights, Southern Cross
   (Capitol), 1975
Best Of (Capitol), 1976
Islands (Capitol), 1977
The Last Waltz (Warner Bros.), 1978
Anthology Volume I (Capitol), 1978
Anthology Volume II (Capitol), 1980
To Kingdom Come – 31 Songs!
   (Capitol), 1989
With Bob Dylan:
Before The Flood (Island), 1974
The Basement Tapes (Columbia), 1975
Rick Danko solo:
Rick Danko (Arista) 1978

JENNIFER BATTEN

US guitarist
Born New York State

Career: Jennifer Batten is one of rock's most versatile and highly acclaimed guitar virtuosos. She started learning the instrument at the age of eight, and, as a young adult, studied at Los Angeles' prestigious Guitar Institute of Technology from 1979. During her early years as a professional, she worked in a wide variety of bands, and also developed and refined a distinctive two-handed tapping technique – demonstrated on her version of John Coltrane's **Giant Steps** (first released on a compilation album in 1989), which she used in 1987 when auditioning for Michael Jackson's live band. Her performance led to her being chosen (from over 100 hopefuls) as one of the two guitarists on Jackson's massive **Bad** tour, which began that September and lasted for over a year, with concerts

RIGHT: *Jennifer Batten is a world class soloist and session player.*

in the Far East, Europe, Australia, and the USA.

After completing the tour, Batten started work on her first solo album, **Above, Below and Beyond**. This came out in 1992, just before she rejoined Michael Jackson for his **Dangerous** tour (she was also featured on his 1996-7 **HIStory** concerts). While on the road, she met veteran British guitarist Jeff Beck (one of her greatest musical heroes), and gave him a copy of her CD. She was subsequently invited to record and tour

with him, and can be heard on his albums **Who Else!** (1999) and **You Had It Coming** (2001).

Batten's second solo disc, Momentum, appeared in 1997; she is currently making a follow-up.

Recommended listening

Above, Below and Beyond (Voss), 1992
Momentum (Mondo Congo), 1997
Who Else! (w/Jeff Beck) (Sony), 1999
You Had It Coming (w/Jeff Beck)
   (Sony), 2001

THE BEATLES

UK group formed 1959

Original line-up: John Lennon, Rickenbacker, Epiphone and Gibson guitars, vocals, guitar; Paul McCartney, guitar (later, Hofner and Rickenbacker basses), vocals; George Harrison, Rickenbacker, Gretsch and Gibson guitars, vocals; Stuart Sutcliffe, bass; Pete Best, drums.

Career: Formed in Liverpool area: influenced strongly by American rock 'n' roll and R&B records brought to port by sailors. After becoming local success, began to work in Hamburg, Germany, where bookings involved playing 8–10 hours per night for little money. However, this experience perfected crowd-pleasing ability (recordings from era are high on energy, short on polish).

Discovered by Liverpool record shop manager Brian Epstein in late 1961, by which time Sutcliffe had left group, preferring to remain in Germany. McCartney then moved to bass, and group became quartet (Sutcliffe died of brain haemorrhage, 1962). Epstein tried to acquire recording contract for Beatles, but without success. Finally, he convinced then minor Parlophone label to provide

audition. George Martin, head of label, signed group in late 1962, but suggested replacement of Pete Best – rest of band not unhappy, and recruited Ringo Starr from Rory Storm and The Hurricanes, fellow Merseyside group.

Prior to this, group had gone through several name changes – initially known as The Quarrymen (after school which Lennon attended), they became Silver Beatles, then simply The Beatles. Sessions for Parlophone proved promising – first single **Love Me Do**, released October 1962, reached No. 17 in UK while follow-up, **Please Please Me**, released early 1962, became huge hit. Similarly titled debut LP topped UK charts. Three further chart-toppers, **From Me To You**, **She Loves You**, and **I Want To Hold Your Hand**, followed in 1963.

US success delayed until 1964 when **I Want To Hold Your Hand** (fifth UK hit) topped US singles chart, beginning deluge of releases in US, almost all becoming major hits. Beatles' success opened floodgates for the "British Invasion," when numerous British acts broke through in US charts, including Rolling Stones, Gerry And The Pacemakers, Dave Clark Five, and many more. Lennon and McCartney were recognized as most potent songwriting partnership of rock 'n' roll era; besides providing all Beatles' hits, they also wrote

ABOVE: *The Beatles make a TV appearance in the mid-1960s.*

for Billy J. Kramer and Peter And Gordon.

Early beat group style evolved by 1966 LP **Rubber Soul** into much more original sound and approach, without affecting commercial success. By late 1966, when psychedelic album **Revolver** appeared, group had given up touring, mostly because hysterical fans made it too risky.

Sergeant Pepper's Lonely Hearts Club Band was released in June 1967. Group also got involved with Indian guru Maharishi Mahesh Yogi; during their attendance at transcendental meditation course in August, Brian Epstein, who had directed group's career throughout hugely successful period, died of alcohol/drug overdose.

Beatles plunged back into work, creating **Magical Mystery Tour** LP and TV film, an extension of **Sergeant Pepper**, and equally influenced by hallucinogenic drugs. It received critical roasting but has subsequently gained more admirers. Although group were now beginning to argue internally, they created remarkable double LP in 1968, known as **The White Album** because of completely white sleeve; it was preceded by singles **Lady Madonna** and **Hey Jude**. Year also saw formation of Beatles' company, Apple

Corps, with record label, shop, and film company. **Yellow Submarine** cartoon movie was created around fictional characters suggested by Beatles' songs.

1969 was final year of Beatles' activities, including fated film project **Let It Be**; this produced two chart-topping singles in title song and **Get Back**. Having left producer and svengali George Martin for **Let It Be**, group worked with him again on their final, classic LP, **Abbey Road** – but opposing business/artistic interests, particularly those of John Lennon and Paul McCartney, were becoming impossible.

Lennon and new wife, Japanese avant-garde artist Yoko Ono, formed splinter group, Plastic Ono Band, which scored with first single, **Give Peace A Chance**. Eventually, in 1970, new manager Allen Klein and famed record producer Phil Spector pulled together **Let It Be** project, but this further annoyed McCartney, whose departure was followed by the group's break-up. Subsequently, each enjoyed solo success to a greater or lesser extent *(see separate entry for George Harrison)*.

Recommended listening

With The Beatles (Parlophone), 1963
A Hard Day's Night (Parlophone), 1964
Beatles For Sale (Parlophone), 1964
Help (Parlophone), 1965
Rubber Soul (Parlophone), 1965
Revolver (Parlophone), 1966
Sergeant Pepper's Lonely Hearts Club Band (Parlophone), 1967
The Beatles (The White Album) (Parlophone), 1968
Abbey Road (Apple), 1969
Let It Be (Apple), 1970
The Beatles 1962–1966 (Apple), 1973
The Beatles 1967–1970 (Apple), 1973
John Lennon solo:
Plastic Ono Band (Apple), 1970
Imagine (Apple), 1971
Sometime In New York City (Apple), 1972
Mind Games (Apple), 1973
Walls and Bridges (Apple), 1974
Rock 'n' Roll (Apple), 1975
Shaved Fish (Apple), 1975
Double Fantasy (Geffen), 1980
Milk and Honey (Geffen) 1984
Paul McCartney (solo and w/Wings):

McCartney (Apple), 1970
Ram (Apple), 1971
Wings Wildlife (Apple), 1971
Band On The Run (Apple), 1974
WIngs Over America (Capitol), 1976
London Town (Capitol), 1978
Tug Of War (Columbia), 1982
Pipes Of Peace (Columbia) ,1983
Press To Play (Capitol), 1986
All The Best! (Capitol), 1987
Off The Ground (Capitol), 1993
Flaming Pie (Capitol), 1997
Run Devil Run (Capitol), 1999
Wingspan (Hits and HIstory) (Capitol), 2001
Driving Rain (Capitol), 2001

JEFF BECK

UK guitarist, composer, vocalist
Born Surrey, June 24, 1944

Career: Studied at Wimbledon Art College. Played lead guitar for Tridents before being recommended to Yardbirds by Jimmy Page as replacement for Eric Clapton. Spent two years with group, before leaving in December 1966 to sign solo deal. Scored singles chart success in 1967 with out-of-character sing-along **Hi Ho Silver Lining**. Also cut version of *Love Is Blue* (1968), and played guitar solo on Donovan's hit **Goo Goo Barabajagal (Love Is Hot)** before forming Jeff Beck Group featuring Rod Stewart, vocals; Ron Wood, bass; Ray Cook (later Mickey Waller), drums. Nicky Hopkins (keyboards) joined later, and group won big reputation in US with **Truth** (1968) and **Beck-Ola** (1969) LPs. Playing biting, R&B-edged heavy rock, group had exciting but tempestuous career, developing reputation for potent music and bawdy life-style. Wood and Stewart split to join Faces in 1969.

Beck planned new group with ex-Vanilla Fudge players Tim Bogert (bass) and Carmine Appice (drums), but when car accident kept Beck out of action for 18 months, the other two formed Cactus.

Beck re-appeared in late 1971 to form new Jeff Beck Group with Robert Tench, vocals, Max Middleton, piano, Clive Chapman, bass, and Cozy Powell, drums. After two albums he declared

band wasn't what he wanted and, on break-up of Cactus, formed trio with Bogert and Appice. This new formation broke up after one album, **Beck Bogert Appice** (1973), and a tour.

Beck retired again until, in 1975, George Martin produced **Blow By Blow** set, which found the guitarist experimenting heavily with jazz/rock fusion. Joining Jan Hammer Group for co-headlining tour (which produced joint album **Live** in 1977), Beck featured Hammer's synthesizer work on his 1976 album for Epic **Wired**.

Yet another inactive period ended in 1980 with appearance of **There And Back** album, again featuring Hammer, plus Tony Hymas, keyboards, Mo Foster, bass, and Simon Phillips, drums (Beck's first all-British band since Yardbirds).

In 1984, Beck joined with Rod Stewart in abortive attempt to form new group, but had US success with Honeydrippers (plus Jimmy Page, Nile Rodgers, and Robert Plant) a year later. Solo albums **Flash** (1985) and **Jeff Beck's Guitar Shop** (1989) both earned Grammys.

1990s projects included **Crazy Legs** (1993) and the groundbreaking **Who Else!** (1999), which combined blues and techno, and featured major contribution from American guitarist Jennifer Batten (qv). Batten also appeared on **You Had It Coming** (2001), and is a member of Beck's current touring band.

Recommended listening

Truth (Columbia), 1968
Beck-Ola (Columbia), 1969
Rough And Ready (Epic), 1971
Jeff Beck Group (Epic), 1972
Beck, Bogert, Appice (Epic), 1973
Blow By Blow (Epic), 1975
Wired (Epic), 1976
Live (with Jan Hammer Group) (Epic), 1977
There And Back (Epic), 1980
Early Anthology (Accord), 1981
Best Of (1967-69) (Fame), 1985
Flash (Epic), 1985
Late 60s (with Rod Stewart) (EMI), 1988
Jeff Beck's Guitar Shop (with Terry Bazzio and Tony Hymas) (Epic), 1989
Crazy Legs (Epic), 1993
Who Else! (Sony), 1999
You Had It Coming (Sony), 2001

GEORGE BENSON

US guitarist, vocalist
Born Pittsburgh, Pennsylvania,
March 22, 1943

Career: Began learning guitar at eight, and played and sang with several Pittsburgh R&B outfits during teens. However, models for guitar style were jazzmen such as Charlie Christian and Wes Montgomery rather than R&B practitioners.

Benson moved to New York in 1963 and joined band of organist Brother Jack McDuff; two years on road with McDuff's funky tenor sax-and keyboard-led outfit honed Benson's guitar style. In mid-60s, recorded for Columbia with own group, before forming working relationship with Creed Taylor's CTI label in 1970, becoming "house guitarist" and releasing albums under own name.

CTI period resulted in recognition of Benson's skills, and moderate success, including Grammy nomination for album **White Rabbit** (1972). His vocal talents, however, were largely ignored.

Real success came when Benson joined Warner Bros in mid-70s, and was teamed with producer Tommy LiPuma. Result was **Breezin'** (1976), a lightweight jazz-funk effort that struck lucrative chord with record-buying public. Eventually going double platinum, it yielded two hit singles in title track (an instrumental) and **This Masquerade**, on which Benson exhibited his attractive Stevie Wonder-influenced voice. Next album, **In Flight** (same year), followed similar formula and also achieved double platinum sales.

Further hit singles and albums ensued, and Benson established himself as major concert draw throughout the world. Always accompanied by the very best musicians, Benson vocalizes to good effect, plays inventive guitar in effortless style, and occasionally combines both in unison scat-singing/guitar improvisations.

Partnership with renowned musician and producer Quincy Jones brought about renewed success with **Give Me The Night** LP (1980), and further hits through early 80s.

One of a handful of jazz musicians to achieve crossover success, Benson still delivers the goods in traditional vein, as witnessed by 1991 Grammy award for **Basie's Bag**. However, he returned to a soul feel for **Love Remembers** (1993), his last Warners album; in the mid-1990s he moved to GRP Records, where his recent output has included **That's Right** (1996), **Standing Together** (1998), and **Absolute Benson** (2000).
Guitars: Ibanez G310, Gibson Super 400 CES.

Recommended listening

Benson Burner (Columbia), 1967
Shape Of Things (A&M), 1968
White Rabbit (CTI), 1972
Breezin' (Warner Bros.), 1976
Summertime: In Concert (CTI), 1977
In Flight (Warner Bros.), 1977
Weekend in L.A. (Warner Bros.), 1978
Give Me The Night (Warner Bros.), 1980
The George Benson Collection (Warner Bros.), 1981
While The City Sleeps (Warner Bros.), 1986
Love Remembers (Warner Bros.), 1993
That's Right (GRP), 1996
Standing Together (GRP), 1998
Absolute Benson (GRP), 2000

BLACK SABBATH

UK group formed 1969

Original line-up: Ozzy Osbourne, vocals; Tony Iommi, Gibson SG and Patrick Eggle guitars; Terry "Geezer" Butler, bass; Bill Ward, drums.

Career: Started in Birmingham as blues band Earth; in late 1969 they changed name to Black Sabbath and recorded first album of same name, which remained in UK charts for 13 weeks.

International success followed quickly with release of 1970 album **Paranoid**; LP and single of same name hit on both sides of Atlantic. Band played first successful American tour in autumn 1970. For the next three years, they toured regularly and recorded prolifically, but in 1973, managerial problems forced cessation of activities. Release of album **Sabotage** (1975) re-established Sabs as major force in heavy metal, a position they have maintained ever since.

Since 1978 band has undergone several personnel changes. Ozzy Osbourne left, only to return a few months later, but in 1979 he departed again to form own band, Ozzy Osbourne's Blizzard of Oz. He was replaced by Ronnie James Dio, formerly singer with Ritchie Blackmore's Rainbow. At the end of 1980 Bill Ward left for personal reasons, and Vinnie Appice, brother of the more famous Carmine, was recruited.

Fluctuating line-up saw Ian Gillan as new vocalist, until he left to rejoin Deep Purple, replaced by Dave Donato. Dio and Appice also split and Ward returned.

In July 1985 the original Sabbath with Ozzy reunited for an appearance at Live Aid in Philadelphia. New singer Glenn Hughes cut the **Seventh Star** album with them in 1986, and the band subsequently toured the UK with Eric Singer (drums), Dave Spitz (bass), Geoff Nichols (keyboards), and Ray Gillen (vocals).

In November 1987 the Sabs released critically acclaimed **The Eternal Idol** with vocalist Tony Martin. For 1989 set **Headless Cross**, line-up comprised Iommi; Cozy Powell, drums; Neil Murray, bass; and Tony Martin. Ronnie James Dio returned as vocalist on **Dehumanizer** (1992), but Ozzy Osbourne was reunited with Sabbath at a live show that November, and (following further personnel changes) he appeared with them again on the double-CD **Reunion**, recorded in 1997 and released the following year. Cozy Powell (who had left the band in 1995) died in a road accident in April 1998; in the last few years Osbourne, Iommi, original bassist Geezer Butler, and Bill Ward have continued to record and perform together as Black Sabbath.

Recommended listening

Black Sabbath (Warner Bros.), 1970
Paranoid (Warner Bros.), 1970
Master of Reality (Warner Bros.), 1971
Black Sabbath 4 (Warner Bros.), 1972
Sabbath Bloody Sabbath (Warner Bros.), 1973
Sabotage (Nems/Warner Bros.), 1975

Heaven And Hell (Warner Bros.), 1980
Born Again (Vertigo), 1983
Seventh Star (Vertigo), 1986
The Eternal Idol (Vertigo), 1987
Headless Cross (IRS), 1989
Tyr (IRS), 1990
Dehumanizer (Reprise/Warner), 1992
Forbidden (IRS), 1995
The Sabbath Stones (compilaton)
   (IRS), 1996
Reunion (Epic), 1998

MARC BOLAN

UK vocalist, guitarist, songwriter
Born Mark Feld, London, July 30,
1947
Died September 16, 1977

Career: In early 60s, then teenage Feld won wide exposure in media as archetypal mod, which led to brief career as male model. Later dropped sharp besuited image for loose-fitting flower clothes, beads and espousal of "flower power." Changed name to Bolan for

debut single **The Wizard** (1966). Briefly joined glam-rock band John's Children, scoring with **Desdemona**.

Joined by Steve Peregrine Took (named for a character in J.R.R. Tolkien's *Lord of the Rings*), Bolan attempted to form five-piece electric band, but hire-purchase company snatched back equipment. Bolan and Took consequently started working in 1968 as acoustic folksy-rock duo Tyrannosaurus Rex. Their albums (**My People Were Fair And Had Sky In Their Hair But Now They're Content To Wear Stars On Their Brows** (1968), **Prophets, Seers And Sages, The Angels Of The Ages** (1968), and **Unicorn** (1969) captured the essence of the period's love-and-peace philosophy. Steve Took quit in 1970, replaced by Mickey Finn (who met Bolan in a health food restaurant). On **Beard Of Stars** (1970), Bolan switched to electric guitar. Later that year, with name shortened to T.Rex, they notched surprise UK No. 2 with soft-rock but uptempo **Ride A White Swan**. Added drummer Bill Legend and bass player Steve Currie in time for next

single **Hot Love**, which topped chart for six weeks in early 1971. **Get It On** became their second No. 1 later same year.

String of UK hits made 1972 big year for T.Rex. In 1973, ex-Beatle Ringo Starr directed movie **Born To Boogie**, but it flopped, and by end of year Bolan's fickle young audiences were deserting him.

The glamour and glitter became tarnished. Bolan left his wife, June Child, to live with black American soul singer Gloria Jones (who bore him a son, Rolan). He put on weight alarmingly, churned out ever less satisfying material, and broke up T.Rex before slinking off to tax exile in Los Angeles.

Bolan undertook comeback tour with Jones early in 1976, and went on to host a weekly TV music show as he fought hard to rebuild career. However, early one September morning in 1977, a car driven by Gloria Jones careered off road just outside London and passenger Bolan was killed, aged 30.

Recommended listening
As Tyrannosaurus Rex:
My People Were Fair... (Regal
   Zonophone), 1968
Prophets, Seers and Sages... (Regal
   Zonophone), 1968
Unicorn (Regal Zonophone), 1969
Beard of Stars (Regal Zonophone),
   1970
As T.Rex:
T.Rex (Fly), 1970
Electric Warrior (Fly), 1971
Bolan Boogie (Fly), 1972
The Slider (EMI), 1972
Greatest Hits Volume 1 (Hallmark),
   1978
Collection (Hallmark), 1978
Solid Gold (Fame), 1979
Unobtainable (Nut), 1980
In Concert (Marc), 1981
Platinum Collection (Cube), 1981
Best Of 20th Century Boy (K-Tel), 1985
Zinc Alloy And The Hidden Rides Of
   Tomorrow (Marc On Wax), 1985
Bolan's Zip Gun (Marc On Wax), 1985
Marc Bolan And T.Rex (Marc On
   Wax), 1987

LEFT: *Marc Bolan at the height of his fame in the early 1970s.*

CHUCK BERRY

US vocalist, guitarist, composer
Born Charles Edward Berry, San Jose,
California, October 18, 1926

Career: Arguably the most influential guitarist and songwriter in the entire history of rock; also an effective vocalist, whose excellent diction ensured maximum impact for his inventive lyrics. Many of his songs became anthems of teenage life.

Family moved to St Louis, Missouri, in 1930s; young Berry gained musical experience in school glee-clubs and church choirs. Trained as a hairdresser, then worked in car factory; performed with small group during evenings and weekends.

In 1955, recorded some songs for audition tape, and travelled north to Chicago to look for successful bluesman MuddyWaters. Muddy suggested Berry take tape to Chess Records. Leonard Chess was interested in embryonic version of **Maybellene** and had the young hopeful record polished version for Chess debut; disc topped R&B chart in 1955, and began prolific succession of hits like **Brown Eyed Handsome Man, Roll Over Beethoven, Sweet Little Sixteen,** and **School Day**.

Berry's records are notable for their lyrical content and distinctive guitar style; most discs had memorable guitar introductions and incisive solos midway. On stage, Berry played solos while hopping around in squatting posture; this came to be described as a "duckwalk."

Stream of hit singles resulted in several movie parts; Chuck was committed to celluloid in *Go Johnny Go* and *Rock Rock Rock*; also featured in film of 1958 Newport Jazz Festival, *Jazz On A Summer's Day* singing **Sweet Little Sixteen**. His performance considered quite revolutionary in such context! After his 1959 conviction for immorality offence (taking underage girl across state lines), Chess still issued Berry singles, but with reduced sales.

Recorded fresh material upon release from custodial sentence in 1964; scored hits with **Nadine, No Particular Place To Go,** and **You Never Can Tell**. Made first overseas tour and played in England with Carl Perkins. Left Chess after financial temptation from Mercury, but only decent Mercury disc was **Club Nitty Gritty** (1966) – others were mainly re-hashes of old hits; returned to Chess in 1969. During 1972 toured England and recorded

LEFT: *A living legend – the great Chuck Berry (and his Gibson ES-335) in full flight*

"live" and studio material; from live set, **My Ding-A-Ling** was issued as single. This version of old blues song with suggestive lyric topped US and UK charts that year (sadly Berry's only No. 1).

As Chess label faded, Chuck cut final **Bio** LP in 1973. Began to concentrate more on tours than recording; gained reputation for being hard to deal with financially. Has become regular attraction at cosmopolitan music festivals. Brief contract with Atlantic yielded solitary 1979 LP **Rock It**, patchy in quality, a commercial failure.

1988 saw interest in rock legend flare yet again with publication of *Chuck Berry: The Autobiography*, and movie *Hail! Hail! Rock And Roll*. However, notoriety was maintained with charges of child abuse, drug and firearm possession in the summer of 1990, the courts imposing a custodial sentence plus two years' probation.

Recommended listening

Hit Singles	US	UK
Maybellene, 1955	5	-
School Day, 1957	3	24
Rock 'n' Roll Music, 1957	8	-
Sweet Little Sixteen, 1958	2	16
Johnny B Goode, 1958	8	-
Carol, 1958	18	-
Let It Rock/Memphis Tennessee, 1963	-	16
No Particular Place To Go, 1964	10	3
You Never Can Tell, 1964	14	23
My Ding-A-Ling, 1972	1	1
Reelin' And Rockin', 1972	27	18

Albums

Golden Hits (Mercury), 1967
Greatest Hits (Archive Of Folk And Jazz Music), 1967
Bio (Chess), 1973
Chuck Berry Volume 1 (Impact), 1979
Chuck Berry Volume 2 (Impact), 1979
Rock It (Atlantic), 1979
Chess Masters (Chess), 1983
Best Of (Vogue, France), 1983
Reelin' And A Rockin' (The Collection), 1985
Greatest Hits (Charly), 1986
Two Dozen Berrys (Vogue, France), 1986
Rock 'n' Roll Rarities (Vogue, France), 1987
21 Greatest Hits (Bescol), 1987
The Chess Box (Chess), 1990

Worth Searching Out

After School Session (Chess), 1958
One Dozen Berrys (Chess), 1958
Golden Decade Volumes 1–3 (Chess), 1973

BON JOVI

US group formed 1982

Original line-up: Jon Bon Jovi, vocals; David Bryan, keyboards; Richie Sambora, Fender Stratocaster guitar; Tico Torres, drums; Alec Such, bass.

Career: Teen idols whose manicured locks and zippy stage outfits caused a torrent of tears at their sell-out stadium concerts during the 80s.

Formed by Jon Bon Jovi (real name Bongiovi), original single **Runaway** (1983) was cut with session musicians, and turntable action on several prominent radio stations persuaded singer to hire permanent group.

The original quintet subsequently survived four multi-platinum albums (1986's **Slippery When Wet** topped 10 million sales), and steady diet of major gigs (having started as support act for ZZ Top and then Kiss). Monster world tour, which included nigh on 240 shows, saw band in Moscow for 1989 *Music For Peace* concert, before exhausted members began hiatus the following year.

Along with Elton John and guitarist Jeff Beck, Bon Jovi (singular) returned to record soundtrack album for *Young Guns II* movie, from which **Blaze of Glory** (1990) earned the permed, teased, and coiffured singer a US No. 1, while Sambora avoided unemployment with work for girlfriend Cher (Jon Bon Jovi had collaborated with the singer on her 1988 hit **We All Sleep Alone**) and 1991 collection **Stranger In This Town**.

Band came together again to record **Keep The Faith** (1992), and continued to tour extensively throughout the 90s, also issuing hits compilation **Cross Road** (1994) and an album of new material, **These Days**, the following year. Jon's solo set, **Destination Anywhere**, appeared in 1997, and was followed in 2000 by a new CD by Bon Jovi the group, **Crush**.

Recommended listening

Bon Jovi (Mercury/Vertigo), 1984
New Jersey (Mercury/Vertigo), 1988
7800 Degrees Fahrenheit
  (Mercury/Vertigo), 1985
Slippery When Wet (Mercury/Vertigo),
  1986
Stranger In This Town
  (Mercury/Vertigo), 1991
Keep The Faith (Polygram/Mercury),
  1992
Cross Road (Best of Bon Jovi)
  (Polygram/Mercury), 1994
These Days (Polygram/Mercury), 1995
Crush (Island Def Jam/Mercury), 2000
One Wild Night (Live 1985–2001)
  (Universal/Island Def Jam), 2001
Jon Bon Jovi solo:
Blaze Of Glory/Young Guns II
  (Mercury) 1990
Destination Anywhere
  (Polygram/Mercury) 1997

BILLY BRAGG

UK singer/songwriter, guitarist
Born Barking, Essex,
December 20, 1957

Career: Bragg was member of punk/R&B band Riff Raff from 1977 to 1980 (their records, on UK indie labels Chiswick and Geezer, included the EP **I Wanna Be A Cosmonaut** (1977) and singles **Every Girl** and **Kitten** (both 1980). After a brief spell in the British Army, he took a temporary job in a record store, and began performing as a soloist. His cheaply

LEFT: *Jon Bon Jovi and Telecaster.*

recorded, seven-track EP, **Life's A Riot With Spy Vs Spy** (1983), was subsequently rejected by virtually every record company until indie outfit Go! Discs decided to give it a shot. The label was rewarded with more than 120,000 sales, and Billy Bragg became an instant cult hero. Stand-out tracks on **Spy Vs Spy** include **A New England**, which became a Top Ten UK single in a cover version (with slightly altered lyrics) by Kirsty MacColl in 1985.

Bragg's first full-length LP, **Brewing Up With Billy Bragg**, appeared in 1984, and was followed by the **Between The Wars** EP (1985) and **Talking With The Taxman About Poetry** (1986), which spawned UK hit single **Levi Stubbs' Tears**. The strongly political content of many of Bragg's songs was matched by his commitment to the UK Labour Party; he participated in its 1985 "Red Wedge" rock tour (part of a nationwide "Jobs For Youth" campaign), and has been a high-profile campaigner for socialism throughout his career. He also raised money for UK Childline charity with his cover version of The Beatles' **She's Leaving Home**, a UK No. 1 single in 1988 (it was released as the flip side of Wet Wet Wet's **With A Little Help From My Friends**).

After the appearance of **Workers' Playtime** (1988), Bragg launched his own Utility label in 1990, but following the completion of 1991 CD **Don't Try This At Home** (which included UK hit single **Sexuality**), he took a five-year break from recording after becoming a father. He eventually returned to the studio to make **William Bloke** (1996), and soon afterwards embarked on a project to provide music for hitherto unpublished lyrics by one of his musical idols, US singer/songwriter and political activist Woody Guthrie (1912–67). He recorded these new songs with US band Wilco, and they appeared in 1998 as **Mermaid Avenue**. A second Bragg/Wilco/Guthrie set followed in 2000, preceded by Bragg's **Reaching To The Converted** solo compilation (1999).

Recommended listening

Life's A Riot With Spy Vs Spy (Go! Discs), 1983

Brewing Up With Billy Bragg (Go! Discs), 1984
Talking With The Taxman About Poetry (Go! Discs), 1986
Workers' Playtime (Go! Discs), 1988
Don't Try This At Home (Go! Discs), 1991
William Bloke (Cooking Vinyl), 1996
Mermaid Avenue (w/Wilco) (Elektra), 1998
Mermaid Avenue Volume II (w/Wilco) (Elektra), 2000

JACKSON BROWNE

UK composer, vocalist, guitarist
Born Heidelberg, Germany,
October 9, 1948

Career: Raised in Los Angeles, Browne moved to New York in 1967 and began playing guitar for Nico. She liked his original songs and used three on her 1968 **Chelsea Girl** album. Soon Browne was placing songs with folk-rock artists such as Johnny Rivers, the Nitty Gritty Dirt Band, and Tom Rush. By the turn of the decade, Browne had attracted the attention of the fledgling Asylum label (whose artists already included Joni Mitchell and other leading names); his 1972 debut album for them, **Jackson Browne**, contained mostly material already recorded by others. Sales were not impressive, but critical reviews were strongly favorable. Browne worked closely with newly formed Eagles, co-writing band's first major hit, **Take It Easy**. His version is on his second LP, 1973's **For Everyman**. Again reviews bordered on ecstatic; again sales bordered on non-existent. Browne seemed doomed to cult status as excellent composer. His low-key stage performance also seemed antithetical to usual excess prevalent in rock.

But Browne's reputation for heartfelt emotion began spreading and, following 1974 release **Late For The Sky**, his back catalog began selling well; however, his next effort was delayed by suicide of his wife. **The Pretender** (1976) seemed to strip Browne to essentials and suddenly he was a star.

Refusing to cash in on success, he

made extended tour of US and Europe, releasing **Running On Empty** in 1977. This album seemed radical departure from past work – it had rough edges not normally associated with Browne. Critics did not know quite what to make of it, and reviews dwelt on the risk Browne had taken in recording under adverse conditions while on tour. The public loved the results and sales boomed.

1980 set **Hold Out** marked return of some order in Browne's personal life, and his involvement with the **No Nukes** live triple album (also featuring Bonnie Raitt, Linda Ronstadt, James Taylor, and others, and recorded at Madison Square Garden in 1979) provided decent funds for US "Safe Energy" committee. Browne's determined anti-nuclear stance made him a regular at fundraising concerts.

Lawyers in Love (1983) ended recording hiatus, but a further three years followed before **Lives In The Balance** surfaced. Both LPs made US Top 50.

After appearing at the special concert, held in 1988 at London's Wembley Stadium and broadcast throughout the world, to mark the 70th birthday of South African leader Nelson Mandela, Browne released the strongly political album **World In Motion** in 1989. There was a lengthy hiatus before the appearance of **I'm Alive** (1993), which was followed, after a further gap, by **Looking East** (1996); but despite the relative infrequency of his recent solo albums, Browne remains active as a live performer.

Recommended listening

Jackson Browne (Asylum), 1971
For Everyman, (Asylum), 1973
Late For The Sky (Asylum), 1974
The Pretender (Asylum), 1976
Running On Empty (Asylum), 1978
Hold Out (Asylum), 1980
Lawyers In Love (Asylum), 1983
Lives In The Balance (Asylum), 1986
World In Motion (Asylum), 1989
I'm Alive (Asylum), 1993
Retrospective (Elektra), 1993
Looking East (Elektra), 1996
The Next Voice You Hear: The Best of Jackson Browne (compilation) (Elektra), 1997

JAMES BURTON

US guitarist
Born Shreveport, Louisiana,
August 21, 1939

Career: Began playing guitar at the age of 12, and quickly made a name for himself at local country music stations. Dale Hawkins' classic single **Suzie Q** (1957), on which Burton played lead, was actually recorded at a radio studio in the guitarist's hometown, Shreveport. As a result of his work with Hawkins, Burton came to the attention of Ricky Nelson, who invited the talented young musician to come to Los Angeles and join his backing band. Burton took the job, and appeared on a string of Nelson's singles between 1958–63, including **Never Be Anyone Else But You** (1959) and **Hello Mary Lou** (1961).

Burton then went freelance, doing a wide variety of session work before replacing Scotty Moore as Elvis Presley's personal guitarist in 1969. Relatively relaxed schedule of sessions, concerts, and cabaret appearances with Presley left time for other projects for Burton and his fellow Presley sidemen, who contributed to two solo LPs by ex-Byrd Gram Parsons: **GP** (1973) and **Grievous Angel** (1974). Parsons' protégée, Emmylou Harris, was also featured on these albums, and after Parsons died from a drugs overdose in September 1973, Burton and other Presley associates became part of her Hot Band.

Burton remained a regular member of the Hot Band until 1976, and following Elvis Presley's death the following year, he began a close association with singer-songwriter John Denver, contributing to many of his albums, live shows, and TV specials. During this period, Burton also worked with rock 'n' roll legend Jerry Lee Lewis.

More recent projects have included extensive touring in *Elvis – The Concert*, a 'virtual' Presley show created with video projections of The King and live accompaniment from Burton and other ex-Presley alumni. In March 2001, Burton was inducted into the Rock and Roll Hall of Fame in New York.

Recommended listening
With Ricky Nelson:
Legacy (Capitol), 2000
With Elvis Presley:
Hits of the 70s (RCA), 1974
In Concert (RCA), 1977
With Gram Parsons:
GP (Warner/Reprise), 1973
Grievous Angel (Warner/Reprise), 1974
With Emmylou Harris:
Pieces of the Sky (Reprise), 1975
Elite Hotel (Reprise), 1976
With John Denver:
John Denver (RCA), 1979

THE BYRDS

US group formed 1964

Original line-up: Roger McGuinn, Rickenbacker lead guitar, vocals; David Crosby, rhythm guitar, vocals; Gene Clark, vocals, tambourine; Chris Hillman, bass; Michael Clarke, drums.

Career: Originally called the Jet Set before arrival of Hillman and Clarke; recorded series of demos for World Pacific, later released in 1969 as **Preflyte**. As trio, cut one unsuccessful single for Elektra, **Please Let Me Love You**, then signed to Columbia as The Byrds. Acclaimed as America's answer to The Beatles, they successfully combined the lyrical genius of Bob Dylan (recording classic cover versions of several of his songs) with The Beatles' melodic expertize to produce an instinctively recognizable style. This was exemplified by million-selling **Mr Tambourine Man**, which topped US and UK charts during Summer 1965.

Generally acknowledged as pioneers of "folk rock," Byrds produced a string of consistently excellent singles during 196–67, including **Turn! Turn! Turn!**, **Eight Miles High**, **So You Want To Be A Rock 'n' Roll Star**, and **My Back Pages**. First two albums consisted mainly of Dylan compositions, and love songs from the prolific Gene Clark.

By early 1966, folk-rock repertoire was extended to include a number of jazz-flavored and hard-rock items. The seminal **Turn! Turn! Turn!** LP (1965) rivalled the output of such contemporaries as The Beatles and The Stones, but Byrds suffered from radio bans; some numbers – notably the classic **Eight Miles High** (also 1965) – were, sometimes unjustly, labelled "drug songs."

In March, career development was further complicated by shock departure of Gene Clark. Continuing as quartet, they released **Fifth Dimension** (1966) – a neat amalgam of folk-rock instrumentation, jazz, and tinges of Indian ragas that fully demonstrated their ability to survive and thrive.

In late 1966, Byrds retired temporarily from live appearances amid speculation that they were breaking up.

1967 was most crucial year in their history, beginning with brilliant **Younger Than Yesterday** LP, which fully demonstrated David Crosby's growing importance as singer/songwriter. More surprisingly, album featured several country-flavored songs from Chris Hillman, the fourth singer/songwriter to emerge from original line-up. Creative

tensions in group led to several flare-ups and a struggle for leadership between McGuinn and Crosby. Loss of management team, Jim Dickson, and Eddie Tickner, only made matters worse.

Arguments over musical direction precipitated Crosby's sacking in October 1967. He was replaced by former Byrd Gene Clark, who lasted only three weeks before quitting due to ever-present fear of flying. Drummer Michael Clarke left in disillusionment shortly afterwards, leaving McGuinn and Hillman to complete the excellent **Notorious Byrd Brothers** album (1968), generally hailed as a creative peak in their illustrious careers.

Early in 1968, McGuinn and Hillman recruited Kevin Kelley (drums) and Gram Parsons (guitar/vocals) and plunged headlong into new musical direction. Although McGuinn was intent on recording an electronic-jazz album, it was Parsons and Hillman who proved strongest in determining group's subsequent musical policy. Country and western style **Sweetheart Of The Rodeo** (1968) was a perfectly timed reaction against the excesses of psychedelia, predating Dylan's **Nashville Skyline** by a year. The Byrds' interest in country music continued, even after Parsons decided to quit on eve of an abortive South African tour.

Late 1968 was another period of flux, culminating in departure of Hillman following a dispute with McGuinn. By end of year, group was almost totally restructured with introduction of bluegrass virtuoso Clarence White (guitar), John York (bass), and Gene Parsons (drums).

From 1969 onwards, McGuinn assumed sole control of Byrds while ex-members went on to fame and fortune in offshoot groups, including Flying Burrito Brothers, Dillard And Clark, Crosby Stills Nash & Young, Manassas, the Souther-Hillman-Furay Band, and Firefall.

Recruitment of bassist Skip Battin (replacing York) produced settled line-up during early 70s, but quality of group's work declined significantly. There were, however, occasional high points, particularly the double album (untitled) which included group's last hit single, 1971's **Chestnut Mare**.

By 1972, several members had drifted into various unproductive solo ventures and group soon disbanded. Original quintet reformed for one album, but results were not encouraging enough to inspire follow-up. During same disastrous year, former members Clarence White and Gram Parsons died in tragic circumstances: White in hit and run accident, Parsons of drugs overdose.

Following uneven set of solo albums, McGuinn, Hillman, and Clark reunited during late 70s, but failed to revive group's career. Apart from Crosby, McGuinn has remained most prominent ex-Byrd, with solo albums such as **Thunderbyrd** (1977), **Back From Rio** (1991) and **Live From Mars** (1996) to his name.

After release of four CD boxed set **The Byrds** (1990), which McGuinn supervised, band was inducted into the Rock and Roll Hall Of Fame.

Recommended listening
Preflyte (Together) (Columbia), 1969
Mr Tambourine Man (Columbia), 1965
Turn! Turn! Turn! (Columbia), 1965
Fifth Dimension (Columbia), 1966
Younger Than Yesterday (Columbia), 1967
Greatest Hits (Columbia), 1967
The Notorious Byrd Brothers (Columbia), 1968
Sweetheart Of The Rodeo (Columbia), 1968
Dr Byrd And Mr Hyde (Columbia), 1969
Ballad Of Easy Rider (Columbia/CBS), 1969
Greatest Hits Volume II (Columbia/CBS), 1971
History Of The Byrds (CBS), 1973
The Byrds Play Dylan (Columbia), 1979
The Original Singles Volume I (Columbia), 1980
The Original Singles Volume II (Columbia), 1982
The Byrds (four CD set) (Columbia), 1990
Roger McGuinn solo:
Cardiff Rose (Columbia), 1976
Thunderbyrd (Columbia), 1977
Back From Rio (Arista), 1991
Live From Mars (Hollywood), 1996

J.J. CALE

American guitarist, singer, songwriter
Born Jean-Jacques Cale,
Oklahoma City, December 5, 1938

Career: Cale made his early reputation on the local Tulsa music scene, before moving to Los Angeles in 1964. There, he worked as an engineer at various LA studios (often collaborating with fellow Okie, and soon-to-be-major name, Leon Russell) while establishing himself as a performer; by 1965, he was playing regular gigs at the famous Whiskey-A-Go-Go on Sunset Boulevard. The following year, Cale made a psychedelic-style LP, **Take A Trip Down Sunset Strip**, as part of The Leather-Coated Minds. During the sessions, he recorded an early version of his classic number **After Midnight**; this was omitted from the album, but eventually released as a B-side. In 1968, Cale relocated to Nashville, but plans to make it as a session guitarist and songwriter there proved abortive, and by the end of the decade, he was back in Tulsa.

Cale's fortunes received a boost when Eric Clapton included **After Midnight** on his first solo album (**Eric Clapton**, 1970); the British guitarist had probably been introduced to the song by his bassist, Carl Radle, who had known Cale in Oklahoma and California. Clapton's cover of **After Midnight** also became a US Top 20 single later in 1970, and the resultant interest in Cale brought him a solo album contract with Leon Russell's Shelter label.

Cale recorded his debut LP, **Naturally**, in Nashville; it was released in 1971, and also spawned a US hit single, **Crazy Mama**. His follow-up set, **Really** (1972) was also largely cut in Music City (although some of it was made at Muscle Shoals, Georgia). Like its predecessor, it showcased Cale's famously laid-back playing and singing – musical characteristics that he combined with an unassuming public profile and unhurried approach to record production.

J.J. Cale LPs such as **Okie** (1974) and **Troubadour** (1976) (whose tracks included **Cocaine** – covered by Eric Clapton on his 1977 **Slowhand** set) sold well throughout the USA and Europe, and in 1976, Cale made his UK debut, appearing at London's Hammersmith Odeon, where he was joined on stage by Clapton and Carl Radle. However, it was three years before he released another LP, and in the early 1980s, he moved from Nashville (where he had built his own studio, Crazy Mama's, some years before) to California, and took a lengthy sabbatical (1984–89) from recording.

He re-emerged with **Travel-Log** (1989), and, in the last 10 years, has produced a string of characteristically stylish records, including **Closer To You** (1994), **Guitar Man** (1996), and, most recently, **Live** (2001), which was recorded on location at some of his recent US and European gigs.

Recommended listening

Naturally (Shelter), 1971
Really (Shelter), 1972
Okie (Shelter), 1974
Troubadour (Shelter), 1976
Shelter (Mercury), 1979
Shades (Mercury), 1981
Grasshopper (Mercury), 1982
#8 (Mercury), 1983
Special Edition (Mercury), 1984
Travel-Log (Silvertone), 1989
#10 (Silvertone), 1992
Closer To You (Delabel), 1994
Guitar Man (Delabel), 1996
Anyway The Wind Blows (anothology)
  (Mercury), 1997
The Very Best of J.J. Cale (anthology)
  (Mercury), 1998
Live (Virgin), 2001

THE CLASH

UK group formed 1976

Original line-up: Joe Strummer, vocals, guitar; Paul Simonon, bass; Mick Jones, guitar; Keith Levine, guitar; Terry Chimes, drums.

Career: Group formed in squat in London's Shepherd's Bush area in May 1976. Simonon and Jones were previously part of prototype punk outfit London SS, and approached Strummer, then with 101ers. Keith Levine became group's second guitarist but was soon replaced. Drummer Chimes completed line-up.

Moving headquarters to disused warehouse in Camden Town, group rehearsed under direction and guidance of manager Bernie Rhodes. An unpublicized appearance with The Sex Pistols was followed by their official debut in August 1976. The publicity afforded The Pistols and punk led to lucrative contract with CBS (Columbia). Move regarded as treason by some hard-core punk fans. Nevertheless, The Clash quickly established themselves as one of the most forceful and committed spokesmen of the new wave; their impact was immediately felt.

First single **White Riot** reached UK No. 38 and was hailed as mini-classic of punk genre. Debut album **The Clash** entered British LP chart at No. 12. During same period, drummer Terry Chimes left, disillusioned with trappings of punk; antipathy felt by other members reflected on LP sleeve where Chimes is renamed Tory Crimes. A lengthy series of auditions followed before Nicky "Topper" Headon was brought in as replacement.

Third single **Complete Control**, a riposte to CBS, was produced by reggae legend Lee "Scratch" Perry and reached Top 30. Tour with Richard Hell and the Voidoids was followed by publicity in the form of group arrests on charges of petty vandalism and shooting racing pigeons. Another tour, appropriately titled **The Clash Out On Parole**, and new single, **White Man in Hammersmith Palais/The Prisoner**, maintained momentum.

Second LP **Give 'Em Enough Rope** hit No. 2 on album charts and provided first Top 20 hit single, **Tommy Gun**. Production by Sandy Pearlman caused further controversy amongst punk elite, who feared that Clash were being transformed into heavy-metal unit. Following split with manager Rhodes, group embarked on first US visit, dubbed the Pearl Harbor Tour. Positive response from US critics helped career prospects.

Returning to UK, began work on film *Rude Boy* (1980). On the day of Britain's General Election (May 11, 1979) **The Cost of Living** (EP) was issued. Included a version of Bobby Fuller's **I Fought The**

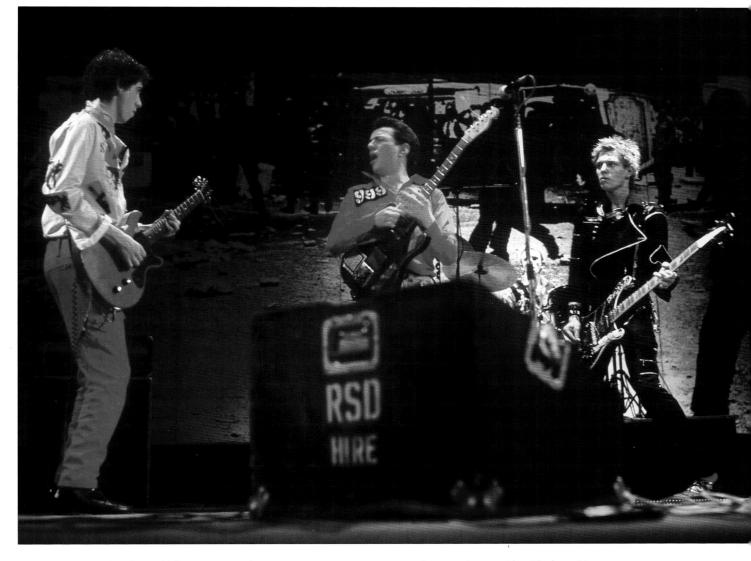

Law. Group's political credibility was promoted further by appearances at Rock Against Racism gigs. Another US tour saw group augmented by Blockheads' keyboardist Micky Gallagher.

Third LP, produced by Guy Stevens, was scheduled as "The New Testament," a pretentious title finally dropped in favour of **London Calling**. Released in Christmas 1979, the work was a strong seller. Next record, **Sandinista**, a triple album, followed same pattern, though less successfully.

US Top 10 breakthrough came with Glyn Johns-produced **Combat Rock** album in 1982. Band then played support on The Who's 1982 farewell tour of US. However, Headon's increasingly idiosyncratic, drug-related behavior resulted in his removal from group on eve

of American appearances. At short notice, Terry Chimes agreed to return to drummer's seat – a position he filled ably until December. The following May, former Cold Fish Peter Howard was named as his replacement, but internal strife continued. Jones left to form own successful band, Big Audio Dynamite, and was replaced by two guitarists, Vince White and Nick Shepherd, at beginning of 1984.

Fallow period was broken by release of delightfully titled 1985 album **Cut The Crap**, but band disintegrated before going on road. Strummer (Latino Rockability War) and Simenon (Havana 3AM) subsequently formed new bands, and Strummer also found an almost permanent spot with the Pogues. Clash enjoyed posthumous success with **Should**

ABOVE: *The Clash putting on a powerful live show in the mid-1970s.*

I Stay Or Should I Go which charted after exposure as jeans theme for TV advertisement.

Recommended listening
The Clash (Columbia,) 1977
Give 'Em Enough Rope (Columbia), 1978
London Calling (Columbia), 1979
Sandinista (Columbia), 1980
Combat Rock (Columbia), 1982
Cut The Crap (Columbia,) 1985
Story Of The Clash Volume 1 (Columbia), 1988
Big Audio Dynamite:
Planet B.A.D.: Greatest Hits (Columbia), 1995

ERIC CLAPTON

UK guitarist, vocalist, composer
Born Ripley, Surrey, March 30, 1945

Career: Brought up by foster-parents. At 15 he started to listen to blues/R&B recordings by Muddy Waters, Chuck Berry, Big Bill Broonzy, and others, and bought first guitar at 17. Taught himself to play while studying at Kingston Art College.

Formed first band in 1963, an R&B outfit called Roosters, which also included at various times Paul Jones and Tom McGuinness, later of Manfred Mann, and Brian Jones, later of Rolling Stones. Band was short-lived, and in late 1963 Clapton spent two weeks with Casey Jones and The Engineers before replacing Anthony "Top" Topham in the recently formed Yardbirds.

While with Yardbirds, Clapton established reputation as blues stylist, and recorded **Five Live Yardbirds** and **Sonny Boy Williamson And The Yardbirds** albums (both 1964). But when band took more commercial direction with 1965 single **For Your Love**, Clapton took off for more purist environment of John Mayall's Bluesbreakers.

Straight-down-the-line blues approach of Mayall's band provided perfect backdrop for Clapton, and the guitarist attracted even more fervent following. Shown to good effect on **John Mayall's Bluesbreakers With Eric Clapton** album (1966), Clapton's playing began to influence other British players; he became widely regarded as *the* guitar hero.

Sitters-in with Bluesbreakers included Jack Bruce and Ginger Baker, bass player and drummer with Graham Bond Organization. Empathy with both musicians led to break from Mayall (Clapton replaced by Peter Green) and formation of Cream in 1967.

With Cream, Clapton enjoyed first major commercial success and full-blown rock star status. Although band was important link in development of heavy rock – the first power trio – it was relatively short-lived, and folded in November 1968.

Period which followed saw Clapton involved with variety of projects, including ill-fated Blind Faith supergroup. He toured and recorded with Delaney And Bonnie, and guested on various other artists' albums before releasing his own first solo LP in 1970. From this time onwards, Clapton tended to play down his former guitar hero persona. He immersed himself in group as Derek of Derek And The Dominos. December 1970 Dominos album **Layla And Other Assorted Love Songs** featured Duane Allman and is regarded by many as

LEFT: *The great Eric Clapton in a typically unassuming onstage pose.*

Clapton's best recorded effort. Single **Layla** – dedicated to then wife of George Harrison, Patti, whom Clapton was later to marry – has achieved classic status.

Nevertheless, Derek And The Dominos were not huge commercial success, and this relative failure plus increasing drug problem took Clapton off music scene for several years. Eventually, with help of friends like Pete Townshend and course of electro-acupuncture, Clapton regained health.

Since 1974, Clapton has pursued an eclectic musical approach, though his love of the blues remains undimmed. Influences on his later career include Don Williams, whose classic **We're All The Way** appears on Clapton's **Slowhand** (1977); J.J. Cale (for compositions like **After Midnight** and **Cocaine** – both hits for Clapton – and for his laid-back vocal and instrumental style); and Bob Marley (Clapton's cover of **I Shot The Sheriff** was a massive US and UK hit single in 1974). This crossover appeal has also been seen to good effect on albums like blockbuster **August** (1986) and **Journeyman** (1989). Clapton also has no fear of uncharted territory, scoring TV series *Edge of Darkness* theme and *Lethal Weapon* movies with Michael Kamen.

The start of the 1990s was blighted with tragedy for Clapton. On August 27, 1990, three of his staff were killed, together with blues guitarist Stevie Ray Vaughan, in a helicopter crash in Wisconsin; and in March the following year, Eric's four-year-old son, Conor, fell to his death from a skyscraper apartment in New York. 1992 single **Tears In Heaven** (from **Unplugged** album), a poignant memorial to Conor, was declared Record of the Year at 1993 Grammy Awards (one of six Grammys awarded to Clapton that year).

Recent releases have included a fine blues set, **From The Cradle** (1994); **Retail Therapy** (with TDF), a surprising excursion into techno territory; the award-winning, pop-oriented **Pilgrim** (1998); and a majestic collaboration with B.B. King, **Riding With The King** (2000), whose title track is a cover version of a classic song by Ry Cooder associate John Hiatt.

Guitars: Gibson Les Paul (with Mayall, Cream); Fender Stratocaster (1970s onwards).

Recommended listening:

With Cream:
Fresh Cream (Atco), 1966
Disraeli Gears (Atco), 1967
Wheels of Fire (Atco), 1968
Goodbye (Atco), 1969

As a soloist/leader:
Eric Clapton (Polydor), 1970
Layla And Other Assorted Love Songs (Atco), 1970
Eric Clapton's Rainbow Concert (RSO), 1973
461 Ocean Boulevard (RSO), 1974
There's One In Every Crowd (RSO), 1975
E.C. Was Here (RSO), 1975
The Blues World Of (Decca), 1975
No Reason To Cry (RSO), 1976
Slowhand (RSO), 1977
Backless (RSO), 1978
Just One Night (RSO), 1980
Another Ticket (RSO), 1981
Time Pieces (Best Of) (RSO), 1982
Money And Cigarettes (Warner Bros.), 1983
Time Pieces, Volume II (RSO), 1983
Behind The Sun (Warner Bros.), 1984
Too Much Monkey Business (Astan), 1984
Backtrackin' (RSO), 1985
Edge of Darkness (soundtrack) (w/Michael Kamen) (BBC), 1985
August (Warner Bros.), 1986
Lethal Weapon (soundtrack) (w/Michael Kamen) (Reprise), 1987
Crossroads (four CD set) (Polydor), 1988
Journeyman (Reprise), 1989
Lethal Weapon 2 (soundtrack) (w/Michael Kamen) (Reprise), 1989
24 Nights (Live from Albert Hall) (Reprise), 1991
Unplugged (Reprise), 1992
Lethal Weapon 3 (soundtrack) (w/Michael Kamen) (Reprise), 1992
From The Cradle (Reprise), 1994
Pilgrim (Reprise), 1998
Lethal Weapon 4 (soundtrack) (w/Michael Kamen) (Reprise), 1987
Riding With The King (Reprise), 2000

GEORGE CLINTON

US vocalist, guitarist, producer,
composer
Born Kannapolis, North Carolina,
July 22, 1940

Career: Arguably the creator of funk,
although James Brown might also have
claim to the rights. Extrovert personality
whose bizarrely intriguing music and
wacky onstage antics have gained him
"legendary" status, if a limited
commercial following.

Founded Parliaments "doo-wop"
vocal group in 1955, who recorded
unsuccessfully for ABC, New Records,
Motown, and Golden World before **(I
Wanna) Testify** charted for Revilot
Records in 1967. Clinton's admiration for
the psychedelic movement of that time
prompted formation of P. Funk
(Parliament-Funkadelic) troupe, whose
wild regalia and repetitive rhythms
intoxicated dance crowd.

Under P. Funk aegis, Clinton (with
bass player William "Bootsy" Collins)
concocted a variety of groups, including
Bootsy's Rubber Band, Funkadelic (who
cut 1978 **One Nation Under A Groove**
set), Parlet, and The Brides of
Funkenstein, and founded own label,
signing distribution agreement with CBS.

Subsequent litigation with Atlantic,
who had bought rights to Revilot
Records, forced Clinton to curtail studio
recordings, and although a solo deal with
Capitol Records (1982) enabled him to
resume career (with bizarrely titled
albums such as **You Shouldn't Nuf Bit
Fish** (1983) and 1985's **Some Of My Best
Friends Are Jokes**), contractual and other
difficulties remained, leading to a
complete absence of new recorded
material in the years 1986–89.

Clinton bounced back with a new
contract from Prince's Paisley Park label,
for which he made **The Cinderella Theory**
(1989) and **Hey Man... Smell My Finger**
(1993). He subsequently signed with
Sony, releasing **The Awesome Power Of
A Fully Operational Mothership**, which
features a number of his former P. Funk
associates, and touring extensively. He
retains a fanatical following, and remains
an inspiration to recent rappers and hip-
hoppers – many of whose discs contain
extensive samples from his back catalog.

Recommended listening
Computer Games (Capitol), 1982
You Shouldn't Nuf Bit Fish (Capitol),
1984
Some Of My Best Friends Are Jokes
(Casablanca), 1985
Best Of (Capitol), 1987
The Cinderella Theory (Paisley Park), 1989
Hey Man... Smell My Finger (Paisley
Park), 1993
The Awesome Power of a Fully
Operational Mothership (550), 1996
Dope Dogs (Dogone/Available), 1998

With Funkadelic:
One Under A Groove (Casablanca), 1978
Music For Your Mother-45's
(Westbound), 1993

BELOW: *Eddie Cochran – one of the
most innovative of all 50s rockers.*

EDDIE COCHRAN

US vocalist, guitarist, composer
Born Albert Lea, Minnesota,
October 3, 1938
Died Bristol, England, April 17, 1960

Career: Spent much of his childhood in
Oklahoma City (which he regarded as his
home town) before moving to LA suburbs
as a teenager. Teamed with Hank Cochran
(unrelated) as Cochran Brothers in 1954;
recorded first single for Ekko label in hillbilly
style. Met songwriter (later manager) Jerry
Capehart in 1956 and signed to Crest
Records in Los Angeles as soloist. When
first Crest single failed, Capehart
negotiated contract with Liberty Records
on strength of Cochran's successful
audition for appearance in movie *The Girl
Can't Help It*. First Liberty single **Sittin' In
The Balcony** (1957) became hit, and album
that followed revealed soft pop style.
Returned, however, to rock 'n' roll with

subsequent singles and biggest US hit **Summertime Blues** (1958).

Two further cameo appearances in typical exploitative rock 'n' roll movies failed to capture dynamic stage performance, but nationwide tours soon established Cochran as teen idol. Visited Britain early in 1960, travelling with his fiancée, Sharon Sheeley, who co-wrote Cochran classic **Somethin' Else** (1959), and Gene Vincent; popularity in UK much increased by spots on *Boy Meets Girl* television show and tour of major UK theatres. During tour many British guitarists were influenced by Cochran's individual guitar style; he was a highly accomplished acoustic and electric player, though some of the subtleties of his studio sound (often built up with multiple overdubs) were inevitably lost in live performance.

Interrupted British tour in April 1960, intending to make brief visit to Los Angeles, but died as result of injuries received in car crash when returning to London for flight (Sheeley and Vincent, also in the vehicle, survived the accident). Posthumous UK No. 1, **Three Steps To Heaven**, marked beginning of cult following (especially in Britain) and subsequent releases included material culled from demo sessions and studio jams. **Guitar**: Semi-acoustic Gretsch.

Recommended listening

Memorial Album (Liberty), 1960
C'mon Everybody (-/Sunset), 1970
Legendary Masters (United Artists), 1971
Very Best Of (15th Anniversary), 1975
Many Sides Of (-/ Rollercoaster), 1979
A Legend In Our Time (Union Pacific), 1979
The Eddie Cochran Singles Album (United Artists), 1979
20th Anniversary Album (-/United Artists), 1980
Gene Vincent And Eddie Cochran – Together Again (Capitol), 1980
Gene Vincent And Eddie Cochran – Rock 'n' Roll Heroes (Rockstar), 1981
Cherished Memories (Liberty/EMI), 1983
25th Anniversary Album (Liberty), 1985
Greatest Hits (Curb), 1990
Early Years (Ace), 1992
Singin' To My Baby/Never To Be Forgotten (Capitol), 1993
Somethin' Else (Razor & Tie), 1998

RY COODER

US guitarist, vocalist, producer, arranger
Born Los Angeles, March 15, 1947

Career: Early enthusiasm for guitar boosted by lessons from leading blues and gospel performers (including Rev. Gary Davis) whom Cooder encountered when they played concerts in LA. Joined backing group for singer Jackie DeShannon in 1964; then became a founder member of the Rising Sons with fellow guitarist Taj Mahal; then had a brief, unhappy stint in Captain Beefheart's Magic Band before switching to session work. Made notable contribution to Rolling Stones' **Let It Bleed** (1969). Cooder also appeared on singles and albums by (among many others) Marc Benno, Crazy Horse, Randy Newman, John Sebastian, and Maria Muldaur.

First solo LP, **Ry Cooder**, released by Reprise in 1970, established Cooder's mean bottleneck guitar style and unique vocals. His solo output for the rest of the decade explored almost every corner of America's popular music heritage, with an emphasis on blues and Tex-Mex. Among many classic albums from this period were **Into The Purple Valley** (1971), which included songs from the Depression era; and **Chicken Skin Music** (1976) – on which he worked for the first time with accordionist Flaco Jimenez. Other members of Cooder's studio/live bands included soul singer Bobby King, singer/songwriter/ guitarist John Hiatt, and LA studio mavens Tim Drummond (bass) and Jim Keltner (drums).

After the unsatisfactory **Jazz** (1978), Cooder's next studio project was strongly R&B-flavored **Bop Till You Drop**, released the following year, and one of the first-ever pop LPs to be recorded/mixed using digital technology. Cooder toured to promote it and its successor, **Borderline** (1980), but over the following years, live appearances decreased markedly, due to his well-known dislike of life on the road, plus a growing involvement with film soundtrack work.

Cooder had previously played on the soundtracks of **Candy** (1968) and **Performance** (1970), but his first full-length movie score was for Walter Hill's **The Long Riders** (1980). He has gone on to provide music for several later Hill films, as well as for (among many others) **Paris, Texas** (1984) and **Crossroads** (1986).

His recorded output since the early 1990s reflects an increasing interest in world music, though he did tour and record as a member of rock band Little Village – also featuring British bassist and songwriter Nick Lowe (Johnny Cash's ex-son-in-law), John Hiatt, and Jim Keltner – in 1992. His 1993 album with Indian *mohan vina* (modified guitar) player V.M. Bhatt, **A Meeting By The River** (Cooder's son Joaquim played percussion on the CD) was followed by Grammy-winning **Talking Timbuktu** with Malian guitarist Ali Farka Toure. Cooder was also a prime mover in the **Buena Vista Social Club** project, which showcased the music of a group of veteran Cuban performers (known affectionately by some of their many fans as "los superabuelos" – the super-grandfathers) via a 1998 Wim Wenders documentary and a bestselling, Grammy-winning CD.

Recommended listening:

Ry Cooder (Reprise), 1970
Into The Purple Valley (Reprise), 1971
Boomer's Story (Reprise), 1972
Paradise And Lunch (Reprise), 1974
Chicken Skin Music (Warner Bros.), 1976
Show Time (live) (Warner Bros.), 1977
Jazz (Warner Bros.), 1978
Bop Till You Drop (Warner Bros.), 1979
Borderline (Warner Bros.), 1980
Southern Comfort (soundtrack) (Warner Bros.), 1981
The Long Riders (soundtrack) (Warner Bros.), 1982
The Border (soundtrack) (Warner Bros.), 1982
Paris, Texas (soundtrack) (Warner Bros.), 1985
Music From Alamo Bay (soundtrack) (Slash), 1985
Blue City (Warner Bros), 1986
Crossroads (Warner Bros), 1986
Why Don't You Try Me Tonight (Warner Bros), 1986
Get Rhythm (Warner Bros), 1987
Johnny Handsome (Warner Bros./ WEA), 1989
Talking Timbuktu (Rykodisc), 1994
Music by Ry Cooder (compilation) (Warner Bros.), 1995
Buena Vista Social Club (Nonesuch), 1997

ELVIS COSTELLO

UK composer, vocalist, guitarist
Born Declan McManus, London,
August 25, 1954

Career: After unsuccessful early career in pub/country-rock band Flip City, Costello (son of erstwhile Joe Loss Band singer Ross McManus) took demo tapes in 1976 to then fledgling Stiff label. Stiff boss Jake Riviera signed Declan, and became his manager. With name change to Elvis Costello, first three singles built strong cult following, and debut LP reached UK Top 20.

June 1977 saw formation of backing group, The Attractions, who toured with Elvis on first Stiff Records UK package, along with Ian Dury, Nick Lowe, Dave Edmunds, and Wreckless Eric. Costello concurrently scored first British Top 20 hit with **Watching The Detectives**.

By early 1978 had made major US impact, and moved with Riviera and Lowe to newly formed Radar label. Three Top 30 hits followed, plus second acclaimed album; third LP released during first days of 1979. Biggest UK hit so far was **Oliver's Army**; and after collapse of Radar in 1979, Riviera set up new F-beat label, launched with successful Costello single, **I Can't Stand Up For Falling Down** (cover of Sam And Dave song). Made further hit singles during 1980, plus classic LP **Get Happy**.

1981 saw release of Billy Sherrill-produced country album **Almost Blue**, which polarized fans; but next year saw return to original abrasive style with **Imperial Bedroom** album.

1984 set **Goodbye Cruel World** was also well received; over next two years Costello toured extensively without regular backing band The Attractions. 1986 album **King Of America**, with accompaniment by US West Coast session men, created new wave of approval, sustained by same year's **Blood And Chocolate**.

Marriage to Cait O'Riordan from The Pogues hardly mellowed Costello, who harangued all and sundry in **Spike** (which included material co-written with Paul McCartney) and **Mighty Like A**

Rose albums. Toured US in 1989 with band featuring former Presley bassist Jerry Scheff and keyboard player Larry Knechtel; next major venture was **The Juliet Letters**, on which he was accompanied by a classical string quartet. **Brutal Youth** CD, released in 1994, featured the Attractions once again, but an important link with Costello's past was broken later that year when singer parted company with long-time manager Jake Riviera. Among recent albums are **Kojak Variety** (1995 – collection of covers), **All This Useless Beauty** (1996), and **Painted From Memory** (1998).

Recommended listening

My Aim Is True (Columbia/Stiff), 1977
This Year's Model (Columbia/F-Beat), 1978
Armed Forces (Columbia/Radar), 1979
Get Happy (Columbia/F-Beat), 1980
Trust (Columbia/F-Beat), 1981
Almost Blue (Columbia/F-Beat), 1981
Imperial Bedroom (Columbia/F-Beat), 1982
Goodbye Cruel World (Columbia /F-Beat), 1984
Punch The Clock (Columbia/F-Beat), 1984
10 Bloody Marys (Demon), 1984
King Of America (Columbia/F-Beat), 1986
Blood And Chocolate (Demon), 1986
Out Of Our Idiot (Demon), 1987
Spike (Warner Bros), 1989
Mighty Like A Rose (Warner Bros.), 1991
The Juliet Letters (Warner Bros.), 1993
Brutal Youth (Warner Bros.), 1994
Kojak Variety (Warner Bros.), 1995
All This Useless Beauty (Warner Bros.), 1996
Painted From Memory (Mercury/Polygram), 1998

ROBERT CRAY BAND

US band formed 1983

Original line-up: Robert Cray, vocals, Fender Stratocaster guitar; Richard Cousins, bass; Peter Boe, keyboards; David Olson, drums.

Career: The Georgia-born son of a serviceman, Cray spent his formative years moving from place to place. Robert Cray Band formed by Cray with bassist Richard Cousins and inspired by blues hero Albert Collins. Worked initially in the Eugene, Oregon area playing club and college dates.

Record deal with Tomato produced album **Who's Been Talkin'**. Three years later came a contract with Hightone Records and two albums, **Bad Influence** and **False Accusations**. Albums and frequent live appearances helped increase profile of the band; in 1986 they signed a lucrative recording deal with Polygram/Mercury and recorded the **Strong Persuader** album.

Cray guested with Tina Turner on her *Break Every Rule* TV special, and toured in the US with Huey Lewis & The News and Eric Clapton. **Strong Persuader** climbed the US charts to become the most successful blues album in American chart history.

Don't Be Afraid Of The Dark LP was a Grammy winner in 1989, the year which also saw Cray's guest appearance on John Lee Hooker's "comeback" album, **The Healer**. Cray teamed with Eric Clapton for the guitar god's two-week-plus dates at London's Royal Albert Hall in 1990; also appeared on Clapton's **Journeyman** LP.

Cray's sixth album, **Midnight Stroll** (1990), featured impressive brass work from legendary Memphis Horns. Cray guested again with John Lee Hooker on veteran bluesman's **Mr. Lucky** (1991), and also enjoyed critical praise and strong sales for his own **I Was Warned** (1992), **Shame + A Sin** (1993), and **Some Rainy Morning** (1995) sets. After releasing **Sweet Potato Pie** (1997), he moved from Mercury to Rykodisc; his first album for the label was Grammy-winning **Take Your Shoes Off**, for which Cray (in his own words) "jumped deeper down into the soul bag." Blues/soul mix also featured on his latest, acclaimed Rykodisc CD, **Shoulda Been Home** (2001).

Recommended listening

Who's Been Talkin' (Tomato), 1980
Bad Influence (Hightone), 1983
False Accusations (Hightone), 1985

ABOVE: *Robert Cray in full flight.*

Strong Persuader (Mercury), 1986
Don't Be Afraid Of The Dark
 (Mercury), 1988
Midnight Stroll (Mercury), 1990
I Was Warned (Mercury), 1992
Shame + A Sin (Mercury), 1993
Some Rainy Morning (Mercury), 1995
Sweet Potato Pie (Mercury), 1997
Take Your Shoes Off (Rykodisc), 1999
Shoulda Been Home (Rykodisc,) 2001
With John Lee Hooker:
The Healer (Silvertone), 1989
Mr. Lucky (Pointblank/Charisma), 1991

CREEDENCE CLEARWATER REVIVAL

US group formed 1967

Original line-up: John Fogerty, vocals, guitar; Tom Fogerty, rhythm guitar; Stu Cook, bass; Doug "Cosmo" Clifford, drums.

Career: Foursome got together in San Francisco Bay area of El Cerritto as Tommy Fogerty and the Blue Velvets. Locally based Fantasy label offered recording deal on proviso that band changed name to the Golliwogs (in attempt to cash-in on current British beat boom). Band agreed and debut single was released in 1965. Further singles followed but none made impact except local hit **Brown Eyed Girl**. Group evolved R&B/cajun "swamp rock" style, and persuaded label's boss Saul Zaentz to agree change of name to Creedence Clearwater Revival.

CCR's 1968 debut album, a mix of standards and John Fogerty originals, made immediate impression. Two singles were lifted simultaneously: a version of Dale Hawkins' **Suzie Q**, and classy reading of Screamin' Jay Hawkins' **I Put A Spell On You**. Band went against then current trend by remaining singles-orientated; their next 45, John Fogerty-penned **Proud Mary**, became instant rock/soul standard, eliciting many notable cover versions. Despite CCR's San Francisco origins, their spiritual home was the Southern bayou country, as classic hits like **Bad Moon Rising**, **Born On The Bayou**, and **Green River** demonstrated.

Cosmo's Factory (1970) included three gold singles (**Travelin' Band**, **Up Around The Bend**, and **Lookin' Out My Back Door**), but cracks were starting to appear in the band. Tom Fogerty quit in 1971 following differences with others, who continued as trio for world tour. John Fogerty's increasing dominance caused further dissension. In what came to be known as "Fogerty's Revenge," he allowed Cook and Clifford equal creative participation in **Mardi Gras** album. Results were lambasted by critics and contributed to band's dissolution in October 1972.

Only John Fogerty has enjoyed substantial post-CCR success. He made his solo debut with **Blue Ridge Rangers** album (1973), and, two years later, had a Top 30 hit single **Rockin' All Over The World**, and a successful LP (**John Fogerty**, 1975). However, 10 years elapsed before the appearance of his next LP – **Centerfield** (1985), one of whose tracks, "Zanz Kant Danz," was a dig at Fantasy's bossman that led to legal difficulties.

Tom Fogerty died of respiratory failure while battling tuberculosis in 1990, and disputes between John Fogerty, Cook, and Clifford dragged on for most of the next decade, with John seeking to prevent his former colleagues from using the Creedence name. John has made two recent solo CDs: **Blue Moon Swamp** (1997) and **Premonition** (1998).

Recommended listening
Creedence Clearwater Revival
 (Fantasy), 1968
Bayou Country (Fantasy), 1969
Green River (Fantasy), 1969
Willie And The Poor Boys (Fantasy),
 1969
Cosmo's Factory (Fantasy), 1970
Pendulum (Fantasy), 1971
Mardi Gras (Fantasy), 1972
Creedence Clearwater Revival box set
 (Fantasy), 2001
John Fogerty solo:
Blue Ridge Rangers (Fantasy), 1973
Centerfield (Warner Bros.), 1985
Eye Of The Zombie (WEA), 1986
Blue Moon Swamp (WEA), 1997

STEVE CROPPER

US guitarist, songwriter, producer
Born Willow Spring, Missouri,
October 21, 1941

Career: Listened mainly to country music as a small child, but was exposed to a much broader spectrum of styles after relocating to Memphis in 1950. Started learning guitar as a teenager, and had an early composition recorded by saxophonist Bill Justis while still in high school. Began engineering course at Memphis State University, but was also active as a musician, playing gigs with his group, the Royal Spades, and also working at nearby Satellite studios (from which the famous Stax label would soon evolve). Contributed to the Mar-Keys' **Last Night** (1961), a hit single recorded at Satellite by a floating group of local musicians, and began spending more time at Satellite/Stax as engineer, session guitarist, and "right hand man" of studio co-owner Jim Stewart.

Other Stax regulars included organist Booker T. Jones, bassist Louis Steinberg (subsequently replaced by Donald "Duck" Dunn), and drummer Al Jackson – they and Cropper formed the so-called "Memphis Group" (MGs), the rhythm section that played on nearly all the label's classic sides. Studio jam led to creation of **Green Onions** (1962), a massive US hit that made the quartet famous in its own right – Booker T. is believed to have been arbitrarily credited as the MGs' leader because he was the youngest of the four performers.

MGs' many subsequent hits included **Groovin'** (1967), **Soul Limbo** (1968), **Hang 'Em High**, and **Time Is Tight** (both 1969); meanwhile, Steve Cropper emerged as key figure in Stax operation – composing and producing songs by many of the label's biggest stars, including Rufus and Carla Thomas, William Bell, Eddie Floyd, Otis Redding, and Wilson Pickett.

In 1970, he ended his long association with the label, setting up a relatively short-lived Memphis studio, TMI (short for Trans-Maximus), and later producing a wide range of rock and blues

ABOVE: *Steve Croppper helped to create the famous "Stax Sound".*

acts, from Jeff Beck and Rod Stewart to John Cougar Mellencamp, Robert Cray, and Joe Louis Walker, in Los Angeles and elsewhere. He has also retained a high profile as a guitarist, appearing with the Blues Brothers Band, Paul Simon, and many other major names.

Long associated with the Fender Telecaster (which he used from the early 60s onwards), Cropper has recently collaborated with Peavey on the specially designed Cropper Classic electric guitar, launched in 1996.

Recommended listening

Complete Stax/Volt singles
  1959–1968 (9 CDs), Atlantic
With the MGs:
Green Onions (Stax), 1962
Mo' Onions (Stax), 1963
Soul Dressing (Stax), 1965
My Sweet Potato (Stax), 1965
And Now!(Stax), 1966
Hip Hug Her (Stax), 1967
Solo albums:
With A Little Help From My Friends (Volt), 1971
Playing My Thang (MCA), 1980
Night After Night (MCA), 1982

CROSBY, STILLS, NASH & YOUNG

US group formed 1968

Original line-up: David Crosby, guitar; Stephen Stills, vocals, guitar; Graham Nash, vocals, guitar.

Career: Band formed without Young, as Crosby, Stills & Nash; Crosby came from Byrds, Stills from Buffalo Springfield, and Nash from top UK group The Hollies. Debut album **Crosby Stills & Nash** released in 1969 to critical and commercial success. Semi-acoustic soft-rock with accent on vocal harmonies, music combined commercial appeal with "sensitivity;" occasional banality camouflaged by slickness. Album went gold and single from it, **Marrakesh Express**, charted in US and UK.

Looking to fill out sound, band recruited another ex-Buffalo Springfield alumnus, Neil Young, then pursuing solo career. Young's chunky guitar and sombre vocals became major asset, and his songwriting ability gave authority to repertoire. **Déjà Vu** (1970), with added talents of bass-player Greg Reeves and drummer Dallas Taylor, also went gold. Album won critical plaudits – especially for Young's distinctive contributions. Lyrical content was timely and in keeping with appearance at Woodstock festival.

Disappointing live set, **Four Way Street**, followed in 1971, but band members were already beginning to take individual direction and CSN & Y folded that year. Crosby and Nash continued to work as duo until late 70s; Stills took up threads of erratically successful solo career; and Young went on to become enigmatic rock superstar.

In 1977, Crosby, Stills & Nash cut reunion album **CSN**, before splitting and regrouping again in 1982.

David Crosby's incarceration (1985–86) on drug-related charges might have sounded death knell for band. However, 1988 saw yet another reformation when they cut their **American Dream** LP, which made US Top 20. 1990 saw the release of a further trio offering, **Live It Up**, but later that year,

Crosby suffered a serious bike accident that was to put him out of action for several months.

Health problems continued to dog Crosby during the 1990s (he received a liver transplant in 1994 and underwent abdominal surgery three years later); however, he, Stills, and Nash have continued to perform and record together. Their 1994 album **After the Storm** was followed by **Looking Forward** (1999), which also featured Neil Young, and the reunited foursome undertook a well-received US tour in 2000.

Recommended listening

Crosby, Stills And Nash (Atlantic), 1969
Déjà Vu (Atlantic), 1970
Four Way Street (Atlantic), 1971
So Far (Atlantic), 1974
CSN (Atlantic), 1977
Replay (Atlantic), 1980
Daylight Again (Atlantic), 1982
Allies (Atlantic), 1983
American Dream (Atlantic), 1988
Live It Up (Atlantic), 1990
After The Storm (Atlantic), 1994
Looking Forward (Reprise), 1999
David Crosby solo:
If I Could Only Remember My Name (Atlantic), 1971
Oh Yes I Can (A&M), 1989
Thousand Roads (Atlantic), 1993
It's All Coming Back To Me Now (Atlantic), 1995
Crosby And Nash:
Graham Nash And David Crosby (Atlantic), 1972
Wind On The Water (ABC), 1975
Whistle Down The Wire (ABC), 1976
Live (ABC), 1977

DICK DALE

US guitarist
Born Boston, Massachusetts,
May 4, 1937

Career: Dale moved from Massachusetts to California as a youngster. By the late 1950s, he and his band, the Del-Tones, were a leading live act in waterfront Los Angeles suburb of Balboa, and Dale had already begun to evolve his distinctive "surf guitar" style – later widely copied

by other West Coast players. A friend and admirer of the legendary guitar- and amp-maker Leo Fender (who was based in nearby Fullerton), Dale was given prototypes of Fender Stratocaster guitar and various amplifiers to try out onstage, and contributed significantly to their development – often testing them to destruction in the process!

Dale enjoyed a minor hit with **Let's Go Trippin'** (1961) and followed it with a handful of other singles, including **Miserlou** (1962) – which, decades later, was memorably featured in Quentin Tarantino's Oscar-winning movie **Pulp Fiction** (1994) – and **Secret Surfin' Spot** (1963). His albums, especially **Surfer's Choice** (1962) and **King of the Surf Guitar** (1963), were also moderately successful, and he had an important influence on many of his Southern Californian contemporaries – notably the Beach Boys. However, a combination of serious illness and bad luck led to a decline in Dale's musical fortunes in the late 1960s, although his records retained a cult following.

He performed and recorded only sporadically in the 70s and 80s (one notable outing was his duet with bluesman Stevie Ray Vaughan on **Pipeline**, featured on the soundtrack of 1987 movie *Back To The Beach*), but made a significant comeback in 1993 with new album **Tribal Thunder**. Since then, he has been in heavy demand, undertaking world tours, providing music for Disneyland, and launching his own signature Fender Stratocaster. Much of his back catalog is now available again on CD compilations like **Better Shred Than Dead** (1997); and recent albums of new material include **Unknown Territory** (1994) and **Calling Up Spirits** (1996).

Recommended listening

King of the Surf Guitar: Best of Dick Dale and the Del-Tones (Rhino), 1986
Better Shred Than Dead (anthology) (Rhino), 1997
Tribal Thunder (HighTone), 1993
Pulp Fiction (soundtrack) (MCA), 1994
Unknown Territory (HighTone), 1994
Calling Up Spirits (Beggars Banquet), 1996

DEEP PURPLE

UK group formed 1968

Original line-up: Rod Evans, vocals; Ritchie Blackmore, guitar; Jon Lord, keyboards; Nick Simper, bass; Ian Paice, drums.

Career: Formed in Germany from remnants of UK band Roundabout (Blackmore; Lord; Dave Curtis, bass; Chris Curtis, vocals; Bobby Clark, drums) as pop-rock outfit. First single (with line-up above), **Hush**, made Top 5 in US, as did next two singles. Early albums also achieved American success. However, band did not gain credibility in homeland until 1970 when Ian Gillan and Roger Glover replaced Evans and Simper for ambitious **Concerto For Group And Orchestra** album, recorded at Albert Hall with Royal Philharmonic Orchestra. New line-up also gained single success with **Black Night** in August of that year.

Pursuing a heavier rock direction, Purple quickly became one of the most successful and influential bands of early 70s; joined Black Sabbath and Led Zeppelin in spreading gospel of multi-decibel, piledriver British rock around the world. Main asset was Ritchie Blackmore, who, although somewhat derivative, established strong reputation as guitar hero.

However, by 1972 band was beset by various ego problems; a year later Gillan left (later to achieve considerable success with his own band), followed shortly by Glover (who went into production). Glenn Hughes, bassist with moderately successful band Trapeze, replaced Glover, while Gillan was replaced by (then) complete unknown David Coverdale. In 1975 Ritchie Blackmore also quit to form Rainbow (where he was later joined by Glover), and American Tommy Bolin, formerly of James Gang, was recruited in his place.

By 1976, audience for Purple's music was beginning to diminish, and band broke up that year. Coverdale, Lord, and Paice eventually went on to become three-fifths of Whitesnake. Glenn Hughes recorded a solo album and undertook session work. Tommy Bolin died suddenly in Miami in 1976.

Fans were delighted when Purple reformed in April 1984 with the classic line up of Gillan, Lord, Paice, Blackmore, and Glover. Their reunion LP **Perfect Strangers**, released in November, was their first studio album in 11 years. It went platinum and their US tour was hailed as the second highest grossing of the year. They played to British fans at Knebworth in 1985, then began a world tour in 1987. With the highly successful **House Of Blue Light** released the same year, it seemed the revived Purple might enjoy a prolonged lease of life.

Despite (temporary) loss of Gillan, who went on to re-record **Walk On The Water** for HM Rock Aid, the band released confident **Slaves And Masters** album in 1990, with Joe Lynne Turner on vocals, fronting stalwarts Blackmore, Lord, Paice, and Glover. Gillan returned to the fold the following year, and Purple's next album, **The Battle Rages On**, was issued in 1993. However, Ritchie Blackmore decided to leave during the subsequent tour (he has since formed a new band, Blackmore's Night); his replacement was ex-Kansas axeman Steve Morse, who made his recording debut with his veteran colleagues on **Purpendicular** (1996). The same line-up also appeared on **Abandon** (1998).

Recommended listening

Shades Of Deep Purple
   (Tetragrammaton/Harvest), 1968
Book Of Taliesyn
   (Tetragrammaton/Harvest), 1969
Deep Purple
   (Tetragrammaton/Harvest), 1969
In Concert (Portrait/Harvest), 1970
Concerto For Group And Orchestra
   (Warner Bros/Harvest), 1970
In Rock (Warner Bros/Harvest), 1970
Fireball (Deep Purple/Harvest), 1971
Machine Head (Warner Bros/Purple),
   1972
Made In Japan (Purple), 1972
Who Do We Think We Are (Purple),
   1973
Burn (Purple), 1974
Stormbringer (Purple), 1974
Come Taste The Band (Purple), 1975
24 Carat Purple (Purple), 1975
Purple Passages (Warner Bros.), 1975
Made In Europe (Purple), 1976
Powerhouse (Purple), 1977
Singles (Harvest), 1978
When We Rock We Rock (Warner
   Bros.), 1978
Deepest Purple (Harvest), 1980
Live In London (Harvest), 1982
Perfect Strangers (Mercury), 1984
Knocking On Your Back Door
   (Polydor), 1985
The Anthology (Harvest), 1985
House Of Blue Light (Polydor), 1987
Nobody's Perfect (Mercury/Polydor),
   1988
Slaves And Masters (RCA), 1990
The Battle Rages On (Giant), 1993
Purpendicular (CMC/Prominent), 1996
Abandon (BMG), 1998

BO DIDDLEY

US vocalist, guitarist, composer
Born Ellas McDaniel, McComb,
Mississippi, December 30, 1928

Career: Raised by mother's cousin, Mrs Gussie McDaniel; taken to Chicago aged five. Studied classical violin for 12 years, but also absorbed music of Baptist church services. Blues/rhythm and blues influences were in complete contrast – balladry of Nat King Cole, humor of Louis Jordan, and guitar of John Lee Hooker. Streets of Chicago also brought young Ellas into contact with Mississippi Delta blues style of Muddy Waters and Little Walter, who gigged in local clubs.

Given guitar by sister as teenager; taught himself to play and formed small group in early 1950s. Played on street corners: Diddley, vocals, guitar; Frank Kirkland, drums; Jerome Green, maraccas; Billy Boy Arnold, harp.

Earned money as boxer, then construction worker, before realizing that music could also pay bills. Auditioned for Chess in 1954, cutting **I'm A Man** and **Bo Diddley**, a landmark with its throbbing jungle rhythm. Disc was released on Checker in spring 1955. A Top 10 R&B hit, it proved to be the first of a string of classic singles. Diddley maintained phenomenal output of original, lyrically unorthodox material with strong humor

ABOVE: *Bo Diddley with one of his many unusually shaped guitars.*

content; **Cracking Up** gave him his first crossover pop hit in summer 1959; then **Say Man** became Top 20 smash.

In early 1960s Diddley's repertoire was used by many British beat groups, songs like **Road Runner**, **Pretty Thing**, **Mona**, **Who Do You Love**, **I Can Tell**, and **You Can't Judge A Book By The Cover** clocking up good mileage. Diddley released prodigious quantity of LPs, mainly during 60s. Material was still mainly original, often predictable, but artist's humor and enthusiasm ooze from the grooves.

Distinctive pair of albums cut in 1967; **Super Blues**, with Bo, Muddy Waters, and Little Walter, and **The Super Blues Band** with Bo, Muddy, and Howlin' Wolf. Around 1971 Bo tried heavier musical context for LP **Another Dimension**, with uncomfortable results; similarly uninspiring was **Big Bad Bo** in 1974. In 1972 and 1973, his stage performance was filmed for footage in movies *Let The Good Times Roll* and *Keep On Rockin'*.

Continued heavy schedule of live shows in US and Europe; disc career less active. With demise of Chess, signed with RCA; cut disappointing LP, **The 20th Anniversary Of Rock 'n' Roll** (1976), and **Not Fade Away**, a flop 45. Shared bill with The Clash on their 1979 American tour, but issued no new studio recordings until 1989, when **Breakin' Through The B.S.** appeared.

As well as regular touring schedule with rock 'n' roll revival packages, Diddley enjoyed television prominence in early 90s with appearance in Nike TV commercial, where he was seen jamming with another Bo, US sports star Bo Jackson. 1993 saw the release of **This Should Not Be** CD; **The Mighty Bo Diddley** followed two years later, and in 1996, a panoply of major names (including Rolling Stones Keith Richards and Ronnie Wood) were featured on his new set, **A Man Among Men**.

Recommended listening

The Best of Bo Diddley: The Millennium Collection (anthology) (MCA), 2000

Have Guitar, Will Travel (Checker), 1960

Bo Diddley (Checker), 1962

Bo Diddley Is A Gunslinger (Checker), 1963

Surfin' With Bo Diddley (also features Billy Lee Riley and the Megatons) (Checker), 1963

Two Great Guitars (w/Chuck Berry) (Checker), 1964

500% More Man (Checker), 1965

Let Me Pass (Checker), 1965

The Originator (Checker), 1966

Super Blues Band (w/Muddy Waters and Little Walter) (Checker), 1967

The Black Gladiator (Checker), 1970

Another Dimension (Chess), 1971

Where It All Began (Chess), 1972

The London Bo Diddley Sessions (Chess), 1973

I'm A Man (live) (MF), 1977

Breakin' Through The BS (Triple X), 1989

This Should Not Be (Triple X), 1993

The Mighty Bo Diddley (Triple X), 1995

A Man Among Men (Code Blues/Atlantic), 1996

BOB DYLAN

US composer, vocalist, guitarist,
harmonica player
Born Robert Allen Zimmerman,
Duluth, Minnesota, May 24, 1941

Career: Quiet, serious Bobby Zimmerman got good grades, participated in school activities, and graduated from Hibbing High in 1959. However, listened to blues and country music, and was more interested in becoming rock 'n' roll star. At University of Minnesota, discovered remnants of beat era in nearby Dinkytown with its folk music coffeehouses. Seeing this as route to success, began playing at local folk clubs. Read Woody Guthrie's *Bound For Glory*, started calling himself Bob Dylan, and invented past as runaway with Okie roots.

Played back-up harmonica on title track of Harry Belafonte's **Midnight Special** album, and for Carolyn Hester. Signed by Columbia Records' John Hammond in October 1961. First album **Bob Dylan** (1962), including own compositions **Song To Woody** and **Talkin' New York**, plus traditional numbers, sold only 5,000 copies in first year.

Dylan predicted direction music was heading and took civil rights/anti-war stance, often using "borrowed" tunes for moralizing topical songs filled with brilliant imagery and caustic irony. By March 1963 reputation was growing, and **The Freewheelin' Bob Dylan** was released (after power struggle between Hammond and Dylan's manager Albert Grossman led to Hammond's departure in mid-recording – he was replaced by Tom Wilson).

Album includes **Blowin' In The Wind**, highlight of Newport Folk Festival that summer when Dylan sang it with Peter, Paul And Mary. Trio's cover version became Top 10 hit, selling 320,000 copies in first eight days of release. Personal relationship developed with Joan Baez and Dylan appeared at her concerts. Becoming hot property, he headlined Carnegie Hall concert; **The Times They Are A-Changin'** album made him hero of protest movement. However, by February

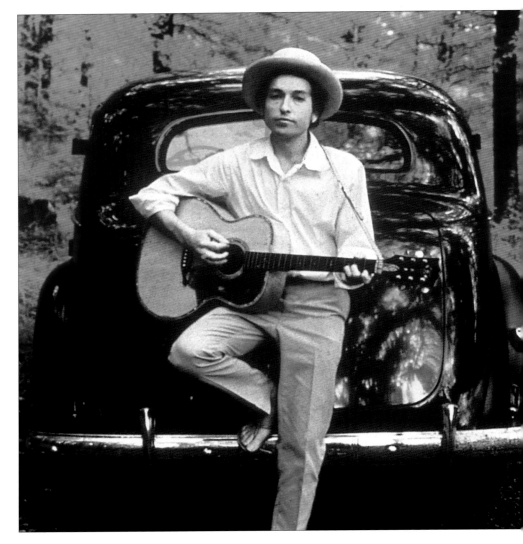

1964 Dylan had become reclusive, using bodyguards and drugs as protection from outside world.

With success as folk singer achieved, Dylan began changing image. During British visits, he heard English rock (and had small role in BBC-TV play). As usual, he had eye on barometer: though acoustic, 1964 LP **Another Side of Bob Dylan** was first step toward rock. Self-pitying and cruel, but vividly powerful, lyrics emphasized personal rather than political sentiments on songs like **All I Really Want To Do** and **It Ain't Me, Babe**. Folk fans and political protesters felt betrayed and album did not do as well as first two.

Spending much time in Woodstock, NY, Dylan wrote 18 new songs for 1965 **Bringing It All Back Home**, which completed switch from folk to rock, and

ABOVE: *Bob Dylan – the greatest singer-songwriter of his generation.*

from traveling to tripping. One side had four solo tracks, including **Mr Tambourine Man** and **It's All Over Now, Baby Blue**; other side with electric guitar and backup band featured **Subterranean Homesick Blues**. Released as single, this surreal, apocalyptic vision ultimately became Dylan's first gold record. The Byrd's two-minute version of **Mr Tambourine Man** went to No. 1 in US and UK, leading new folk-rock trend.

Although losing fans among protesters, Dylan gained wider audience of alienated young people who responded to funky music and sneering rejection of American Dream. May 1965 film *Don't Look Back* showed onstage and backstage dramas, including split with Baez, during

Dylan's English tour. Returning to US, recorded **Like A Rolling Stone**, which gave him international stardom, with Mike Bloomfield on guitar and Al Kooper on organ. Single was released before rest of **Highway 61 Revisited** (1965); album was produced by Bob Johnston.

Unveiling electric sound and Carnaby Street clothes at Newport and Forest Hills that summer, Dylan was booed by audience who saw prancing rock 'n' roller as sell-out. Next single **Positively 4th Street** was described as "most vicious song ever to reach the Hit Parade." Double album **Blonde On Blonde** (1966) was characterized by intense, poetic songs of drugs, dreams and nightmares about identity. Toured with The Hawks, later called The Band, and married Sara Lowndes. Dylan admitted to being a millionaire, with over 10 million records sold.

In July 1966, shortly after his 25th birthday, motorcycle crash led to 18-month disappearance; while recuperating in Woodstock from broken neck, rumors of death, disfigurement, and drug addiction abounded. During this period Dylan recorded **Basement Tapes** with The Band (not officially released until eight years later). Early 1968 saw his appearance at benefit concert for Woody Guthrie, the birth of his first child, and release of **John Wesley Harding**, recorded in Nashville with country instrumentation. Voice had mellowed, lyrics were more accessible and gave hint of compassion, and tunes were melodic. **Nashville Skyline** (1969) continued songs in praise of living and gave last Top 10 single with **Lay Lady Lay**. During summer 1969 he split with Grossman; performed for huge crowds at Isle of Wight and Woodstock Festivals.

Moving back to Greenwich Village, released two disappointing records in 1970, although **Self Portrait** became seventh gold album. Over next two years kept low profile, while books, fanzines, and Dylanology clubs interpreted his words and scavengers searched his garbage for significance. Meanwhile, bootleg records proliferated, Dylan's book *Tarantula* was published, and he visited Israel. Performed at Madison Square Garden benefit for Bangladesh; recorded both electric and acoustic versions of George Jackson single,

and did sessions for friends.

Went to West Coast for small role in film *Pat Garrett And Billy The Kid* (1973), and wrote score for it, including **Knocking on Heaven's Door**. When Columbia contract expired, recorded **Planet Waves** (1974) for Asylum; tour with The Band resulted in exciting live album **Before The Flood** (same year). Re-signing with Columbia, recorded **Blood On The Tracks** (also '74). Filled with pain and bitterness (his marriage was breaking up), album was seen as return to form after recent simplistic good-time music. After recording new album **Desire** (1975), toured with old friends and stars of the 1960s in 1975–76 Rolling Thunder Revue. Dylan praised as charismatic entertainer; television special and live album **Hard Rain** (1976) released. During tour Dylan also created four-hour, poetically rambling film *Renaldo And Clara*, screened in 1978.

At end of 1970s Dylan became born-again Christian. Somewhat self-righteously aimed moralizing at non-believers (including fellow rock 'n' rollers). First post-conversion album **Slow Train Coming** (1979) featured talented instrumentalists. Later albums added gospel flavour, but didn't create much commercial excitement.

Subsequent albums received patchy critical and commercial acceptance, but Dylan's live pulling power remained undiminished, as evidenced by 1986 tour with Tom Petty And The Heartbreakers, and 1987 outings with fellow 60s legends The Grateful Dead. Began annual pilgrimage to UK in 1989 (sell-out dates in London and Birmingham) and for 1991 gigs introduced new band featuring Tony Garnier (bass), Cesar Diaz (guitar), John Jackson (guitar) and Ian Wallace (drums).

Some would say typecast, Dylan appeared as clapped-out middle-aged rock star in appalling *Hearts Of Fire* movie (1987), but went on to enjoy success as member of occasional Traveling Wilburys troupe, with George Harrison, Jeff Lynne, Tom Petty, and, before his death, Roy Orbison.

In the early 1990s, Dylan released two albums of traditional material, **Good As I Been To You** (1992) and **World Gone Wrong** (1993), which again drew mixed reviews. However, his 1997 set, **Time Out**

of Mind (featuring new songs, and produced by Daniel Lanois, who had previously worked with U2 and – outstandingly – on Emmylou Harris' 1995 **Wrecking Ball** CD) was given a warmer reception. Dylan remains a powerful, enigmatic figure who has lost little of his power to surprise and (sometimes) perplex his audiences.

Recommended listening

Bob Dylan (Columbia), 1962
Freewheelin' Bob Dylan (Columbia), 1963
Times They Are A-Changing' (Columbia), 1964
Another Side Of Bob Dylan (Columbia), 1964
Bringing It All Back Home (Columbia), 1965
Highway 61 Revisited (Columbia), 1965
Blonde On Blonde (Columbia), 1966
John Wesley Harding (Columbia), 1968
Nashville Skyline (Columbia), 1969
Self Portrait (Columbia), 1970
New Morning (Columbia), 1970
Pat Garrett And Billy The Kid (soundtrack) (Columbia), 1973
Dylan (Columbia), 1973
Planet Waves (Columbia), 1974
Blood On The Tracks (Columbia), 1974
Basement Tapes (Columbia), 1975
Desire (Columbia), 1975
Hard Rain (Columbia), 1976
Street Legal (Columbia), 1978
Slow Train Coming (Columbia), 1979
Saved (Columbia), 1980
Shot Of Love (Columbia), 1981
Infidels (CBS), 1983
Empire Burlesque (CBS), 1985
Oh Mercy (Columbia), 1989
Under The Red Sky (Columbia), 1990
Good As I Been To You (Columbia), 1992
World Gone Wrong (Columbia), 1993
Time Out Of Mind (Columbia), 1997
The Essential Bob Dylan (Columbia), 2000

THE EAGLES

US band formed 1971

Original line-up: Glenn Frey, vocals, guitar; Randy Meisner, vocals, bass; Bernie Leadon, guitar, vocals; Don Henley, drums, vocals.

Career: Frey and Henley met as members of Linda Rondstadt's backing band. Following recruitment of ex-Poco member Meisner and former Flying Burrito Brother Leadon, four flew to London to record first album as Eagles for Asylum.

Album **The Eagles** (1972) made major impact, as did single **Take It Easy**, co-written by Frey and stablemate Jackson Browne. **Desperado** (1973) consolidated success, and crystallized Eagles' image as laid-back California outlaws. By now band had become major live attraction, adding large orchestra for some concerts.

Having contributed to sessions for third album **On The Border** (1974), guitarist Don Felder added as fifth member. Band went from strength to strength, breaking British market for first time in 1975 with single **One Of These Nights**. Same year saw first No. 1 single in US, **Best Of My Love**.

During mid-70s band could do no wrong, achieving status of mega-group with across-board appeal. Heaped with gold and platinum records, showered with awards, only problem was meeting demand for product and live appearances. Strain proved too much for Bernie Leadon, who quit at end of 1975 to pursue unspectacular solo career. Slightly surprising choice of replacement was former James Gang guitarist Joe Walsh who had more recently been pursuing solo career. Walsh's songwriting/guitar work gave their "laid-back" California sound a shot in the arm. In 1977 Randy Meisner also quit to go solo, and in came Timothy B. Schmit, another former Poco stalwart.

By the end of the decade, by which time line-up had been further augmented by long-time friend Joe Vitale on keyboards, Eagles had become one of the most successful American recording acts of the 70s. Band sold 40 million albums worldwide since inception; **Hotel**

ABOVE: *The man who put the "twang" in pop guitar – Duane Eddy.*

California sold nine million in year of release (1977), **Greatest Hits** compilation seven million. All concerts during decade were immediate sell-outs, and 1980 **Live** double LP was an impressive reminder of their onstage potency.

However, by now The Eagles had (temporarily) ceased to exist as a functioning unit.

1982 saw both Glenn Frey and Don Henley have success with solo releases (Henley's **Dirty Laundry** (1982) in particular becoming major hit), but group reunion, though often rumored, did not take place until 1994, when Frey, Felder, Henley, Schmit, and Walsh embarked on their "Hell Freezes Over" tour, which continued into 1995 and spawned album (and video) of same name. In 1998, they was joined by ex-members Meisner and Leadon for a one-off New York show celebrating group's induction into Rock 'n' Roll Hall of Fame. Quintet undertook US and UK tours in 1999–2000, but internal problems have recently re-emerged: Felder was sacked from the band in February 2001, and is currently suing Frey and Henley for unfair dismissal.

Recommended listening

The Eagles (Asylum), 1972
Desperado (Asylum), 1973
On The Border (Asylum), 1974
One Of These Nights (Asylum), 1975
Their Greatest Hits (Asylum), 1975
Hotel California (Asylum), 1976
The Long Run (Asylum), 1979
Eagles Live (Asylum), 1980
Hell Freezes Over (Geffen), 1994
1972–1999 (Elektra), 2000
Don Henley solo:
I Can't Stand Still (Asylum/-), 1982
Building The Perfect Beast (Geffen), 1985

DUANE EDDY

US guitarist, composer
Born Corning, New York,
April 28, 1938

Career: Raised in Phoenix, Arizona, Eddy played guitar from five, and, as a teenager, worked in local dance bands before coming under influence of ace guitarist Al Casey.

After tuition from another guitar maven, Jim Wybele, Eddy was signed by local DJ Lee Hazlewood – later a recording star/producer himself – and Lester Sill in 1957. He cut debut **Movin 'n' Groovin'** in 1958 with his backing band The Rebels (Larry Knechtel, Steve Douglas, and Al Casey).

Eddy developed unique "twangy" guitar sound by utilizing various tremolo and reverb effects (some of them devised by the resourceful Hazlewood, who made use of old water tanks and other unlikely objects to create a distinctive sound) and by playing melody on the bass strings of his guitar. As much a part of his records' appeal were the raunchy sax solos of Steve Douglas and Jim Horn and the rebel yells of Ben De Moto. The overall effect was potent blend of rock 'n' roll, R&B, and Southern states' influences.

Second release **Rebel Rouser** (1958) went gold and led to string of big sellers (12 million records sold by 1963, total sales having now topped 30 million from some 25 singles, 21 of which made UK charts). More than half his hits were self-penned.

Eddy acted in TV western series *Have Gun Will Travel*, and movies *Because They're Young* (his theme for which was 1960 million-seller), *A Thunder Of Drums*, and *The Wild Westerner*. He also composed the theme for 1961 movie *Ring Of Fire*.

Eddy has continued to tour extensively, either solo or as part of "revival packages," and enjoyed brief chart resurrection with re-recording of **Peter Gunn** (1987) in collaboration with UK group The Art Of Noise. The track won Best Instrumental Grammy in 1987, and prompted Capitol Records to sign artist for self-titled album, produced by Jeff Lynne and featuring Ry Cooder, Paul McCartney, and George Harrison.
Guitar: Gretsch 6120.

Recommended listening

Movin' n' Groovin' (-/London), 1957
Have Twangy Guitar, Will Travel
  (Jamie), 1958
Especially For You (Jamie),
  1958
Twang's The Thang (Jamie),
  1959
Songs For Our Heritage
  (Jamie), 1960
$1,000,000 Worth Of Twang
  (Jamie), 1961
Girls, Girls, Girls (Jamie), 1961
$1,000,000 Worth Of Twang Volume
  2 (Jamie), 1962
Twistin' (Jamie), 1962
In Person (Jamie), 1962
16 Greatest Hits (Jamie), 1962
Pure Gold (RCA), 1965
Best Of (RCA/Camden), 1965
Twangy Guitar (RCA), 1970
Duane Eddy Guitar Man (-/GTO), 1975
Twang Twang (anthology), (Rhino) 1994
His Twangy Guitar and the Rebels (See
  for Miles), 1995
Best Of/Lonely Guitar (One Way), 1998
Deep In The Heart of Twangsvil (Bear
  Family), 1999

DAVE EDMUNDS

UK vocalist, guitarist, composer,
producer
Born Cardiff, Wales, April 5, 1944

Career: Served eight-year musical apprenticeship in various local bands. Formed Love Sculpture with John Williams, bass, and Bob Jones, drums; their frenetic rock instrumental adaptation of Khachaturian's **Sabre Dance** reached No. 6 on UK chart in 1968 and was band's only hit. Love Sculpture broke up following American tour.

With assistance from producer Kingsley Ward, Edmunds built his own Rockfield Studio in Monmouthshire, Wales. There, he learned how to reproduce sounds of his favorite oldies. Re-make of Smiley Lewis's R&B classic **I Hear You Knocking** gave him three-million selling UK No. 1 in 1970. Debut album **Rockpile** (1972) also featured John Williams and former Amen Corner leader Andy Fairweather Low.

Besides own work, Edmunds produced Brinsley Schwarz, Ducks Deluxe, Flamin' Groovies, Shakin' Stevens And The Sunsets, and American legend Del Shannon. Recreating classic Phil Spector "Wall Of Sound," had further hits of own with versions of Spector oldies **Baby I Love You** and **Born To Be With You**.

Former Brinsley Schwarz member Nick Lowe contributed to Edmunds' debut album with Swan Song label, **Get It** (1975). Lowe also became member, with Billy Bremner (vocals, guitar), of Rockpile road band formed by Edmunds, and featured heavily on 1980 LP **Seconds Of Pleasure**.

1979 **Repeat When Necessary** album included chart singles **Girls Talk**, **Queen Of Hearts**, and **Crawling From The Wreckage**. Edmunds enjoyed further UK Top 30 hit with version of Guy Mitchell's **Singing The Blues** in following year.

During latter part of 80s and into early 90s, Edmunds foresook personal ambition for production and session duties for a variety of performers, including kd lang, Stray Cats, Everly Brothers and Status Quo; took time out for his own **Closer To The Flame** set in 1989, and undertook selected gigs. Released **Plugged In** CD in 1994, and has subsequently toured extensively and provided music for movies and commercials.

Guitars: Gibson 335, Gibson J200 acoustics, Fender Telecaster, Martin D45.

Recommended listening

Subtle As A Flying Mallet (RCA), 1975
Get It (Swan Song), 1975
Tracks On Wax (Swan Song), 1978
Repeat When Necessary (Swan Song),
  1979
Twangin' (Swan Song), 1981
Best Of (Swan Song), 1981
D.E. 7 (Columbia), 1982
I Hear You Rockin' (Arista), 1987
Anthology (1968-90) (Rhino), 1993
KBFH Presents (King Biscuit), 1999
Pile of Rock – Live (Sanctuary), 2001
With Love Sculpture:
Classic Tracks 68–72 (One-Up), 1974
With Rockpile:
Seconds Of Pleasure (Columbia/
  F-Beat), 1980
Original Rockpile, The Volume II
  (Harvest), 1987

239

FAIRPORT CONVENTION

UK group formed 1967

Original line-up: Simon Nicol, guitar, vocals; Richard Thompson, guitar, vocals; Ashley "Tyger" Hutchings, bass; Shaun Frater, drums; Judy Dyble, autoharp, vocals.

Career: Pioneers of UK folk-rock, although in a long and varied career they have embraced a wide diversity of styles. Original line-up (above) played debut gig in Spring 1967. By November, Martin Lamble (drums) and lead singer Ian Matthews were recruited for first album, **Fairport Convention** (1968). Early repertoire consisted of contemporary American folk-rock and original material. Dyble was replaced by Strawbs' Sandy Denny in 1968, and group began eventual conversion to traditional British folk music. **What We Did On Our Holidays** (1969) revealed Thompson as major songwriting talent, while demonstrating healthy balance of original interpretations of traditional songs and excellent Joni Mitchell and Bob Dylan covers.

Matthews quit in January 1969, and was replaced by established folkie Dave Swarbrick (fiddle, vocals), who became Fairport's longest serving member. Later that year, traditionally based **Unhalfbricking** was succeeded by **Liege And Lief**, generally acknowledged as Fairport Convention's finest work.

In June 1969, after a Birmingham gig, the group's van skidded from motorway and Lamble was killed. By the end of the year, Sandy Denny had quit to form Fotheringay, while Ashley Hutchings left to start Steeleye Span. New members Dave Mattacks (drums) and Dave Pegg (bass) kept unit stable for a year during which **Full House** and **Live At The L.A. Troubadour** were recorded. The former revealed the Swarbrick/Thompson partnership at its best. By January 1971, Thompson had departed to pursue highly acclaimed career with wife Linda (and later as a soloist). Following two more British folk-rock albums, **Angel Delight** and **Babbacombe Lee**, the last of the original Fairports, guitarist Simon Nicol, left to form Albion Country Band with Ashley Hutchings.

During 1972, group went through unprecedented period of flux, but the next year, they released two albums, **Rosie** and **Nine**; latter proved their best post-Thompson effort. Group's somewhat fading credibility was improved by dramatic return of Sandy Denny in late 1973. **Live Convention** was followed by **Rising For The Moon**, a showcase for Denny insufficiently integrated into group context.

Mattacks left to join Etchingham Steam Band, and in January 1976 Denny returned to solo career. Lucas and Donahue also quit, precipitating Fairport's demise. New members were recruited, including Bruce Rowland (drums), Bob Brady (piano), Dan Ar Bras (guitar), and Roger Burridge (mandolin, fiddle). Final Island album, **Gottle O'Geer** (1976), originally intended as Swarbrick solo, was recorded as contractual filler. A brief period with Vertigo resulted in two average works, **The Bonny Bunch Of Roses** (1977) and **Tipplers Tales** (1978), before anti-climactic **Farewell Farewell** (1979). Former Fairports all succeeded at various levels with spin off/solo ventures. Sandy Denny died tragically on April 21, 1978, after falling downstairs at a friend's house.

Since 1980, Fairport have held regular reunion concerts, and they continue to record and tour sporadically. Although their later work is patchy in comparison with earlier pioneering achievements, their influence on development of British electric folk music is inestimable.

Recommended listening

Fairport Convention (A&M), 1968
What We Did On Our Holidays (Island), 1969
Unhalfbricking (A&M), 1969
Liege And Lief (A&M), 1969
Live At The LA Troubadour (Island), 1969
Full House (A&M), 1970
Angel Delight (A&M), 1971
Babbacombe Lee (A&M), 1971
A History of Fairport Convention (Island), 1972
Rosie (A&M), 1973
Nine (A&M), 1973
Fairport Live – A Moveable Beast (Island), 1974
Rising For The Moon (Island), 1974
Gottle O'Geer (Antilles), 1976
Fairport Chronicles (A&M), 1976
The Bonny Bunch Of Roses (Vertigo), 1977
Tipplers Tales (Vertigo), 1978
Farewell Farewell (Simons), 1979
Heyday (Hannibal), 1987
In Real Time (Island), 1987
Expletive Delighted (Varrick), 1987

FLEETWOOD MAC

UK group formed 1967

Original line-up: Peter Green, Gibson Les Paul guitar, vocals; John McVie, bass; Mick Fleetwood, drums; Jeremy Spencer, guitar, vocals.

Career: Peter Green formed band when he, McVie, and Fleetwood quit John Mayall's Bluesbreakers. For short period McVie considered re-joining Mayall and Fleetwood Mac's debut performance at UK's Windsor Festival (August 1967) featured temporary bassist Bob Brunning.

First LP (**Fleetwood Mac**, 1968) featured straight-ahead blues; after releasing follow-up, **Mr. Wonderful**, band added third guitarist, Danny Kirwan. UK/US tours and substantial chart success followed, including No. 1 UK single **Albatross** (1969), and concert favourite **Oh Well**. However, in Summer 1970, Green left the band after severe nervous breakdown.

Band gradually recovered self-confidence after this blow; but in February 1971, Jeremy Spencer shocked his colleagues with conversion to religious cult, Children of God. Like Green, he renounced his past and swore to leave rock business. Green stepped in to help Mac complete US tour. Permanent guitar duties were assumed in April 1971 by Bob Welch, and with him Mac released spotty **Future Games** and underrated **Bare Trees**.

Next casualty was Kirwan who was fired in summer 1972 because of growing disenchantment with road life. Welch's influence took Mac from blues-based

ABOVE: Fleetwood Mac, 1970, with guitarist Peter Green in white robe.

rock towards softer California sound. This trend was accelerated by Kirwan's replacements, Americans Bob Weston (guitar, vocals) and Dave Walker (vocals). Mac released **Penguin** in 1973, indicating McVie's fascination for the Antarctic bird, which became band's symbol.

By June 1973 Walker had left to work with Kirwan, and band floundered. **Mystery To Me** was critically disappointing; Weston left after recording this LP, and resulting internal upheavals caused cancellation of US autumn 1973 tour. Their manager formed bogus group to tour in their place at start of 1974. Band seemed to disappear for good as litigation ensued over various claims to name Fleetwood Mac. They reappeared with **Heroes Are Hard To Find** (1974), but Bob Welch left shortly after.

Legend has it that Mick Fleetwood was checking out LA studio to record Mac's next album when he was introduced to Lindsey Buckingham, who was working next door with Stevie Nicks. Fleetwood asked them to join his group, and result was smash hit LP, **Fleetwood Mac** (1975). Any doubts about Mac's ability to sustain this success was

dispelled by **Rumours** (1977). Album followed break-up of John and Christine McVie's marriage, as well as Fleetwood's; Buckingham and Nicks also broke off long-term relationship during this period.

New success of Mac pushed band into realm of superstars. Certain air of self-indulgence appeared in long-awaited **Tusk** (1979). **Fleetwood Mac Live** (1980) broke no new ground and Mac seemed to lose direction again as Nicks, Fleetwood, and Buckingham all released solo offerings.

Demise of group looked permanent as individual careers took hold, particularly Stevie Nicks', but the lure of the dollar proved hard to resist, and 1987 saw release of brand new album **Tango In The Night**.

When Buckingham refused to tour to support **Tango**, Mac recruited ace guitarists Billy Burnette (son of late rock 'n' roll star Johnny) and Rick Vito. Ironically, Buckingham changed his mind and featured on US dates before embarking on solo career.

With Nicks and McVie enjoying individual successes, their joint decision to quit Fleetwood Mac following 1990 **Mask** world tour was hardly surprising. Three years later, the band (with Nicks, Buckingham, and McVie) reunited for a one-off appearance at Bill Clinton's

Presidential Inaugural concert, and various line-ups have subsequently resurfaced for occasional concerts and the albums **Time** (1995) and **The Dance** (1997).

Recommended listening

Fleetwood Mac (Epic), 1968
Mr. Wonderful (Epic), 1968
English Rose (Epic), 1969
Then Play On (Reprise), 1969
Kiln House (Reprise), 1970
Future Games (Reprise), 1971
Bare Trees (Reprise), 1972
Penguin (Reprise), 1973
Mystery To Me (Reprise), 1974
Heroes Are Hard To Find (Reprise), 1974
Fleetwood Mac (Reprise), 1975
Rumours (Warner Bros.), 1977
Tusk (Warner Bros.), 1979
Fleetwood Mac Live (Warner Bros.), 1980
Tango In The Night (Warner Bros.), 1987
Behind The Mask (Warner Bros.), 1990
Time (Warner Bros.), 1995
Live At The BBC (Sanctuary), 1995
The Dance (Warner Bros.), 1997
1967–69 Complete Blue Horizon Sessions (6 CD set) (Sire), 1999

PETER FRAMPTON

UK vocalist, guitarist, composer
Born Beckenham, England,
April 22, 1950

Career: British pop music press traditionally seized cute faces to pump up, and cherubic-faced Peter Frampton was their choice for "Face of 68" teen idol. He was then leader of The Herd who hit with **From The Underworld** (1967), **Paradise Lost** (1968), and **I Don't Want Our Loving To Die** (1968). But Frampton sought recognition as talented musician rather than mere pin-up. He quit Herd to form highly rated Humble Pie with Steve Marriott, Greg Ridley (bass) and Jerry Shirley (drums); band displayed impressively hard-driving R&B-influenced style.

In 1971 Frampton left to pursue more melodic and romantic direction with increasing emphasis on tasteful guitar work and songs with potent hooklines. He also guested on George Harrison's **All Things Must Pass**, Harry Nilsson's **Son Of Schmilsson**, and other projects.

First solo album, **Frampton**, featured Ringo Starr, Billy Preston, Klaus Voorman, former Herd cohort Andy Brown, ex-Spooky Tooth member Mike Kellie, and Rick Wills from Cochise. Kellie and Wills were drafted into Frampton's new band Camel with Mick Gallagher, ex-Bell 'n' Arc. Kellie soon moved back to re-formed Spooky Tooth, being replaced by American drummer John Siomos (ex-Mitch Ryder).

Camel toured US and concentrated on American market until break-up in 1974. Frampton continued to record solo albums and tour with various back-up bands, scoring bestselling live album with 1975 **Frampton Comes Alive!** LP, which included hit singles **Show Me The Way**, **Baby I Love Your Way**, and **Do You Feel**. Mick Jagger, Stevie Wonder, and other names helped on 1977 success **I'm In You**.

In 1978, a near-fatal car crash put him temporarily out of action, and by mid-80s it seemed as though his solo career had gone into headspin. However, he returned to limelight with David Bowie

in 1987, as member of megastar's touring band, and cut **When All The Pieces Fit** album in 1989. In 1991, he was reunited with Steve Marriott, recording five tracks which were Marriott's last completed work before his death on April 20 that year (as the result of a fire at his home). Frampton subsequently released a new solo album (**Peter Frampton**, 1994) and his recent CDs include **Frampton Comes Alive II** (1995) and **Live in Detroit** (2000).

Recommended listening

Wind Of Change (A&M), 1972
Frampton's Camel (A&M), 1973
Frampton (A&M), 1975
Frampton Comes Alive! (A&M), 1975
I'm In You (A&M), 1977
Where I Should Be (A&M), 1979
Super Disc Of Peter Frampton
   (-/A&M), 1979
Breaking All The Rules (A&M), 1981
The Art Of Control (A&M), 1982
Premonition (A&M), 1986
When All The Pieces Fit (Atlantic/-),
   1989

FREE

UK group formed 1968

Original line-up: Paul Kossoff, Gibson Les Paul guitar; Simon Kirke, drums; Andy Fraser, bass; Paul Rodgers, vocals.

Career: Kossoff and Kirke were in second division band Black Cat Bones. They saw Rodgers perform with Brown Sugar and asked him to join. Andy Fraser (then only 15) was in John Mayall's Bluesbreakers but dissatisfied with jazz direction. Mutual friend contacted him and the four got together for jam session; first evening produced four songs and group decided to make unit permanent.

Veteran UK blues musician Alexis Korner encouraged and supported the fledgling band, christening them Free At Last; but after being signed to Island Records, their name was shortened to Free. First LP (**Tons of Sobs**, 1968) made only minor impact, but second, **Free** (1969), won massive UK and US support when released later the following year;

All Right Now single (taken from third album, **Fire and Water**) went Top 10 on both sides of the Atlantic in 1970. However, sudden success created friction as members jostled for limelight, and after **Highway** album (also 1970), band temporarily broke up. Rodgers' subsequent attempts at a solo career flopped, as did Fraser's. Kirke and Kossoff recorded **Kossoff, Kirke, Tetsu And Rabbit** LP (1971) with Texan keyboards player Rabbit Bundrick and bassist Tetsu Yamauchi.

In 1972 original band re-formed for **Free At Last** album. During tour Kossoff's drug habit and Rodgers/Fraser fights split group again. Kossoff and Fraser left, Tetsu and Rabbit replacing them. This line-up recorded **Heartbreaker** (Kossoff helped with guitar work). Single from LP, **Wishing Well**, prompted tour. Kossoff started but again collapsed and Wendell Richardson (ex-Osibisa) stepped in. At end of US tour, Free folded for good.

Fraser failed to follow up success with either Andy Fraser Band or Sharks. Kossoff died in 1976 of drug-induced heart failure shortly after launching his band **Back Street Crawler**. Tetsu joined Rod Stewart's Faces, and Rabbit did session work and made two solo LPs before joining Who as tour "member" from 1978-82. Rodgers and Kirke set up Bad Company.

Certainly one of UK's finer bands, with understated, sparse arrangements and high energy spirit, Free had far-ranging influence. Unfortunately, talent failed to reach its potential; drugs and egos doomed Free from the start. But, by way of a more pleasant footnote, the 1991 re-release of **All Right Now**, featured in chewing gum ad, returned Free to the UK charts, with hastily compiled **Best Of** package also making UK Top 10.

Recommended listening

Tons Of Sobs (A&M/Island), 1969
Free (A&M/Island), 1969
Fire And Water (A&M/Island), 1970
Highway (A&M/Island), 1970
Live (A&M/Island), 1971
Free At Last (A&M/Island), 1972
Heartbreaker (A&M/Island), 1973
Best Of (A&M/-), 1975

Completely Free (compilation)
(A&M/Island), 1983
Best Of Free – All Right Now (Island),
1991

RORY GALLAGHER

UK guitarist, vocalist, composer
Born Ballyshannon, County Donegal,
Ireland, March 2, 1949
Died London, June 14, 1995

Career: One of rock's true grafters. Raised in Cork; played in local bands until 15. Joined the Fontana Showband, which played pop hits to enthusiastic dance-hall crowds. In 1963, acquired his trademark 1961-vintage Fender Stratocaster – which he used almost exclusively for the rest of his life.

With Charlie McCracken, bass, and John Wilson, drums, formed Taste, high-energy blues/rock trio. Band learned trade in Hamburg and home country before moving to UK in 1969. Taste earned ecstatic reviews for Gallagher's dazzling guitar technique; but his central role led to tension with his two colleagues. Wilson often refused to take stage for group encores, leaving Gallagher and McCracken to appease audience. Trio split in 1971, and Gallagher took to road with Wilgar Campbell, drums, and Gerry McAvoy, bass, using own name as band title. Line-up completed three successful albums before Campbell was replaced by Rod De'Ath. Lou Martin was added on keyboards.

Pursuing a hectic touring schedule, Rory Gallagher Band secured reputation in Europe and America. They released a stream of respectably selling albums, with several memorable highlights: among them was live album **Irish Tour '74**, which captured gregarious Gallagher at his best. Director Tony Palmer filmed gigs for his movie *Rory Gallagher – Irish Tour '74*, which premiered at prestigious Cork Film Festival that year.

RIGHT: *Rory Gallagher with the battered Fender Stratocaster he used throughout his career.*

After 1976 set **Calling Card**, De'Ath and Martin quit. Drummer Ted McKenna (ex-Alex Harvey band) joined for **Photo Finish** (1978). 1980 world tour provided live cuts for **Stage Struck**. Album showed Gallagher still loved the road. 1982 **Jinx** collection maintained enthusiastic studio approach, although barren period followed before **Fresh Evidence** (1990).

Complete absence from both UK/US singles charts during recording career belies Gallagher's popular appeal. He toured tirelessly, and was capable of bringing even the most staid of audience to its feet during his powerful, blues-laden solo sets. Sadly, Gallagher's health began to give way in the 1990s. He was taken ill while appearing in Europe in 1994, and received a liver transplant the following April, but died two months afterwards.

Guitars: Fender Stratocaster, Martin acoustic, mandolin.

Recommended listening

Rory Gallagher (-/Polydor), 1971
Deuce (-/ Chrysalis), 1971
Live In Europe (live) (Chrysalis), 1973
Blueprint (Chrysalis), 1973
Tattoo (Chrysalis), 1973
Irish Tour '74 (live) (Chrysalis), 1974
In The Beginning (-/Emerald Gem), 1974
Against The Grain (Chrysalis), 1975
Calling Card (Chrysalis), 1976
Photo Finish (Chrysalis), 1978
Top Priority (Chrysalis), 1979
Stage Struck (live) (Chrysalis), 1980
Jinx (Chrysalis), 1982
Defender (Demon Solo), 1987
Fresh Evidence (IRS/Castle), 1990
With Taste:
Taste (Atco/Polydor), 1969
On The Boards (Atco/Polydor), 1970
Live Taste (-/Polydor), 1971
Live At The Isle Of Wight (-/Polydor),
1972
Taste (-/Polydor), 1977

LOWELL GEORGE

US guitarist, vocalist, composer
Born Hollywood, California,
April 13, 1945
Died Arlington, Virginia, June 29, 1979

Career: George played in mid-60s folk-rock group Factory, and, two years later, was briefly in The Standells and the Seeds. He then joined Frank Zappa, playing on both **Hot Rats** (1969) and **Weasels Ripped My Flesh** (1970).

During this period, he wrote and recorded several demos, including **Willing** and **Truck Stop Girl** – the latter subsequently covered by The Byrds. Numerous other US acts also picked up on George's songs, including Linda Ronstadt and Commander Cody. This growing level of interest eventually led to recording deal with Warners, and George formed Little Feat with Bill Payne, keyboards, vocals; Roy Estrada, bass; and Richard Hayward, drums.

First album **Little Feat**, released in 1971, attracted some critical acclaim, though sales were poor. Same fate befell follow-up **Sailin' Shoes** (1972), in spite of increased media coverage. Disillusioned, Estrada left to join Captain Beefheart's Magic Band. The other members re-grouped in new six-piece line-up, including Ken Gradney (bass), Sam Clayton (congas), and Paul Barrere (guitar). Third album **Dixie Chicken** (1973) also brought minimal success, and members finally lost interest and drifted into other projects.

George was in constant demand as sessioneer/songwriter, but declined invitation to join projected group with John Sebastian and Phil Everly as well as similar request from Jackson Browne. Contributed to albums by (among others) The Meters, Jimmy Webb, Carly Simon, John Sebastian, Nilsson, and Robert Palmer.

Little Feat re-formed in 1974 to cut excellent **Feats Don't Fail Me Now**. Followed with critically acclaimed tour of England as part of *Warner Bros. Music Show* in early 1975. (They were to return to England in May 1976 to support The Who at Charlton Football Ground.)

During group's final years, Lowell George's role appeared to diminish; he contributed only three songs to **The Last Record Album** (1975), including the memorable **Long Distance Love**.

Hepatitis precluded any extensive involvement in Feat's next album, **Time Loves A Hero** (1977), generally regarded as least impressive. Live double, **Waiting For Columbus** (1978), was also poor in relation to earlier work, which was hardly surprising since George was traveling separately during tours. George produced Grateful Dead's **Shakedown Street** in the same year.

Group finally split in April 1979 while recording final album. George, meanwhile, had begun solo career with average **Thanks I'll Eat It Here**, better work being anticipated in the future. However, On June 29, 1979, he died, aged 34, from drug-induced heart failure in Arlington, Virginia; last gig had taken place at George Washington University, Washington DC the previous evening.

Recommended listening

Little Feat (Warner Bros.), 1971
Sailin' Shoes (Warner Bros.), 1972
Dixie Chicken (Warner Bros.), 1973
Feats Don't Fail Me Now (Warner
  Bros.), 1974
The Last Record Album (Warner
  Bros.), 1975
Time Loves A Hero (Warner Bros.),
  1977
Waiting For Columbus (Warner Bros.)
  1978
Down On The Farm (Warner Bros.), 1979
Hoy-Hoy! (Warner Bros.), 1981
Lowell George solo:
Thanks, I'll Eat It Here (Warner Bros.)
  1979

GRATEFUL DEAD

US group formed 1966

Original line-up: Jerry Garcia, Gibson Les Paul and SG, Fender Stratocaster, Travis Bean and various custom-made guitars; Phil Lesh, bass; Ron "Pigpen" McKernan, keyboards; Bob Weir, Gibson ES-335 guitar; Bill Kreutzmann (aka Bill Sommers), drums; Robert Hunter, lyrics.

Career: Grateful Dead emerged from San Francisco's hippie scene. Garcia joined up with Hunter at San Mateo Junior College in early 60s. While playing folk and blues in local spots, they came across Weir and McKernan. Garcia met Kreutzmann when working in a record store.

Kreutzmann and Pigpen formed rock band Zodiacs, while Garcia and Hunter joined David Nelson (later New Riders Of The Purple Sage) and Pete Albin (later Big Brother & The Holding Co.). This collection played bluegrass as Wildwood Boys and Hart Valley Drifters.

Garcia then formed Mother McCree's Uptown Jug Champions with Pigpen and Weir. Pigpen convinced band to change to electric blues and came up with name Warlocks. Kreutzmann and bassist Phil Lesh joined soon afterwards.

Warlocks became associated with author Ken Kesey and his so-called Merry Pranksters, and were the "house band" at his mid-60s Acid Tests, during which participants took LSD and other psychedelic drugs. In 1966 the band chose new name, Grateful Dead; this period saw evolution of their soon-to-be-familiar extended concert format, incorporating lengthy improvisations.

Grateful Dead signed to Warner Bros. in 1967, and recorded their debut LP in three days.

Unsatisfied with its sound, Garcia took six months to complete follow-up, **Anthem Of The Sun** (1968), on which Mickey Hart joined as second drummer. **Aoxomoxoa** (1969) put band even deeper into debt as Warner Bros. had yet to recover studio costs for second release. Problem was inability to capture atmosphere of band on stage – solved by next effort, a double live set, **Live Dead** (1969).

Band now entered what many consider to be classic period, as their studio work switched from drawn-out jams to shorter, structured songs. **Workingman's Dead** and **American Beauty** (both 1970) reflect this approach and remain among Dead's best efforts.

Embezzlement charges against band's manager (Hart's father) caused Hart to leave band; but these problems did not affect success of **The Grateful Dead** (aka "Skull and Roses"), band's

ABOVE: *Jerry Garcia onstage, 1980s.*

1986, following which he had to relearn many of his basic playing skills. He recovered sufficiently to appear on **In The Dark** (1987), and the Dead gained a Top 30 placing with their final studio album, **Built To Last** (1989). Despite Mydland's 1990 death from drug overdose, the Dead soldiered on with Bruce Hornsby and (later) Vince Welnick on keyboards.

Early 1990s saw further tours, live albums and side projects, but Garcia's physical condition was again deteriorating, and his death from a heart attack on August 9 1995 led to the band's own demise.

Recommended listening

Grateful Dead albums:

Grateful Dead (Warner Bros.), 1967
Anthem Of The Sun (Warner Bros.), 1968
Aoxomoxoa (Warner Bros.), 1969
Live Dead (Warner Bros.), 1969
Workingman's Dead (Warner Bros.), 1970
American Beauty (Warner Bros.), 1970
The Grateful Dead ("Skull and Roses") (Warner Bros.), 1971
Europe '72 (Warner Bros.), 1972
History Of The Grateful Dead, Volume 1 – Bear's Choice (Warner Bros.), 1973
Wake Of The Flood (Grateful Dead), 1973
Live From The Mars Hotel (Grateful Dead), 1974
Blues For Allah (Grateful Dead), 1975
Steal Your Face (Grateful Dead), 1976
Terrapin Station (Arista), 1977
What A Long Strange Trip It's Been (Warner Bros.), 1977
Shakedown Street (Arista), 1978
Go To Heaven (Arista), 1980
Reckoning (Arista), 1981
Dead Set (Arista), 1981
In The Dark (Arista), 1987
Dylan And The Dead (CBS), 1989
Built To Last (Arista), 1989
Without A Net (live) (Arista), 1990

Other Garcia records:

Garcia (Grateful Dead), 1972
Compliments of Garcia (Grateful Dead), 1974
Cats Under The Stars (Arista), 1978
Jerry Garcia/David Grisman (Acoustic Discs), 1991

second live album, released in 1971. **Europe '72** (1972) was live triple LP featuring some of Pigpen's last days with Dead, and introducing new pianist Keith Godchaux and his wife Donna (vocals). Pigpen had alcohol-related liver disease that was shortly to force his retirement; he died in May 1973.

Band launched their own label with a new studio-recorded set, **Wake Of The Flood** (1973). Individual members' outside activities took attention away from group: however, **Blues For Allah** (1975) proved Dead's continuing potency; it also marked Mickey Hart's return to fold.

In March 1976 Dead and The Who were paired by promoter Bill Graham for massive 100,000-strong two-day outdoor concert in Oakland, California.

Band strove for different approaches on **Terrapin Station** (1977), first Dead LP to use outside producer (Keith Olsen); Lowell George took over for **Shakedown Street** (1978).

That year, Dead travelled to Egypt for three special concerts in front of Great Pyramid. In 1979, the Godchauxs quit (Keith was to die in a road accident in July 1980); **Go To Heaven** (1980) introduced new keyboardist Brent Mydland. 1981 saw appearance of two live double albums, **Reckoning** (acoustic) and **Dead Set** (electric). Well received – but Jerry Garcia's health and addiction problems were now causing serious concern. A near-fatal diabetic collapse left him in a five-day coma in

BUDDY GUY

US guitarist, singer, composer
Born George Guy, Lettsworth,
Louisiana, July 30, 1936

Career: Made his early reputation on thriving Baton Rouge, Louisiana, blues scene as a soloist and sideman for Lightnin' Slim. Relocated to Chicago in 1957, where he gained early recognition for winning a "Battle of the Blues" at city's Blue Flame Club. The other contestants were big-name guitarists Otis Rush and Magic Sam, and harmonica ace Junior Wells – later a frequent playing partner of Guy's. After recording debut for Artistic/Cobra (which went out of business before his singles for them could make much impact), Guy signed with Chess, enjoying considerable success with classic, soulful tracks such as **First Time I Met The Blues** (1960), **I Found A True Love** (1961), and **Worried Blues (Stick Around)** (1963). Despite growing reputation, however, Guy did not give up his day job; he continued to work regular shifts as a tow-truck driver until 1967, when he and Junior Wells began touring.

Now signed to Vanguard, and with a more overtly soul-flavored singing and playing style, Guy began to develop a substantial following among rock fans. In the 1970s, he frequently supported The Rolling Stones and Eric Clapton on concert dates, and his playing was recognized as a major influence on Jimi Hendrix (it was also to inspire Stevie Ray Vaughan). Unfortunately, such acclaim – and Guy's powerful onstage presence – did not always lead to big record sales, and his albums were few, far between, and sometimes patchy in quality until the release of **Damn Right, I've Got The Blues** on Silvertone in 1991. A Grammy winner (like its 1993 successor, **Feels Like Rain**), **Damn Right** included contributions from Clapton (who has described Guy in *Musician* magazine as "By far and without a doubt the best guitar player alive"), Mark Knopfler and other luminaries. Among Guy's other recent CDs are **Slippin' In** (1994), **Live: The Real Deal** (1996), and his latest set, **Sweet Tea** (2001). He can be heard regularly "in the flesh" at his own club, Legends, in downtown Chicago.

Recommended listening

The Treasure Untold (Charly Blues Masterworks Vol. 11) (compilation of classic 1960–1966 sides) (Charly R & B), 1992
A Man And The Blues (Vanguard), 1968
Hold That Plane! (Vanguard), 1972
Buddy Guy & Junior Wells Play The Blues (Atco), 1972
Complete JSP Recordings 1979-82 (3 CDs) (JSP), 2000
Damn Right, I've Got The Blues (Silvertone), 1991
Feels Like Rain (Silvertone), 1993
Slippin' In (Silvertone), 1994
Live: The Real Deal (Silvertone), 1996
Sweet Tea (Silvertone), 2001

BILL HALEY

US vocalist, guitarist, composer
Born William John Clifton Haley Jr.,
Detroit, July 6, 1927
Died February 9, 1981, Harlingen,
Texas

Career: Bill Haley's career lived up to the name of his backing group, The Comets. It was his classic single **Rock Around The Clock** (whose sales of 20 million-plus copies make it one of the most successful records of all time) which really triggered off the rock 'n' roll revolution when featured in 1955 movie *The Blackboard Jungle*.

Moving to Booth-Winn, Pennsylvania, at the age of four, and raised on his parents' farm, Haley played hillbilly music at local country fairs as teenager, and spent two years in early 1940s as guitarist in cousin Lee's band. Cut first solo record, **Candy Kisses**, in 1945, when 18.

After four years with various country and western bands, in 1949 Haley became a DJ at radio station WPWA in Chester, Pennsylvania. Formed own group, the Four Aces of Swing, for live music broadcasts. Aces went on to record for various companies (they even cut a single for Atlantic, soon to be famous for its stable of soul artists) before signing to Dave Miller's Essex label in Philadelphia.

Jackie Brenston's 1951 R&B hit **Rocket 88** has sometimes been cited as the first rock 'n' roll record, and Haley made a lackluster version of it for white audiences in rockabilly style, selling 10,000 copies. He then notched 75,000 for a more spirited rendition of **Rock The Joint**, another R&B cover.

Sensing innate commercial potential of R&B/C&W hybrid, Haley stopped recording hillbilly material, changed band's name to the Comets, and made national charts in 1953 with **Crazy Man Crazy**, a pulsating record which formulated his successful and instantly recognizable style.

Already long past teens, his moon-shaped face crowned by a soon-to-be-famous kiss curl, Haley fronted band of seasoned musicians: Johnny Grande (piano); Joey Ambrose (sax); Franny Beecher (guitar); Billy Williamson (steel guitar); Marshall Lytle (bass); and Dick Richards (drums). Although belonging to different age group, they touched chord of rising youth cult, and suddenly became hottest property in music business.

Rock Around The Clock, recorded in April 1954 after move from Essex Records to Decca, was cut as favor to Haley's manager Dave Myers, who had written song 18 months earlier for Sunny Dae. Released late 1954, record reached No. 17 in UK in January 1955, then quickly dropped from the chart. After follow-up **Shake Rattle And Roll** (re-make of Joe Turner R&B hit) scored on both sides of the Atlantic, **Rock Around The Clock** was reissued, topping the charts in June (USA) and October (UK). It has subsequently been re-released several times, most recent Top 30 revival being 1974, when it reached No. 12 in UK.

Haley's American success was surpassed in UK, where in February 1957 he was mobbed by many thousands of fans on arrival at London's Waterloo Station in a train specially chartered by the *Sunday Mirror* newspaper. Cinema audiences had rioted at showing of two exploitation movies *Rock Around The Clock* and *Don't Knock The Rock* in which Haley starred. Concert tour produced similar scenes, with theater seats being ripped out and fans going into hysterics.

However, despite sometimes wild live act which saw saxophonist Rudy Pompelli (who had replaced Joey Ambrose in 1955) cavorting all over the stage and playing flat on his back, group couldn't hide the fact that they were essentially middle-aged musicians pandering to kids. With arrival of Elvis Presley, Haley's comet burned out, since these kids now had a hero of their own generation. A chubby-faced, rather sedate, happily married man, he could offer a measure of musical excitement but none of the sex appeal of his younger rival. His music also soon lost its edge, later recordings lapsing into lightweight MOR genre.

Moving to Rio Grande Valley, Haley contented himself with occasional nostalgia-circuit gigs with Comets. He was set for one such tour in Fall 1980, but it was called off due to his illness, and in November he was admitted to hospital with a suspected brain tumor. Three months later, the first hero of rock 'n' roll – a man who sold nearly 70 million records – was dead at the early age of 54.

Recommended listening
Rock The Joint! (Essex recordings, 1951–54), (Rollercoaster)
Best of Bill Haley & His Comets (MCA), 2000.

BELOW: *Bill Haley in the 1970s – still rocking around the clock.*

EDWARD VAN HALEN

US guitarist, composer
Born Nijmegen, Netherlands,
January 26, 1957

Career: Dutch-born Van Halen brothers, Alex and Edward, relocated to USA in 1962 with family. They grew up in Pasadena, California, and showed early aptitude for music (Alex as drummer and Edward as guitarist). While still at high school, formed group (originally known as Mammoth but subsequently rechristened Van Halen) with singer David Lee Roth and bassist Mike Anthony (both born in Mid-West). Band became popular local attraction through combination of loud and energetic heavy metal and Roth's very tight trousers! Due to inability to attract record deal, began promoting own gigs; used every possible attention-grabbing trick – like parachuting into stadium in successful attempt to upstage the headlining band.

By 1977, group were attracting audiences of 3,000. Warner Bros. A&R man Ted Templeman saw them playing Hollywood club and signed them immediately.

Their first album, **Van Halen**, was released in 1978. Like its successors, it achieved major US chart success, and showcased Eddie Van Halen's stunning guitar virtuosity. Using specially "hotrodded" instruments *(see pages 108–109)*, he played at lightning speed and deployed advanced techniques like two-handed tapping. Eddie displayed his extraordinary playing skills not only with his own band, but on the famous solo he contributed to Michael Jackson's bestselling single, **Beat It** (1982).

At end of 1985, following triumph with LP **1984** (which included smash hit single **Jump**), Roth left to pursue solo ambitions, scoring considerable success. Van Halen reconstituted with veteran metal merchant Sammy Hagar and went on to record biggest album of career, multi-platinum-selling **5150**. Disc also spawned US hit single **Why Can't This Be Love?**

Band took two years off before returning with 1988 set **OU812**, which topped US album chart. Van Halen returned to road in September of same year for two-month American tour.

Next Van Halen CD, **For Unlawful Carnal Knowledge** (1991) debuted at No. 1 in *Billboard* album chart. Surprisingly, collection did not overwhelm critics, although single cuts **Top Of The World** and **The Dream Is Over** saw

unit in prime form. However, after further success with live set **Right Here, Right Now** (1993) and studio-recorded **Balance** (1995), Sammy Hagar quit the group; replacement vocalist Gary Cherone appeared on **Van Halen 3** (1998) but left soon afterwards; there have been persistent rumors that original singer David Lee Roth may rejoin.

Edward Van Halen's health has recently given some cause for concern; he had a hip replacement operation in 1996, and in 2000-2001 he underwent successful treatment for cancer. He has since reassured his fans about his condition, and seems set to give us many more years of powerful and innovative guitar playing.

Recommended listening
   Van Halen band albums:
   Van Halen (Warner Bros.), 1978
   Van Halen II (Warner Bros.), 1979
   Women And Children First (Warner Bros.),
      1980
   Fair Warning (Warner Bros.), 1981
   Diver Down (Warner Bros.), 1982
   1984 (Warner Bros.), 1983
   5150 (Warner Bros.), 1986
   OU812 (Warner Bros.) 1988
   For Unlawful Carnal Knowledge (Warner
      Bros.), 1991
   Van Halen Live: Right Here, Right Now
      (2 CDs) (Warner Bros.), 1993
   Balance (Warner Bros.), 1995
   Best of Volume 1 (Warner Bros.), 1996
   Van Halen 3 (Warner Bros.), 1998
   Edward Van Halen solo/as guest artist:
   on Beat It by Michael Jackson (Thriller CD)
      (Epic), 1982
   with Brian May and Friends on Star Fleet
      Project (EMI), 1983
   on soundtrack to movie *The Wild Life*
      (MCA), 1984
   with Roger Waters on soundtrack to movie
      The Legend of 1900 (Sony), 1999
   David Lee Roth solo:
   Crazy From The Heat (Warner Bros.), 1985
   Eat 'Em And Smile (Warner Bros.), 1986
   Skyscraper (Warner Bros.), 1988
   A Little Ain't Enough (Warner Bros.), 1991
   Your Filthy Little Mouth (Reprise), 1994
   David Lee Roth: The Best (Rhino), 1997
   DLR Band (Sumthing Distribution), 1998

RIGHT: *The fastest guitarist in the West – Edward Van Halen and his hotrodded axe.*

GEORGE HARRISON

UK vocalist, guitarist, composer
Born Liverpool, February 25, 1943
Died Los Angeles, California,
November 29, 2001

Career: As youngest member of Fab Four, George spent several years in shadow of Lennon and McCartney, and in early days was rarely allowed to demonstrate his considerable songwriting talent on Beatles records. His only A-side for the group, **Something**, came from their final LP, **Abbey Road** (1969). However, he had already released a solo record – soundtrack for film *Wonderwall*, the first album to appear on Apple label – in 1968, and his experimental **Electronic Sounds** was issued the following year, just before Beatles split.

In late 1969, Harrison became involved with US white soulsters Delaney And Bonnie, touring and recording with them. Curiously, though, Harrison was last of four Beatles to release a conventional, song-based solo album; he remedied this with triple set, **All Things Must Pass**, in 1970. It was an immediate success, and a single from it, **My Sweet Lord**, became an international chart-topper. However this song was to become notorious in view of court case over its similarity to **He's So Fine**, 60s hit for the Chiffons. Harrison lost case and in late 70s had to pay damages of more than half a million dollars to publishers of **He's So Fine**.

During later Beatle years, Harrison became fascinated by Indian culture and religion, leading to interest in transcendental meditation and the sitar. This aspect of his work was mostly absent from **All Things Must Pass**, but when leading Indian sitar player Ravi Shankar asked for help for starving people of Bangladesh in form of charity concert, Harrison was eager to oblige. With star-studded line-up, including Bob Dylan, Eric Clapton, Billy Preston, Leon Russell, and Ringo Starr, Harrison organized "The Concert For Bangla Desh" at Madison Square Garden, New York on August 1, 1971. The event was recorded and filmed (live album – another triple set – was released the following year and became a US and UK bestseller), with all proceeds going to assist victims.

Next solo LP, **Living In the Material World** (1973), was also a commercial success, and title track from his 1974 set **Dark Horse** reached the US singles charts. However, with punk now on the horizon, critical opinion was turning against Harrison, and subsequent contractual problems relating to the launch of his own label (Dark Horse), plus increasing involvement in other activities (including motor racing and movie-making), did nothing to improve his generally disappointing music-making during this period.

Three-year gap between **Thirty Three & 1/3** (1976); and next LP, **George Harrison**. Harrison was rarely seen in public at this time, but emerged following John Lennon's murder with tribute single **All Those Years Ago**, on which Paul McCartney and Ringo also guested. Follow-up LP, **Somewhere In England** was released in 1981, while **Gone Troppo** LP and **Wake Up My Love** single came out (with little promotional support) the following year.

Surprising return to charts in 1987, thanks to single **Got My Mind Set On You** from **Cloud Nine** LP, prefaced formation of **Traveling Wilburys** outfit with Bob Dylan, Jeff Lynne, Tom Petty, and, before his death, Roy Orbison. Harrison also guested on Petty's **Full Moon Fever** and Eric Clapton album **Journeyman** (both 1989).

Harrison's last solo album, **Live In Japan**, appeared in 1992. Six years later, he revealed that he had been undergoing treatment for cancer, and following a recurrence of the disease, he died at a friend's house in Los Angeles on November 29, 2001.

Recommended listening
Wonderwall Music (Apple), 1968
Electronic Sounds (Apple), 1969
All Things Must Pass (Apple), 1970
Concert For Bangladesh (Apple), 1972
Living In The Material World (Apple), 1973
Dark Horse (Apple), 1974
Extra Texture (Apple), 1975
33 & 1/3 (Dark Horse), 1976
George Harrison (Dark Horse), 1979
Somewhere In England (Dark Horse), 1981
Gone Troppo (Dark Horse), 1982
Cloud Nine (Dark Horse), 1987
Best Of 1976–89 (Dark Horse), 1989
Live In Japan (Warner Bros./Dark Horse), 1992
With Traveling Wilburys:
Volume 1 (Wilbury), 1988
Volume 3 (Wilbury), 1990

P.J. HARVEY

UK singer, guitarist, songwriter
Born Polly Jean Harvey, Yeovil, Somerset, October 9, 1969

Career: Rural upbringing in English West Country; her parents, both music lovers, introduced her to a wide range of rock and pop (including Captain Beefheart's classic 60s and 70s recordings – a key influence). Played sax at school; took up guitar as a teenager, and appeared with locally based bands before forming trio PJ Harvey in 1991 with bassist Stephen Vaughn and drummer Robert Ellis. Debut single **Dress** (issued that year on independent Too Pure label) gained considerable airplay, as did its 1992 follow-up **Sheela-Na-Gig** (name refers to ancient carvings of sexually explicit female figures found on walls of churches and other buildings in Britain and Ireland). Album **Dry** appeared soon afterwards, and won critical plaudits in Britain and USA (*Rolling Stone* magazine made Harvey their Best New Female and Best Songwriter that year).

However, pressure of work left Harvey exhausted, and she was obliged to take several months off in Summer/Fall 1992 to recuperate, before starting work on new album **Rid Of Me** (her first for Island label). This appeared in 1993, and proved highly successful; but later that year, Harvey split up the PJ Harvey trio (although she has continued to work regularly with drummer Ellis), and released **4-Track Demos**, recorded by herself at home, and featuring raw, viscerally powerful versions of material from **Rid Of Me** (including title track).

Harvey's first "solo" studio album, **To Bring You My Love**, came out in early

ABOVE: *A young George Harrison (left) pictured beside John Lennon.*

1995, adding further to her reputation; she toured extensively to support it, and the following year saw collaborations on a variety of other artists' CDs, including **Dance Hall At Louse Point** by John Parish (co-producer of **To Bring You My Love** and several of her subsequent records), and **Murder Ballads** by Nick Cave, with whom she was rumored to be having a relationship.

Harvey's next solo set, **Is This Desire?** appeared in 1998; among her projects during the year was film acting debut in

The Book Of Life, directed by Hal Hartley, in which she played Mary Magdalene. She also toured Europe, UK and USA, and in 1999, moved to New York for six months. Her experiences there led to the songs featured on **Stories From The City, Stories From The Sea**, recorded back home in England and issued in late 2000.

A uniquely powerful performer and songwriter, Harvey is undoubtedly one of the most significant British rock artists to emerge in the last decade.

Recommended listening

Dry (Pure), 1992
Rid Of Me (Island), 1993
4-Track Demos (Island), 1993
To Bring You My Love (Island), 1995
Dance Hall At Louse Point (with John Parish) (Island), 1996
Is This Desire? (Island), 1998
Stories From The City, Stories From The Sea (Island), 2000
With John Parish in Automatic Dlamini:
From A Diva To A Diver (Rosemont), 1992
As guest artist:
with Nick Cave:
Murder Ballads (Mute), 1996
on September Songs: The Music of Kurt Weill (Sony), 1997

JIMI HENDRIX

US guitarist, vocalist
Born Johnny Allen Hendrix (name changed to James Marshall Hendrix in 1946), Seattle, Washington, November 27, 1942
Died London, September 18, 1970

Career: The most legendary guitarist in rock music, Jimi Hendrix spent early years, following military service, as back-up musician for such R&B luminaries as Ike and Tina Turner, Solomon Burke, Jackie Wilson, Tommy Tucker, Sam Cooke, Little Richard, Wilson Pickett, The Isley Brothers, and King Curtis.

Settling in New York, Hendrix was heard playing in club by then girlfriend of Rolling Stones' Keith Richards, who persuaded former Animals' bass player turned manager, Chas Chandler, to check him out. Chandler decided to forgo own playing career and sold his bass guitars to buy equipment for Hendrix. He took the young musician to London and embarked on major publicity campaign, bringing The Beatles, Pete Townshend, and Eric Clapton to "in" clubs to see Hendrix's outrageously flashy performances.

A master showman, Hendrix exploited tricks learned from watching T. Bone Walker, Johnny "Guitar" Watson, and other black American musicians, playing the guitar behind his neck or with his teeth, and experimenting with a whole new range of sound effects on his Fender Stratocaster. Polydor Records rushed to sign him, and 1967 debut single **Hey Joe** and LP **Are You Experienced?** (recorded with The Jimi Hendrix Experience, also featuring British musicians Noel Redding, bass, and Mitch Mitchell, drums) stormed UK charts. Later the same year, the Experience made their US debut at the Monterey Pop Festival, California. Hendrix's guitar-burning act there (preserved in film *Monterey Pop*) left the audience stunned.

Hendrix reached zenith of commercial success and artistic creativity with classic

Left: *Hendrix and his Stratocaster.*

Axis: Bold As Love (1967) and **Electric Ladyland** (1968) LPs. After masterful appearance at Woodstock in August 1969, the Jimi Hendrix Experience broke up amid welter of personal and business problems, as well as drug-linked difficulties with the authorities. Mostly, however, Hendrix felt cornered by the style of music.

Under some pressure from Black Power movement in US, Hendrix decided to form Band Of Gypsys (with Billy Cox, bass; Buddy Miles, drums) but, despite phenomenal powers as a concert-draw, group was short-lived; Hendrix walked out on 19,000 fans in middle of second number at the band's Madison Square Garden gig in January 1970. That summer Hendrix played to nearly a quarter of a million people at the Isle of Wight Festival (backed by Cox and former Experience drummer Mitch Mitchell); this was Jimi's last major concert – a disappointing affair that met with a poor response from critics.

Three years of incredibly hard touring, recording, and drink and drug abuse took their toll, and on September 18, 1970, Hendrix died from inhaling his own vomit after an overdose of pills.

For 20th anniversary of his death in 1990, both Hendrix's sidemen Mitch Mitchell (*The Hendrix Experience*) and Noel Redding (*Are You Experienced?*) had biographies published – two of several volumes issued during period casting a critical eye over the wayward genius.

At times verging on the self-indulgent, Hendrix's guitar work nevertheless displayed unrivaled genius, opening up new musical horizons for a generation of rock musicians, while his vocals oozed raw power. Hendrix seems certain to retain his place as one of the most influential and popular artists in the history of rock.

Guitar: Fender Stratocaster.

Recommended listening

Hit Singles	US	UK
Hey Joe, 1967	-	6
Purple Haze, 1967	-	3
The Wind Cries Mary, 1967	-	6
Burning Of The Midnight Lamp, 1967	-	18
All Along The Watchtower, 1968	20	5
Voodoo Chile, 1970	-	1

Albums

a) LPs released during Hendrix's lifetime:
Are You Experienced (Track/Reprise), 1967
(recent CD reissue includes extra tracks formerly released on singles)
Axis: Bold As Love (Track/Reprise), 1967
(US version released a month after UK disc, in January 1968)
Electric Ladyland (Track/Reprise), 1968
Smash Hits (Reprise), 1969
Band Of Gypsys (Track/Capitol), 1970

b) Posthumous releases and compilations:
Monterey (*one side only; other side featured Otis Redding*) (Reprise), 1970
The Cry Of Love (Reprise), 1971
Rainbow Bridge (*live recordings from 1968–1970*) (Reprise), 1971
Jimi Hendrix at the Isle Of Wight (Polydor), 1971
Hendrix In The West (Reprise/Polydor), 1972
Soundtrack Recordings from the film *Jimi Hendrix* (Reprise), 1973
Loose Ends (Polydor), 1974
Crash Landing (Reprise), 1975
Midnight Lightning (Reprise/Polydor), 1976
10th Anniversary Box (Polydor), 1980
Nine To The Universe (Polydor/Reprise), 1980
The Jimi Hendrix Concerts (Reprise), 1982
Kiss The Sky (Polydor), 1984
Jimi Plays Monterey (Reprise), 1986
Live at Winterland (Rykodisc), 1987
Radio One (material from BBC sessions) (Rykodisc), 1988
Cornerstones 1967–70 (Polydor), 1990
The Ultimate Experience (Polydor), 1992
Blues (MCA), 1994
First Rays Of The New Rising Sun (MCA), 1997
Experience Hendrix – The Best of Jimi Hendrix (MCA), 1997
BBC Sessions (*features same material as "Radio One" (see above) plus additional tracks*) (MCA), 1998

BUDDY HOLLY

US vocalist, guitarist, composer
Born Charles Hardin Holley, Lubbock,
Texas, September 7, 1936
Died Clear Lake, Iowa,
February 3, 1959

Career: During 1954–55, Holly appeared on hometown radio station KDA with his performing partner Bob Montgomery. He also worked as a warm-up/support act for visiting package shows; one night, he was spotted by a Nashville talent scout while performing at a concert headlined by Bill Haley, and signed to Decca.

Dissatisfaction with company and producers encouraged Holly to record independently at Norman Petty's Clovis, New Mexico, studio. Master tape of **That'll Be The Day**, made there in 1957, was subsequently sold to New York subsidiaries of Decca where group recordings featuring Holly and The Crickets (Joe B. Mauldin, bass; Niki Sullivan, guitar, replaced by Tommy Allsop in 1959; Jerry Allison, drums) were released on Brunswick; Holly's solo efforts appeared on Coral. Resulting hits gave Holly dual career; he sang mostly his own songs, or those of his fellow Crickets, notably Allison.

Several US package tours and short visit to Australia preceded tour of UK in March 1958. Many UK musicians were impressed with his guitar style and the then unknown Fender Stratocaster guitar – which, together with horn-rimmed glasses, became Holly's trademark.

Management problems and move to New York following marriage to Maria Elena Santiago in 1958 forced split with Crickets (who went on to record many more LPs without Holly). Recorded trendsetting session with Dick Jacobs Orchestra in New York and planned to collaborate with Ray Charles Band.

Royalty disputes and lack of funds forced Holly into uncomfortable ballroom tour through frozen Mid-West states during early 1959. Halfway through tour, Holly chartered small plane with Ritchie Valens and Big Bopper to escape discomfort of tour buses. All three were killed when plane crashed into snow-covered field in Iowa.

Single coupling **It Doesn't Matter Any More** and **Raining In My Heart** from orchestral session subsequently became biggest solo hit. Although Holly then disappeared from US chart, his popularity in Britain ensured continuation of hits for several years.

The Holly legend was surprisingly well-served by movie industry, when Gary Busey's uncanny interpretation of artist in *The Buddy Holly Story* (1978) was outstanding critical success. The actor later purchased Holly's horn-rimmed specs and acoustic guitar at a New York auction of Holly memorabilia.

The musical *Buddy*, written by British playwright Alan Janes, opened in 1989 at London's Victoria Palace Theatre, and subsequently transferred to the Strand Theatre, where it celebrated its 10th anniversary in October 1999. The show is still running there, and a total of over 4,000 performances of it have now taken place in the UK and USA.

Recommended listening

Hit Singles	US	UK
That'll Be The Day*, 1957	1	1
Peggy Sue, 1957	3	6
Listen To Me, 1958	-	16
Oh Boy*, 1958	10	3
Maybe Baby*, 1958	17	4
Rave On, 1958	37	5
Think It Over*, 1958	27	11
Early In The Morning, 1958	32	17
It Doesn't Matter Anymore, 1959	13	1
Peggy Sue Got Married, 1959	-	13
Baby I Don't Care, 1961	-	12
Reminiscing, 1962	-	17
Brown Eyed Handsome Man, 1963	-	3
Bo Diddley, 1963	-	4
Wishing, 1963	-	10
*With Crickets		
Crickets:		
Don't Ever Change, 1962	-	5
My Little Girl, 1963		-17

Albums

The Chirping Crickets (Brunswick), 1957
Buddy Holly (Coral), 1958
That'll Be The Day (Decca), 1958
The Buddy Holly Story (Coral), 1959
The Buddy Holly Collection (MCA), 1993
Greatest Hits (MCA). 1996
20th Century Masters: The Best of Buddy Holly (MCA), 1999
Very Best of Buddy Holly (Dressed To Kill – UK import), 2000

JOHN LEE HOOKER

US vocalist, guitarist, composer
Born Clarkesdale, Mississippi,
August 22, 1917
Died June 21, 2001, Los Altos,
California

Career: Proving the old adage "it's never too late to become a pop star," John Lee Hooker survived some lean times before enjoying an extraordinary "Indian Summer" of chart success, recognition, and respect in the last 10 years of his life.

The blues pioneer moved to Detroit in 1943, cutting the million-selling single **Boogie Chillun** for Modern in 1948. Unusually, he maintained a solid output for a variety of labels (including Stateside, Chess, ABC, and Vee-Jay) for two decades before gaining attention during British "beat boom" of early 60s. His classic tracks **Dimples** and **Boom Boom** launched a thousand UK R&B bands, and the artist enjoyed a resurgence of popularity that seemed unlikely to be repeated.

With his career seemingly winding down, Hooker still recorded throughout the 70s and 80s, with sets for Atlantic and Tomato Records; re-issues also appeared in stores. During this period, Hooker also popped up in a cameo role in *Blues Brothers* movie (1980), which was followed by soundtrack contribution to Spielberg's *The Colour Purple* (1986).

His work with Bonnie Raitt, Carlos Santana, and Robert Cray, among others, propelled the septuagenarian back into prominence in 1989 with **The Healer** set, from which **I'm In The Mood** duet with Raitt won a Grammy award. Hooker then found himself the unlikely star of a couple of international television advertisements, and a favourite with MTV producers. Hooker was recipient of "John Lee Hooker Night" at 1990 Benson & Hedges Blues Festival, held at Madison Square Gardens,

ABOVE: *The boogie man – John Lee Hooker, armed with his Gibson 335.*

and was inducted into Rock 'n' Roll Hall Of Fame in January 1991. His album **Mr. Lucky** (on which he was again joined by an impressive roster of rock and blues luminaries) appeared later that year, and the good times continued to roll for Hooker throughout the rest of the decade – in which he toured extensively, and made three further excellent, star-studded CDs: **Boom Boom** (1992), **Chill Out** (1995), and **Don't Look Back** (1997). He continued performing until shortly before his death.

Recommended listening

The Legendary Modern Recordings
   1948–54 (Ace/Flair), 1993
Half A Stranger (recordings from
   1948–55) (Mainstream), 1991
Complete 50s Chess Recordings
   (MCA), 1998
The Vee-Jay Years 1955–64 (Charly),
   1992
The Ultimate Collection (Rhino), 1991
The Healer (Silvertone), 1989
Mr. Lucky (Pointblank/Charisma), 1991
Boom Boom (Pointblank/Virgin), 1992
Chill Out (Pointblank/Virgin), 1995

Don't Look Back (Pointblank/Virgin),
   1997
The Best of Friends (compilation
   album) (Pointblank/Virgin), 1999

THE JAM

UK group formed 1976

Original line-up: Paul Weller, vocals, bass; Steve Brookes, guitar; Bruce Foxton, guitar; Rick Buckler, drums.

Career: Above quartet got together while at school in Woking, Surrey, to play rock 'n' roll and R&B. Youth and social club gigs followed; after Steve Brookes left, Weller switched to guitar, Foxton to bass.

This new line-up made London debut in summer 1976, displaying image based on early 60s "mod" look, and playing sharp, well-crafted rock songs that showed songwriter Weller's debt to Pete Townshend. Although band had little in common with most other new wave outfits, Jam won contract as part of mass record company signings that followed "summer of punk."

First single **In The City** hovered around bottom of UK chart, but follow-up **All Around The World** (both 1977) made No. 13. In meantime, debut album, also called **In The City**, and released the same year, made No. 20 in album chart. During next three years band became chart regulars with both singles and LPs, establishing themselves as one of most interesting new outfits of late 70s. Weller set direction of band, and showed himself to be perceptive writer and spokesman.

1980 saw further triumphs for The Jam, with first No. 1 single **Going Underground/The Dreams Of Children** and title of Best Group in the *New Musical Express* Readers' Poll. Next single, **Start**, also made No. 1.

Despite massive success during 1982 – they swept board in all UK polls and toured Britain and Europe to universal acclaim – Weller announced that band would fold at end of year. Apparently he found Jam's format too constricting and wished to move on to other things. During December, group undertook farewell tour to usual ecstatic crowds, and

retired from scene. 1982 LP, **The Gift**, entered UK charts at No. 1. Jam singles/sleeves are such collectors' items that Polydor have re-issued entire catalog three times.

Although they never achieved more than cult status in US, The Jam, always an intense live act, were major UK stars during their short existence. Success was largely due to Paul Weller, who has subsequently found success with The Style Council, and with solo albums such as **Wild Wood** (1993), **Stanley Road** (1995), and **Heliocentric** (2000).

Recommended listening

Hit Singles	US	UK
All Around The World, 1977	-	13
Down In The Tube Station At Midnight, 1978	-	15
Strange Town, 1979	-	15
When You're Young, 1979	-	17
The Eton Rifles, 1979	-	3
Going Underground/Dreams Of Children, 1980	-	1
Start, 1980	-	1
Funeral Pyre, 1981	-	4
Absolute Beginners, 1981	-	4
Town Called Malice/Precious, 1982	-	1
Just Who Is The Five O'Clock Hero, 1982-	-	8
The Bitterest Pill (I Ever Had To Swallow), 1982	-	2
Beat Surrender, 1982	-	1

Albums

In The City (Polydor), 1977
This Is The Modern World (Polydor),
   1977
All Mod Cons (Polydor), 1978
Setting Sons (Polydor), 1979
Sound Affects (Polydor), 1980
The Gift (Polydor), 1982
Dig The New Breed (live) (Polydor),
   1982
Snap (Polydor), 1983
Compact Snap (Polydor), 1983
The Peel Sessions (Strange Fruit),
   1990
Greatest Hits (Polydor), 1991
Extras (Polydor), 1992
Live Jam (Polydor), 1993
Days of Speed (acoustic Weller album
   featuring new versions of some Jam
   classics) (Independiente), 2001

JEFFERSON AIRPLANE/STARSHIP

US group formed 1965

Original line-up: Marty Balin, vocals; Paul Kantner, guitar; Signe Anderson, vocals; Jorma Kaukonen, guitar; Jack Casady, bass; Skip Spence, drums.

Career: Balin and Kantner met on San Francisco's folk coffee-house circuit in early 1965. Balin felt it was time to return to his roots and explore rock 'n' roll of Elvis, Jerry Lee Lewis, and Little Richard. Anderson and Kaukonen joined him in the nascent Jefferson Airplane, and Casady, a long-time friend of Balin's, was invited to become the group's bassist. Spence was recruited in mid-65, and Airplane began building local reputation as band that played folk lyrics to rock beat. Top San Francisco promoter Bill Graham helped foster exciting, vibrant image for band by providing priority booking at new Fillmore Hall. This led to RCA contract: Airplane were the first alternative/hippie band on the Bay Area music scene to be signed.

Spencer Dryden replaced Spence (later to form Moby Grape) while band recorded **Jefferson Airplane Takes Off** (1966). National promotion helped "folk-rock" sound achieve gold LP status and aroused industry interest in West Coast bands. Anderson left due to pregnancy, and Kantner recruited Grace Slick from Great Society, band that used to open for Airplane.

This classic line-up scored big US hit with **Somebody To Love** (1967). This song and **White Rabbit** (same year) were old Great Society numbers. Slick's vocals made them, and whole of the 1967 **Surrealistic Pillow** LP, a haunting, emotive experience. To band's delight, critics and fans fell in love with album, which remains essential listening for anyone interested in the 60s West Coast scene.

Sudden success meant band could live in communal bliss, but community living also brought problems. **After Bathing At Baxter's** (1967) had fewer of Balin's songs and more new sounds and experimentation, much of which now seems dated.

Slick and Kantner had become lovers; when they began assuming full leadership roles, Balin backed off. **Crown Of Creation** (1968) reduced Balin's role even further by including weak Slick song, **Lather**, and non-rock David Crosby song, **Triad**. Daring at time of release, and containing some good harmony, this LP is high point of early Airplane.

Bless Its Pointed Little Head (1969) was average live set. Next album, **Volunteers** (released the same year), pushed band into forefront of counter-culture's political stance. Considering shallow, preachy tone, LP has remained surprisingly interesting. Balin felt band was becoming too big and too smooth and quit. Several US tours followed (including playing at Stones' Altamont concert), then band seemed to lose all

LEFT: *Jorma Kaukonen at an outdoor concert with the Jefferson Airplane.*

sense of direction. Balin's loss, Slick's pregnancy with Kantner's child, and Dryden's departure left Airplane grounded. Kaukonen and Casady began electric blues/country band, Hot Tuna. At first a part-time affair, project eventually removed duo from Airplane altogether. In telling omen for the future, Slick and Kantner used several famous Bay Area-based buddies (including Jerry Garcia and David Crosby) to record 1970 LP **Blows Against The Empire**, which they credited to "Paul Kantner and the Jefferson Starship."

Airplane returned with Joey Covington (drums) on 1971 **Bark** LP. State of Airplane is reflected by superior Slick-Kantner solo, **Sunfighter**, released at same time. With one more sub-par set, 1972's **Long John Silver**, Airplane finally crashed. David Frieberg, ex-Quicksilver Messenger Service, added vocals on live but uninspired **Thirty Seconds Over Winterland** (1973). Then with no formal announcement, Airplane disappeared. Casady and Kaukonen worked full time turning Hot Tuna into early heavy-metal band. Slick, Kantner, and Frieberg produced weak solo effort, and Slick released unsatisfactory **Manhole** LP (1973).

Next, Slick and Kantner decided to re-form band. Using Frieberg, "Papa" John Creach (fiddler Hot Tuna had introduced to Airplane on **Bark**), ex-Turtles' John Barbata (drums), Peter Sears (bass), and Craig Chaquico (guitar), new formation took name Jefferson Starship.

US tour, using early Airplane and solo material, convinced Slick and Kantner that band was viable proposition. **Dragonfly** (1974) wasn't overly brilliant but sold well. More importantly, it had one Balin credit and indicated reunion with his creative influence; Balin began appearing with Starship and contributing efforts to recording sessions. However, he refused to sign with group or formally commit self to Starship. His **Miracles** became mammoth US hit in summer 1975 and pushed LP **Red Octopus** to US No. 1 (Airplane/Starship's first after 10 years of work).

The success of **Octopus** obviously influenced sales of next LP, **Spitfire**

(1976), but album was inferior and seemed a sell-out/cash-in. **Earth** (1978) reflected growing personal problems and confusion over what to do next. Slick, Balin, and Barbata all left and there seemed no reason to continue.

Kantner recruited Aynsley Dunbar, drums, and Mickey Thomas, vocals; their 1979 effort, **Freedom At Point Zero**, was first line-up not to feature female vocals. Next came **Modern Times** (1980), with Slick provided some backing vocals. Having resolved bout with alcohol and various personal problems, she rejoined full time on 1982's **Winds Of Change** (after release of two solo LPs).

Break-up of Kantner/Slick's personal relationship led to Kantner leaving group June 1984 amid much acrimony; resultant law suits forced band to abbreviate name in March 1985 to Starship for **Knee Deep In The Hoopla** album.

With a line-up now missing Kantner (who formed KBC band), Frieberg, Slick, and Company enjoyed a US No. 1 single in 1985 with **We Built This City** from the **Knee Deep** LP. Further success was attained with **Nothing's Gonna Stop Us Now** (1987), a rip-roaring pop anthem.

In 1989, Jefferson Airplane was re-launched when Slick reunited with Kantner, Casady, Balin, and Kaukonen for self-titled album. Meanwhile, Starship (Thomas, Sears, Baldwin, Chaquico, Brett Bloomfield, bass, and Mark Morgan, keyboards) soldiered on, and enjoyed modest success with **Love Among The Cannibals** set (August 1989). But Sears was another casualty in ongoing cast change, while Thomas took time out when hospitalized after bust-up in San Franciscan bar.

News of the reborn band prompted readers of *Rolling Stone* magazine to vote the event "Most Unwelcome Comeback" in 1990, though various Airplane/Starship-derived groupings have gone on to tour and record together in the following years. Since the mid-90s, Grace Slick has focused increasingly on her painting skills, exhibiting at her San Francisco Bay-side home town of Tiburon and elsewhere.

Recommended listening

Hit Singles	US	UK
As Airplane:		
Somebody To Love, 1967	5	-
White Rabbit, 1967	8	-
As Starship:		
Miracles, 1975	3	-
With Your Love, 1976	12	-
Runaway, 1978	12	-
Count On Me, 1978	8	-
Jane, 1979	14	-
We Built This City, 1985	1	12
Nothing's Gonna Stop Us Now, 1987	1	1
It's Not Over, 1987	9	-
It's Not Enough, 1989	12	-

Albums

As Airplane:

Jefferson Airplane Takes Off (RCA), 1966

Surrealistic Pillow (RCA), 1967

After Bathing At Baxter's (RCA), 1968

Crown Of Creation (RCA), 1968

Bless Its Pointed Little Head (RCA), 1969

Volunteers (RCA), 1969

Worst Of (RCA), 1970

Bark (Grunt), 1971

Thirty Seconds Over Winterland – Live (Grunt), 1973

Jefferson Airplane (Epic) 1989

As Starship:

Dragon Fly (Grunt), 1974

Red Octopus (RCA), 1975

Spitfire (Grunt), 1976

Earth (Grunt), 1978

Gold (Grunt), 1979

Freedom At Ground Zero (Grunt), 1980

Modern Times (Grunt), 1981

Winds Of Change (Grunt USA), 1982

Nuclear Furniture (Grunt USA), 1984

Knee Deep In The Hoopla (RCA), 1985

Love Among The Cannibals, 1989

Kantner-Slick:

Blows Against The Empire (RCA), 1970

Sunfighter (Grunt), 1971

Recent releases:

Jefferson Starship At Their Best (greatest hits) (BMG/RCA), 1993

Jefferson Starship: Deep Space/Virgin Sky (Intersound), 1995

Jefferson Airplane/Starship Hits (2 CD compilation) (BMG/RCA), 1998

JOURNEY

US group formed 1973

Original Line-up: Gregg Rolie, vocals, keyboards, guitar; Neal Schon, guitar; George Tickner, guitar; Ross Valory, bass; Aynsley Dunbar, drums.

Career: Rolie and Schon were together in Santana when jazz influence created musical conflict of interest. They ran across Walter "Herbie" Herbert, who was attempting to assemble supergroup to play San Francisco Bay area. Valory had played with Steve Miller and Dunbar with an impressive range of rock and blues bands – including John Mayall, Jeff Beck, and Frank Zappa's Mothers of Invention. Tickner was excellent session musician.

For first gig, Journey played San Francisco's Winterland on last day of 1973. Interest from Columbia Records followed extensive touring, and first LP, **Journey**, appeared in Spring 1975. Lack of response was discouraging, and Tickner and Valory left band. Valory soon returned, however, and Journey continued year-round touring.

Next two albums (**Look Into The Future** and **Next**) were released in 1975 and 1976, but generated little interest. Manager Herbert suggested addition of lead vocalist Steve Perry, leaving Rolie free to fill out band's sound. **Infinity** (1978) can be considered Journey's first real album, with powerful vocals and synthesiser riffs. Perry also earned band US Top 20 hit, **Lovin' Touchin' Squeezin'** (1979).

Live shows shifted from interminable solos to tight format. Such restraint never fitted Dunbar's style, and he quit. Steve Smith (who had played with Infinity tour opener Ronnie Montrose) took Dunbar's place. Subsequent albums increased band's popularity, though not with critics, who dismissed Journey as "commercial." Renewed interest in band's history resulted in compilation LP, **In The Beginning** (1979). **Captured** (issued the following year) is strong live set, and **Escape** (1981) introduced keyboard player Jonathan Cain. He is also songwriter, and co-wrote that year's hit single, **Who's Crying Now**.

Escape achieved multi-platinum status, and, with band's reputation secure, Schon ventured into extra-curricular projects, most notably with Jan Hammer and Sammy Hagar. Vocalist Perry also took time out, scoring both with Kenny Loggins on **Don't Fight It** single (1982), and as a soloist on **Street Talk** (1984), from which **Oh Sherrie** made No. 3 in US singles charts.

Band re-grouped for **Only The Young** single in 1985, but following year's **Raised On Radio** LP featured on Schon, Perry and Cain on the credits. Although album spawned four chart singles, including **I'll Be Alright Without You** in 1987, Journey's career stuttered, and, with Perry actively focusing on solo projects, group's future was put on hold.

Journey came together again in 1996, with **Trial By Fire** album and subsequent tour, which was to be swansong for Perry and Smith. They were later replaced by vocalist Steve Augeri and drummer Deen Castronovo, who are featured on the band's **Arrival** CD, released in 2001.

Recommended listening

Journey (Columbia), 1975
Look Into The Future (Columbia), 1976
Next (Columbia), 1977
Infinity (Columbia), 1978
Evolution (Columbia), 1979
Departure (Columbia), 1980
Captured (live) (Columbia), 1980
Escape (Columbia), 1981
Frontiers (Columbia), 1983
Raised On Radio (Columbia), 1986
Time3 (compilation) (Columbia), 1992
Trial By Fire (Columbia), 1996
Arrival (Columbia), 2001

JOY DIVISION/ NEW ORDER

UK group formed 1977

Original line-up: Ian Curtis, vocals; Bernard Albrecht (later Sumner) (né Dicken), guitar; Stephen Morris, drums; Peter Hook, bass.

Career: In 1977 Curtis, Albrecht, and Morris came together, calling themselves Warsaw. Early career consisted of obscure gigging throughout Manchester. They changed name to Joy Division, though there was never anything joyful about their sound, Curtis' flat voice being backed by depressing dirge-like instrumentals. Indications of things to come appear on live 10-inch compilation album **Short Circuit** (1978). This features **At A Later Date**, recorded the previous year, while the band were still known as Warsaw.

Joy Division released four-track EP **An Ideal For Living** in Summer 1978 on own label Enigma. (Also released as 12-inch on Anonymous Records.) Band's real potential for stark, sheer realism appeared on their work for the new Manchester-based Factory label. **A Factory Sample** (same year) was EP to show off label's new talent, and two Joy Division tracks **Glass** and **Digital** were disc's high point.

National interest stirred by Martin Hannett-produced **Unknown Pleasures** (1979), a bleak yet powerful debut album. A pair of out-takes given to Fast Records (Edinburgh) were subsequently released on **Earcom Two** compilation. Another two releases from this period, **Atmosphere** and **Dead Souls**, appeared in 1,000 copy editions on the small French Sordid Sentimentale label.

Joy Division's 1979 UK tour with Buzzcocks earned ecstatic response from critics and audience alike, but the suicide of Curtis in May 1980 curtailed planned US tour. Single **Love Will Tear Us Apart** and second album appeared after his death. Another out-take, **Komankino/ Incubation**, appeared as free flexi-disc from Factory. Excellent **Still** release (1981) included live/studio material, covering the band's entire career.

Joy Division had agreed to "kill" the name should any member leave the group, and remaining line-up thus became New Order, with guitarist Albrecht also rechristening himself Bernard (Barney) Sumner.

By early 80s ethos of band had begun to change, with more dance-orientated sound coming to fore. New appeal was reflected in success of Top 30 UK entry **Temptation**. Further commercial progress was made in 1983 when band scored with **Blue Monday**, single which went on to sell more than a million worldwide.

Signed to Quincy Jones' Qwest label in the States, New Order debuted with **The Perfect Kiss** in 1984, but had to wait a further three years before US chart success with **True Faith** single.

New Order went on to develop cult status with **Low Life** LP (1985) and double set **Substance**, a compilation of re-mixed singles. **Technique** album (1989) saw band debut at No. 1 in UK charts. Now well into the party spirit, band scored with UK No. 1 single **World In Motion** (1990), a clever rap/dance mix released to coincide with World Cup soccer finals. Although happy to indulge in solo projects – Hook formed Revenge for one-off album **One True Passion** (1989), and Bernard Sumner featured in Electronic with Johnny Marr and Neil Tennant – New Order's collective talent is a thing to wonder at. However, they have worked together tantalisingly rarely in the last decade. Their 1993 UK tour, in the wake of the appearance of the **Republic** album, was riven by personal and business tensions (some of them related to the impending collapse of Factory Records), and following its completion, the band members are believed to have been scarcely on speaking terms. This state of affairs has, thankfully, now been remedied, and in Fall 2001, following the release of their long-awaited CD, **Get Ready**, New Order embarked on their first UK tour for eight years.

Recommended listening
Joy Division albums:
Unknown Pleasures (Factory), 1979
Closer (Factory), 1980
Still (Factory), 1981
New Order albums:
Movement (Factory), 1981
Power, Corruption And Lies (Factory),
  1983
Low Life (Factory), 1985
Brotherhood (Factory), 1986
Substance (Factory), 1987
Technique (Factory), 1989
Republic (Factory), 1993
Get Ready (London), 2001

LEFT: *Guitarist Bernard Sumner (aka Albrecht) was born Bernard Dicken.*

B.B. KING

US vocalist, guitarist, composer
Born Itta Bena, Indianola, Mississippi,
September 16, 1925

Career: Truly living up to his name, Riley B. "Blues Boy" King has majestically dominated the blues scene for over 35 years. Astute management and an ear for the modern have maintained enthusiastic concert crowds and undiminished reverence for his abilities.

King has appeared with the finest of musicians, from black American greats The Crusaders to rock stars like Eric Clapton and Leon Russell. He has recorded hits in a hotel room, in a garage, and in the world's foremost studios. His material has ranged from pure blues to rock numbers, pop songs, and even Broadway standards – all of which have benefited from his unique, inimitable musical approach.

His emergent playing style was heavily influenced by both T-Bone Walker and the jazz of Charlie Christian; like them – but unlike many Mississippi Delta guitarists – B.B. does not use a bottleneck or slide, but relies on his left-hand fingers to create bends and vibrato. Joining radio WGRM in Greenwood, Mississippi, in late 50s, he was spotted by blues harmonica great Sonny Boy Williamson II (aka Rice Miller) who took him to the more important Memphis station WDIA. There, King became resident DJ and was dubbed "The Beale Street Blues Boy," later shortened to "B.B." by station manager Don Kearn.

King's recording debut came with **Miss Martha King** (1949). Then talent scout Ike Turner signed him to Modern Records' RPM subsidiary where he enjoyed 11-year stint, soaring to No. 1 on R&B charts in 1950 with **Three O'Clock Blues**, which featured Turner on piano, Hank Crawford on saxophone, and Willie Mitchell on trumpet.

Quickly becoming the most in-demand artist on blues circuit, King quit WDIA. (His show was taken over by Rufus Thomas, who went on to fame as a soul singer.)

King's eloquent guitar lines, with their torrent of notes, are perfectly matched to his emotive vocals, which combine falsetto wailing and a rich, gospel-flavored tenor (a reflection of his pre-Memphis days, when he regularly sang in gospel groups.) Despite a couple of quirks (he rarely plays rhythm, and never sings and plays simultaneously), King is an absolute master of his chosen genre, and has influenced countless other guitarists, notably Buddy Guy, Otis Rush, and Eric Clapton.

In 1961 he switched to major ABC-Paramount label, for which he made classic albums like the seminal **Live At The Regal** (1964), arguably his greatest-ever recording. He moved to MCA in 1969, and almost immediately enjoyed a stunning artistic and commercial success with smash US hit single **The Thrill Is Gone**, featuring a superbly effective string arrangement. It came from the **Completely Well** album, released the same year, and was followed by a string of collaborations (some better judged than others) with rock-based performers, reflecting King's substantial following among younger, white audiences.

King kept up a tireless recording and touring schedule throughout the 1970s and 80s, playing shows in Europe, Africa, and Asia – and, in 1979, even appearing in the USSR. His role as an international ambassador and elder statesman for the blues was reflected in the Lifetime Award he received at the Grammy Awards ceremony in 1988. This recognized him as "one of the most original and soulful of all blues guitarists and singers;" the previous year he had become one of the few bluesmen to be inducted into the Rock 'n' Roll Hall of Fame.

However, King's career is far from over. He and his trademark Gibson semi-solid guitar, "Lucille," continue their musical odyssey onstage and in the studio; recent albums have included a **Blues Summit** (1993) with appearances by Robert Cray, Buddy Guy, John Lee Hooker, and others, **Deuces Wild** (1997), and **Riding With The King** (2000). The latter two discs both feature Eric Clapton, a close friend since the 1970s.

Recommended listening

Hit Singles	US	UK
The Thrill Is Gone, 1970	15	-
When Love Comes To Town (with U2), 1989	-	6

Albums

Live At The Regal (MCA), 1965
His Best: The Electric B.B. King (MCA/ABC), 1969
Live And Well (MCA/ABC), 1970
Completely Well (MCA/ABC), 1970
Live At Cook County Jail (MCA/Probe), 1971
Back In The Alley (MCA/ABC), 1973
Alive In London (with the Crusaders) (MCA), 1982
Midnight Believer (MCA), 1984
Spotlight On Lucille (Ace), 1986
Completely Well (MCA), 1987
One Nighter Blues (Ace), 1987
Rarest B.B. King (Blues Boy), 1987
Across The Tracks (Ace), 1987
King Of The Blues (MCA), 1988
Live At San Quentin (MCA), 1990
There's Always One More Time (MCA), 1991
Blues Summit (MCA), 1993
Deuces Wild (MCA), 1997
Blues On The Bayou (MCA), 1998
Best of B.B. King: Millennium Collection (MCA), 1999
Riding With The King (with Eric Clapton) (Reprise), 2000
Makin' Love Is Good For You (MCA) 2000
With Pat Metheny, Dave Brubeck, Heath Bros:
Live 1987 (Kingdom Jazz), 1987
With Bobby Bland:
Together For The First Time (MCA), 1974
Together Again (MCA), 1976

RIGHT: *Master bluesman B.B. King with his Gibson guitar "Lucille."*

KING CRIMSON

UK group formed 1969

Original line-up: Robert Fripp, guitar, mellotron; Ian McDonald, reeds, keyboards; Greg Lake, bass, vocals; Peter Sinfield, lyricist; Mike Giles, drums.

Career: Evolved from Giles, Giles And Fripp, a pop-influenced trio from Dorset that recorded two singles and one barely noticed album, **The Cheerful Insanity Of Giles Giles And Fripp**. Group split in November 1968, Peter Giles temporarily quitting business; while brother Mike and Fripp founded King Crimson. With new members McDonald and Lake (aided by lyricist Sinfield) rehearsals were completed below café in London's Fulham Road. Debut gig at Speakeasy (April 1969) established small cult following, dramatically increased following appearance at Rolling Stones' celebrated Hyde Park concert in July. First album, **In The Court Of The Crimson King** (1969) received ecstatic response and established unit as one of most progressive of era. From this point on, group were dogged by series of personnel changes and upheavals.

An 11-day US tour in November/ December 1969 took its toll; on return to London both Giles and McDonald quit. While seeking permanent line-up, Fripp employed a number of session men/friends to complete second LP **In The Wake Of Poseidon** (1970). Giles returned as bassist, jazzer Keith Tippett played piano, Mel Collins added saxophone, and Gordon Haskell contributed vocals. Sinfield was by this time credited as lyricist, light show operator, and synthesizer player. Prior to album's release Fripp had declined invitations to join Yes and Aynsley Dunbar's Blue Whale. Lukewarm response afforded **Poseidon** meant that only Collins and Haskell were retained for third album (**Lizard**, issued in 1970), aided by drummer Andy McCullough. After recording sessions, Haskell and McCullough quit.

Fripp and Sinfield again restructured group, with Mel Collins, Ian Wallace (drums), and Boz Burrell, a singer whom Fripp taught to play bass. Following release of **Islands** in 1971, Sinfield left to reappear as Roxy Music's producer. Less than successful US tour killed off remaining members of Crimson, leaving live **Earthbound** as final comment.

Fripp returned to England and, following period of hibernation, introduced another unit, comprising Bill Bruford (former Yes drummer), bassist John Wetton (ex-Family), percussionist Jamie Muir and David Cross (violin, mellotron). The power and promise of line-up was fully revealed on excellent **Larks' Tongues In Aspic** (1973) and vindicated in concert. Unfortunately, Muir quit, leaving four-piece Crimson to record **Starless And Bible Black** (1974).

In July 1974, Crimson closed tour with concert at New York's Central Park, captured for posterity on second live album, **USA**. In September, Fripp officially announced that Crimson no longer existed. A posthumous album, **Red**, was released in 1974 and saw return of original member Ian McDonald.

Between 1974–80, Fripp worked with number of artists, most notably Eno (they collaborated on **No Pussyfooting** (1973) and **Evening Star**, released two years later). Projects with Peter Gabriel and David Bowie also attracted great interest, leading to newfound respect.

In 1981, Fripp reformed King Crimson with Adrien Belew (guitar, lead vocal), Robert Fripp (guitar), Tony Levin (bass, vocals), and Bill Bruford (drums). Album **Discipline** was released in September 1981 amid critical arguments about whether Crimson were an anachronism, a seminal progressive rock band, or both. **Beat**, released following year, was first Crimson studio album to have same personnel on two consecutive releases. However, this incarnation of the band broke up in 1984, after the release of **Three Of A Perfect Pair**, and though Fripp remained involved with numerous other projects, King Crimson lay dormant until 1993. The group resumed

BELOW: *The Kinks guesting on a British TV show in the mid-1960s.*

touring soon afterwards, and issued their **Thrak** album in 1995; another new CD, entitled The **ConstruKction of Light,** followed in 2000.

Recommended listening

In The Court Of The Crimson King (Island), 1969
In The Wake Of Poseidon (Island), 1970
Lizard (Island), 1970
Islands (Island), 1971
Earthbound (Island), 1972
Lark's Tongues In Aspic (Island), 1973
Starless And Bible Black (Island), 1974
USA (Island), 1975
Red (Island), 1974
Discipline (EG/Polydor), 1981
Beat (EG/Polydor), 1982
Three Of A Perfect Pair (Polydor), 1984
Thrak (Virgin), 1995
The Construktion of Light (Virgin), 2000
Robert Fripp solo:
Exposure (EG), 1987
Let The Power Fall (EG), 1987

THE KINKS

UK band formed 1964

Original line-up: Ray Davies, vocals, guitar; Dave Davies, guitar, vocals; Peter Quaife, bass; Mick Avory, drums.

Career: Dressed in red huntsman's jackets and sporting mod haircuts, The Kinks were introduced to the British public as an image-heavy beat band. Debut Pye single **Long Tall Sally** was straight copy of Beatles' cover of Little Richard's classic; it bombed, as did follow-up **You Do Something To Me**, which only sold 127 copies. The rough, propulsive **You Really Got Me** was something quite different. Close in form to The Kingsmen's **Louie, Louie**, it had an R&B edge which British audiences were looking for at time and shot to No. 1.

Producer Shel Talmy had found a golden vein and exploited it well over next 18 months with string of chart singles, mostly written by Ray Davies. From straightforward pop songs, Davies started composing ever more pictorial lyrics, strongly British in inspiration yet with a wide appeal. The humorous **Dedicated Follower Of Fashion** (released in 1966, and taking off fashion fanatics of the period), the following year's atmospheric **Waterloo Sunset** (which proved songs didn't have to have American locations to be effective), and others showed depth of his writing talent, which some rated equal to that of Lennon/McCartney.

As band began touring less, Ray Davies involved himself in solo projects, including score for *The Virgin Soldiers* movie (which appeared in 1969). Brother Dave had solo UK hit (backed by Kinks and issued as Kinks single in US) in 1967 with **Death Of A Clown**. This was included along with **Waterloo Sunset** and the funny yet perceptive **David Watts** on brilliant **Something Else By The Kinks** album (1967), marking end of group's partnership with Shel Talmy.

With Ray Davies now producing, the Kinks followed Beatles and others into realms of concept albums, notably with **(The Kinks Are) The Village Green Preservation Society** (1968) and following year's **Arthur (Or The Decline And Fall Of The British Empire)**. In 1970 group returned to singles charts with **Lola**, a song about transvestism and a hit on both sides of Atlantic. **Kinks Part 1: Lola Versus Powerman And The Moneygoround** (1970) had biting lyrics about rampant manipulation prevalent in pop music scene. Meanwhile, Ray Davies completed soundtrack of *Percy* and had main role in television play *The Long Distance Piano Player*.

Getting out of current management deal and Pye record contract, group signed with RCA. Opening album for the label, **Muswell Hillbillies**, appeared in 1971, but sold poorly.

Ironically, group's US following was burgeoning. Increasingly theatrical in concept, with strong roots in music-hall traditions, The Kinks' subsequent albums were often somewhat grandiose projects. **Sleepwalker** (1977) found group switching to Arista Records and album was another in a string of Stateside successes.

In 1979 group recorded **Low Budget**, their first venture in an American studio, and the following year issued **One For The Road**, a live double LP of their best-known material, recorded while on tour in US; a version of **Lola** from this set made US Hot 100 in 1980.

By 1983 and **Give The People What They Want** album, Ray Davies' writing abilities seemed in decline, despite unexpected **Come Dancing** single hit and later **Think Visual** (1986) and **UK Jive** (1989) LPs. Unable to give up life of the road, band continued gigging; US tour in 1989 featured new drummer Bob Henrit (ex-Argent) and, on keyboard, Mark Haley.

The 1990s have seen Ray and brother Dave pursuing solo projects, but there have been no new Kinks releases since the **Phobia** album, issued in 1993, and its successor, **To The Bone** (for which the group performed new versions of some of their classic songs in front of an invited audience at their own Konk Studio in London)

Recommended listening

The Kinks (Reprise), 1964
Kinda Kinks (Reprise), 1965
The Kink Kontroversy (Reprise), 1966
Face To Face (Reprise), 1966
Village Green Preservation Society (Reprise), 1968
Arthur (Or The Decline And Fall Of The British Empire) (Reprise), 1969
Lola Versus Powerman And the Moneygoround Part One (Reprise), 1970
Muswell Hillbillies (RCA), 1971
Everybody's In Show-Biz (RCA), 1972
Preservation Act I (RCA), 1973
Preservation Act II (RCA), 1974
Soap Opera (RCA), 1975
Schoolboys in Disgrace (RCA), 1975
Sleepwalker (Arista), 1977
Misfits (Arista), 1978
Low Budget (Arista), 1979
One For The Road (Arista), 1980
Give The People What They Want (Arista), 1981
State of Confusion (Arista), 1983
Word Of Mouth (Arista), 1984
Think Visual (MCA), 1986
The Road (MCA), 1987
UK Jive (MCA), 1989
Phobia (Columbia), 1993
To The Bone (Konk), 1994

MARK KNOPFLER

UK guitarist, singer, songwriter
Born Glasgow, Scotland,
August 12, 1949

Career: Knopfler spent most of his childhood in Newcastle, northern England, took an early job as a local newspaper reporter, and subsequently studied English Literature at Leeds University. He had been active as a guitarist and singer since his teens, and in 1973, he moved to London, where he joined blues band Brewer's Droop (whose drummer, Pick Withers, was a future Dire Straits member), combining his musical activities with part-time teaching and lecturing. Briefly a member of Café Racers, but by mid-1977, he was rehearsing and sharing a south London apartment with his brother David (also a guitarist) and bassist John Illsley. Withers was invited to complete line-up of what was soon to be Dire Straits.

In July 1977, band made demos of a number of Mark's songs (including early version of **Sultans of Swing**); these received airplay from London DJ Charlie Gillett, and led to a record deal and high-profile gigs, including support spot on Talking Heads' 1978 UK tour. Dire Straits recorded first, eponymously titled LP later that year; on its release, it became an international bestseller, while **Sultans Of Swing** (featured on the album) became a massive US/UK hit single the following year.

After second, also hugely successful LP, **Communiqu**é, Hal Lindes replaced David Knopfler, and Withers was a further casualty when Terry Williams (ex-Man, Rockpile) took the drum seat after **Love Over Gold** album (1982). Session keyboard player Alan Clark had been added permanently for this latter set.

The archetypal touring unit, Dire Straits nonetheless had difficult periods on the road, with Knopfler ever more uncomfortable with role as rock superstar. His independent projects, producing Bob Dylan's **Infidels** (1983), and scoring movies such as *Local Hero*, *Cal*, and *Comfort And Joy*, had observers speculating on the group's future.

Two-year sabbatical ended with release of studio album **Brothers In Arms** (1985) which prompted 12-month world tour, and augmentation of Dire Straits line-up which saw Guy Fletcher replace Clark. Self-deprecatory single **Money For Nothing** (taken from **Brothers**) earned band first US No. 1 and permanent spot on MTV.

The following year, Dire Straits were star attraction at

Left: *Mark Knopfler onstage with one of his favorite guitars, custom-made by Rudy Pensa.*

Nelson Mandela 70th Birthday Concert held at London's Wembley Stadium. However, Knopfler's priorities increasingly shifted towards lower-key musical projects, including the Notting Hillbillies, in which he reunited with pre-Straits colleague, guitarist Steve Phillips: other members were Knopfler's manager, Ed Bicknell, on drums; Guy Fletcher on keyboards, Brendan Croker (guitar and vocals); and Marcus Cliffe (bass). Hillbillies' debut album, **Missing… Presumed Having A Good Time** (1990) surprised pundits (and Knopfler himself) by making UK album listings; they also toured to wide acclaim.

Knopfler's other 1990 release was **Neck And Neck**, a guitar duet CD with veteran Nashville picker Chet Atkins (qv), but the following year Dire Straits sprang back into action with new album, **On Every Street**, and massive worldwide tour, which continued through 1992. However, there have been no further band gigs or new studio recordings, and Knopfler now seems to have settled down to a highly successful solo career. His albums **Golden Heart** (1996) and **Sailing To Philadephia** (2000) have been warmly received, and he is also active as a producer and guest player on a wide range of projects.

Recommended listening

Dire Straits Hit Singles	US	UK
Sultans Of Swing, 1979	4	8
Romeo And Juliet, 1981	-	1
Private Investigations, 1982	-	2
Twisting By The Pool, 1983	-	14
So Far Away, 1985	-	20
Money For Nothing, 1985	1	4
Brothers In Arms, 1985	-	16
Walk Of Life, 1986	13	2
Your Latest Trick, 1986	-	26
Calling Elvis, 1991	-	21

Albums

Dire Straits (Warner Bros./Vertigo), 1978
Communiqué (Warner Bros./Vertigo), 1979
Making Moves (Warner Bros./Vertigo), 1980
Love Over Gold (Warner Bros./Vertigo), 1982
Alchemy (Live) (Warner Bros./Vertigo), 1984
Brothers In Arms (Warner Bros./Vertigo), 1985
On Every Street (Vertigo), 1991
On The Night(live) (Vertigo), 1993
Live At The BBC (material from late 70s) (Vertigo), 1995
Notting Hillbillies:
Missing… Presumed Having A Good Time (Warner Bros./Vertigo), 1990
Mark Knopfler solo:
Neck And Neck (with Chet Atkins) (Columbia), 1990
Screenplaying (music from Knopfler's various film soundtracks) (Warner Bros.), 1993
Golden Heart (Vertigo), 1996
Sailing To Philadelphia (Mercury) 2000

KISS

US group formed 1973

Original line-up: Ace Frehley, guitar; Paul Stanley, guitar; Gene Simmons, bass; Peter Criss, drums.

Career: Kiss began by taking Lou Reed/David Bowie glitter rock and pushing it to extreme. Band obliterated members' past by hiding behind comic-book costumes and greasepaint. With first concerts, Kiss managed to alienate rock press, offend parents, and win undying loyalty of New York's younger rock fans.

Albums emphasized gothic, bigger-than-life aspects of rock music. Live shows had massive drum kits rising 40 feet into air and explosives flashing everywhere, while Simmons spat fire (real) and blood (fake), or just rolled out

his foot-long tongue. Critics wondered what this had to do with the music, while kids made Kiss hottest-selling band of decade.

Debut LP, **Kiss**, appeared in 1974. Band made major early impact in Japan – Japanese credits were included on sleeve of second album, **Hotter Than Hell**, which appeared later the same year. After **Dressed To Kill** (1975) came **Alive!**; this included massive hit single **Rock And Roll All Nite**, and showed band was not all flash. Next LP, 1976's **Destroyer**, proved even more of a surprise by including excellent ballad, **Beth**. Superhero/hidden identity ploy enhanced by band's refusal to be photographed or interviewed without make-up; a comic-book history of the band was included in **The Originals**, a special 1976 re-issue of their first three LPs. Next two album covers, **Rock And Roll Over** (1976) and **Love Gun** (1977), also had colorful comic-style covers instead of usual pictures.

ABOVE: *Kiss and make-up; Simmons, Stanley, and Frehley in action.*

By 1977, Kiss management had organized fans into Kiss Army and provided them with range of Kiss memorabilia and products. Disdain of other bands and managers had suspicion of jealousy. First sign that Kiss fans were possibly outgrowing their heroes came in 1978. Amid much publicity, four solo LPs, one from each member of Kiss, went platinum before day of release – but all four began appearing in bargain bins shortly afterwards. **Dynasty** (1979) and **Unmasked** (1980) lacked outrageousness of early Kiss. Peter Criss quit, claiming face could no longer cope with make-up; band had first photos taken without it.

Surprisingly, Criss's replacement, Eric Carr, filled position well, and band produced an excellent but relatively unsuccessful new album, **The Elder**

(1981), which seemed to be rock-opera soundtrack for non-existent movie. Such a concept would drag down any album during this period, and **The Elder** flopped. **Creatures Of The Night** (1982) returned to old Kiss style; problem was finding audience for it. One puzzling aspect is why this most visual of bands hasn't translated well into video age, though **Creatures Of The Night** video is superb.

Personnel changes marked uncertain period for band. Frehley left, and Vince Cusano took permanent guitar spot. Cusano then quit after world tour, with Mark Norton added. But Norton, who works under stage name Mark St. John, suffered debilitating illness and ex-Blackjack guitarist Bruce Kulick took most temporary guitar job in town.

In mid-80s, band abandoned garish stage make-up, deciding that their musical ability should stand on its own merits. **Lick It Up** (1983) was first "naked" album, while 1984 set **Animalize** made US and UK Top 10.

Following 1987 **Crazy Nights** LP, Kiss embarked upon North American tour with veterans Cheap Trick in support; also visited UK in 1988. With Frehley's band Frehley's Comet enjoying US success, Kiss faltered for a couple of years before regaining Top 10 status with **Forever** single (composed by Paul Stanley with Michael Bolton) in 1990.

The band has weathered many stylistic storms to attain place near top of commercial league, although death of drummer Eric Carr from cancer in November 1991 clouded future. Eric Singer took his place, and Kiss' subsequent 90s releases included **Revenge** (1992), **Alive III** (1993), and **Psycho-Circus** (1998). The latter featured the band's "classic" line-up (with Peter Criss replacing Singer, plus Frehley, Simmons and Stanley); but there have been no new albums since, and in 2001, Criss left the group.

Recommended listening

Kiss (Casablanca), 1974
Hotter Than Hell (Casablanca), 1974
Dressed To Kill (Casablanca), 1975
Alive! (Casablanca), 1975
Destroyer (Casablanca), 1976
Rock And Roll Over (Casablanca), 1976

Love Gun (Casablanca), 1977
Kiss Alive II (Casablanca), 1978
Dynasty (Casablanca), 1979
Unmasked (Casablanca), 1980
The Best Of The Solo Albums (Casablanca), 1981
The Elder (Casablanca), 1981
Creatures Of The Night (Casablanca) 1982
Lick It Up (Mercury), 1983
Animalize (Vertigo), 1984
Double Platinum (Casablanca), 1985
Asylum (Vertigo), 1985
Crazy Nights (Vertigo), 1987
Smashes, Thrashes and Hits (Mercury), 1988
Hot In The Shade (Mercury), 1989
Revenge (Mercury), 1992
Alive III (Mercury), 1993
Psycho-Circus (Mercury), 1998

LEO KOTTKE

US guitarist, singer, composer
Born Athens, Georgia,
September 11, 1945

Career: Learned to play several instruments as a child, but focused on guitar after first experimenting with one at the age of 11, while recuperating from a serious illness. Overcame eardrum damage, sustained in early adulthood after accident with firecracker and excessive exposure to sound of guns on firing range, and began making a name for himself as a virtuoso acoustic guitarist (and rather less polished vocalist – he has famously likened his singing to "geese farts on a foggy day").

Gained early reputation during late 60s in coffee-houses around his adopted hometown, Minneapolis; signed by eccentric, highly influential player/label owner John Fahey, who released Kottke's **6 and 12-String Guitar** in 1969; **Circle 'Round The Sun** followed in 1970, and the following year saw Leo's debut on Capitol, **Mudlark**.

Kottke's six LPs for Capitol contain a mixture of original compositions, classical arrangements, imaginative covers (including a version of The Byrds' **Eight Miles High**), and numbers associated with his mentor, Fahey. This rich diversity,

plus his powerful, incisive picking style, brought Kottke wide popularity, and he toured extensively throughout the USA and Europe, as a headliner and support to big-name acts such as The Mothers of Invention, Procol Harum, and the Mahavishnu Orchestra.

A move to Chrysalis Records (his first release for them, **Leo Kottke**, appeared in 1976) saw his success continue – but by the 1980s, his vigorous approach to the guitar had taken its toll on his muscles and fingers. He began to suffer from what he described (in an 1994 interview with journalist James Jensen) as "a kind of paralysis you would get from tendonitis… I would last about five to 10 minutes into [a concert] and it would set in and I really couldn't play." The only remedy was a radical change in technique, as Kottke switched from fingerpicks to bare right-hand fingertips and nails. This transformation coincided with the guitarist's move from Chrysalis to the Private Music label, and his new, softer tone can be heard on his first CD for the company, **A Shout Towards Noon** (1986). Fortunately, he made a full recovery from his physical problems, and remains one of today's most innovative acoustic players.

Recommended listening

6 and 12-String Guitar (Tacoma), 1969
Circle 'Round The Sun (Symposium), 1970
Mudlark (Capitol), 1971
Greenhouse (Capitol), 1972
My Feet Are Smiling (live) (Capitol), 1973
Ice Water (Capitol), 1974
Dreams And All That Stuff (Capitol), 1974
Chewing Pine (Capitol), 1975
Leo Kottke (Chrysalis), 1976
Burnt Lips (Chrysalis), 1978
Balance (Chrysalis), 1979
Guitar Music (Chrysalis), 1981
Time Step (Chrysalis), 1983
A Shout Towards Noon (Private), 1986
Regards From Chuck Pink (Private), 1988
My Father's Face (Private), 1989
That's What (Private), 1990
Great Big Boy (Private), 1991
Peculiaroso (Private), 1993
Standing In My Shoes (Private), 1997
One Guitar, No Vocals (Private), 1999

LOS LOBOS

US group formed 1973

Original line-up: Cesar Rosas, vocals, guitar; David Hidalgo, vocals, guitar, accordion; Conrad Lozano, bass; Louie Pérez, drums.

Career: Group were schoolfriends in Los Angeles; started out as acoustic ensemble dedicated to playing Mexican music –

original name was Los Lobos del Este de Los Angeles (the Wolves of East Los Angeles). Switched to electric instruments and were joined by Steve Berlin (sax) for vinyl debut, 1983 EP **...And A Time To Dance**. First full-length album, **How Will The Wolf Survive?** released in 1984. Its irresistible Tex-Mex style brought wide acclaim on both sides of the Atlantic; follow-up, **By The Light of the Moon** (1987) was also a critical success. Later that year, *La Bamba*, a film about Ritchie Valens, the Latino pop star killed in the

same plane crash as Buddy Holly in 1959, was released. Its soundtrack featured music by Carlos Santana, Miles Goodman – and Los Lobos, whose version of the movie's title song (Valens' most famous number) gave them an unexpected American and British No. 1.

The band did not allow their chart-topping status to deflect them from their musical path. In 1988, they issued the all-Spanish language **La Pistola Y El Corazón** (The Pistol and the Heart), and continued to develop their own distinctive, highly individual brand of Mexican-American fusion throughout the 1990s, on albums like **The Neighborhood** (1990), **Kiko** (1992), **Colossal Head** (1996), and **This Time** (1999).

Hidalgo and Perez have also worked with the Latin Playboys, while Rosas (probably the highest-profile band member) is a member of Los Super Seven (with Hidalgo), and has released a fine solo album, **Soul Disguise** (1999).

Recommended listening

> How Will The Wolf Survive? (WEA), 1984
> By The Light Of The Moon (WEA), 1987
> *La Bamba* (soundtrack) (WEA), 1987
> La Pistola Y El Corazón (WEA), 1988
> The Neighborhood (WEA), 1990
> Colossal Head (WEA), 1996
> This Time (WEA), 1999
> Just Another Band From East L.A. – A Collection (WEA compilation), 1993

NILS LOFGREN

US vocalist, composer, guitarist, pianist
Born Chicago, June 21, 1951

Career: Lofgren's parents moved to Maryland when he was a teenager. He and his brother began playing in local Washington DC bands, where Nils' talents came to attention of Crazy Horse; they featured him on their self-titled first album, released in 1971. This

Left: *Cesar Rosas has found success with Los Lobos and as a soloist.*

association led to work with Neil Young, who used Lofgren on his 1970 album **After the Goldrush**.

18-year-old Lofgren returned to DC to set up own band, Grin. (From this era, 1971 LP **1+1** or compilation **The Best Of Grin** are worth a listen.) Grin had split by 1973, and Lofgren was happy to join Neil Young's *Tonight's The Night* tour.

Lofgren spent good part of 1974 re-forming Grin and watching it fall apart again. His track record ensured modicum of interest when his solo debut, **Nils Lofgren** was released in 1975. Subsequent tour developed cult following and Lofgren seemed ready for stardom. But even the excellent 1976 **Cry Tough** and a tour as opening act for Boston failed to gain expected results. **Night After Night** (1977) was an impressive live set, and **Nils** (1979) received a lot of US airplay, but didn't chart well. Lofgren rejoined Neil Young on the Canadian's 1982 **Trans** LP, and also became a member of his touring band. The economy and style of Lofgren's playing (demonstrated by his solo albums for the Backstreet label in the early 80s, and also by his work for Bruce Springsteen on The Boss's acclaimed 1985 world tour) makes his relative lack of premier league success all the more perplexing.

Ever the accommodating sideman, Lofgren joined with Ringo Starr for ex-Beatles 1989 US extravaganza *Tour For All Generations*, and maintained position with Springsteen (he was featured on 1987 **Tunnel Of Love** LP and world tour). Lofgren returned to solo recording (following earlier collapse of Towerbell label for whom he cut 1985 **Flip** and 1986 **Code Of The Road** LPs) with **Silver Lining** in 1991 on Essential Records. **Valentine** single from album saw Starr and Springsteen make guest appearance. Lofgren's subsequent 90s releases included **Crooked Line** (1992) and **Damaged Goods** (1996).

Recommended listening
> 1+1 (SpinDizzy/Epic), 1971
> Nils Lofgren (A&M), 1975
> Cry Tough (A&M), 1976
> Night After Night (A&M), 1977
> Nils (A&M), 1979

> The Best Of (A&M), 1981
> Night Fades Away (Backstreet), 1981
> Wonderland (Backstreet), 1983
> Flip (Towerbell), 1985
> Code Of The Road (Towerbell), 1986
> Silver Lining (Essential), 1991
> Crooked Line (Essential), 1992
> Damaged Goods (Essential), 1996

LYNYRD SKYNYRD

US group formed 1965

Original line-up: Ronnie Van Zant, vocals; Gary Rossington, guitar; Allen Collins, guitar.

Career: Originally formed in Jacksonville, Florida, as high-school trio, named after their authoritarian PE teacher, Leonard Skinner. By 1972, full line-up completed with Leon Wilkeson (bass), Billy Powell (keyboards), and Robert Burns (drums). Discovered playing Southern bars and clubs by Al Kooper, who immediately signed them to his Sounds Of The South label. Session bassist Ed King (ex-Strawberry Alarm Clock) brought in by Kooper as full-time member. First album, **Pronounced Leh-nerd Skin-nerd** (1973), received favorable response. Closing cut from album, **Free Bird**, later became group anthem, achieving minor chart placings in US and UK following several re-releases.

Career boosted by playing support on The Who's 1973 US tour. Quickly established themselves as one of America's most celebrated boogie bands, boasting three guitarists. Next album, **Second Helping** (1974), went gold. Set included US hit single, **Sweet Home Alabama**, their famous riposte to Neil Young's scathing **Southern Man** and **Alabama** put-downs. Third album, **Nuthin' Fancy**, released in 1975, also went gold. Included US Top 30 hit **Saturday Night Special**.

Extensive touring schedules drained group's energies, prompting Burns' departure, replaced by Artimus Pyle. Not surprisingly, seasoned sessioneer Ed King left shortly afterwards. Undeterred, Skynyrd kept on boogieing and their increasingly raucous behavior inspired strong, devoted following.

On October 20, 1977, a week after the release of the notable **Street Survivors** LP, Skynyrd embarked on lengthy US tour. Their private plane took off from Greenville, South Carolina, en route for Baton Rouge, Louisiana; approaching Gillsburg, Mississippi, the plane crashed in a wood, 200 yards from an open field. Casualties included Ronnie Van Zant, Steve Gaines, roadie Dean Kirkpatrick, and backing singer Cassie Gaines. The tragedy shook the rock world, for the group had always been much loved for their aggressive, uncompromising approach: MCA quickly stopped release of **Street Survivors** LP with its prophetic cover showing the band members surrounded by flames. Even Neil Young sang **Sweet Home Alabama** at one of his concerts in their memory.

In 1979, spirit of LS was reborn with Rossington Collins Band, formed by remaining members of group, plus vocalist Dale Krantz, guitarist Barry Harwood, and drummer Dell Hess. Aggregation cut a couple of albums for MCA before splitting up, although 1987 saw re-formation for Lynyrd Skynyrd celebration tour, with Van Zant's brother Johnny, founder of .38 Special, fronting the outfit. MCA subsequently issued a live double album of the concerts, **Southern By The Grace Of God**, although Collins' death in 1990 from respiratory problems further clouded group's history. However, Skynyrd have remained in business – touring US and UK, and issuing a number of successful albums, including **The Last Rebel** (1993), **Endangered Species** (1994), and – more recently – **Lyve From Steeltown** (1998) and **Edge of Forever** (1999).

Recommended listening
> Pronounced Leh-nerd Skin-nerd (MCA), 1973
> Second Helping (MCA), 1974
> Nuthin' Fancy (MCA), 1975
> Gimme Back My Bullets (MCA), 1976
> One More From The Road (double live) (MCA), 1976
> Street Survivors (MCA), 1977
> Southern By The Grace Of God (MCA), 1988
> Lynyrd Skynyrd 91 (Atlantic), 1991
> The Last Rebel (Atlantic), 1993
> Edge of Forever (Sanctuary), 1999

269

JOHNNY MARR

UK guitarist, composer
Born John Maher, Manchester,
October 31, 1963

Career: The 1980s were not exactly a golden era for guitarists in UK bands: a strong distaste for virtuoso axemen had arisen in the punk period, and was still widespread, while synthesisers and drum machines were increasingly dominating the musical landscape. Johnny Marr was one of the few prominent British guitar players to emerge during this period, and his striking, colorful work with The Smiths and on subsequent projects have helped to redefine the instrument's role in contemporary pop.

Marr was an untypical product of the thriving Manchester scene, combining a fascination for 60s and 70s folk-rock and soul with more modern tastes and influences. In 1982, he teamed up with another unusual local figure, singer and lyricist Stephen Patrick Morrissey; their songwriting partnership was to form the core of The Smiths. Recruiting a bassist (Andy Rourke) and drummer (Mike Joyce), they released their debut single, **Hand In Glove**, the following year. Its success in the indie charts brought The Smiths wide attention, and provoked mixed responses from audiences and critics. Some found their music wimpish and fragile, others poetic and powerful, but the band quickly established a loyal following, signing to Rough Trade and embarking on sessions for their debut album with ex-Teardrop Explodes/Fashion member Troy Tate as producer. Tate's efforts were subsequently dumped when group met John Porter, who re-recorded material for the LP, titled **The Smiths** and issued in early 1984. Extensive UK tour hurried LP to instant No. 2 position in Britain, with gold status quickly following. **What Difference Does It Make?** single reached the Top 20 that February; a version of **Hand In Glove** by 60s pop icon Sandie Shaw (backed by Marr, Joyce, and Rourke) was a lesser hit a few months afterwards, and the band themselves enjoyed two further 1984 Top 30 successes, **Heaven Knows I'm Miserable Now** and **William It Was Really Nothing**.

British singles success continued throughout 1985, and the band's new album, **Meat Is Murder**, expounding their vegetarian lifestyle, entered UK album charts at No. 1 later that year. However, this stream of bestselling, critically acclaimed records, including 1986 LP **The Queen Is Dead**, could not disguise rumblings of discontent within group. A second guitarist, Craig Gannon, joined The Smiths briefly in 1986, and by the following year, the rift between Morrissey and Marr (who was already in demand as a session player) had split the band. Their final studio album, **Strangeways Here We Come** (1987) had been preceded by an impressive live double, **Louder Than Bombs**.

Johnny Marr subsequently adopted "have guitar, will travel" approach, gigging with Pretenders, Bryan Ferry, Midge Ure, Talking Heads, and Paul McCartney, among others. He later joined The The, and collaborated in Electronic aggregation with (among others) New Order's Bernard Sumner. Their 1990 single **Getting Away With It** made the UK Top 20, and was followed by **Get The Message** (1991), **Disappointed** (1992), and (more recently) the CDs **Raise The Pressure** (1996) and **Twisted Tenderness** (1999). Marr's other activities include a guest appearance on British folk guitar veteran Bert Jansch's impressive **Crimson Moon** album (2000).

Recommended listening
 Smiths albums:
 The Smiths (Sire), 1983
 Meat Is Murder (Sire), 1985
 The Queen Is Dead (Sire), 1987
 Strangeways Here We Come (Sire), 1987
 The Very Best of The Smiths (WEA), 2001
 Other records:
 Bryan Ferry: Bête Noire (WEA), 1987
 Talking Heads: Naked (WEA), 1988
 Kirsty MacColl: Kite (IRS), 1989
 Electronic: Raise The Pressure (WEA),
  1996
 Electronic: Twisted Tenderness (Koch),
  1999
 Bert Jansch: Crimson Moon (Castle)
  2000

RIGHT: *A new-style guitar hero –*
Manchester's Johnny Marr.

BOB MARLEY

Jamaican vocalist, guitarist, composer
Born Robert Nesta Marley, St Anns,
Jamaica, 1945 (passport gave exact
date as February 6, but Marley said
this was inaccurate)
Died Miami, Florida, May 11, 1980

Career: Son of an English army captain
and Jamaican mother, Bob Marley was
undoubtedly the greatest figure in the
evolution of reggae music.

While at Jamaica's Stepney School,
became friendly with Winston Hubert
McIntosh and Neville Livingstone; as
Peter Tosh and Bunny Wailer, they were
later to join Marley in The Wailers.

At 16, Bob cut his solo debut record,

Judge Not (co-written with mentor Joe
Higgs) at Ken Khouri's Federal Studio in
Kingston. Then with Leslie Kong
producing, he covered Brook Benton's
One Cup Of Coffee after seeing the
American soul star in concert with Dinah
Washington.

Teaming with Tosh and Wailer, plus

BELOW: *The late, great Bob Marley.*

272

Junior Braithwaite and Beverly Kelso, Marley formed The Wailin' Wailers; they signed to Clement "Coxsone" Dodd's Studio One label and sold more than 80,000 copies of first single **Simmer Down** (1965).

Backed by studio band Skatalites, quintet worked through ska and rock-steady eras towards dawn of reggae style. However, they broke up in 1966 following wrangles over payment for their recordings.

Marley joined his mother in Delaware, US, and worked in Chrysler car factory before returning to Jamaica to avoid service in Vietnam. Reuniting with Tosh and Wailer, Marley recorded again with Leslie Kong who, via his association with Desmond Dekker, had become a major name on the island's music scene. (Between 1967 and 1969, Kong co-wrote and produced Dekker's smash hits **007**, **Israelites**, and **(Ah) It Mek**.) Trio also worked with Lee "Scratch" Perry (aka The Upsetter), who helped form Marley's distinctive style.

Espousing teachings of Jamaican politico/folk legend Marcus Garvey, Marley and friends became devout Rastafarians. In 1968 Marley was busted for possession of marijuana, the first of many subsequent clashes with the Jamaican establishment.

Quitting Perry's label, trio took his ace musicians, brothers Carlton and Aston "Family Man" Barrett, with them and formed own short-lived Wailing Soul label. When Bunny Wailer was sent to prison for a year following another drugs bust, Marley signed as songwriter to American soul star Johnny Nash's JAD label. He helped Nash develop unique blend of soul and reggae which gave the American singer a UK hit with **Stir It Up** (1972).

Marley used resultant income to set up Tuff Gong label with Tosh and Wailer, and subsequently won an international deal with Island Records, thanks to that company's Jamaican-born boss Chris Blackwell.

Blackwell's carefully orchestrated promotion put Bob Marley and Wailers in vogue with rock critics, musicians, and audiences alike. **Catch A Fire** album (1972) led to well-received UK visit and Stateside tour with Sly And The Family

Stone. Though not quite so strong, follow-up set **Burnin'** (1973) did include **I Shot The Sheriff**, later covered very successfully by Eric Clapton.

Wailer and Tosh then quit group; though they remained firm friends with Marley, they were unhappy with Island deal. Marley brought in his wife Rita plus Judy Mowatt and Marcia Griffiths (the I-Threes) as back-up vocalists, and in 1974 released classic **Natty Dread** album. This set the seal on his growing reputation as Jamaica's most important artist. Superb **Live!** LP (1975), recorded at London's Lyceum, included version of **No Woman No Cry**, which became major UK pop hit, as well as brilliant **Lively Up Yourself**.

Marley's stature as spokesman for Jamaican masses – his songs were often full of social and political comment – made him target of political gangs. In December 1976 he was shot four times in the arm by a group who burst into his home on eve of concert he was to give for then ruling left-wing PNP party led by Michael Manley. Bob appeared at concert, but immediately afterwards went into exile in Miami, remaining absent from Jamaica for 18 months. Recorded 1977 album **Exodus** partly in that city, partly in London.

Marley's return to homeland was triumphant. In April 1978, before 20,000 people at Kingston's National Stadium, he joined Manley and political rival Edward Seaga in symbolic handshake at concert which commemorated visit to Jamaica 12 years earlier by Emperor Haile Selassie of Ethiopia, figurehead of the Rastafarian movement. Marley also appeared in a special concert to celebrate birth of the new African nation of Zimbabwe. Same year saw release of his album **Kaya**; **Survival** set followed in 1979.

Towards end of his 1980 world tour Marley collapsed following performance at New York's Madison Square Gardens and was rushed to hospital. Three years earlier he had had a cancerous toe removed, but now it seemed the cancer had spread. Despite treatment at famed Josef Issels Clinic in Bavaria, Germany, Marley's condition was incurable. He died during May 1980 at Cedars Lebanon Hospital in Miami, where he had flown to visit his mother en route for Jamaica.

Further tragedy befell the Marley clan when both Carlton Bennett and Peter Tosh were killed in 1987.

A few years later, a complex and bitterly contested ownership battle arose over Bob Marley's estate, which includes Tuff Gong studios (administered by Rita Marley since Bob's death), publishing rights, pressing plant, and The Bob Marley Museum. By mid-1991, it seemed likely that MCA Records would assume control of all these assets, despite counter bids by Barbados-based ex-Equals leader, performer, and studio owner Eddy Grant, and by Marley's natural beneficiaries, whose claim was underwritten by former Island Records supremo Chris Blackwell. However, the Marley camp eventually won the day, and has proved highly effective in protecting and sustaining the memory and legacy of Jamaica's favorite musical son.

Meanwhile, Marley's son Ziggy (who, in December 1991, named his new-born daughter Justice after hearing the outcome of the battle over the family's heritage) has become a major star in his own right, cutting Grammy-winning albums for EMI and Virgin with his band, the Melody Makers, which also includes three of Bob's other children, Cedella, Sharon, and Stephen.

Recommended listening
 Catch A Fire (Island), 1972
 Burnin' (Island), 1973
 African Herbsman (BCI), 1973
 Natty Dread (Island), 1974
 Live! (Island), 1975
 Rastaman Vibration (Island), 1976
 Exodus (Island), 1977
 Kaya (Island), 1978
 Babylon By Bus (live) (Island), 1978
 Survival (Island), 1979
 Uprising (Island), 1980
 Chances Are (material from late
  60s/early 70s) (Warner Bros.), 1981
 Confrontation (Island), 1983
 Legend (compliation) (Island), 1984
 Rebel Music (compilation) (Island), 1986
 Talkin' Blues (1970s radio material),
  (Island) 1991
 Songs Of Freedom (limited edition)
  (Island), 1992
 Natural Mystic (BCI), 1995
 Best of The Early Years (Sanctuary),
  2001

273

LEFT: *Don McLean, most famous as the composer of* American Pie.

Capitol (1988). He has made numerous other live and studio albums, including a recent CD of songs by country music great Marty Robbins (2001), but will surely be best remembered for **American Pie**, which returned to UK charts in October 1991, nearly 20 years after first release, and was memorably covered by Madonna in 2000.

In 1999, the Martin company, whose guitars McLean has used throughout his career, produced a limited edition instrument in his honor *(see pages 140–141 for more details)*.

Recommended listening

Tapestry (Mediarts), 1970
American Pie (UA), 1972
Don McLean (UA), 1972
Playin' Favourites (UA), 1973
Homeless Brother (UA), 1974
Solo (live) (UA), 1976
Prime Time (Arista), 1977
Chain Lightning (EMI), 1978
Believers (Millennium), 1981
Dominion (EMI), 1982
The Best of Don McLean (EMI), 1988
Love Tracks (Capitol), 1988
For The Memories (Vols. 1 & 2)
 (Gold Castle), 1989
Headroom (Curb), 1991
Don McLean Christmas (Curb), 1991
Classics (Curb), 1992
American Pie and Other Hits (EMI), 1992
Favorites and Rarities (EMI), 1992
River Of Love (Curb), 1995
Christmas Dreams (Curb), 1997
Don McLean Sings Marty Robbins
 (Don McLean Records), 2001

DON McLEAN

US vocalist, guitarist, composer
Born New Rochelle, New York,
October 2, 1945

Career: Developed early interest in all forms of American music, particularly folk. On leaving school in 1963, started singing and playing in clubs.

By end of 60s, McLean had built up excellent reputation within his field and become a prolific songwriter. After spending two years knocking on record company doors, he made his debut album, **Tapestry**, in 1970; it was rejected by no less than 34 labels before being released by Mediarts, a small firm that soon folded (although record was later reissued by United Artists, who signed him in 1971).

Breakthrough came with late 1971 release of extraordinary single, **American Pie**. Despite McLean's folky background, record was symbolic 'history' of rock 'n' roll, using evocative images tied to highly commercial hook-line. Record was worldwide smash, catapulting McLean to instant stardom. Follow-up, **Vincent** (1972), a highly personal song

celebrating genius of painter Vincent Van Gogh, was almost as successful. Both numbers (which also appeared on McLean's bestselling 1972 **American Pie** album) were excellent showcases for his attractively plaintive voice and tasteful acoustic guitar work.

Career received further boost in 1973 with MOR singer Perry Como had huge hit with **And I Love You So**, a song from **Tapestry**. In the meantime, McLean had become in-demand live performer, years of small-time gigs paying off in controlled, well-paced performances.

During remainder of 70s, McLean consolidated career, although he was never elevated to "bed-sit philosopher" status of singer-songwriters such as Cat Stevens and Leonard Cohen. Surprisingly, he became more popular in UK than in homeland, and regular tours in Great Britain were always sell-outs.

In 1980, his career entered new phase with massive pop success of cover of Roy Orbison's classic **Crying**. True to form, single entered UK charts before US showed interest. McLean maintained heavy performing workload, returning to studio during 80s for **Believers** LP (1981) and country-styled **Love Tracks** for

METALLICA

US group formed 1981

Original line-up: Lars Ulrich, drums; James Hetfield, guitar, vocals; Lloyd Grant, guitar; Dave Mustaine, guitar; Ron McGovney, bass.

Career: Riff-laden HM thrash merchants whose response to the increasingly refinement of mainstream pop was a noise bombardment in the finest hard rock traditions.

Formed in San Francisco by Danish immigrant Ulrich, ex-member of British HM group Diamond Head, Metallica recorded track for 1981 **Metal Massacre** compilation album. Band's own debut LP, **Kill 'Em All** (1983) saw McGovney and Mustaine replaced by Cliff Burton (ex-Trauma) and Kirk Hammett respectively. Grant had also quit, returning to session work.

1984 set **Ride The Lightning** earned band deal with Elektra Records, and contract with Def Leppard management company Q-Prime; **Master of Puppets** LP followed in 1986. That year, Metallica spent six months on the road supporting Ozzy Osbourne, but their heavy touring schedule was temporarily curtailed by death of Burton, killed in road accident involving band's coach. Jason Newstead was chosen as his replacement.

Dissatisfaction with studio recording prompted band to "return to basics" and 1987 **Garage Days Revisited** EP (taped in Ulrich's workshop) charted in UK after strong support and publicity from Vertigo, Metallica's UK record company.

Group's growing reputation was confirmed when tour (1988) had them headlining alongside mega-bands The Scorpions and Van Halen; LP **...And Justice For All** (1988) was subsequent Top 10 hit in UK and USA. Successive Grammy awards (1990 and 1991) for Best Metal Performance and dynamic 1991 album **Metallica** provided band with distinctive profile in the murky and often confusing world of heavy metal. They consolidated their position throughout the rest of the 1990s with worldwide concerts, bestselling CDs – including **Load** (1996), **Re-load** (1997), and **S&M** (1999) – and an impressive range of music industry/metal awards, plus numerous gold and platinum discs. The band has also been among the most vociferous opponents of Internet music piracy – suing creators of Napster software on 2000 for "enabling and allowing its users to trade copyrighted songs," and also taking legal action against universities whose students were allegedly downloading material by Metallica and others. The group (and co-plaintiff, rapper Dr. Dre) reached an out-of-court settlement with Napster in July 2001.

Recommended listening

Kill 'Em All (Music For Nations), 1983
Ride The Lightning (Elektra/Music For Nations), 1984
Master Of Puppets (Music For Nations), 1986
Garage Days Revisited (EP) (Elektra), 1987
...And Justice For All (Elektra), 1988
Metallica (WEA), 1991
Live Shit: Binge And Purge (WEA), 1993
Load (WEA), 1996
Re-Load (WEA), 1997
S&M (WEA DVD w/San Francisco Symphony Orch.), 1999

STEVE MILLER

US guitarist, vocalist, composer
Born Milwaukee, Wisconsin,
November 5, 1943

Career: Began playing guitar at age four under auspices of legendary Les Paul and T-Bone Walker, both friends of Miller's father. Formed first band, The Marksmen Combo, before teens – it included future collaborator/vocalist/guitarist Boz Scaggs.

Miller enrolled at University of Wisconsin to study literature, and, after spending a year in Denmark, moved to Chicago, where he spent much of his time jamming with blues greats Muddy Waters, Buddy Guy, Junior Wells, and Otis Rush. Returning to his adopted home state of Texas, Miller worked as janitor for a local studio, cutting demos in spare time, before heading for San Francisco in 1966.

Recruiting Lonnie Turner (bass), Tim Davis (drums), and James "Curly" Cooke (guitar), he formed Steve Miller Band, which attained strong local following, and appeared at Monterey Pop Festival in Summer 1967. Signed to Capitol Records that year, band released first album **Children Of The Future** in May 1968, with Scaggs re-joining Miller (replacing Cooke) and Jim Peterman providing keyboards. Stunning **Sailor** set (1969) included classic material **Living In The USA**, **Gangster Of Love**, and haunting **Song For Our Ancestors**. Various personnel changes saw Scaggs go solo and Peterman turn to production.

Overcoming serious bout of hepatitis (one of several extended breaks due to health problems), Miller progressed steadily through 70s with gold albums **The Joker** (1973) and **Fly Like An Eagle** (1976). A four-year hiatus ended in 1981 with **Circle Of Love** album, Miller returning from extended period spent farming his estate in Oregon.

1982 set **Abracadabra** returned him to pinnacle of charts; but blues set **Living In The 20th Century** (1987) was his best work during decade, and paid tribute to veteran/major influence Jimmy Reed.

Miller's career was resurrected again in 1990 when **The Joker** topped UK singles chart after exposure as theme for jeans commercial. Subsequent **Best Of...** set, from most productive period (1968–73), made Top 50 in British album chart.

Recommended listening

Children Of The Future (Capitol), 1968
Sailor (Capitol), 1969
Brave New World (Capitol), 1969
Your Saving Grace (Capitol), 1969
Number Five (Capitol), 1970
Rock Love (Capitol), 1971
Recall The Beginning – A Journey From Eden (Capitol), 1972
Anthology (Capitol), 1973
The Joker (Capitol), 1973
Fly Like An Eagle (Capitol/Mercury), 1976
Book Of Dreams (Capitol/Mercury), 1977
Best Of 1968–73 (Capitol), 1977
Greatest Hits 74–78 (Capitol/Mercury), 1978
Circle Of Love (Capitol/Mercury), 1981
Abracadabra (Capitol/Mercury), 1982
Steve Miller Band Live (Mercury), 1983
Italian X Rays (Mercury), 1984
Living In The 20th Century (Capitol), 1986
Born 2 B Blue (Capitol), 1988
Best Of (Capitol), 1991
Wide River (Capitol), 1993
Box Set (3 CD compilation) (Capitol), 1994

JONI MITCHELL

Canadian vocalist, composer,
guitarist, pianist
Born Roberta Joan Anderson,
Fort McLeod, Alberta, Canada,
November 7, 1943

Career: Attended Alberta College Of Art with intention of becoming commercial artist, but subsequently developed serious interest in folk music/songwriting. Securing gig at the Depression coffeehouse, Joni gradually gained confidence. Following performance at Mariposa Folk Festival in Ontario, she wrote her first song, **Day After Day**. Professional career began in Toronto, where she quickly became a leading figure of the Yorktown set.

Married Chuck Mitchell in June 1965; couple moved to Detroit, achieving some acclaim as duo on local folk circuit. After break-up of marriage, Joni continued as soloist, securing engagements in New York; signed to Reprise in 1967. Under aegis of Elliot Roberts, she gained widespread reputation as star songwriter with a series of covers of her material by Judy Collins, Gordon Lightfoot, Johnny Cash, Tom Rush, Fairport Convention, and others.

Employing services of ex-Byrd David Crosby as producer, Mitchell recorded her self-titled debut LP, released in 1968. Early albums (including her 1969 follow-up, **Clouds**) were essentially acoustic, melodic works, sharpened by poetic lyrics. Although a product of the singer/songwriter boom of the late 1960s, Mitchell revealed a maturity and incisiveness that separated her from most of her contemporaries. While others wallowed in their own narcissism, Mitchell was careful to bring a cutting edge to many of her lines. She continually struggled to find meaning in her much-publicized broken relationships, without falling into self-indulgence.

Third album, **Ladies Of The Canyon** (1970), provided the breakthrough that Mitchell needed for continued success in the 70s. Sales were boosted by surprise hit single, **Big Yellow Taxi**, and cover versions of **Woodstock** by Crosby, Stills, Nash & Young and Matthews Southern Comfort (who took song to No. 1 in UK). More importantly, **Ladies Of The Canyon** included piano accompaniment alongside her acoustic guitar work.

Successive albums, **Blue** (1971), **For The Roses** (1972), and 1974's **Court And Spark**, showed greater confidence in her own writing and a willingness to explore new musical ideas. Introduction of Tom

BELOW: *Singer-songwriter Joni Mitchell onstage in the 1990s.*

Scott on wind instruments on **For The Roses** revealed first recorded signs of an interest in jazz as possible avenue for later work. Significantly, the only non-Mitchell song of the set was a re-make of Annie Ross's **Twisted**.

By 1975, Mitchell was moving too fast for many of her older fans. **The Hissing Of Summer Lawns**, in many respects her best work to date, featured an array of new musical effects, including synthesizer and the African drums of Burundi. The lyrics contained many of the old themes presented from different points of view. By this time, her songwriting talent was probably unmatched by any artist in rock, bar Dylan. In spite of such achievements, her more myopic critics were crying for a return to the folky songs of the late 60s. Instead, Mitchell pushed forward; **Hejira** (1976) was another dense work, less tuneful than its predecessor, but still commercially successful.

Her attraction to jazz was fully expressed in late 70s LPs **Don Juan's Reckless Daughter** and, more noticeably, **Mingus**. Realizing, perhaps, that her interests were becoming increasing incompatible with the mainstream rock audience, Mitchell threatened to retire at the end of decade to devote more energy to her first love, painting. (Virtually all her album sleeves feature her original artwork.)

Just as it seemed that her career was nearing a close, Mitchell re-emerged in 1982 with **Wild Things Run Fast** on David Geffen's label. Surprisingly, the album was a return to the more melodic work of the early 70s, and fared well chart-wise. Three-year recording break was ended by release of 1985 set **Dog Eat Dog**, whose sharp lyrical content took swipes at everything from US evangelism to domestic bliss.

Now further enmeshed in painting career, Mitchell again remained aloof from the recording studio before contractual obligations resulted in critically acclaimed 1988 album **Chalk Mark In A Rain Storm,** marking 20th anniversary of her debut LP. Despite artistic commitments – her abstracts command high prices, and there have been several exhibitions of her

photographs – Mitchell continues to record, and has toured more frequently in recent years; she entered 90s with a new album for Geffen, **Night Ride Home**, before returning to Reprise for **Turbulent Indigo** (1994) and **Taming The Tiger** (1998).

Recommended listening

Joni Mitchell (Reprise), 1968
Clouds (Reprise), 1969
Ladies Of The Canyon (Reprise), 1970
Blue (Reprise), 1971
For The Roses (Asylum), 1972
Court And Spark (Elektra/Asylum), 1974
Miles Of Aisles (Asylum), 1974
The Hissing Of Summer Lawns (Asylum), 1975
Hejira (Asylum), 1976
Don Juan's Reckless Daughter (Asylum), 1977
Mingus (Asylum), 1979
Shadows And Light (Asylum), 1980
Wild Things Run Fast (Geffen), 1982
Dog Eat Dog (Geffen), 1985
Chalk Mark In A Rain Storm (Geffen), 1988
Night Ride Home (Geffen), 1991
Turbulent Indigo (Reprise), 1994
Taming The Tiger (Reprise), 1998

NIRVANA

US group formed 1987

Original line-up: Kurt Cobain, guitar and vocals; Krist Novoselic, bass; Dale Crover, drums.

Career: Cobain and Novoselic, both residents of Aberdeen, Washington, a logging town near the state's Pacific coast, shared a fascination for 1980s punk/hardcore. Their early bands went through various names and personnel changes (and originally featured Cobain as drummer); first Nirvana line-up eventually emerged in 1987. The group built up a following among college audiences (especially in nearby city of Olympia), and recorded demos that led to release of their first single, **Love Buzz**, on Seattle's Sub Pop label in 1988. Debut album, **Bleach**, followed in 1989, and

helped to spread band's reputation – which extended to the UK when Nirvana visited the country for a short tour in late 1989. By this time, drummer Chad Channing had taken over from Crover; Channing was subsequently replaced by Dave Grohl (although Dan Peters, from Sub Pop labelmates Mudhoney, stood in on Nirvana's 1990 double-A-side single, **Sliver/Dive**).

Following major record deal with DGC, Nirvana's **Nevermind** album appeared in 1991. Single from it, **Smells Like Teen Spirit**, brought the band Top 10 success in UK in early 1992 (extensive gigging, plus support from music press, had helped to boost their British and European profile), and **Nevermind** itself quickly became a multi-million seller. Cobain married his pregnant girlfriend, Courtney Love (front woman of Hole, and daughter of ex- Grateful Dead road manager Hank Harrison) that February; lurid publicity about the couple's personal lives and alleged drug use was to dog them for the rest of Cobain's short life.

Cobain's poor physical condition (he suffered from chronic gastric problems) led to his hospitalization during Nirvana's Summer 1992 UK tour. Despite these ailments and other difficulties, work continued on a new single, **Oh The Guilt** (1992), and the band's third album, **In Utero**, followed in 1993. Both were highly successful.

Sadly, however, the ominous titles and themes of Cobain's songs from this period (**In Utero's Rape Me**, and **I Hate Myself And I Want To Die**, featured on a 1993 Beavis and Butt-Head compilation) were now increasingly reflected in his troubled mental state. Repeated drug overdoses and suicide threats led to demands from Novoselic and Grohl that he should urgently seek treatment for his problems; but before this could happen, Cobain shot himself at his home in Seattle on April 5, 1994. Nirvana's **Unplugged in New York** set was released posthumously later that year.

Recommended listening

Bleach (Sub Pop), 1989
Nevermind (DGC), 1991
In Utero (DGC), 1991
Unplugged in New York (DGC), 1994

JIMMY PAGE

UK guitarist, composer
Born Heston, Middlesex,
January 9, 1944

Career: Jimmy Page began his career as a session guitarist, appearing on records by the Kinks, the Rolling Stones, Georgie Fame, and The Who. Already rated as one of London's top studio musicians by 1966, when he joined The Yardbirds – initially as replacement bass player for Paul Samwell-Smith. Soon afterwards, however, Yardbirds' guitar player Jeff Beck quit as well, and Page took over his role.

The group, which broke up in Summer 1968, had been scheduled to tour northern Europe later that year. Page formed "The New Yardbirds" to fulfil these bookings: stand-in line-up comprised session bass player John Paul Jones, who had previously worked with Stones, Lulu, Dusty Springfield, and many others; Birmingham-based drummer John Bonham; and ex-Band Of Joy vocalist Robert Plant.

On their return from Scandinavia, the quartet decided to remain together, and, with the help of manager Peter Grant, they chose the name Led Zeppelin (allegedly suggested by The Who's Keith Moon, who had also been considering a collaboration with Page). Grant quickly secured recording contract with Atlantic, and band's debut album, **Led Zeppelin**, was released in 1968; it went gold early following year. Mixture of blues and rock riffs filled void left by Cream; superb musicianship and Plant's macho bare-to-the-waist image saw them streets ahead of US contemporaries. Album's crisp production set it apart from other bands' inferior, muddy-sounding hard rock efforts. Single **Good Times Bad Times**, culled from LP, earned Zeppelin first US Top 100 entry.

Reputation secured by **Led Zeppelin II** (1969), which included band's anthem **Whole Lotta Love**, a US Top 10. Band never had singles success in UK, though **Love** was theme for BBC's *Top Of The Pops* TV show for several years.

Zeppelin completed major tour of US in 1973, compounding success of further albums **III** (1970) and **IV** (1971). Tracks **Immigrant Song** (from **III**) and now all-time classic **Stairway To Heaven** (from **IV**) extracted phenomenal reaction from audiences. Band now really at their at

LEFT: *Session man turned rock virtuoso – Jimmy Page plays his double-neck Gibson.*

peak, with Grant turning down deals which conflicted with long-term strategy.

Group spent over a year away from studio after release of **Houses Of The Holy** (1973). Returned in 1975 with **Physical Graffiti**. Album was packaged in "moveable" sleeve, revealing various objects/individuals in windows of tenement block, and was as impressive musically as visually.

Zeppelin's own label Swan Song launched with release of **Graffiti**; other acts, including Bad Company, Maggie Bell, and Pretty Things, also signed to label. 1975 saw Plant injured in car crash during Greek holiday. His incapacity kept band off road for two years, although album **Presence** (1976) maintained momentum and appeased fans. LP had biggest advance orders ever in US, going platinum upon issue.

In 1976 movie/soundtrack album **The Song Remains The Same** released. Film captured explosive stage act to the full, despite some "live" footage being shot at Pinewood Studios, England.

On their massive 1977 US tour, Zeppelin grossed over a million dollars for New York shows (at Madison Square Garden) alone. Ten dates were cancelled, however, when Plant had to fly home following the sudden death of his young son.

Ninth album **In Through The Out Door** cut in Sweden at end of 1978. Unlikely hosts in frozen North were Abba, who had invited band to record in their studio. Major outdoor concert at stately home Knebworth House in August 1979 saw band re-conquer homeland. **In Through The Out Door** LP was released shortly afterwards. Album's unique packaging (wrapped in brown paper and featuring six different covers) won major marketing award in US.

After death of drummer John Bonham (following a drinking session) in 1980, band officially folded, though there have been occasional reunions, with Bonham's son Jason taking over drum duties. 1985 saw Page and Plant appearing with Nile Rodgers and Jeff Beck as the Honeydrippers, and reaching US No. 3 with single **Sea Of Love**. US success was also forthcoming for short-lived Page/Paul Rodgers band The Firm.

In the early 1990s, Page collaborated with vocalist David Coverdale, drummer Denny Carmarsi (ex-Heart), and bassist Ricky Phillips (ex-Bad English), touring and issuing 1992 CD **Coverdale/Page**. He reunited with Plant for **No Quarter – Unledded** (1994) and **Walking Into Clarksdale** (1998), and has recently appeared in concert and on record with the Black Crowes (**Live At The Greek**, 2000).

TED NUGENT

US guitarist, bandleader, vocalist, composer
Born Detroit, December 13, 1949

Career: Self-styled "wild man of rock," Nugent's antics (including hunting with bow and arrow and wearing a loin cloth) have almost justified epithet. He acquired first guitar at eight; joined first major band, Amboy Dukes, in 1965. Dukes played quasi-psychedelic music appropriate to times, but with extra Detroit metal quotient. Group scored US Top 20 hit in summer 1968 with **Journey To The Centre Of The Mind**.

Group continued through early 70s, but had limited success, and Nugent eventually signed as a soloist with Epic in 1975. His first LP for the company (**Ted Nugent**) featured Derek St Holmes, rhythm guitar, vocals; Rob Grange, bass; and Cliff Davies, drums; it soon made the Top 30.

1976 album **Free For All** included Meat Loaf (then a less-than-household name) as guest vocalist, and was also a chart success. By 1978 LP **Weekend Warriors**, there were other personnel changes, although Davies remained as drummer and sometimes producer, bowing out after 1981 live LP **Intensities**

In Ten Cities.

During 1982, Nugent switched labels to Atlantic, forming new band with drummer Carmine Appice (ex-Vanilla Fudge), and previous sidemen Dave Kiswiney, bass, and vocalist Derek St Holmes. Decade was less successful for the mad axeman, and, following 1988 set, **If You Can't Lick 'Em... Lick 'Em**, he set up Damn Yankees combo with Jack Blades (bass), drummer Mike Cartellone, and Tommy Shaw (ex-Styx) on guitar; their eponymous LP was released in 1990. The Yankees enjoyed US Top 5 status with single **High Enough** (1991), while their album made US Top 20, but the group split after a follow-up CD, **Don't Tread**, which appeared the following year.

In the last 10 years, Nugent has become increasingly involved with various pro-hunting, pro-firearms, and environmental groups. However, he remains committed to music, releasing a new solo album, appropriately titled **Spirit of the Wild**, in 1995, and continuing to tour, most notably with Kiss in 2000 and Lynyrd Skynyrd in 2001.
Guitar: Gibson Byrdland.

Recommended listening
Amboy Dukes (Mainstream), 1967
Amboy Dukes – Journey To The
  Center of the Mind (Mainstream),1968

Amboy Dukes – Marriage On The
  Rocks (Mainstream), 1970
Ted Nugent (Epic), 1975
Free For All (Epic), 1976
Cat Scratch Fever (Epic), 1977
Double Live Gonzo (Epic), 1978
Weekend Warriors (Epic), 1978
State Of Shock (Epic), 1979
Scream Dream (Epic), 1980
Intensities In Ten Cities (Epic), 1981
Great Gonzos! The Best of Ted
  Nugent (compilation) (Epic), 1981
Nugent (Atlantic) 1982
Penetrator (Atlantic) 1984
Little Miss Dangerous (Atlantic), 1986
If You Can't Lick 'Em... Lick 'Em
  (Atlantic) 1988
Damn Yankees (Atlantic), 1990
Damn Yankees – Don't Tread
  (Atlantic) 1992
Out Of Control (compilation) (Sony)
  1993
Spirit Of The Wild (Atlantic), 1995
Motor City Madness (Sony), 1996
Full Bluntal Nugity (Spitfire), 2001

CARL PERKINS

US vocalist, guitarist, composer
Born Lake City, Tennessee,
April 9, 1932
Died Jackson, Tennessee,
January 19, 1998

Career: Began performing country and blues material in Tennessee in late 1940s. By early 1950s had evolved own style, apparent in first recordings for Flip and Sun labels in Memphis in 1955. At first, he was encouraged to record country material by Sun boss Sam Phillips, but turned to rockabilly, and achieved distinction of first national rockabilly hit with own composition **Blue Suede Shoes** in 1956. Major setback to career came when he was hospitalized that year following serious car crash on way to first major television appearance in New York; unable to consolidate chart success.

Despite quality material and distinctive vocal and guitar style, Perkins was overshadowed by Elvis Presley (who

Left: *Ted Nugent with his Gibson Byrdland and a wall of amplification.*

covered **Blue Suede Shoes** with great success), and was neglected at Sun in favour of Jerry Lee Lewis. Moved to Columbia with fellow Sun artist Johnny Cash in 1958 in joint deal, only to find himself overshadowed again, this time by Cash, and, despite minor hit with **Pointed Toe Shoes** in 1959, star status eluded him.

Death of elder brother Jay was further setback, and Perkins turned increasingly to drink. Signed to Decca in 1963, visiting Europe and recording with The Beatles, who regarded him as hero. Cut good material for various labels during 60s and became integral part of Johnny Cash Road Show, touring extensively. Encouraged by Cash, turned towards Christianity and away from pills and booze. Perkins split with Cash in 1976 in order to return to touring and recording independently.

During the 1980s, Perkins was frequent "guest" on albums and at concerts, and worked with Paul McCartney (**Tug Of War** LP), Johnny Cash, and Jerry Lee Lewis (**The Survivors** album – 1982). In 1985, George Harrison, Ringo Starr, Eric Clapton, and Dave Edmunds joined him on stage for a *Carl Perkins And Friends* show to commemorate 30th anniversary of the recording of **Blue Suede Shoes**. He was inducted into Rock 'n' Roll Hall Of Fame in 1987,and continued to record and perform throughout much of the 90s, despite deteriorating health.

Guitars: Gibson Switchmaster, Fender Telecaster.

Recommended listening

Dance Album of Carl Perkins (Sun) 1958
Whole Lotta Shakin' (Columbia), 1958
Carl Perkins On Top (Columbia), 1969
Boppin' The Blues (Columbia), 1970
My Kind of Country (Mercury), 1973
The Survivors (Columbia), 1982
Li'l Bit Of Gold (compilation) (Rhino), 1988
Born To Rock (Universal), 1989
Carl Perkins and Sons (BMG), 1993
Take Me Back (BMG), 1993
Disciple In Blue Suede Shoes (BMG), 1993
Go, Cat, Go! (BMG), 1996
The Essential Sun Collection (2 CD compilation) (Recall), 1999

The Man and the Legend (compilation) (Magnum), 2000

TOM PETTY AND THE HEARTBREAKERS

US group formed 1976

Original line-up: Tom Petty, vocals, Fender Stratocaster, Rickenbacker 12-string guitars; Stan Lynch, drums, vocals; Mike Campbell, guitar; Benmont Tench, keyboards, vocals; Ron Blair, bass.

Career: Petty grew up in Gainsville, Florida, and played for local group Epics in high school. He then held variety of low-paid jobs while playing bass in Gainsville's premier band Mudcrutch, where he encountered Campbell and Tench.

Mudcrutch moved to Los Angeles to seek fame and fortune in April 1974, but folded after a flopped single. However, trio kept in touch and in early 1976 were working on some of Tench's demos with Lynch and Blair (also from Gainsville) when they decided to try again, this time as The Heartbreakers. Group signed with Shelter Records and released first, eponymously titled LP in 1976.

Critical praise, exciting live shows, and plenty of radio play ensured swift recognition for Heartbreakers, who responded by recording even stronger LP, **You're Gonna Get It!**, in 1978. Just as it seemed they were making it (1979 single **Don't Do Me Like That** gave them first Top 10 hit), Shelter Records collapsed. Band became deeply involved in legal problems, and Petty himself was forced to file for bankruptcy.

1979's **Damn The Torpedoes** reflected The Heartbreakers' tenacity and resilience in both title and sound. Stevie Nicks used group on her 1981 **Bella Donna** solo LP; and they continued to gather momentum throughout 80s, with successful albums like **Long After Dark** (1982), and **Southern Accents** (1985). Double LP **Pack Up The Plantation** (same year) emanated from band's gigs at Los Angeles' Wiltern Theater, but also included two Tom Petty/Stevie Nicks vocal duets from an LA Forum show back in 1981.

Following 1987's **Let Me Up (I've Had Enough)**, Petty became increasingly involved in non-Heartbreakers projects, including the formation of the Traveling Wilburys (with George Harrison, Jeff Lynne, Roy Orbison, and Bob Dylan).

1989 **Full Moon Fever** solo CD saw Petty at his artistic peak; it made the UK Top 10 and spawned **I Won't Back Down**, **Running Down A Dream**, and **Free Fallin'** hit singles. He joined forces with The Heartbreakers again for **Into The Great Wide Open** (1991), but **Wildflowers** (1994) was nominally another solo effort (though it also featured backing from several band members). The next Petty/Heartbreakers project was their soundtrack music for Edward Burns' 1996 movie *She's The One* (which starred Jennifer Aniston and Cameron Diaz); their most recent album, **Echo**, appeared in 1999, and a new CD is rumored to be due in 2002.

Recommended listening

Hit Singles	US	UK
Don't Do Me Like That, 1979	10	-
Refugee, 1980	15	-
The Waiting, 1981	19	-
You Got Lucky, 1983	20	-
Don't Come Around, 1985	13	-
I Won't Back Down, 1989	12	28
Free Fallin', 1990	7	-
With Stevie Nicks:		
Stop Draggin' My Heart Around, 1981	3	-

Albums

Tom Petty And The Heartbreakers (Shelter), 1976
You're Gonna Get It! (Shelter), 1978
Damn The Torpedoes (Backstreet), 1979
Hard Promises (Backstreet), 1981
Long After Dark (Backstreet), 1982
Southern Accents (MCA), 1985
Pack Up The Plantation Live! (MCA), 1985
Let Me Up (I've Had Enough) (MCA), 1987
Full Moon Fever (MCA), 1989
Into The Great Wide Open (MCA), 1991
Wildflowers (WEA), 1994
She's The One (soundtrack) (WEA), 1996
Echo (WEA), 1999

PINK FLOYD

UK group formed 1966

Original line-up: Syd Barrett, vocals, guitar; Roger Waters, bass; Richard Wright, keyboards; Nick Mason, drums.

Career: Barrett and Waters attended Cambridge High School for boys, along with future member David Gilmour. Barrett moved to art college in London before forming short-lived duo with Gilmour. Waters, meanwhile, was studying architecture in London and had formed Sigma 6 with Mason and Wright.

Group evolved into T. Set, Meggadeath, and Screaming Abdabs, finally bringing in jazz guitarist Bob Close and Barrett. Latter dubbed group The Pink Floyd Sound, a name said to have been inspired by Georgia bluesmen Pink Anderson and Floyd Council. As they moved towards psychedelic music, Close was ousted.

Floyd spent late 1966 playing at variety of early underground haunts in the capital, including The Marquee, the London Free School's Sound/Light Workshop at All Saints Church Hall, Notting Hill, and, most notably, The Roundhouse. By end of year they were regular headliners at UFO, London's foremost hippie club. With new managers Peter Jenner and Andrew King, secured contract with EMI, recording first single in January 1967. **Arnold Layne**, written by Barrett, was amusing tale of transvestite who steals underwear. Novel sound and theme ensured Top 20 placing in UK charts, establishing Floyd as most successful group to emerge from Britain's underground scene.

During May 1967, ambitious *Games For May* was staged at London's Queen Elizabeth Hall, complete with quadraphonic sound system. Games For May, re-titled **See Emily Play**, was released as single and reached UK No. 6 in July.

In August, first LP, **Piper At The Gates Of Dawn**, demonstrated Syd Barrett's dominant role in group. Barrett's lead guitar work was impressive, neatly complementing Wright's unusual keyboard style – but prior to first US tour, Barrett's behavior became increasingly erratic, possibly a side-effect of over-use of hallucinogens. In succeeding months, condition worsened; at some performances he would not play at all, remaining motionless on stage. By February 1968, Gilmour was brought in as replacement, Barrett finally leaving in April.

Without Barrett's lyrics, group had little chance of succeeding as singles act. Instead they concentrated on live work, appearing regularly at Middle Earth, and headlining free concert at London's Hyde Park in July. Second album, **A Saucerful Of Secrets** (1968), demonstrated ability to survive. Used Waters' instrumental, electronic, and choral work to great effect, particularly during **Set The Controls For The Heart Of The Sun**.

Band also displayed a growing interest in soundtrack composition, making musical contributions to movies *More* (1969), *The Committee* (1969), *Zabriskie Point* and *The Body* (both 1970), and *The Valley* (**Obscured By Clouds** album) (1972).

Released double LP **Ummagumma**, featuring two live sides (recorded at Mothers Club, Birmingham, and Manchester College of Commerce, in June 1969) backed by studio contributions from every member. Work was self-indulgent in parts and erratic in quality. A period of relative quiet ended with release of **Atom Heart Mother** (1970) which topped UK LP charts; successful concerts followed, including free concert in Hyde Park.

Early in 1971, Floyd appeared at Crystal Palace Garden Party in South London amid fireworks and rain. Premiered **Return To The Son Of Nothing**, an extended melodic rock improvisation that finally emerged as **Echoes**, key track on their 1971 LP **Meddle**.

The band's next major album project, **The Dark Side Of The Moon**, issued in 1973, was the culmination of various ideas explored by the band over the years. It underlined the dark pessimism in Waters' songwriting, perhaps consciously rejecting the escapist romanticism that had characterized and destroyed Barrett. Bleakness of theme was offset by stunning production, unparalleled for its period. An aesthetically rewarding venture, album also became their biggest seller. Remained in UK lists for over two years, and became a fixture in the US charts for more than a decade.

Following album's release, group played at London's Earls Court, then retired for six months. Much of 1974 was occupied with studio work, but Floyd returned to the States for a short tour in 1975, before playing badly received set in UK at Knebworth.

Wish You Were Here album was finally issued in September 1975 after two and a half years' work. Press reaction proved unfavorable – but sales-wise, it was another triumph. During 1976, group toured Europe and USA, and completed work on **Animals**, released January 1977. Further solo projects followed amid rumours of impending dissolution. **The Wall**, which appeared in 1979, provided another phenomenal seller, and included a Christmas single chart-topper, **Another Brick In The Wall (Part 2)**. Spin-off film *The Wall*, starring Bob Geldof of Boomtown Rats, received a more mixed reception.

Prophetically titled 1983 album **The Final Cut** emphasized Waters' dominance of group with further bleak visions of present day society. From early underground following, group had gone on to worldwide acclaim – but long-simmering internal tensions now came to a head, leading to an acrimonious split and subsequent litigation between Waters and his ex-colleagues.

Amid these legal wrangles, individual band members pursued their own musical projects. Waters' solo debut, **The Pros and Cons of Hitchhiking**, came out in 1984, and was followed, two years later, by his soundtrack for the movie version of cartoonist Raymond Briggs' bleak tale of nuclear destruction, *When The Wind Blows*. Meanwhile, Gilmour (who had made his first, self-titled LP in 1978, and had also been involved in freelance studio playing and production) also issued a new album (**About Face**, 1986).

In 1987, Wright, Gilmour, and Mason came together again to tour with Floyd paraphernalia, including their celebrated

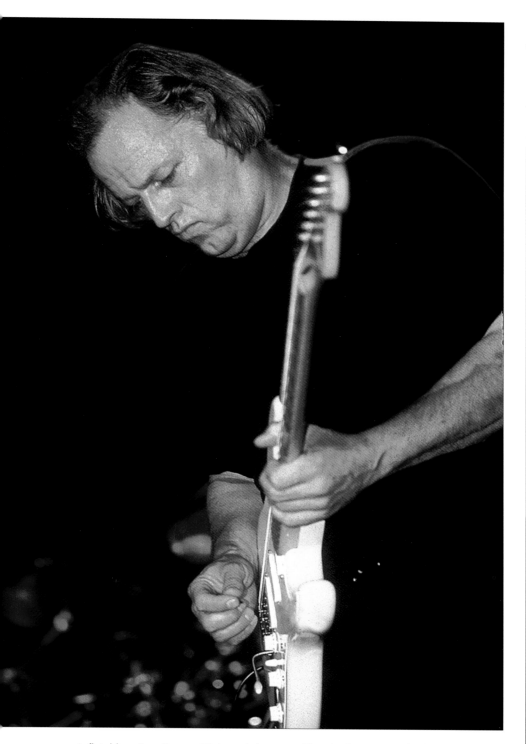

leader), **The Division Bell** (1994) and **Pulse** (1995), as well as occasional tours and solo activities.

Recommended listening

Pink Floyd albums:
The Piper At The Gates Of Dawn
  (Tower), 1967
A Saucerful Of Secrets (Tower), 1968
Ummagumma (Harvest), 1969
Atom Heart Mother (Harvest), 1970
Relics (Harvest), 1971
Meddle (Harvest), 1971
Obscured By Clouds (Harvest), 1972
The Dark Side Of The Moon
  (Harvest), 1973
Wish You Were Here (Columbia),
  1975
Animals (Columbia), 1977
The Wall (Columbia), 1979
A Collection of Great Dance Songs
  (compilation) Columbia), 1981
The Final Cut (Columbia), 1983
Works (Capitol), 1983
A Momentary Lapse Of Reason
  (Columbia), 1987
Delicate Sound Of Thunder
  (Columbia), 1988
The Division Bell (Columbia), 1994
Pulse (Columbia), 1995
Echoes (Best of) (Capitol), 2001
With various artists:
Zabriskie Point (soundtrack) (MGM),
  1970
Syd Barrett solo:
Best of Syd Barrett – Wouldn't You
  Miss Me? (Capitol), 2001
David Gilmour solo:
David Gilmour (Columbia), 1978
About Face (Columbia), 1986
Nick Mason solo:
Fictitious Sports (Columbia), 1981
Profiles (with Rick Fenn) (Columbia),
  1985
Roger Waters solo:
The Body (Harvest), 1970
The Pros And Cons Of Hitchhiking
  (Columbia), 1984
Radio K.A.O.S. (Columbia/Harvest),
  1987
The Wall: Berlin (Mercury), 1990
Amused To Death (Columbia), 1992
In The Flesh (live) (Columbia), 2000

inflatable pig. Roger Waters (whose second solo album, **Radio KAOS**, had just been released) hit the road almost simultaneously with a rival series of gigs, using archive Floyd film footage as visual back-up. The two factions continued to record and perform, with Gilmour, Wright, and Mason issuing **A Momentary Lapse Of Reason** (1987) and **Delicate Sound Of Thunder** (1988) as Pink Floyd, but without Waters – who staged his own spectacular live version of **The Wall** in Berlin in 1990. Subsequent album and video of this event were bestsellers in both US and UK.

The later 90s have seen Waters' grandiose **Amused To Death** CD (1992), and two Pink Floyd albums (David Gilmour is now the group's official

THE POLICE

UK group formed 1977

Original line-up: Sting (Gordon Sumner), vocals, bass; Henri Padovani, guitar; Stewart Copeland, drums.

Career: Trio was formed by drummer Copeland, previously with UK group Curved Air. Idea was to combine post-punk principles of simplicity and spontaneity with coherence and melodic sense. Copeland recruited Sting from Newcastle jazz and rock scene, and pair pulled in Padovani on guitar.

Band made recording debut in 1977 with single **Fall Out**, on Illegal Records, an independent label formed by Copeland with brother Miles. Padovani left after only a few months; replaced by Andy Summers, veteran of Zoot Money's Big Roll Band, The Animals, Soft Machine, and Kevin Ayers.

Roxanne single (A&M, 1979) brought The Police major attention. Combining reggae-styled verse with rocking harmony chorus, record eventually went silver. It was first of string of highly distinctive hits, and the band's albums were as successful as their singles: **Outlandos D'Amour** (1978), **Regatta De Blanc** (1979), and **Zenyatta Mondatta** (1980) all achieved platinum status.

Group also gained reputation as exciting live act, touring worldwide to wild acclaim in 1980–81. **Six Pack**, a package of the first five Police singles plus new release **The Bed's Too Big Without You**, reached No. 17 in the UK singles charts in mid-1980.

1981 saw **Ghost In The Machine** LP riding high in charts, and hit singles from album soaring; **Every Little Thing She Does Is Magic** gave them their fourth UK No. 1, while **Invisible Sun** reached No. 2. By now, band members were becoming involved in solo activities. Sting had already had major acting parts in The Who film *Quadrophenia* and BBC-TV's *Artemis '81*, and received further acclaim for his lead role in Dennis Potter's *Brimstone And Treacle*, which featured his memorable performance of **Spread A Little Happiness** (1982) – also a hit. The

same year, Andy Summers recorded moderately successful instrumental LP, **I Advance Masked**, with King Crimson's Robert Fripp in 1982, while Stewart Copeland also pursued recording/composition projects.

Return to group work came in spring 1983. **Synchronicity** LP and single **Every Breath You Take** flew to No. 1 both sides of the Atlantic. **Synchronicity** was third Police LP in a row to enter UK album charts at No. 1. It was also to be their last album together: band have never officially split up, but Sting's decision to go solo effectively put paid to prospects of further regular collaborations with Summers and Copeland.

Sting's subsequent, stellar achievements are two numerous to mention here – but his two colleagues have also had highly successful post-Police careers. Recent Andy Summers albums (frequently displaying jazz and Latin influences) include **Synaesthesia** (1995), **Green Chimneys** (1999), and **Peggy's Blue Skylight** (2000); and 2002 will see the debut of the HotFlash trio, in which he will appear alongside former Cream bassist Jack Bruce and drummer Dennis Chambers. Copeland's activities have also been wide-ranging and innovative: he has composed film scores, ballet and opera music, played in the band Animal Logic with virtuoso bassist Stanley Clarke, and is currently a member of Oysterhead with Phish guitarist Trey Anastasio and Primus bassist Les Claypool.

Recommended listening

Hit Singles	US	UK
Roxanne, 1979	32	12
Can't Stand Losing You, 1979	-	2
Message In A Bottle, 1979	-	1
Walking On The Moon, 1979	-	1
So Lonely, 1980	-	6
Six Pack, 1980	-	17
Don't Stand So Close To Me, 1980	10	1
De Do Do Do, De Da Da Da, 1980	10	5
Invisible Sun, 1981	-	2
Every Little Thing She Does Is Magic, 1981	3	1
Spirits In The Material World, 1982	11	12
Every Breath You Take, 1983	1	1
Wrapped Around Your Finger, 1983	-	7
Synchronicity II, 1983	16	17
King Of Pain, 1984	3	17

Albums
Outlandos D'Amour (A&M), 1978
Regatta De Blanc (A&M), 1979
Zenyatta Mondatta (A&M), 1980
Ghost In The Machine (A&M), 1981
Synchronicity (A&M), 1983
Every Breath You Take – The Album (A&M) 1986
Stewart Copeland solo:
The Rhythmatist (A&M), 1985
The Equalizer (IRS/MCA), 1988
Stewart Copeland with Animal Logic:
Animal Logic (MCA/Virgin), 1989
Andy Summers solo:
XYZ (A&M), 1987
Mysterious Barricades (Private), 1989
The Golden Wire (Private), 1989
Charming Snakes (Private), 1990
World Gone Strange (Private), 1991
Synaesthesia (CMP), 1995
Green Chimneys (RCA), 1999
Peggy's Blue Skylight (RCA), 2000
Andy Summers with Robert Fripp:
I Advance Masked (A&M), 1982
Bewitched (A&M), 1984

QUEEN

UK group formed 1972

Original line-up: Brian May, self-made "Red Special" guitar; Roger Taylor, drums; Freddie Mercury, vocals; John Deacon, bass.

Career: Evolved from Smile, featuring Brian May, Tim Staffell, and Roger Taylor; when group folded, Staffell persuaded flatmate Freddie Mercury to join May and Taylor in new venture. Several months later Deacon was added. Group underwent strenuous rehearsals, playing occasionally at Imperial College, London (where May had been post-graduate astronomy student). Lucrative contract with EMI was followed by debut single **Keep Yourself Alive** (1973), which flopped, although first album, **Queen** (same year), displayed clever musical

LEFT: *Brian May of Queen with his home-made "Red Special" guitar.*

singles; the same year, May joined with Ian Gillan, Robert Plant, and Bruce Dickinson to record version of **Smoke On The Water** for Rock Aid Armenia.

Rumors about Mercury's state of health had been in circulation for some time, but were apparently confounded by the release of **Innuendo** in 1991. LP debuted at No. 1 in UK album charts, while six-minute-plus title track topped single listings. However, that November, a terse press release stated that singer had contracted AIDS. Two days later, he was dead, victim of broncho-pneumonia, exacerbated by the killer disease. The remaining members of Queen announced that they would celebrate his life "in the style to which he was accustomed." Ironically, at time of Mercury's demise, Queen's current single was **The Show Must Go On**.

Recommended listening

Queen (Elektra/EMI), 1973
Queen II (Elektra/EMI), 1974
Sheer Heart Attack (Elektra/EMI), 1974
A Night At The Opera (Elektra/EMI), 1975
A Day At The Races (Elektra/EMI), 1976
News Of The World (Elektra/EMI), 1977
Jazz (Elektra/EMI), 1978
Live Killers (Elektra/EMI), 1979
The Game (Elektra/EMI), 1980
Flash Gordon (soundtrack) (Elektra/EMI), 1980
Greatest Hits (Elektra/EMI), 1981
Hot Space (Elektra/EMI), 1982
The Works (Elektra/EMI), 1984
The Miracle (Capitol/Parlophone) 1989
Innuendo (Hollywood/Parlophone), 1991
Brian May solo:
Star Fleet Project (EMI), 1983
Freddie Mercury solo:
Mr Bad Guy (CBS), 1985
Roger Taylor solo:
Fun In Space (Elektra), 1981
Strange Frontier (EMI), 1984
Roger Taylor and The Cross:
Shove It (Virgin), 1988

balance between glam rock and Zeppelin-style heavy metal. Group eventually hit charts in early 1974 with **Seven Seas of Rhye**, and the same year two further LPs, **Queen II** and **Sheer Heart Attack**, were issued. Latter attracted critical commendation for ingenious arrangements, courtesy of producer Roy Thomas Baker. Success of fifth single **Killer Queen** (1974) placed Queen in enviable position of achieving following from both Top 20 fans and hard rock enthusiasts.

Most of 1975 spent preparing **A Night At The Opera**; single taken from it, **Bohemian Rhapsody** (1975), was ultimate kitsch epic, showcasing Mercury's falsetto vocals, May's brilliant guitar work, and the group's distinctive harmony singing. It became Christmas chart-topper for nine weeks.

Queen seemed to change image and musical style with every new song during this period. Subsequent hits included **We Are The Champions** (1977), later adopted by sports fans (and politicians) across the world; rockabilly spoof **Crazy Little Thing Called Love** (1979); and pop-styled **Another One Bites The Dust** in 1980.

New decade saw chart success continue: **Flash** (1980 – from *Flash Gordon* movie which group scored), and 1984's **Radio Ga Ga** and **I Want To Break Free** were to become classics. Members also embarked on solo projects. Taylor cut **Fun in Space** LP (1981); May collaborated with Eddie Van Halen on **Star Fleet** project; Mercury contributed to Giorgio Moroder's soundtrack for *Metropolis* movie and enjoyed UK Top 20 single with **I Was Born To Love You** (1985); while Deacon's group, The Immortals, featured on score of 1986 *Biggles* film.

Prodigious performers, Queen were kings of stadium circuit during early 80s. However, following European tour in 1986, group temporarily disbanded as Taylor formed The Cross, while Mercury recorded passionate version of **The Great Pretender** (1987), duetted with Spanish opera diva Montserrat Caballé on **Barcelona** (same year), and penned theme for *Time* musical. Meanwhile, May produced spoof **Bohemian Rhapsody** single by Bad News (1987) and tracks for actress girlfriend Anita Dobson.

Queen reunited in 1989 for **The Miracle** LP, which spawned a trio of hit

BONNIE RAITT

US guitarist, vocalist, composer
Born Los Angeles, California,
November 8, 1949

Career: Grew up in artistic family in LA (her father, John, was a distinguished actor/singer). Moved to Cambridge, Massachusetts, area in 1967 as student, but dropped out of college two years later to pursue musical career. Raitt selected Dick Waterman as manager because of his association with various blues artists, her childhood heroes.

Eponymously titled 1971 debut LP established pattern of using wide variety of material and musicians for each recording, and also showcased Raitt's masterly blues guitar playing. Subsequent albums displayed growing maturity, understanding, and warmth, as she interpreted blues classics alongside her own numbers and other well-chosen contemporary songs. These included Jackson Browne's **Under The Falling Sky** and Eric Kaz's **Love Has No Pride** – both from her second LP, **Give It Up** (1972) – and Allen Toussaint's **What Is Success** on 1974 **Streetlights** set.

These discs were well received, but not big sellers. However, Raitt achieved some serious commercial success with her **Sweet Forgiveness** album (1977), from which revival of Del Shannon's classic **Runaway** was Top 40 hit. **The Glow** (1979) was carefully conceived follow-up, and included more original compositions; but after **Green Light** set (1982), Raitt spent four years in wilderness before prophetic **Nine Lives** was issued.

Frustration at state of her career, as well as self-confessed drink and drug problems, saw artist in virtual exile until Don Was-produced **Nick Of Time** (1989) for Capitol Records earned two million-plus sales, the US No. 1 spot, and a handful of Grammys, including Album Of The Year. A plethora of guest musicians, including Herbie Hancock, David Crosby, and Graham Nash, prompted Raitt into superlative performance; she also featured prominently on John Lee Hooker's **The Healer** album (1980),

before going on to work with Emmylou Harris, B.B. King, and other major names.

Following US tour and several charity gigs, Raitt returned to studio and cut **Luck Of The Draw** (1992), another massive seller and Grammy-winner. Subsequent releases, **Longing In Their Hearts** (1994) and **Fundamental** (1998), have further consolidated her status as one of the most highly respected musicians on the contemporary US scene.

Recommended listening

Bonnie Raitt (Warner Bros.), 1971
Give It Up (Warner Bros.), 1972
Takin' My Time (Warner Bros.), 1973
Streetlights (Warner Bros.), 1974
Home Plate (Warner Bros.), 1975
Sweet Forgiveness (Warner Bros.), 1977
The Glow (Warner Bros.), 1979
Green Light (Warner Bros.), 1982
Nine Lives (Warner Bros.), 1986
Nick Of Time (Capitol), 1989
The Bonnie Raitt Collection (Warner Bros.), 1990
Luck Of The Draw (Capitol), 1991
Longing In Their Hearts (Capitol), 1994
Road Tested (live) (Capitol), 1995
Fundamental (Capitol), 1998

R.E.M.

US band formed in 1981

Original line-up: Bill Berry, drums, backing vocals; Peter Buck, Rickenbacker guitar; Mike Mills, bass, backing vocals, keyboards; Michael Stipe, vocals, lyrics.

Career: Mike Mills and Bill Berry met while at High School in Macon, Georgia, and subsequently moved c.70 miles north to city of Athens to attend university; there, they encountered fellow student Michael Stipe and record store employee Peter Buck.

The four budding musicians came together as R.E.M. (the letters stand for "rapid eye movement"), playing gigs around Athens with a repertoire that initially comprised cover versions of songs such as **Needles And Pins**, The Sex Pistols' **God Save The Queen**, and **California Sun**. In 1981, the group made

an independent single, **Radio Free Europe/Sitting Still** (1981); on the strength of this, they were signed by the IRS label, which released their already-recorded EP **Chronic Town** in 1982.

Debut album, **Murmur**, appeared in 1983, and was a major critical success, winning the coveted title of *Rolling Stone* Record of the Year. It sold respectably (reaching No. 36 in the US album charts), and the band were soon in demand for concerts throughout America. They also made their European debut, undertaking TV and live work in Britain.

Keeping up an energetic schedule of gigs and recordings, R.E.M. released a second LP, **Reckoning**, in Summer 1984. It sold slightly better than its predecessor (just scraping into the US Top 30), and after a UK tour to promote the record, band decided to make their next album, **Fables Of The Reconstruction**, in London. Sessions for this took place in early 1985 with veteran folk-rock producer Joe Boyd, and disc (another moderate seller) appeared that Summer. The harder-edged **Life's Rich Pageant**, their biggest commercial success to date, was issued the following year.

Release of R.E.M.'s fifth album, **Document** (recorded in Nashville and mixed in Los Angeles) in Fall 1987 coincided with major UK gig at London's Hammersmith Odeon. Band co-produced the record with Scott Litt; it brought them to the brink of major league rock stardom, and spawned a Top 10 US single, **The One I Love** (it reached only No. 51 in the UK hit parade).

In 1988 R.E.M. signed with Warner Bros. in a multi-million dollar deal, and debuted for that label with **Green** in October of same year; world tour commenced four months later, by which time band were enjoying a US Top 10 hit single with **Stand**, taken from the new album.

After several years of prolific output, R.E.M. took a short break from group recording during 1989, leaving members free to pursue their own projects: these included Buck's contribution (with UK

RIGHT: *Peter Buck, guitarist with million-selling Georgia band R.E.M.*

singer-songwriter and ex-Soft Boy Robyn Hitchcock) to Byrds' tribute album **Time In Between**. Period also saw Mills, Berry, and Warren Zevon cut **Hindu Love Gods** set, while Stipe produced **White Dirt** CD for The Chickasaw Mudpuppies, and guested on Syd Straw's **Surprise**.

Band's next album, 1991 set **Out Of Time**, enjoyed massive critical and commercial success, and topped both US and UK album charts. It also contained memorable hit singles **Shiny Happy People**, **Losing My Religion**, and **Near Wild Heaven**. Subsequent albums **Automatic For The People** (1992) and **Monster** (1994) were more somber in mood, but also multi-platinum sellers. However, the following year's international tour by the band was plagued with difficulties: Berry and Mills were both taken seriously ill on the road, while Stipe suffered a hernia, and, like his colleagues, had to undergo immediate emergency surgery. Despite some cancellations, the tour was completed, and the musicians were soon well enough to record their next album, **New Adventures in Hi-Fi**, released in 1997.

That Fall, Bill Berry announced that he was leaving the group. He has not been officially replaced: R.E.M.'s 1998 CD, **Up**, (which received mixed reviews) featured electronic percussion, and their latest album, **Reveal** (2001) includes contributions from a stand-in drummer, Joey Waronker. While Berry's departure was apparently a surprise to his colleagues, it has had no appreciable effect on their commitment or continuing success – as recent, triumphant live shows and still-buoyant record sales have demonstrated.

Recommended listening

Murmur (IRS/A&M), 1983
Reckoning (IRS), 1984
Chronic Town (EP) (IRS), 1984
Fables Of The Reconstruction (IRS), 1985
Life's Rich Pageant (IRS), 1986
Document (IRS), 1987
Green (Warner Bros.), 1988
Eponymous (IRS/MCA), 1988
Out Of Time (Warner Bros.), 1991
Best Of (IRS), 1991
Automatic For The People (Warner Bros.), 1992
Monster (Warner Bros.), 1994
New Adventures In Hi-Fi (Warner Bros.), 1996
R.E.M. In The Attic (EMI/Capitol), 1997
Up (Warner Bros.), 1998
Reveal (Warner Bros.), 2001

THE ROLLING STONES

UK group formed 1963

Original line-up: Mick Jagger, vocals; Keith Richards, guitar, vocals; Brian Jones, guitar, vocals; Bill Wyman, bass; Ian Stewart, piano; Charlie Watts, drums.

Career: Jagger and Richards first met at primary school in Kent, then went their separate ways. In 1960, when Richards was attending Dartford Art School and Jagger the London School of Economics, they discovered mutual interest in blues and R&B. Pair moved in and out of ever-changing group line-ups comprising London's infant blues scene of the time.

Future Rolling Stones personnel coalesced around Alexis Korner's Blues Incorporated, pioneer British blues outfit that had regular gig at Ealing Blues Club, West London. Cheltenham-born guitarist Brian Jones occasionally sat in with them, and by 1962 Jagger was their regular singer; he was also rehearsing with Jones, Richards, and other like-minded musicians, including pianist Ian Stewart.

In June 1962, Blues Incorporated were booked for BBC radio broadcast; budget only allowed for six players, so Jagger stepped down and deputized for Blues Incorporated at London's Marquee Club, where he and his colleagues were billed as Brian Jones And Mick Jagger And The Rollin' Stones. Stones line-up was completed the following year, when Charlie Watts made move from Blues Incorporated, and Bill Wyman joined on bass after audition.

New band's reputation spread quickly by word of mouth, and they came to attention of former PR man Andrew Loog Oldham; he became their manager and negotiated record contract with Decca. (First move was to oust pianist Stewart on the grounds that he looked too "normal" – although he was to remain "sixth Stone," playing on records and at gigs, until his death in 1984.)

LEFT: *Keith Richards and his trademark, five-stringed Telecaster.*

Debut single, version of Chuck Berry's **Come On** (1963) brought band to notice of public and, particularly, of media. Oldham pushed Stones as "bad boys" (compared to "lovable moptop" Beatles), and they swiftly became cult figures. First album **The Rolling Stones**, largely covers of R&B material, reached top of UK charts in April 1964. June that year saw US tour and first UK chart-topper, their version of Bobby Womack's **It's All Over Now**.

However, from 1965 all singles were Jagger/Richards compositions, and band developed distinctive pop-rock style that still kept strong blues undertones. **The Last Time** (1965) made US Top 10, and paved way for first US/UK No. 1, the classic **(I Can't Get No) Satisfaction** (same year).

By end of 60s, Stones had become international attraction, second only to Beatles in importance. They were surrounded by almost permanent aura of notoriety: **Let's Spend The Night Together** (1967) was censored by the Ed Sullivan TV show; Jagger's relationship with Marianne Faithfull provided gossip-column titillation; and he, Richards, and Jones were all busted for drug possession. Pressures became too much for Jones, whose departure from the band in 1969 was followed, less than a month later, by his death from drowning while under the influence of drink and drugs. His replacement was Mick Taylor, formerly with John Mayall Band.

Musically, apart from 1967 flirtation with psychedelia on **Their Satanic Majesties Request** album, band had gone from strength to strength. **Beggars Banquet** (1968) and **Let It Bleed** (1969) were both classic rock albums, regarded by many critics as Stones' best ever.

By the 70s, the Stones, now something of a rock 'n' roll institution, were living the lives of jet-setting tax exiles and establishing new records for massively attended live performances. In 1974 Mick Taylor quit, to be replaced by Ronnie Wood, ex-Faces. There was some toning down of former "rebel" image, but band continued to put out worthwhile albums (after 1971, on their own Rolling Stones label) that generally contained a couple of classics each, and maintained standard of singles with

numbers like **Brown Sugar** (1971) and **It's Only Rock And Roll** (1974)

At the end of the decade, though, the Stones seemed to lose some of their momentum. **Emotional Rescue** (1980) and **Tattoo You** (1981) saw band in solid but uninspiring mood, although the latter LP topped US chart and preceded a record-breaking American tour. Following mediocre **Undercover** (1983), quintet signed with CBS for **Dirty Work** set (1986) which spawned powerful version of Bob & Earl's R&B classic **Harlem Shuffle**. A long break until **Steel Wheels** LP and tour (1989) allowed group members to consolidate solo ambitions, although 1991 live LP **Flashpoint** maintained collective profile.

Jagger cut **She's The Boss** (1985) and **Primitive Cool** (1987), and enjoyed chart duet with David Bowie on **Dancing In The Street** (from *Live Aid*) in 1985. Wyman enjoyed hit single with **(Si Si) Je Suis Un Rock Star** (1981), while Richards recorded **Talk Is Cheap** for Virgin in 1988, toured US in the same year, and acted as musical director for Chuck Berry's *Hail Hail Rock 'n' Roll* concert video. Watts appeared frequently with his jazz quintet and cut big-band LP, **The Charlie Watts Orchestra Live** (1986). Wood (whose solo set **1,2,3,4** had been released in 1981) pursued painting career, presenting an exhibition of work in autumn of 1987. Guitarist suffered severe leg injuries in 1990 after car accident.

Never far from the front pages, The Stones caused controversy with anti-Gulf War single, **Highwire**, in March 1991, and signed a 60 million dollar deal with Virgin Records that December. Their first CD for the label, **Voodoo Lounge**, appeared three years later; on it, bassist Darryl Jones replaced Wyman, who had left in 1993 after becoming weary of touring and recording with the band. He and his former colleagues have continued to develop their own projects over the last decade: Richards has worked extensively with his **X-Pensive Winos** combo, issuing a solo album, **Main Offender**, in 1992; Watts' jazz activities have taken up increasing amounts of his time and energy; while Jagger's **Wandering Spirit** CD appeared in 1993. However, The Stones show no sign of

calling it a day just yet: their tours can still sell out stadiums, and recent records, including the **Stripped** set (1995) and their latest studio offering, **Bridges To Babylon** (1997), have been well received by fans and critics.

Recommended listening

Rolling Stones albums:
The Rolling Stones (London), 1964
Rolling Stones No. 2 (London), 1965
Out Of Our Heads (London), 1965
Aftermath (London), 1966
Big Hits (High Tide & Green Grass) (compilation) (London), 1966
Got Live If You Want It (London), 1967
Between The Buttons (London), 1967
Flowers (London), 1967
Their Satanic Majesties Request (London), 1967
Beggars Banquet (London), 1968
Let It Bleed (London), 1969
Get Yer Ya Ya's Out! (live) (London), 1970
Sticky Fingers (Rolling Stones), 1971
Exile On Main Street (Rolling Stones), 1972
Goat's Head Soup (Rolling Stones), 1973
It's Only Rock 'n' Roll (Rolling Stones), 1974
Made In The Shade (compilation) (Rolling Stones), 1975
Black and Blue (Rolling Stones), 1976
Some Girls (Rolling Stones), 1978
Emotional Rescue (Rolling Stones), 1980
Tattoo You (Rolling Stones), 1981
Still Life (Rolling Stones), 1982
Undercover (Rolling Stones), 1983
Dirty Work (Columbia), 1986
Steel Wheels (Columbia), 1989
Flashpoint (live) (Columbia), 1991
Voodoo Lounge (Virgin), 1994
Stripped (Virgin), 1995
Bridges To Babylon (Virgin), 1997
No Security (live) (Virgin), 1998
Mick Jagger solo:
She's The Boss (WEA), 1985
Primitive Cool (WEA), 1987
Wandering Spirit (WEA), 1993
Goddess In The Doorway (Virgin), 2001
Keith Richards solo:
Talk Is Cheap (Virgin), 1988
Main Offender (Virgin), 1992

TODD RUNDGREN

US vocalist, composer, guitarist, producer
Born Upper Darby, Pennsylvania, June 22, 1948

Career: Greatly influenced by "British Invasion" spearheaded by Beatles and Rolling Stones; acquired first electric guitar at 17. First band was Woody's Truck Stop (for less than a year); by 1968 he had left to form The Nazz, legendary Philadelphia group whose three LPs, made between 1968 and 1970, are now regarded as prime collectors' items (they were subsequently re-issued by Rhino Records). However, Todd left Nazz in mid-1969, and was soon developing a formidable reputation as a producer/engineer. Early clients included The Band, Paul Butterfield Blues Band, and Jesse Winchester, and between these sessions, Rundgren was also laying the groundwork for his own solo career.

Had great success during 1972 with LP **Something/Anything?** (which included his classic single **I Saw The Light**, a major US hit, and his only British Top 30 success) plus production of LPs by Sparks (then known as Halfnelson) and Badfinger. 1973 saw release of his second solo album **A Wizard, A True Star**; that year, Rundgren also produced the New York Dolls' eponymously titled first LP (though his approach did not meet with the band's approval!), and had happier studio encounters with Grand Funk Railroad and Fanny. In 1974, after issuing another solo set, **Todd**, he formed Utopia, whose first album appeared a few months later. Until the mid-80s, Rundgren would put out both band and solo records, though the personnel on these discs often overlapped. His musical style was eclectic and unpredictable, though it spawned occasional hits such as 1978's **Can We Still Be Friends?** During this period, however, his biggest commercial success was as a producer – most notably for Meat Loaf on multi-platinum **Bat Out Of Hell** (1977). Among other high-profile clients were Hall and Oates, Tom Robinson, The Tubes, and Patti Smith.

Utopia's **Adventures in Utopia** (1980) proved to be the group's biggest seller, and the early 80s saw Rundgren maintaining a busy schedule of performances and recordings, while also experimenting with new technology, including digital video. After making solo sets **Healing** (1981) and **The Ever Popular Tortured Artist Effect** (1983), and **Swing To The Right** (1982), **Oblivion** (1984), and **P.O.V.** (1985) with Utopia, he split the band, signed a new solo contract with Warner Bros., and issued **A Cappella** (1985). As the name (an Italian musical term used to refer to unaccompanied singing) suggests, this record was created using only vocals, with electronic assistance from multi-track recording and samplers.

That December, Rundgren enjoyed minor UK chart success with **Loving You's A Dirty Job But Somebody's Gotta Do It** (his duet with Welsh rock ballad queen Bonnie Tyler); his next album, **Nearly Human**, appeared in 1989, and was followed by a live set, **Second Wind** (1991). His continuing fascination with cutting-edge media was reflected in 1993's **No World Order**, an interactive audio-visual project; its follow-up, fittingly titled **The Individualist**, was released in CD-plus format two years later. However, Rundgren has not entirely abandoned more conventional musical activities: he has made fairly frequent concert appearances with Ringo Starr's "All-Starr Band" (he first toured with them in 1992, and was also part of the 1999 and 2001 line-ups); and has also taken part in a recent international Beatles tribute tour with The Who's bassist John Entwistle, Ann Wilson (ex-Heart) and Alan Parsons.

Recommended listening
With The Nazz:
Nazz (Screen Gems), 1968
Nazz Nazz (Screens Gems), 1969
Nazz III (Screen Gems), 1970
Solo and with Utopia:
Runt (Ampex), 1970
The Ballad of Todd Rundgren (Bearsville), 1971
Something/Anything (Bearsville), 1972
A Wizard, A True Star (Bearsville), 1973
Todd (Bearsville), 1973

Todd Rundgren's Utopia (Bearsville), 1974
Initiation (Bearsville), 1975
Another Life (Bearsville), 1975
Faithful (Bearsville), 1976
Ra (Bearsville), 1977
Oops! Wrong Planet (Bearsville), 1977
Hermit Of Mink Hollow (Bearsville), 1978
Back To The Bars (Bearsville), 1978
Adventures In Utopia (Bearsville), 1980
Deface The Music (Bearsville), 1980
Healing (Bearsville), 1981
Swing To The Right (Bearsville), 1982
Utopia (Bearsville), 1982
The Ever Popular Tortured Artist Effect (Bearsville), 1983
Oblivion (WEA), 1983
A Cappella (WEA), 1985
Nearly Human (WEA), 1989
Second Wind (live) (WEA), 1991
No World Order (Food For Thought), 1993
The Individualist (TR-i), 1995

CARLOS SANTANA

US guitarist, bandleader, composer
Born Autlán de Navarro, Mexico, July 20, 1947

Career: After immigrating to California from Tijuana as a child, Santana emerged as major local rock musician during San Francisco's 1960s Haight-Ashbury flower-power era; guested on seminal **The Live Adventures Of Mike Bloomfield And Al Kooper** album (1969), then put together own band. Brought Latin flavour to rock through use of conga player Mike Carrabello and award-winning Central American percussionist José "Chepito" Areas alongside Gregg Rolie (keyboards, vocals), David Brown (bass), and Mike Shrieve (drums).

Reputation was already made before 1969 debut album **Santana**, which sold a million copies in US alone. Band's appearance in *Woodstock* concert that year, performing **Soul Sacrifice**, was one of the great moments of rock.

Oye Como Va, penned by Latin-music great Tito Puente, helped second album **Abraxas** (1970) to equally big sales. **Santana III** (1971) brought

LEFT: *Carlos Santana, seen here with his Paul Reed Smith electric guitar.*

The Healer, which appeared in 1989.

For **Spirits Dancing In The Flesh** (1990), the Santana line-up comprised Thompson, Peraza, bassist Benny Rietveld, Scottish vocalist Alec Ligertwood, and drummer Walfredo Reyes Jr. Neither this set, nor its follow-ups **Milagro** (1992) and **Brothers** (1994), sold especially well; but the veteran musician's fortunes were transformed by **Supernatural** (1999) – an extraordinary commercial and artistic triumph on which Carlos and his band were joined by a succession of major names, including Eric Clapton, Wyclef Jean, and Lauren Hill. The album has sold over 20 million copies to date, and spawned two major singles: **Smooth** and **Maria Maria**.

Recommended listening

Santana (Columbia), 1969
Abraxas (Columbia), 1970
Santana III (Columbia), 1972
Caravanserai (Columbia), 1972
Welcome (Columbia), 1973
Lotus (Columbia), 1974
Greatest Hits (Columbia), 1974
Borboletta (Columbia), 1974
Amigos (Columbia), 1976
Moonflower (Columbia), 1977
Inner Secrets (Columbia), 1978
Marathon (Columbia), 1979
Oneness (Columbia), 1979
Swing Of Delight (Columbia), 1980
Zebop! (Columbia), 1981
Shango (Columbia), 1982
Havana Moon (Columbia), 1983
Beyond Appearances (Columbia), 1985
Freedom (Columbia), 1987
Blues For Salvador (Columbia), 1987
Viva Santana! (Columbia), 1988
Spirits Dancing In The Flesh
(Columbia), 1990
Milagro (Polygram), 1992
Sacred Fire (Polygram), 1993
Brothers (Guts and Grace/Island), 1994
Supernatural (Arista), 1999
With John McLaughlin:
Love, Devotion, Surrender (Columbia),
1973
With Alice Coltrane:
Illuminations (Columbia), 1974

Santana's guitarist protégé Neil Schon and percussionist Coke Escovedo into band. Live album featuring jams with Buddy Miles, released the following year, was less satisfying. Its appearance coincided with disbanding of original Santana group in wake of Santana's espousal of teachings of guru Sri Chinmoy at instigation of jazz-rock guitarist John McLaughlin; Santana adopted name Devadip.

Latin/jazz/rock fusion **Caravanserai** LP (1972) used Rolie and Schon, along with studio musicians; but they were not included in new band in 1973. This placed Santana originals Areas and Shrieve alongside Tom Coster, keyboard, James Mingo Lewis and Armando Peraza, percussion, and Doug Rauch, bass. Besides own band's work, Santana recorded 1973 **Love, Devotion, Surrender** album in partnership with John McLaughlin, and **Illuminations** (1974) with Alice Coltrane.

Various line-up changes saw Santana return from heady experimentation to simpler roots, which put albums back among best sellers. However, in 1977 Carlos ditched existing band, except Coster; Schon and Rolie went on to form Journey. Guitarist then signed management deal with former Woodstock and Fillmore promoter Bill Graham. Maintained prodigious output, which, by 1982, had resulted in 14 LPs in 15 years.

Carlos Santana enjoyed single success with **Winning** (1981) and **Hold On** (1982), and also embarked on further collaborative work – **Havana Moon** (1983) included contribution from country singer-songwriter Willie Nelson.

After 20th anniversary concert in San Francisco in 1986, Santana's **Freedom** album (1987) and subsequent tour featured Buddy Miles (on vocals) as well as Rolie, Coster, bassist Alfonso Johnson, and percussionists Graham Lear, Armando Peraza, Orestes Vilato, and Raul Rekow. The same year saw the release of a Grammy-winning solo set **Blues For Salvador**. Several of Carlos's 1988 live shows included jazz sax star Wayne Shorter, and the guitarist subsequently guested on John Lee Hooker's classic album

MICHAEL SCHENKER GROUP

European group formed 1980

Original line-up: Michael Schenker, guitar; Gary Barden, vocals; Simon Phillips, drums; Mo Foster, bass; Don Airey, keyboards.

Career: Schenker (born Saustedt, West Germany, January 10, 1955) joined brother's band, Scorpions (qv), who opened for British rockers UFO on one of their early German tours in 1973. UFO were impressed enough to ask Schenker to join them. He stayed from 1974 to 1979, then reunited briefly with the Scorpions before attempting to launch a band of his own. Rehearsals began with Gary Barden and Denny Carmassi on drums, as well as Billy Sheehan on bass – but project fell apart after Schenker was hospitalized. However, within a year, had formed Michael Schenker Group (often abbreviated to MSG) with original line-up shown above; their self-titled debut album, produced by Roger Glover of Deep Purple, appeared in 1980.

Although strong, line-up was never meant to be permanent, and Schenker recruited touring unit of Barden, Chris Glen on bass, drummer Cozy Powell, and his own replacement in UFO, Paul Raymond.

In 1981, this grouping produced unsuccessful **MSG** LP, and there were more personnel changes – although old line-up was featured on live double-LP, **One Night At Budokan** (also 1981). Raymond left for full-time duties with UFO, and Graham Bonnet stepped in for vocalist Barden, featuring on MSG's **Assault Attack** album (1982). However, Bonnet's vocals on the disc failed to live up to his live efforts, and Barden returned as lead singer, while Ted McKenna replaced Cozy Powell. Further dissension led to break-up of group in 1984, a year after the release of their **Built To Destroy** LP.

Michael Schenker forged a new working relationship with Irish singer/songwriter Robin McAuley. The new McAuley Schenker Group, featuring

German drummer Bodo Schopf, bassist Rocky Newton, and second guitarist Mitch Perry, made their debut at the European Monsters Of Rock Festival in 1987 and released their album **Perfect Timing** that October. Schenker was happy to reduce his "guitar hero" role to allow room for McAuley to develop as writer and performer.

Following disappointing 1989 set **Save Yourself** for Capitol Records, Schenker guested with pick-up outfit Contraband, before recording **M.S.G.** (1992) and **"Unplugged" Live** (1993), the last two MSG sets to feature McAuley. Schenker's other 90s albums included **Written In The Sand** (1996), **Story Live** (1997), and 1999's **Thank You With Orchestra**, which showcases his acoustic guitar playing. He also appears on UFO's **Walk On Water** (1997) and **Covenant** (2000) CDs, and his most recent MSG disc is **Be Aware Of Scorpions** (2001).

ABOVE: *Michael Schenker onstage.*

Recommended listening
The Michael Schenker Group (Chrysalis), 1980
MSG (Chrysalis), 1981
One Night At Budokan (Chrysalis), 1981
Dancer (Chrysalis), 1982
Assault Attack (Chrysalis), 1983
Built To Destroy (Chrysalis), 1983
Portfolio (Chrysalis), 1987
Perfect Timing (Capitol), 1987
Rock Will Never Die (Chrysalis), 1988
Save Yourself (Capitol), 1989
M.S.G. (EMI), 1992
Unplugged Live (EMI), 1993
Written In The Sand (Positive Energy), 1996
Story Live (Positive Energy), 1997
Thank You With Orchestra (Positive Energy), 1998
Into The Arena 1972–95 (2 CD compilation) (Raven), 2000
Be Aware Of Scorpions (SPV), 2001

SCORPIONS

German group formed 1970

Original line-up: Michael Schenker, guitar; Rudolph Schenker, guitar; Klaus Meine, vocals; Lothar Heimbeer, bass; Wolfgang Dziony, drums.

Career: Long-established German heavy-metal crew who have survived major changes in personnel to remain in front-line of head-banging fraternity.

Schenker brothers united in 1970 after stints in low-key groups, and cut **Lonesome Crow** album two years later. Michael left band to join UFO (replacement Uli Jon Roth) before second album **Fly To The Rainbow** for RCA (1974), which also saw Jürgen Rosenthal on drums and new bassist Francis Buchholz. Rosenthal's stint was brief, and the drum chair was occupied, in turn, by Rudy Lenners and Herman Rarebell.

After period of inactivity, but with German and Japanese markets clamoring for more product, settled line-up (Rudy Schenker, Meine, Buchholz, Matthias Jabs on guitar and Rarebell) embarked on sustained period of success, commencing with **Lovedrive** (1979), which featured guest guitarist Michael Schenker, then **Animal Magnetism** (1980), **Blackout** (US Top 10 in 1982), and 1984's **Love At First Sting**.

Persistent gigging (including Russian tour in 1988 and appearance at Roger Waters' 1990 live presentation of *The Wall* in Berlin) maintained Scorpions' profile, and their **Crazy World** album, released in 1990, eventually became a multi-million seller. **Face The Heat** (1993) also sold well, and the band's next studio album was **Pure Instinct**, issued in 1996. **Eye II Eye** followed in 1999, and the band's most recent CD (also featuring the Berlin Philharmonic Orchestra!) is **Moment of Glory** (2000).

Recommended listening

Lonesome Crow (Brain), 1972
Fly To The Rainbow (RCA), 1974
In Trance (RCA), 1976
Virgin Killer (RCA), 1977
Taken By Force (RCA), 1978
Lovedrive (Mercury), 1979
Best Of (RCA), 1979
Tokyo Tapes (RCA), 1979
Animal Magnetism (Mercury), 1980
Rock Galaxy (RCA), 1980
Love At First Sting (Mercury/Fame), 1984
World Wide Live (Mercury), 1985
Crazy World (Mercury), 1990
Face The Heat (Mercury), 1993
Pure Instinct (WEA), 1996
Eye II Eye (Koch), 1999
Moment Of Glory (EMI), 2000

THE SEX PISTOLS

UK group formed 1975

Original line-up: Steve Jones, guitar, vocals; Glen Matlock, bass; Paul Cook, drums; Johnny Rotten (John Lydon), vocals.

Career: Budding musicians Jones, Cook, and Matlock used to hang around Sex, the London clothes store that Malcolm McLaren ran with designer Vivienne Westwood. There, they met John Lydon, who was invited to become their vocalist after an impromptu audition in the shop. McLaren became the quartet's manager: he and Westwood molded their anarchic image, renamed Lydon "Rotten," and coined moniker Sex Pistols.

Pistols were promoted as angry young men, radically opposed to "established" rock (especially the pretentious excesses of hippie/progressive bands), and with a "two-fingers" attitude to society. Their first gig took place in London in November 1975; subsequent concerts were musically crude but full of explosive energy – not only enhancing band's reputation for being "anti" everything, but frequently provoking audience violence.

In October 1976 (after a ferocious bidding war), McLaren secured a recording contract for the Pistols with EMI, who released their **Anarchy In The UK** single on November 26. A few days later, the Pistols were provoked into swearing on live Thames TV program; resultant uproar brought the group blanket front page national newspaper coverage, and heralded the start of the "punk" revolution.

EMI hurriedly dropped band, having already paid them £40,000. A&M stepped in to sign them, but withdrew from the contract (after handing over £75,000) shortly afterwards. By time Virgin offered £50,000 advance in May 1977, Pistols had collected over £150,000 for their **Anarchy** single (which was only a minor hit in the UK charts).

In early 1977, Matlock was replaced as bassist by Rotten's friend Sid Vicious (Simon Beverley). Sid could barely play, and most of the bass parts on subsequent Pistols recordings (including their classic 1977 album **Never Mind The Bollocks**...) were either the work of Matlock or Steve Jones. LP spawned major hits **God Save The Queen** (especially controversial in the year of Queen's Silver Jubilee), **Pretty Vacant**, and **Holidays In The Sun** (all 1977). However, UK gigging became practically impossible, as Pistols' notoriety earned them bans from many venues, and after a chaotic American tour in January 1978, Rotten announced their break-up. Other three carried on temporarily, even using infamous Great Train Robber, Ronald Biggs, for vocal or two. However, in October 1978, Vicious was arrested in New York for murder of girlfriend, Nancy Spungen. He died in overdose incident in February 1979 while awaiting trial.

Lydon, the highest profile surviving Sex Pistol, has enjoyed considerable success with his band Public Image Ltd. (PiL). The careers of Cook, Jones, and Matlock have been more erratic, though they all continue to perform and record.

Recommended listening

Never Mind The Bollocks, Here's The Sex Pistols (Warner Bros./Virgin), 1977*
The Great Rock 'n' Roll Swindle (Virgin), 1979
Some Product: (Carri On Sex Pistols) (Virgin), 1979
Flogging A Dead Horse (Virgin), 1980
Live At Chelmsford Top Security Prison (Restless), 1990
Archive (Rialto), 1997

*Only "official" LP released while band was working as a unit

THE SHADOWS

UK group formed 1959

Original line-up: Hank Marvin, Fender Stratocaster guitar; Bruce Welch, Fender Telecaster guitar; Jet Harris, bass; Tony Meehan, drums.

Career: In 1958 Marvin and Welch were members of Cliff Richard's backing group The Drifters. By following year personnel had stabilized as above, and group had changed name to Shadows to avoid confusion with American Drifters.

Although band continued to back Richard, they started to record independently from 1959. During a 1960 British tour, Jerry Lordan, artist appearing on same bill, gave them instrumental piece he had written called **Apache**. Their version of the number reached No. 1 in July 1960, and set pattern for string of instrumental successes that continued until the late 60s – including **Kon-Tiki** (1961), **Wonderful Land** (1962), and **Foot Tapper** (1963). Formula for success was simple yet effective: Marvin's guitar would carry melody, while other members provided clipped, efficient backing.

During Shadows' major hit-making years, several personnel changes took place. Tony Meehan left in 1961 to be replaced by Brian Bennett. Jet Harris quit in 1962 and almost immediately joined up with Meehan again – duo produced three Top 10 singles in 1963 before Harris retired from scene due to ill health. For short while Harris was replaced in Shadows by Brian "Liquorice" Locking; he was succeeded by John Rostill.

After 1968, when singles success began to dry up, members got involved in other musical activities: Hank Marvin, Bruce Welch and John Farrar subsequently formed successful trio; Welch wrote for and produced Cliff Richard; Farrar produced Olivia Newton-John; and Brian Bennett became in-demand session musician. However, The Shadows continued to record and work together sporadically, with various bass players – even representing Britain in the 1975 Eurovision Song Contest (humiliatingly, they came second to a little-known Dutch group).

In 1977, **20 Golden Greats** compilation album topped UK charts, and in early 1979, the group enjoyed a Top 10 single with version of **Don't Cry For Me Argentina** from Andrew Lloyd Webber's musical *Evita*. Its follow-up, a cover of Stanley Myers' **Cavatina** (the instrumental theme from the 1978 movie *The Deer Hunter*, originally made famous by classical guitarist John Williams) was also a British hit. Later singles graced the lower reaches of the charts, and both The Shadows and Hank Marvin himself continued to make highly successful (though increasingly bland) new albums throughout the 80s and 90s, while re-issues of their earlier work have been perennial bestsellers.

Although their style of music has not had much direct impact on the course of British pop – few guitarists actually play *like* Hank Marvin – Shadows encouraged generation of young men to take up instruments and make music for themselves. Marvin's importance has been acknowledged by many of today's leading rock stars, some of whom (including Mark Knopfler, Andy Summers, and even Tony Iommi of Black Sabbath) came together in 1996 on the album **Twang! – A Tribute To**

LEFT: *Hank Marvin – a Fender Stratocaster user since the 1960s.*

Hank Marvin and the Shadows, which included their versions of some of the group's classics.

Recommended listening

> The Shadows (EMI), 1961
> Dance With The Shadows (EMI), 1963
> The Sound of The Shadows (EMI), 1965
> Twenty Golden Greats (EMI), 1977
> String of Hits (EMI), 1979
> Change of Address (Polydor), 1980
> XXV (Polydor), 1983
> Moonlight Shadows (Polydor), 1986
> The Shadows Collection (Pickwick), 1989
> Themes and Dreams (Polydor), 1991
> The First 20 Years At The Top (3 CDs) (EMI), 1995
> The Hit Sound of The Shadows (Connoisseur), 2001

PAUL SIMON

US composer, vocalist, guitarist
Born Newark, New Jersey,
October 13, 1941

Career: Simon and singer Art Garfunkel met while fellow high school students in New York, singing together in the Peptones before enjoying a US hit single, **Hey Schoolgirl** (composed by Simon) as "Tom and Jerry" (Garfunkel was "Tom Graph," Simon "Jerry Landis") in 1957–58. After failing to capitalize on this success, the pair pursued separate projects (though they continued to collaborate occasionally), and Simon used a variety of pseudonyms, including Jerry Landis, Paul Kane, and True Taylor, as he struggled to make it as a songwriter and solo performer while attending college and law school.

In the early 1960s, Simon, previously a fairly mainstream pop performer, was influenced by the folk music boom then sweeping America and Europe. In 1964, he traveled to London, playing to small but enthusiastic audiences, and absorbing new styles and songs. Back home in New York, he and Garfunkel recorded their first album as Simon and Garfunkel, **Wednesday Morning 3 A.M.** (1964), a folky set that initially sold poorly. Simon

returned to Britain as a soloist the following year; during his stay he cut **The Paul Simon Songbook** LP in London, and learned the traditional *Scarborough Fair* from English folk singer/guitarist Martin Carthy. Meanwhile, back in New York, producer Tom Wilson had added an electric backing to Simon and Garfunkel's **The Sound of Silence** (track from **Wednesday Morning**); on its release as a single in late 1965, the re-arranged song became a US hit, establishing Simon and Garfunkel as major stars.

They had a string of subsequent successes: their second album, **Sounds of Silence**, appeared in 1966, and was followed later the same year by **Parsley, Sage, Rosemary and Thyme**. Its title comes from the lyrics of **Scarborough Fair**, featured on the album and also, together with **Sound of Silence**, **Mrs. Robinson**, and other classics, on the duo's soundtrack to the Oscar-winning movie *The Graduate* (1967).

S&G's **Bookends** LP was released in 1968, and their final album together, **Bridge Over Troubled Water**, in 1970. No longer close friends, they have seldom performed together since; and Simon's subsequent work as a soloist has displayed increasing eclecticism and complexity. 1972 album **Paul Simon** not only provided US/UK hit single, **Mother And Child Reunion**, but reached No. 1 in UK album charts. Dixie Hummingbirds gospel group and top session musicians featured on follow-up **There Goes Rhymin' Simon** (1973), which spawned further hits; subsequent tour provided material for **Live Rhymin'**, released in 1974.

In 1975, **Still Crazy After All These Years** blended musical changes with starkly precise personal songs. Containing US No. 1 single **50 Ways To Leave Your Lover**, album won two Grammys (Best Album and Best Male Pop Vocal Performance).

In 1980, following acting debut in *Annie Hall*, Simon produced, starred in and provided music for disappointing **One-Trick Pony**. Next solo album was **Hearts And Bones** (1983), originally planned as a Simon and Garfunkel reunion.

Simon's musical interests were now expanding to include South African music, and – after lengthy sessions in America

and Johannesburg – his classic **Graceland** album, with its distinctive contributions from vocal group Ladysmith Black Mambazo, appeared in 1986. It included the hit single **You Can Call Me Al**, earned a Grammy award, and prompted similar examination of indigenous music in South American-inspired **The Rhythm Of The Saints** (1990).

Early 90s saw Simon active as live performer and producer, and working on musical *The Capeman*; album of songs from the show was released in 1997, the year before it opened (to poor reviews) on Broadway. However, Simon's most recent studio album, **You're The One** (2000) enjoyed a warmer critical reception and excellent sales.

Recommended listening

> **Simon & Garfunkel:**
> Wednesday Morning 3 AM (Columbia), 1964
> Sounds Of Silence (Columbia), 1966
> Parsley, Sage Rosemary and Thyme (Columbia), 1966
> Bookends (Columbia), 1968
> *The Graduate* (soundtrack) (Columbia), 1968
> Bridge Over Troubled Water (Columbia) 1970
> **Solo:**
> The Paul Simon Songbook (Columbia), 1965
> Paul Simon (Columbia), 1972
> There Goes Rhymin' Simon (Columbia), 1973
> Live Rhymin' (Columbia), 1974
> Still Crazy After All These Years (Columbia), 1975
> Greatest Hits, Etc. (Columbia), 1977
> One Trick Pony (soundtrack) (Warner Bros.), 1980
> Hearts and Bones (Warner Bros.), 1983
> Graceland (Warner Bros.), 1986
> Negotiations And Lovesongs (1971–86) (Warner Bros.), 1988
> The Rhythm Of The Saints (Warner Bros.), 1990
> Paul Simon's Concert In The Park (Warner Bros.), 1991
> 1964-93 (3 CD compilation) (Warner Bros.), 1993
> Songs From The Capeman (Warner Bros.), 1997
> You're The One (Warner Bros.), 2000

MARTIN TAYLOR

UK guitarist
Born 1956, Harlow, Essex

Career: The son of British Trad and Dixieland jazz bassist Buck Taylor, Martin took up the guitar at the age of four. He had already been inspired by listening to records of the great gypsy jazz guitarist Django Reinhardt (1910–53), and was soon performing in public with local bands. Turning professional at the age of ˜16, Taylor took a job as a member of the orchestra on the liner *Queen Elizabeth II*, playing guitar on the voyage from England to New York, and then spending six months entertaining passengers on Caribbean cruises.

On his return to London, Taylor cut his first solo album, **Taylor Made** (1978), and also performed and recorded in a duo with veteran player Ike Isaacs (1918–95), his partner on the LP **After Hours** (1979). Issacs had previously worked regularly with jazz violinist (and former colleague of Django Reinhardt in the Quintet of the Hot Club of France) Stéphane Grappelli, and in 1979 Taylor was invited to become the guitarist in Grappelli's touring band. He stayed with Grappelli until 1990, making over 20 albums with him, and playing many of the numbers made famous by Reinhardt. Between these engagements, Taylor was also working as a soloist, and alongside distinguished jazz artists such as clarinetist Buddy DeFranco (**Groovin'**, 1984; **Garden of Dreams**, 1987) and composer/saxophonist John Dankworth. Taylor's album **Sarabanda**, recorded in Los Angeles and released in 1987, further boosted his reputation, as did his stint with Charlie Byrd and Barney Kessel as a stand-in member (replacing Herb Ellis) of the "Great Guitars" trio during the early 1990s.

Taylor's 1993 set **Artistry**, produced by rock guitarist Steve Howe of Yes, brought him substantial commercial success, topping the UK jazz charts for almost two months. The following year he formed his *Spirit of Django* ensemble, whose eponymous 1994 debut album was another UK bestseller. During this period, Taylor was also collaborating with virtuoso US mandolinist David Grisman (**Tone Poems II**, 1995) and top country player Chet Atkins (**Portraits**, 1996).

Taylor is now recognized as one of the world's leading guitarists, and recently became the first British jazz player in 30 years to sign a solo contract with US label Columbia/Sony. His first

ABOVE: *Top UK jazz player Martin Taylor with a Vanden semi-acoustic.*

release for the company was 1999's **Kiss And Tell** (also the title of his recently published autobiography), followed in 2001 by **Nitelife**.

TEN YEARS AFTER

UK group formed 1967

Original line-up: Alvin Lee, Gibson ES-335 guitar, vocals; Chick Churchill, keyboards; Leo Lyons, bass; Ric Lee, drums.

Career: One of major bands to emerge from mid-60s blues revival movement in UK. Formed by Alvin Lee and Lyons who met in English city of Nottingham and worked together in Hamburg, Germany, for a time. On returning to Britain, they met Ric Lee (no relation) and formed Jaybirds. Adding Chick Churchill, changed name and came to critics' attention via appearances at London's Marquee Club. Group signed to Decca's Deram subsidiary, which put out first album, **Ten Years After**, in 1967.

Famed American promoter Bill Graham heard LP and booked group for his Fillmore Auditorium venues in US. Subsequent albums **Undead** (1968) and **Stonedhenge** (1969), plus appearance at massive 1969 Woodstock rock festival (and in the *Woodstock* movie, which showcased their 11-minute opus **I'm Going Home**) established world reputation for fast and furious blend of blues and heavy rock. Same year saw release of **Ssssh** LP; its follow-up, **Cricklewood Green** (1970) contained the band's only UK hit single, **Love Like A Man**.

Band went on to record **Watt** album (also 1970) before issuing the more reflective **A Space In Time** (1971), which featured electronic effects. But by 1973,

Lee was disillusioned with group's direction and exhaustive tour schedule (a record 28 US tours before they broke up), and describing band as "a traveling jukebox."

Members took time off for solo projects and Alvin Lee retired to 15th-century country home to build studio and record with gospel singer Mylon Lefevre. Churchill's solo album **You And Me** appeared in 1973. **Recorded Live** set (same year) was live album compiled from Ten Years After concerts in Amsterdam, Rotterdam, Frankfurt, and Paris.

1974 saw the band record their swansong album, **Positive Vibrations**, and make a sell-out concert appearance at London's Rainbow Theatre. It proved to be their last British gig; that Fall, Lee set off to tour world as Alvin Lee And Co., and the following May, he declared Ten Years After defunct. However, just one month later Ten Years After were back on road for US tour to fulfil contractual obligations before final split.

All four musicians have remained active in various branches of the music business, and Ten Years After have played reunion gigs (and occasionally recorded together) in recent years.

RICHARD THOMPSON

UK composer, guitarist, singer
Born London, April 3, 1949

Career: After establishing his reputation as a member of Fairport Convention (qv), Thompson left the band in 1971. While appearing on one-off projects with other Fairport alumni, such as **The Bunch** and **Morris On** (both 1972), he pursued a solo career, and released a series of

influential but poor-selling LPs, showcasing his compelling, often bleak songs, and inspired acoustic and electric guitar work: **Henry The Human Fly** (1972), **I Want To See The Bright Lights Tonight** and **Hokey Pokey** (1974), and **Pour Down Like Silver** (1975). These all featured his partner (later his wife) Linda on vocals; the couple's conversion to Islam in the mid-70s led to a prolonged absence from the studios, and was followed by the overtly religious **First Light** (1978) on which Richard first used synth guitar, and **Sunnyvista** (1979). Two years later, Richard issued his virtuoso instrumental album **Strict Tempo!** (featuring mainly folk and jazz tunes), and 1982 saw the appearance of what was to be the final Richard and Linda Thompson LP, **Shoot Out The Lights**. The pair split acrimoniously later that year.

After re-marriage to an American, Thompson divided his time between the USA and Britain. He found somewhat greater (though still limited) commercial success for his 80s and 90s albums, especially after his late 80s record deal with Capitol, pairing him with producer Mitchell Froom (husband of singer-songwriter Suzanne Vega), who has also worked with Elvis Costello, Bonnie Raitt, and other major names. 1990s CDs such as **Rumor and Sigh** (1991) and **you? me? us?** (1996) proved that Thompson had lost none of his genius for combining rock and folk influences, and on the tour to promote his 1999 album, **Mock Tudor**, he was joined on stage by his and Linda's son Teddy, himself a talented singer-songwriter-guitarist.

U2

UK group formed 1979

Original line-up: Bono "Vox" Hewson, vocals; Dave "The Edge" Evans, guitar, keyboards; Adam Clayton, bass; Larry Mullen, drums.

Career: Inspired by London's new, young bands in 1976, Bono and The Edge decided to form own group in Dublin. Friends Clayton and Mullen joined, and name U2 was chosen, with implication that every fan could join in the music as well.

Bono described band as beginning with three chords, but with special enthusiasm. Pub gigs led to local record contract with CBS. Two singles, released in Ireland only, led to cult following in Britain. Island Records became interested and signed band, releasing **11 O'Clock Tick Tock** single in 1980. UK critics now began falling over themselves to cite U2 as the next big thing; when **Boy** LP was released in late 1980, U2 were hailed as *the* hope for rock's future. Band ignored press and pushed on, establishing close rapport with audiences.

1981 single **Gloria** received heavy airplay and made UK Top 50. When **October** LP was released (same year), journalistic backlash set in, with critics carping that U2 were really just another 1960s-style band because of basic guitar, bass, and drum sound. Group continued to disregard what was written about them, and their following continued to grow.

1982 tour introduced music from forthcoming **War** album, which subsequently entered UK listings at No. 1, and established band's credentials in US. First major British single success, **New Years Day,** made UK Top 10 in early 1983. Live **Under a Blood Red Sky** set (same year) was followed in 1984 by **The Unforgettable Fire**; and the band's involvement with Band Aid single **Do They Know It's Christmas?** (1984) and the following year's *Live Aid* concert further boosted their appeal.

In 1987, U2 undertook an extensive international tour to promote **The Joshua Tree** (issued that year), and even

appeared on the cover of *Time* magazine. A book about the band, *Unforgettable Fire,* written by former professional soccer player Eamon Dunphy, was also a bestseller, and U2's major league status was confirmed when they won Grammys in 1988 for Best Album and Best Group, and were also honored at BRIT awards as Best International Group. During same year, Bono and The Edge featured on Roy Orbison's final album, **Mystery Girl**.

Double set **Rattle And Hum** (1988), produced by Jimmy Iovine, and mixing live and studio recordings, topped both US and UK charts, achieving multi-platinum status. Its accompanying movie, directed by Philip Joanou, was also critically and commercially acclaimed. The LP spawned hit singles **Desire**, **Angel Of Harlem**, and funky **When Love Comes To Town** (with B.B. King).

Group toured Australia in 1989, and also featured in televised New Year's Eve concert in Dublin. Further Grammy and BRIT awards preceded arrest of Clayton for drug possession, although he avoided conviction after making charitable donation to the Woman's Aid Group of Ireland.

In the absence of any new material, U2 members took time out in 1990 for solo activities, reuniting to contribute to Cole Porter anthology **Red Hot + Blue** and associated video to benefit international AIDS charity.

Returning to the production team of Daniel Lanois and Brian Eno, who had worked with band on **The Unforgettable Fire** and **The Joshua Tree**, U2 completed **Achtung Baby** album for late 1991 release. Lanois described the record as "rougher and harder than anything they've done before." Early in 1992, the band launched their *Zoo TV* tour, fitting in sessions for a new CD, **Zooropa**, during gaps in their performing schedule. No further "official" U2 albums were to appear until **Pop** (1997), although The Passengers' **Original Soundtracks I** (1995) involved all four group members, plus Brian Eno and various star guests, including operatic tenor Luciano Pavarotti. 2000 saw the issue of U2's latest CD, **All That You Can't Leave Behind**, and the following year they embarked on their *Elevation 2001*

tour – a three-leg, eight-month extravaganza, including gigs throughout America and Europe.

Recommended listening
Boy (Island), 1980
October (Island), 1981
Under A Blood Red Sky (Island), 1983
The Unforgettable Fire (Island), 1984
The Joshua Tree (Island), 1987
Zooropa (Island), 1993
Best of U2 1980–90 (Island), 1998

STEVIE RAY VAUGHAN

US guitarist, singer, composer
Born October 3, 1954, Dallas, Texas
Died August 27, 1990, East Troy, Wisconsin

Career: Although he spent much of his childhood in Dallas, Stevie Ray Vaughan (like his older brother Jimmie, another distinguished blues guitarist) had his musical roots in Austin, some 200 miles to the southwest. He moved to the city as a teenager, and played in numerous local bands before forming the first incarnation of his own group, Double Trouble, there in 1980.

Already well-known in the Austin area, Double Trouble were talent-spotted in 1981 by veteran record producer Jerry Wexler (famous for his work with Ray Charles, Aretha Franklin, and other soul and blues greats). Wexler was instrumental in getting the band onto the bill of the major international Festival of Jazz and Blues at Montreux, Switzerland, the following year. Double Trouble's appearance there led to a recording contract with Epic – and also to an invitation from David Bowie, who had been in the audience, for Stevie Ray Vaughan to contribute to his forthcoming LP **Let's Dance**.

1983 saw the release first of Bowie's record, and then of Double Trouble's debut, **Texas Flood**. Both were massively successful, and the band toured tirelessly to capitalize on their sudden breakthrough, finding time between gigs to record a follow-up album, **Couldn't Stand The Weather**, which appeared in mid-1984. However, the pressure of such widespread acclaim was to prove almost too much for Stevie Ray Vaughan. Suffering from drink- and drug-related problems, he was forced to take a break from performing in 1986, after an arduous period in which he and his group had completed both a new studio LP (**Soul to Soul**, 1985) and a double album of concert recordings, **Live Alive** (1986).

Following his return from rehab (he

BELOW: Stevie Ray Vaughan.

remained drug-free and sober for the rest of his life), Vaughan resumed his daunting work schedule, duetting with surf guitarist Dick Dale (qv) in the movie *Back To The Beach* (1987), playing live shows throughout the USA, and working on Double Trouble's new album **In Step**, which appeared in 1989. It was awarded a Grammy early the following year, and Vaughan and the band, now major stars, toured almost constantly that Summer. The guitarist met his death in a helicopter

crash shortly after completing a show in East Troy, Wisconsin, on August 27, 1990. His last completed album – a joint effort with his brother Jimmie, **Family Style** – was issued two months later.

Recommended listening
Texas Flood (Epic), 1983
Couldn't Stand The Weather (Epic), 1984
Live Alive (Epic), 1986
Greatest Hits (Epic), 1995

STEVE VAI

US guitarist, composer
Born Nassau County, New York, June 6, 1960

Career: Steve Vai is a highly convincing guitar hero, with impeccable hard rock credentials, and a lightning-fast technique. However, the range and subtlety of his playing have always set him apart from more run-of-the-mill heavy metal pyrotechnicians, and his solo albums contain some of the innovative and exciting music making to be heard on the contemporary scene.

A dedicated guitarist since his teens, he studied privately with Joe Satriani (a highly successful player in his own right, Satriani is just four years Vai's senior; his other pupils include Kirk Hammett of Metallica), then at Berklee School of Music in Boston, Massachusetts. On completing his course there, he became a regular member of Frank Zappa's band, contributing to albums such as **Tinseltown Rebellion** (1981), **The Man From Utopia** (1983), **Them Or Us** (1984 – incorporating Zappa's unforgettable paean to his young, blue-haired sideman, *Stevie's Spanking*), and **Thing-fish** (1985).

In 1984, Vai released his first solo disc, **Flex-Able** (recorded at his LA home); later that year, he replaced Swedish-born axeman Yngwie Malmsteen in heavy rock band **Alcatrazz**, appearing on their 1985 **Disturbing The Peace** LP before joining David Lee Roth for the massively successful **Eat 'Em And Smile** (1986) and its follow-up **Skyscraper** (1988). Next came a short (1989–90) stint with Whitesnake; while touring with the group, and contributing to their 1989 **Slip Of The Tongue** CD, Vai was also developing material for his own new solo album, **Passion & Warfare**. This was released, to wide acclaim, in 1990; and throughout the following decade, Vai continued to work as a soloist and bandleader while guesting on various high-profile rock records (including Alice Cooper's 1991 set **Hey Stoopid**, which also featured Joe Satriani).

Vai's other 90s solo albums, **Sex & Religion** (1993), **Alien Love Secrets** (1995), **Fire Garden** (1996), and **The Ultra Zone** (1999) have all showcased his flamboyant, but distinctively lyrical guitar style (he uses a seven-stringed electric, and makes skilled use of its extended compass). He has also collaborated with jazzman Chick Corea on a 1996 album of numbers from Leonard Bernstein's *West Side Story*, and toured with Satriani, Eric Johnson, and (latterly) John Petrucci in G3, an unusual aggregate in which three featured star players share the bill, performing separately and together. Recent G3 gigs include appearances in Mexico and Asia.

Vai's latest solo releases are the live double CD, **Alive in An Ultra World** (2001) and a comprehensive set of rare/reissued/archive material, **The Secret Jewel Box** (same year).

Recommended listening

Flex-Able (Urantia), 1984
Passion and Warfare (Relativity/Sony), 1990
Sex & Religion (Relativity/Sony), 1993
Alien Love Secrets (Relativity/Sony), 1995
Fire Garden (Epic/Sony), 1996
G3 Live In Concert (Epic), 1997
The Ultra Zone (Epic), 1999

RIGHT: *Steve Vai, seen here with the Ibanez guitar he helped to design, is one of the most innovative players on today's rock scene.*

WHITESNAKE

UK group formed 1978

Original line-up: David Coverdale, vocals; Micky Moody, guitar; Bernie Marsden, guitar; Jon Lord, keyboards; Neil Murray, bass; David Dowle, drums.

Career: Coverdale joined 1973 Deep Purple line-up, staying until 1976. Following year saw release of his solo LP, **Whitesnake**. It sold poorly, but Coverdale had more success with next solo project, **Northwinds** (1977). Once legal problems (which had temporarily prevented him from working in his native UK) were resolved, Coverdale formed a new band, naming it Whitesnake. Their debut album, **Trouble**, appeared in 1978; sound was basic R&B-influenced rock, pioneered decade before by Deep Purple and others.

Love Hunter LP (1979) continued in same style, but that year drummer Dowle was replaced by Ian Paice (ex-Purple). Band's 1980 single, **Fool For Your Loving**, was a Top 20 UK hit, proving band could appeal to mass audience, while **Ready An' Willing** album (1980) sold well enough to encourage issue of double live set, **Live In The Heart Of The City**, later that year. However, Whitesnake's next studio offering, **Come An' Get It** (1981) revealed a fundamental problem: music was loud and energetic, but sounded unchallenging and over-familiar. 1982's **Saints & Sinners** saw revised line-up, and personnel changes continued to affect the band. Most significant of these was departure of Lord upon re-formation of Deep Purple in 1984.

Whitesnake's fortunes received boost with **Slide It In** (1984), and its follow-up, 1987's **Whitesnake** (their first album for EMI) went platinum. Line-up during this period was Coverdale, guitarists Adrian Vandenberg and Viv Campbell, bassist Rudy Sarzo, and drummer Tom Aldridge. With permed locks and erotic posturing, quartet enjoyed extravagant MTV video exposure and hysterical scenes on major US gigs. Group lost Campbell for **Slip Of The Tongue** LP (1989) (he was replaced by Steve Vai); album made both US and UK Top 10, and was followed by a triumphant world tour, including bill-topping appearance at 1980 UK *Monsters Of Rock* festival. Subsequent lack of product and Coverdale's involvement with Jimmy Page in new project saw Whitesnake take a lengthy break. They re-emerged in 1997 with a different line-up and a moderately successful CD, **Restless Heart** – but since then, Coverdale has continued to focus on his solo career.

Recommended listening

Trouble (United Artists), 1978
Love Hunter (United Artists), 1979
Ready An' Willing (Mirage/United Artists), 1980
Live In The Heart Of The City (Mirage/United Artists), 1980
Come An' Get It (Atlantic/Liberty), 1981
Saints & Sinners (Liberty), 1982
Slide It In (Liberty), 1985
Whitesnake (EMI), 1987
Slip Of The Tongue (Geffen/EMI), 1989
Greatest Hits (Geffen), 1994
Restless Heart (EMI), 1997

THE WHO

UK group formed 1964

Original line-up: Pete Townshend, guitar, vocals; Roger Daltrey, vocals; John Entwistle, bass, vocals; Keith Moon, drums.

Career: In 1962, while still at school in West London, Townshend and Entwistle joined Daltrey's band The Detours – a five-piece, which went through several singers and guitarists until Daltrey switched from guitar to vocals. They then became a quartet with Townshend on lead, Entwistle on bass, and Dougie Sandom on drums, later renaming themselves The Who.

Publicist Pete Meaden decided Who were perfect for early 60s "mod" audience; he convinced band to change name to High Numbers, dressed them in the latest Carnaby Street fashions, and wrote and produced an unsuccessful single (**I'm The Face**) for them in 1964. By now, Sandom had left the band. Various temporary drummers filled in before Keith Moon was hired (after showing up at a gig and announcing that he could play better than their current sticksman).

Would-be manager Kit Lambert visited the Railway Hotel in Harrow to see High Numbers in September 1964; he and partner Chris Stamp subsequently took over from Meaden, and band reverted to the Who name. It was at this venue that Townshend smashed his first guitar, accidentally breaking the neck of his Rickenbacker on a low ceiling, and going on to trash the rest of the instrument deliberately. His antics provoked huge audience excitement; and guitar and drum destruction soon became a regular feature of Who gigs.

Band got recording contract in early 1965, and began working with Kinks' producer Shel Talmy. First single, **I Can't Explain**, went to No. 8 in UK that Spring. **Anyway Anyhow Anywhere** also made UK Top 10 on its release a few months later, while a third 1965 7-inch, **My Generation**, surpassed others in sales (reaching No. 2 in UK), and in notoriety, with its controversial lyric, "Hope I die before I get old."

Despite these hit singles, and a bestselling first LP, **My Generation** (1965), Who remained in debt, thanks to continued instrument smashing. There were also internal power struggles, and management/producer problems – including legal battle with Shel Talmy over **Substitute** (1966), their next single. After this was settled, Lambert produced **I'm A Boy** (also 1966), a UK No. 2. Later that year, band had first US hit, **Happy Jack**, followed by 1967 successes with **Pictures Of Lily**, and **I Can See For Miles**. 1967 also saw Who's first live dates in America; these included tours supporting Herman's Hermits, TV/radio spots, and an appearance at California's Monterey Pop Festival.

In 1969, Who released their long-awaited double LP, **Tommy**. A "rock opera" with spiritual overtones, chronicling the adventures of a deaf, dumb, and blind boy, it was dedicated to Townshend's guru, Meher Baba. Band spent two years performing *Tommy*

live, taking it to several European opera houses, and also to America's Woodstock Festival.

In 1970 group released outstanding **Live At Leeds**; but attempts at another concept LP, *Lifehouse*, failed, and remains were salvaged for **Who's Next** (1971), produced by Glyn Johns. On **Quadrophenia** (1973), band returned to sound of their early days, once again examining adolescence through medium of mod culture. Piece received a mixed reception, and it seemed that none of The Who's current work could match success of *Tommy* – Ken Russell's 1975 film of the opera, with Daltrey in title role, comprehensively upstaged band's new

album, **Who By Numbers** (same year).

A long lull in recording preceded **Who Are You** in 1978 – LP and single of same name proved to be Who's biggest sellers for almost a decade. Untimely death of Keith Moon that September forced band to consider folding, but by early 1979, they had recruited ex-Faces drummer Kenney Jones in his place. Year saw extensive touring and two successful Who movies: band biography *The Kids Are Alright*, and *Quadrophenia*. However, tragedy struck on December 3, 1979, when 11 fans were crushed to death at Who concert in Cincinnati. Band again contemplated disbanding, but continued US tour well into 1980.

Face Dances LP (1981) contained The Who's first new material in three years; single **You Better, You Bet** made US Top 20, although band were now making little impact in UK. Personal and professional problems drove Townshend to drink and drugs, but he eventually recovered from his addictions, and was able to finish work on next Who LP **It's Hard** (1982), with producer Glyn Johns.

Despite warm reception for album, band decided to call it a day later that year, going out in style with US Farewell Tour grossing 40 million dollars. They reunited for *Live Aid* in 1985 at Wembley Stadium, and have subsequently come together for other occasional tours and special events.

Recommended listening

My Generation (Track), 1965
A Quick One (Track) (released as Happy Jack in the USA), 1966
The Who Sell Out (Track), 1967
Magic Bus (Track), 1968
Tommy (Track), 1969
Live At Leeds (Track), 1970
Who's Next (Track), 1971
Meaty Beaty Big and Bouncy (greatest hits compilation) (Track), 1971
Quadrophenia (Track), 1973
Odds and Sods (Track), 1974
The Who By Numbers (Polydor), 1975
The Story Of The Who (Polydor), 1976
Who Are You (Polydor), 1978
The Kids Are Alright (Polydor), 1979
Face Dances (Polydor), 1981
It's Hard (Polydor), 1982
The Singles (Polydor), 1984
30 Years of Maximum R & B (4 CD set) (MCA), 1994
Live At The Isle of Wight (Columbia), 1996
My Generation: The Very Best of The Who (MCA), 1996
Best Of (Millennium Collection) (MCA), 1999
BBC Sessions (radio material) (MCA), 2000
Pete Townshend solo:
Who Came First (Track), 1972
Empty Glass (Atlantic), 1980
Best of Pete Townshend (compilation) (Atlantic), 1996

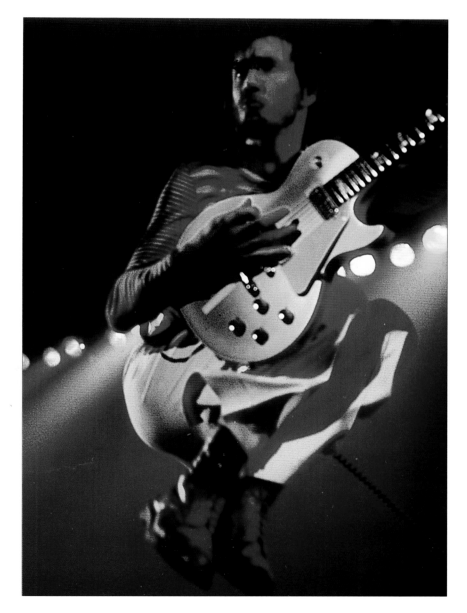

LEFT: *Pete Townshend, temporarily airborne with his Gibson Les Paul.*

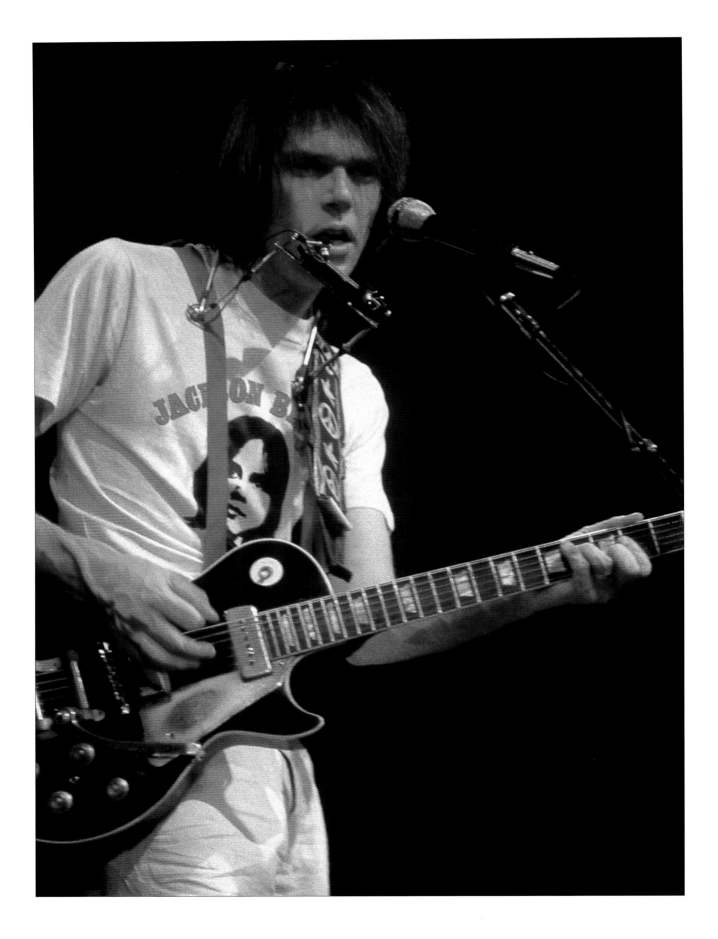

NEIL YOUNG

Canadian vocalist, composer, guitarist
Born Toronto, Ontario,
November 12, 1945

Career: Son of a well-known Toronto sports writer, who gave Neil ukelele for Christmas in 1958. He eventually graduated to banjo, and switched to guitar soon afterwards; early influence was Hank Marvin of the Shadows. After playing in short-lived group The Jades, Young joined first real band, Squires, in 1963, and by the following year, he had begun to arrange and write for them. During this period, encountered singer/ guitarists Stephen Stills and Richie Furay (subsequently to be his colleagues in Buffalo Springfield). Also met another important musical associate, bassist Bruce Palmer, and through him became a member of the Mynah Birds (led by Ricky Matthews, who later found fame as Rick James in 1980s). The group visited Detroit in 1965 for recording session at Motown Records; however, arrest of Matthews as deserter from US Navy destroyed any chance of a contract with the label.

In early 1966, Young moved to Los Angeles with Palmer (using an old hearse to drive over 3,000 miles across country from Toronto). The two Canadians re-united with Stills and Furay following a chance meeting in downtown LA, and joined them in The Herd, with drummer Dewey Martin (ex-Dillards). Group was soon renamed Buffalo Springfield, and began gigging in spring 1966. After meeting Byrds, Springfield became embroiled in LA folk-rock and country-rock scenes.

Despite several line-up changes (Palmer departed and later returned, Young left and rejoined, bassist/vocalist Jim Messina joined early 1968), Buffalo Springfield survived until May 1968, leaving three excellent LPs and five hit singles, one of which, **For What It's Worth**, made US Top 10.

Now working in folk-inspired singer-songwriter genre, Young acquired record

LEFT: *Neil Young with electric guitar – and Jackson Browne T-shirt!*

deal with Reprise. First solo LP (**Neil Young**) was released in 1969. He then formed band Crazy Horse, which provided electric backing for his second album, **Everybody Knows This Is Nowhere** (same year). That Summer, Young joined Crosby, Stills and Nash, appearing with them at 1969 Woodstock Festival, as well as on 1970 **Déjà Vu** LP, and double live set **Four Way Street** (1971). However, he simultaneously maintained his solo career with **After The Goldrush** (1970), and after parting company with CSN (though they would subsequently reunite in the studio and onstage), released his massively successful album **Harvest** (1972).

Young's next major project, the autobiographical movie **Journey Through The Past**, demonstrated his unwillingness to follow an easy commercial path. The film received an uncertain reception, and melancholy songs and performances permeated much of Young's output during 1973–74 – possibly a reaction to the drug-related death of Crazy Horse guitarist Danny Whitten in 1972.

Late 1975 LP **Zuma** saw return to form of earlier LPs, with attacking guitar solos and distinctively powerful vocals from Young. Briefly collaborated with Stephen Stills, but union proved to be short-lived. Next solo album, **American Stars 'n' Bars** (1977), included assistance from Linda Ronstadt and Emmylou Harris, joining stellar list of guests on previous Young records, such as Crosby, Stills and Nash, Jack Nitzsche, Rick Danko and Levon Helm (The Band), Nils Lofgren, and others. Three-LP set **Decade**, a self-compiled retrospective, appeared later the same year, and was followed in 1978 by **Comes A Time**, which encountered many delays due to track changes, remixes, cover art alteration, etc. New era arrived with **Rust Never Sleeps** (1979) and **Live Rust** (released same year), once again with backing from Crazy Horse. Concept included major tour, made into film *Rust Never Sleeps*, premiered in July that year.

Young then worked at length on movie project *Human Highway*, while releasing two poorly received albums, **Hawks and Doves** (1980) and **Re*Ac*tor** (1981). In 1982, began using synthesizers and electronic instruments; eventually

invited many of past friends from backing bands to assist him in making **Trans** (1982), including Nils Lofgren, guitar; Ben Keith, pedal steel, keyboards; Bruce Palmer, bass; Joe Lala, percussion; and Ralph Molina, drums. Group toured in support of **Trans** album, but Young's musical experiments were alienating some long-standing fans, and distressing his record label, Geffen, from whom he parted company after a series of inconsistent, stylistically unpredictable albums: **Everybody's Rockin'** (1983), **Old Ways** (1985), **Landing On Water** (1986), and **Life** (1987).

Latter album was made with Crazy Horse, who also featured on Young's highly acclaimed **Ragged Glory** (1990) – released after a CSNY reunion (1988's **American Dream**) and solo efforts **This Note's For You** (same year) and **Freedom** (1989). Young maintained liaison with his old back-up band for bizarre live double album **Weld** (made during *Ragged Glory* tour) in 1991, before returning to the mood and style of nearly two decades earlier on **Harvest Moon** (1992) a belated "follow up" to his 1972 **Harvest** LP.

Crazy Horse also appeared on Young's **Broken Arrow** album and tour (1996), and on the following year's movie/live double CD **Year of the Horse**. The endlessly unpredictable Canadian's other 90s projects have included a musical liasion with grunge meisters Pearl Jam (1995's **Mirror Ball**), and a further CSNY project, **Looking Forward** (1999). Young's most recent solo effort is 2000's **Silver and Gold**.

Recommended listening
Neil Young (Reprise), 1968
After The Goldrush (Reprise), 1970
Harvest (Reprise), 1972
Zuma (Reprise), 1975
Decade (2 CDs) (WEA), 1977
Rust Never Sleeps (Reprise), 1979
Live Rust (Reprise), 1979
Ragged Glory (WEA), 1990
Harvest Moon (WEA), 1992
Unplugged (WEA), 1993
Mirror Ball (with Pearl Jam) (WEA) 1995
Year of the Horse (2 CDs) (WEA), 1997
Silver and Gold (WEA), 2000

FRANK ZAPPA

US composer, guitarist, vocalist
Born Francis Vincent Zappa Jr.,
Baltimore, Maryland, December 21,
1940
Died Los Angeles, California,
December 4, 1993

Career: Raised on East Coast until age 10, then moved to West Coast with family. Early musical interests ranged from avant-garde classical to 1950s doo-wop. Practical experience included high-school band Blackouts, collaborations with Don Van Vliet (also ex-Blackout and renamed Captain Beefheart by Zappa), and operating his own primitive recording studio in Cucamonga, California.

In 1963, Zappa joined and then took over an existing local group, the Soul Giants, which, according to legend, played first gig in its reshaped form on Mothers Day 1964. This suggested name change to "The Mothers" – although band's record label later demanded that they should be known as "The Mothers of Invention."

Mothers' debut album, satirical, bizarre **Freak Out**, appeared in early 1966, earning Zappa a reputation as rock's sharpest sociologist. The highly intelligent interviews he gave revealed distaste for any trends or fashions. With altered line-up, he and the band recorded **Absolutely Free** (1967), which questioned lack of freedom in modern society. **We're Only In It For The Money** (same year) took a swipe at hippies and some of their musical favorites, including Beatles' **Sgt. Pepper** and Jimi Hendrix's **Hey Joe**.

Zappa's modern classical influences were reflected on his free-form solo LP, **Lumpy Gravy** (also 1967). That year, he began work on two simultaneous recording projects. **Cruising With Ruben And The Jets** appeared in 1968, and provided return to satire of early albums – though Zappa's loving reproduction of 50s doo-wop on the record is as much a musical tribute as a lampoon. **Uncle Meat** (1969), soundtrack for never-completed movie, displayed his fascination for all forms of media.

Burnt Weeny Sandwich (1970)

proved to be "original" Mothers' last studio album. Zappa formally announced band's demise in October 1969: ex-members Lowell George and Roy Estrada went on to form Little Feat. Zappa retained former Mother Ian Underwood (guitar, keyboards) for second solo album **Hot Rats** (1969). On record, it was often hard to distinguish between his personal and "Mothers" projects; situation was further confused by appearance of several Mothers on his "solo" set **Chunga's Revenge** (1970). 1971 saw ambitious orchestral/rock collaboration **200 Motels**, and emergence of a new Mothers line-up, captured on live albums **Fillmore East, June 1971** (1971) and **Just Another Band From LA** (1972). At the end of 71, Zappa embarked on an accident-prone European tour (band's equipment was destroyed in fire at Montreux, Switzerland; and a few days later, Zappa sustained serious injuries when he was pushed from stage at Rainbow Theatre, London). Despite these problems, he continued to release substantial amounts of material throughout this period, though some critics accused him of losing his musical and satirical bite, and his lyrics became increasingly scatological in content.

New record deal with Warners coincided with Zappa's increased determination to have a hit record. 1973's **Overnite Sensation** missed mark, but **Apostrophe** (1974) finally rose high in US charts. Next two LPs, **Roxy And Elsewhere** and **One Size Fits All** (both 1974) were live sets, as was much of following year's **Bongo Fury**, which featured reunion with old friend Captain Beefheart – their first collaboration since the late 60s.

Comparative lull following appearance of **Zoot Allures** (1976), coinciding with legal wrangles between Zappa and Warners, ended with the launch of Frank's own new label (Zappa Records), and the release of a swift succession of albums, including **Sheik Yerbouti** (1979), **Joe's Garage Act 1** (1979), and **You Are What You Is** (1981). **Ship Arriving Too Late To Save A Drowning Witch** (1982) contains **Valley Girl** single by Zappa and Moon Unit (his daughter) – song's lyrics make witty use of Southern California's teenage slang.

As well as working in rock genre with

associates/sidemen including guitarist Steve Vai, Zappa also became involved in classical composition in the 1980s, and began making extensive use of the Synclavier sampling keyboard in the studio. However, admirers of his distinctive guitar style were more interested in his three-CD set of solos, **Shut Up 'N' Play Yer Guitar**, culled from onstage performances, and first released in 1981. Decade also saw Zappa participating in political campaigns (notably struggle against moves to censor rock lyrics), and acting as adviser to Czech president Václav Havel, a long-time Zappa fan. Sadly, Frank's activities were curtailed after he was diagnosed with prostate cancer in 1991; the disease led to his death just two years later, at the age of only 52.

Recommended listening

Uncle Meat (Bizarre/Reprise), 1969
Hot Rats (Bizarre/Reprise), 1969
Burnt Weeny Sandwich
  (Bizarre/Reprise), 1969
Weasels Ripped My Flesh
  (Bizarre/Reprise), 1970
Chunga's Revenge (Bizarre/Reprise), 1970
The Mothers: Fillmore East, June 1971
  (Bizarre/Reprise), 1971
200 Motels (United Artists), 1971
Just Another Band From LA
  (Bizarre/Reprise), 1972
Waka Jawaka – Hot Rats
  (Bizarre/Reprise), 1972
Grand Wazoo (Bizarre/Reprise), 1972
Overnite Sensation (DiscReet), 1973
Apostrophe (DiscReet), 1974
One Size Fits All (DiscReet), 1975
Bongo Fury (DiscReet), 1975
Zoot Allures (DiscReet), 1976
Sheik Yerbouti (DiscReet), 1979
Sleep Dirt (DiscReet), 1979
Orchestral Favourites (DiscReet), 1979
Joe's Garage Act I (Zappa/CBS), 1979
Joe's Garage Acts II And III
  (Zappa/CBS), 1979
Tinsel Town Rebellion (Barking
  Pumpkin/CBS), 1980
You Are What You Is (Ryko), 1981
Shut Up 'N' Play Yer Guitar (Ryko), 1981
Ship Arriving Too Late To Save A
  Drowning Witch (Ryko), 1982
Them Or Us (Ryko), 1984
Jazz From Hell (Ryko), 1986

Left: *Dusty Hill (left) and Billy Gibbons of Texas rockers Z.Z.Top.*

touring as boogie band, ZZ Top now headlined massive concerts, and 1975's **Fandango!** followed **Tres Hombres** to platinum; extracted single **Tush**, with its raunchy euphemisms, merited heavy airplay. Following **Tejas** LP (1976) and massive *World Wide Texas Tour*, ZZ Top decided to take a vacation which turned into a three-year hiatus in career.

Deguello LP returned trio to prominence in 1979, and they subsequently enjoyed international chart success with 1983 set **Eliminator** and 1985 follow-up **Afterburner**. Single **Gimme All Your Lovin'** (1983) heralded renewed Top 30 chart action, and their stylish videos became a permanent fixture on MTV. Band took further break before release of **Recycler** album in 1990, during which time it was announced that **Eliminator** and **Afterburner** had combined sales approaching 15 million.

Repaying debt to their roots, ZZ Top provided funding for Delta Blues Museum in Clarksdale, Mississippi, and were feted by town council during Memphis leg of 1991 American tour. In the last decade, they have continued to perform and record to wide acclaim: albums like **Antenna** (1994) and **Rhythmeen** (1996) have been bestsellers, and in 1999, the band celebrated three decades of music-making with their latest CD, appropriately titled **XXX**.

Recommended listening

First Album (Warner Bros.), 1971
Rio Grande Mud (Warner Bros.), 1972
Tres Hombres (Warner Bros.), 1973
Fandango! (Warner Bros.), 1975
Tejas (Warner Bros.), 1976
Best Of (Warner Bros.), 1977
Deguello (Warner Bros.), 1979
El Loco (Warner Bros.), 1981
Eliminator (Warner Bros.), 1983
Afterburner (Warner Bros.), 1985
Recycler (Warner Bros.), 1990
Antenna (RCA), 1994
One Foot In The Blues (Warner Bros.), 1994
Rhythmeen (RCA), 1996
XXX (RCA), 1999

ZZ TOP

US group formed 1969

Original line-up: Billy Gibbons, guitar, vocals; Dusty Hill, bass, vocals; Frank Beard, drums.

Career: In late 1960s, Gibbons was guitarist in Moving Sidewalks, local Houston, Texas band. When they fell apart, he and manager Bill Ham planned new group. Beard joined and recommended Hill. ZZ Top quickly evolved a potent, high energy blues/rock mix, establishing formidable reputation as a live act, and challenging other, better-known bands to match their performance.

First Album (1970) received only local interest, but **Rio Grande Mud** (1972) reflected growing audience, eventually going gold. **Tres Hombres** (1973) consolidated their success, and provided US hit single **La Grange**. Forever

HARDWARE

In the 1930s, electric players sometimes had to plug their instruments into makeshift amplifiers assembled from phonograph and radio components. But before long, dedicated (though still primitive) sound gear for guitars was available – and in the post-war years, its power and quality began to increase rapidly, thanks to the efforts of manufacturers like Leo Fender, many of whose classic 1950s and 60s amp designs are still in use today. In this section, we look at the early history of guitar equipment, and go on to discover how more recent developments like 100-watt stacks, effects pedals, and digital technology have expanded the range of sounds available to musicians in the studio and onstage.

GUITARS AND ELECTRICITY – FROM BREED TO BEAUCHAMP

Most of the scientific principles underlying the operation of the electric guitar were discovered and first applied during the 19th century; and the instrument's most immediate ancestor is probably the "apparatus for producing musical sounds by electricity" patented in 1890 by a US naval officer called George Breed.

Breed based his invention on a modified acoustic guitar, whose strings pass between the poles of a magnet, and across a metal bridge connected to a conducting wheel housed in a box at the tailpiece. This wheel, turned by a clockwork motor, is linked, via a contact-spring, to a battery wired up to the guitar's frets. When the player presses a string against a fret, an electrical circuit is completed. Voltage from the battery passes to the contact-spring; the conducting wheel, brushing against it, creates a charge that is introduced, via the bridge, into the magnetic field surrounding the strings. This makes the fretted string vibrate, sounding the selected note.

The Breed guitar (no examples have survived) uses electricity to make sounds, though not to project or boost them; it was several decades before the emergence of the more sophisticated technology needed to accomplish this. In 1907, Lee DeForest invented the triode, a vacuum tube capable of amplifying weak electrical signals. However, high quality sound reproduction only became a reality in the late 1920s, with the advent of the moving-coil loudspeaker, and the first true electric guitar followed in 1930.

This was the famous "Frying Pan," created by three Los Angeles-based designers who later marketed their invention under the Electro brand name: George Beauchamp (also an important figure in the

Part of George Breed's 1890 patent specification for "An Apparatus for Producing Musical Sounds by Electricity." (Courtesy US Patent & Trademark Office)

"Frying Pan" Hawaiian guitar
The original c.1930 prototype model, carved from a
single piece of maple (production Frying Pans were
made of aluminum).
(Courtesy Rickenbacker International Corporation)

development of the resonator guitar – see pages 166–167), Paul Barth,
and Adolph Rickenbacker. The instrument's massive horseshoe-shaped
magnets (similar to Breed's) surround its metal strings; below the strings is
a coil of wire wrapped around a metal plate. Striking the strings creates a
disturbance in the magnetic field around them; this is converted to a
current by the coil and fed (via two screw terminals visible beneath the
left-hand magnet) to an amplifier and speaker.

ELECTRO IN THE 1930s

The *"Frying Pan"* electric Hawaiian guitar went on the market in 1932. Later that year, George Beauchamp, Paul Barth, and Adolph Rickenbacker (whose company was named the Electro String Instrument Corporation in 1934, and subsequently became known as Rickenbacker) brought out a wooden-bodied *"Spanish"* model that also used Beauchamp's horseshoe-style pickup. For most of the 1930s, Electro was the most prominent and innovative developer and manufacturer of electric instruments and amplifiers (though National, Gibson, and other American firms were soon providing stiff competition). The Electro/Rickenbacker range included wooden, metal, and plastic-bodied fretted instruments, electric violins and basses, often sold as *"sets"* with small combo amps like the metal-covered 1930s model shown here.

The company promoted their revolutionary new products with colorfully worded ads like this one, from 1934: *"A miracle has come to pass in the realm of beautiful tone. The soft, fairy-voiced Hawaiian guitar, the tinkling mandolin, the ethereal Spanish guitar – all have been liberated, dignified, and given their rightful place among orchestral instruments... Touched with the magic wand of electric genius, the quality they lacked has been conferred upon them – volume! Controlled volume – more than sufficient for the largest orchestra."*

Rickenbacker/Electro combo amp, 1930s (note mis-spelling of "Rickenbacher" on decal). (Courtesy Rickenbacker International Corporation)

Rickenbacker/Electro archtop with horseshoe pickup (body made by Kay Musical Instruments, Chicago), 1937. (Courtesy Rickenbacker International Corporation)

Electro's technical and marketing success was largely due to Adolph Rickenbacker himself. A skilled engineer, whose extensive industrial experience had included a spell at Hotpoint, where he had pioneered advanced injection-moulding techniques, he was among the first manufacturers to make some of his guitars and fiddles from "non-traditional" materials such as Bakelite. He was also able to reduce costs by sourcing components (and sometimes entire instruments, like the wooden-bodied archtop shown here) from other companies; and his considerable personal fortune (he was the only Electro director to be independently wealthy) undoubtedly kept the business afloat during its early years.

By the end of the decade, Rickenbacker had helped to turn electric guitars and amplifiers from gimmicks to accepted tools of the popular musician's trade. The firm was forced to abandon instrument-making during the War years, but soon resumed its major role on the guitar scene after the end of hostilities in 1945.

FENDER AMPS – 1948–60

Leo Fender began making guitars, pickups, and amplifiers with his first business partner, Clayton O. Kauffman (known as "Doc") in the mid-1940s. By early 1946, their fledgling firm, K&F, was producing 40 instruments a week, and when Kauffman bowed out of the business later that year, Leo set up on his own as the Fender Electric Instrument Company. He was soon developing and manufacturing a growing range of lap steels (his first "Spanish" guitar, the Broadcaster, did not appear until 1950) and amps.

There was nothing fancy about early Fender amplifiers. Often supplied (like Electro amps) as part of a "set" with an instrument, they were cheap and compact, and used simple circuits derived from diagrams published by RCA, who made the vacuum tubes that drove the devices. Nevertheless, they sold well, and one of Leo's biggest successes in the late 40s came with the student "Champion" range. The first Champion was the 800 model, launched in 1948,

Fender Concert, early 1960s.
(Courtesy John Henry's, London)

Fender Champion 600, c.1949.
(Courtesy Real Guitars, San
Francisco)

and fitted with an
8-inch (20.3-cm)
loudspeaker. It
boasted Fender's
distinctive, recently
developed "TV-front"
cabinet design, which was
also used a year later for a
new Champion, the 600
(illustrated here). Its amplification stage was identical to its predecessor's, but
it had a smaller, 6-inch (15.2-cm) speaker, a 3-watt output, and a distinctive
brown-and-cream Naugahyde covering (normally used on furniture). The
example shown in our photo has lost its leather carrying handle, but is still in
working order after more than 50 years – a tribute to the "extremely rugged
construction" mentioned in the original publicity for the amp.

   The Champion (later renamed Champ) became a mainstay of Fender's small
amp range. Like the firm's more powerful, professional models, it underwent
substantial changes during the 1950s, as Leo fine-tuned his circuitry in the
search for better sound, and "TV-front" amps were replaced by "wide-panel"
units featuring oblong speaker apertures, and then by "narrow-panel" amps
with a much larger grille area. In 1959, Fender redesigned its cabinets again,
introducing angled, front-facing control panels and Tolex coverings. The 40-
watt Concert amp shown opposite (a slightly later "blackface" model) is one
of several perennially popular combos dating from this period.

THE FENDER BASSMAN

The Bassman is one of Fender's most influential amps, and has gone through many modifications since its launch, as a companion to the company's Precision bass guitar, in 1952. The original "TV-front" Bassman was fitted with a 15-inch (38-cm) loudspeaker, designed to handle signals either from a Fender bass or an "electrified" traditional stand-up instrument. It also boasted a 26-watt output – small by modern standards, but offering nearly twice the power of the company's other professional amplifiers of the time.

This unit underwent a makeover in 1953, when its "TV front" was replaced with Fender's new, wide-panel styling. Two years later, more substantial alterations were introduced: the model gained a "narrow-panel" face, its 15-inch (38-cm) speaker was replaced with four 10-inch (25.4-cm) cones, and its power output was upped to 60 watts. A subsequent feature was the provision of "bright" and "normal" input channels, added to allow the amp to be used by a six-string guitarist and bassist simultaneously. However, the "bright" sound was so good for lead guitar that many rock 'n' roll and country players started buying Bassmen in preference to regular guitar combos.

Fender Bassman 100 amplifier, 1970s.
(Courtesy John Henry's, London)

Further changes to the Bassman came in the early 60s, with the launch of a separate "piggyback" amp head (similar to the one shown on the left), combined with a speaker cabinet (not illustrated) containing a single 12-inch (30.5-cm) driver. First produced with "brownface" control panels, these units were later refinished in "blackface" and "silverface" stylings.

In 1965, Fender was taken over by CBS (see next two pages), and the firm's new corporate bosses began to introduce heavily modified, often inferior versions of some of the company's classic amps and guitars. Various Bassmen, some with transistorized circuitry, remained in production during the CBS period, but since the company's change of management in 1985, many of the Leo Fender's original designs have been returned to production. These include the "Vintage Series" Bassman shown in our second picture: with its narrow-panel front, tweed finish, and authentic sound and specification, it is almost indistinguishable from the 1959 model on which it is based.

Fender '59 Bassman combo, 2001. (Courtesy Fender Musical Instruments Corp.)

THE FENDER TWIN REVERB AND TWO-TONE

The Twin Reverb, launched in 1963, is perhaps second only to the Bassman in the affections of Fender lovers. It is a superb amp for rock, blues, or country playing: compact yet powerful, delivering (in its original version) no less than 85 watts of sound through its two 12-inch (30.5-cm) speakers, and equipped with two channels – "clean" and "vibrato" – which are each switchable between normal and "bright" tone quality. The "vibrato" found on this and other Fender amps is actually a tremolo effect, providing variations in volume whose speed and intensity are controlled via two knobs on the front panel (true vibrato is a pitch fluctuation). The amp's "reverb" is generated by an internal spring unit – a simple but effective device whose characteristic, "twangy" sound is hard to emulate using more sophisticated technology!

This classic model was one of the last amplifiers designed by Leo Fender for the company he had founded almost two decades earlier.

Fender Vintage Series '65 Twin Reverb combo, 2001. (Both photos courtesy Fender Musical Instruments Corp.)

*Soon after he left the firm in 1965, its incoming owners, CBS, decided
to launch a line of transistorized amps under the Fender marque –
some of which were to share their names (though not their features)
with well-established, tube-powered Fender products like the Twin
Reverb. Leo's former associate, Forrest White (who had been appointed
Manufacturing Operations Director at Fender/CBS), could not stop the
plans from going ahead, and eventually resigned in protest at them. As
he and other Fender "old-timers" predicted, the new range proved to
be a disaster. However, the original, all-tube Twin Reverb survived
(with some modifications), and like the Bassman, it remains in
production at Fender's headquarters in Corona, California.*

*As well as their replicas and reissues of early Fender amplifiers, the
company also makes an impressive range of new designs, some
contemporary in inspiration, but others ingeniously "retro"-looking –
like the Custom Shop Two-Tone also shown here. A hand-built, all-
tube, 15-watt combo with a single 10-inch (25.4-cm) speaker, the
Two-Tone's Tolex finish and chrome control panel add to its "period"
appearance, and it is described in the current Fender catalog as
"one of the most unique custom pieces we've produced."*

THE FENDER VIBROLUX AND PROSONIC

According to former Fender Vice-President Forrest White's authoritative history of the firm, the original Vibrolux amplifier was designed by Leo Fender in Spring 1956, and introduced later the same year. A smaller version of the 15-watt Tremolux model (which had been launched in 1955), the Vibrolux had only a 10-watt output and a single 10-inch (25.4-cm) speaker, but offered, in the company's words, "outstanding performance characteristics and design features at a conservative price." In the 1960s Vibroluxes gained some extra power and a reverb unit, but the amp is no longer available in any of its "vintage" specifications. Instead, it has been revived by the modern Fender Corporation as a 40-watt combo, boasting two 10-inch (25.4-cm) speakers, twin ("normal" and "bright") channels, and improved reverb and vibrato. The Vibrolux Reverb currently retails at just over $1,400.

Another impressive product in Fender's current "Professional Tube Series" is the Prosonic, which is manufactured in two configurations: a combo unit and a separate amp and cabinet (as shown here). Both models have the same 60-watt power output, but while the combo contains two 10-inch (25.4-cm)

Fender Custom Vibrolux Reverb combo, 2001. (Both photos courtesy Fender Musical Instruments Corp.)

speakers, the Tone Master enclosure supplied for the "piggyback" version packs a more formidable punch, with four 12-inch (30.5-cm) drivers. The company's publicity waxes lyrical over both models' capabilities, describing them as a cross between "a classic Fender amplifier [and] a flame-thrower," with dual selectable channels and "cascading gain" circuitry that "can take you from vintage clean to swampy grunge with the spin of your guitar's volume knob." Fortunately for potential customers' backs, the Tone Master cabinet is on casters – the combined weight of the speaker and amp head is over 120 lb (54.4kg)!

Fender Prosonic Head and Tone Master enclosure, 2001.
(Both photos courtesy Fender Musical Instruments Corp.)

THE FENDER BLUES JUNIOR AND HOT ROD DeVILLE

Since taking over from CBS in 1985, Fender's new management team, under the leadership of Bill Schultz, have shown great respect for their company's heritage – producing impressive replicas and reissues of vintage designs, but also maintaining a spirit of adventure and innovation by developing exciting new products. Some of the best of these are directly inspired by Leo Fender's work, like the current range of "American Tube Series" combos, two of which are featured here.

The smallest American Tube Series amps, the Pro Junior and Blues Junior, are modelled on the classic Champion/Champ units, originally conceived by Leo Fender for practice or student use, but often favored by professionals for studio work. (Devotees of the Champ sound, with its characteristically meaty distortion, include Rolling Stone Keith Richards and former Beatle George Harrison.) The

Pro Junior, which features just two control knobs, a 15-watt output, and a single 10-inch (25.4-cm) speaker, is intended as a

Fender American Tube Series Blues Junior, 2001. (Both photos courtesy Fender Musical Instruments Corp.)

simple, high-quality recording amp. Its bigger brother, the Blues Junior
(featured in our photo) has the same power output, but boasts a larger
12-inch (30.5-cm) speaker, reverb, and some other tonal refinements,
including a switchable "Fat" circuit for extra impact.

The two Juniors and more powerful Hot Rod models that make up
the rest of the range all share the same distinctive "narrow-panel"
design used on many 1950s classic Fender amps. The Hot Rod Deluxe
is a 40-watt, three-channel combo with reverb and a single 12-inch
(30.5-cm) speaker. Next in the Hot Rod series is the DeVille 410
illustrated opposite. This puts out 60 watts into its four 10-inch
(25.4-cm) speakers, and offers a three-channel preamp with "drive"
circuitry for controlled overload, reverb, and an effects loop that
makes it easy to patch in pedals or other external devices. The
DeVille 212 differs from the 410 only in its speaker configuration,
containing two 12-inch (30.5-cm) cones.

*Fender American Tube
Series Hot Rod
DeVille 410, 2001.
(Both photos courtesy
Fender Musical
Instruments Corp.)*

THE MARSHALL STACK

Jim Marshall, founder of Marshall Amplification, is the only English rock equipment-maker to achieve "household name" status in an industry dominated by Americans. Famous for his "stacks" (comprising two or more speaker cabinets with a high-powered tube amp perched on top of them) and for many other technical innovations in his chosen field, he has been active in the music business for most of his life – although he first got involved in amplifier design and construction by a somewhat roundabout route.

Born in London in 1923, Marshall suffered from tuberculosis as a child; his illness kept him from school and made him unfit for military service, but he became fascinated by engineering, working as a toolmaker at an aircraft factory during the late 1940s, while pursuing his passion for music by taking dancing and drumming lessons. He eventually made a name for himself as a jazz and big-band drummer, and was also in demand as a teacher, running his own thriving drum school. In 1960, he opened a retail store selling percussion instruments. After expanding into guitar and amplifier sales, he started to design and build his own, extra-powerful tube-based amps and speaker cabinets, moving to bigger premises as demand increased. His early customers included Pete Townshend, whose jazz musician father was an old friend of Marshall's. In 1965, the young guitarist, then enjoying his first taste of fame with The Who, asked Marshall to build him a 100-watt amp with no less than eight 12-inch (30.5-cm) speakers. Such a large number of drivers could not be accommodated in a single cabinet, so Marshall constructed two speaker units for them, designed to stand one on top of the other – and, as he subsequently put it, "the Marshall Stack was here!"

Soon, more and more leading players – among them Eric Clapton and Jimi Hendrix (whose drummer, Mitch Mitchell, was a former Marshall drum school pupil) – were also using the stack. Available in various configurations, it has since become a perennial favorite with musicians and audiences, and is widely regarded as the finest rock amplification system ever made.

Marshall JCM 900 100-watt amplifier, with two "Lead 1960" cabinets, each containing four 12-inch (30.5-cm) speakers, 2000.
(Courtesy Guitar Village, Farnham)

MARSHALL – FOUR DECADES OF EXCELLENCE

Since the mid-60s, Marshall has grown steadily, moving to bigger premises (the firm is now based in a 70,000ft² factory in Bletchley, about 40 miles (64km) northwest of London), and expanding its range of products. It currently makes both tube and transistorized amplification for guitars and basses (including amp heads and cabinets, combos, and rack-mounted gear), as well as a variety of effects and accessories, and it received the Queen's Award For Export Achievement in 1984.

Though its equipment is associated with so many leading rock names, only one guitarist, Slash of Guns N' Roses, has ever had a Marshall model actually named for him. A long-time

fan of the company's gear, he ordered 10 identical replacements for his favorite, long discontinued, late 1980s amp when planning a tour in 1996. As Jim Marshall told Vintage Guitar *magazine, "After all that time, we [needed] to do some research and development to find all the right components to do them all over again, which would be very costly. I said that the only way I could do it would*

Marshall limited edition JTM Bluesbreaker combo, 1997.
(Both photos courtesy John Henry's, London)

be to produce a limited edition of 3,000… and I let Slash put his signature on the front with mine, which is the first time I'd ever done that." The resultant "JCM Slash Signature Model," produced in a striking snakeskin vinyl covering, was described by the company as a "deadly accurate reissue" of the 1980s original, and in less than a year, all 3,000 of them had been sold.

Most of Marshall's other "special edition" amps, like the unusual, white finish JTM Bluesbreaker combo shown opposite (the initials, which have appeared on many Marshall products since the 60s, stand for "Jim and Terry Marshall" – Terry is Jim's son) were made to commemorate landmark dates in the company's history, such as its Silver Jubilee in 1987 and 35th anniversary in 1997. More "one-off" models are doubtless being planned for Marshall Amplification's 40th birthday celebrations in 2002. Meanwhile, the company continues to prosper, and, in the words of its website, "to hold true to the tradition of excellence instilled in it by its founder."

Marshall Master Model 50-watt amp head, 1970s. (Both photos courtesy John Henry's, London)

VOX AND THE AC30

While Marshall is now Britain's best-known amp manufacturer, another company, Vox, was the UK's leading suppliers of high-quality band gear – including amplifiers, electric organs, guitars and basses – for much of the 1960s. The firm had its origins in the Jennings Organ Company, set up by amateur musician and instrument dealer Tom Jennings in 1951. By the mid-50s, Jennings, with support from his old friend, engineer Dick Denney, had diversified into amp-making, and after enjoying considerable success with the small AC15 combo (see next two pages), they produced a prototype 30-watt guitar amp, the AC30, in 1958.

Among the first purchasers of the new amp were The Shadows, who acquired three

AC30s in 1959. During the year, various modifications were made to the unit's design, and it was fitted with a new, specially designed speaker (named the Vox "Blue"). In this form, it

Vox AC30 combo, 2001
(Courtesy Korg UK Ltd.)

went on to dominate the UK pop and rock records of the period: The Shadows featured it on all their classic instrumental hits (including Apache, FBI, and Wonderful Land), and it was also famously used by The Beatles (see photo) and The Rolling Stones.

The AC30 offered three, individually adjustable channels (each with high and low sensitivity inputs) – "normal," "brilliant," and "vibtrem" – and boasted a distinctively rich, meaty tone. At a time when American amps were almost impossible to obtain in Europe, it was simply the best and most powerful model available to British musicians until the advent of Marshall. Even after the appearance of larger amps, many players remained faithful to their AC30s (Brian May of Queen uses "stacks" of them onstage and in the studio!) – although subsequent changes in specification, and the eventual introduction of solid state circuitry, were later to have an adverse effect on the combo's performance and sales.

Recently, however, Vox (now owned by Korg UK) has resumed production of the "classic" AC30, incorporating the original features and distinctive finish that made the amp a classic; one of these new models – which are once again proving to be best sellers – is shown here.

The Beatles were among the many famous early users of the AC30, which is clearly visible in the centre of this photo.

THE VOX AC15 AND PATHFINDER

As explained on the previous pages, the AC15 was Vox's first big-selling amplifier. Designed by Jennings Musical Instruments' Chief Engineer, Dick Denney, it was introduced in 1958, and was quickly adopted by many leading British musicians, including Bert Weedon (famous for his classic Play In A Day *guitar tutor), and Hank B. Marvin of The Shadows. The AC15's apparently low output (15 watts) is misleading; like its small US-built equivalents (such as the Fender Vibrolux), it packed a considerable punch, and players needing extra power could always use two (or more) AC15s together – though this became unnecessary when the AC30 appeared the following year!*

Despite its small size, the AC15 has remained in the Vox catalog for many years, and in 1996, a "new" version of it – restoring some of the features that had previously been abandoned for reasons of cost or because of difficulties in obtaining components – was launched by Vox's current owners, Korg. There are some extra refinements on this reissued model (which is shown opposite): a spring reverb has been added, as well as master volume and tone controls, but the unit still boasts its original 12-inch (30.5-cm)

Vox AC15 combo.
(Both photos courtesy
Korg UK Ltd.)

Vox Pathfinder combo.
(Both photos courtesy Korg UK Ltd.)

speaker and tremolo circuitry, and is proving particularly popular as a high quality recording amp.

For guitarists seeking the Vox sound in a smaller, cheaper package, the company produces its compact Pathfinder combo (also illustrated here). Unlike the tube-driven AC30 and AC15, it is a transistorized unit; many players consider that solid state components lack the warmth and richness of valves, but the Pathfinder retains a good deal of the classic Vox sound, and is capable of holding its own not just as a practice amp, but also in the studio and onstage. It has a 15-watt output, an 8-inch (20.3-cm) speaker, and boost and tremolo circuits (controllable from the amp itself, or via a footswitch).

VOX'S VALVETRONIX AMPS

Vox's latest venture is its new "digital modelling" amplifier, the Valvetronix, currently available in 60-watt (AD60VT) or stereo, 2 x 60-watt (AD120VT) configurations. Digital modelling (currently being developed by a number of other manufacturers) allows a single unit to replicate the tonal characteristics of several different types of amp: the Valvetronix offers no less than 16 sonic "flavors" (all selectable from its control panel). Among them are "UK 70s, 80s, and 90s," a "virtual" AC15 and AC30, "US HiGain" and "Boutique Overdrive." The Valvetronix relies on microchip technology for these simulations; Vox's new owners, Korg, have a long and distinguished track record in this area, and the AD60 and 120's preamps also incorporate Korg-derived "pedal" effects, including wah-wah, fuzz, treble boost, and compression.

It is the Valvetronix models' unique power amp stages that sets them apart from the plethora of other "magic boxes" offering instant replicas of classic sounds. They are tube driven: in its publicity, Vox explains that "all of the great sounding amps we've modelled are valve amps, [and our] technology enables the AD60VT and AD120VT to produce the high dynamic range associated with these traditional [units] – something a solid-state amp simply couldn't do." Vox's patented

Valve Reactor system also incorporates a special solid state power circuit, coupled to the Valvetronix's output transformer, which adapts the amp's performance to model each of the simulated sounds more accurately.

As well as their ability to mimic a wide cross-section of different amp types, the Valvetronix combos boast many other features: both have on-board guitar tuners, a comprehensive range of inputs and outputs, and custom-voiced Celestion speakers (Celestion, one of the UK's leading speaker manufacturers, were also responsible for the classic "Blue" driver fitted to the Vox AC30). The AD60VT and AD120VT represent an innovative and exciting new departure for Vox and Korg. Time and customer reaction will tell whether they have succeeded in creating what their website claims to be "the best of all worlds… a versatile amp that [can] superbly re-create every detail, every nuance of a collection of the world's most sought after guitar amplifiers."

Vox Valvetronix AD60VT and AD120VT digital modelling combos. (Courtesy Korg UK Ltd.)

GIBSON'S GOLDTONE SERIES: THE GA-15 AND GA-30RV

Gibson has been in the guitar- and amp-manufacturing business since the 1930s, but over the last few years, it has been better known for its instruments than its sound equipment. However, the company has recently won considerable acclaim for its new "Goldtone" tube-powered guitar amplifiers. These are divided into two types: the basic Goldtone models, which Gibson describe as "no nonsense, compact, [and] purist... [with] the minimum controls necessary to produce a good range of sounds, from clean to overdriven;" and the more feature-rich "Super Goldtones." Examples of both are shown here.

The Goldtone GA-15, with its 15-watt output and 10-inch (25.4-cm) speaker, is the baby of the family, with a single channel, switchable between normal and "bright" modes. It has only two control knobs (volume and tone), though the tone circuit is not the standard high frequency roll-off device found on most other amps,

Gibson Super Goldtone GA-30RV combo. (Both photos courtesy John Henry's, London)

*Gibson Goldtone
GA-15 combo.
(Both photos courtesy
John Henry's, London)*

*but a dual-gang potentiometer that gradually reduces the midrange frequencies
and boosts the treble as it is turned clockwise.*

*The "Super Goldtone" GA-30RV has a higher power rating (30 watts through
10-inch (25.4-cm) and 12-inch (30.5-cm) speakers) and a more elaborate front
end. It boasts two preamplifiers (see inset photo of control panel): preamp 1
delivers a cleaner sound, with a degree of controlled distortion at higher volumes;
while preamp 2 offers a range of more overdriven tones. The preamps can be used
separately or together, and there is also a "boost" circuit, and a six-spring
Accutronics reverb with individual level controls for each preamp. Many of the
amp's functions can be controlled from a footswitch.*

*The GA-30RV is also available in a stereo, 2 x 15-watt version (the 30RVS)
which has earned plaudits from several top American players. Joe Perry of
Aerosmith has recently been touring and recording with one, and Mick Jagger also
used a 30RVS on sessions for his 2001 solo album,* Goddess in the Doorway.

THE GIBSON GA-60RV AND GA-30RVH

Gibson's CEO, Henry Juszkiewicz, has recently described his company's range of Goldtone and Super Goldtone amps as "setting a higher standard and giving the musician unparalleled tone, flexibility, and quality." The GA-60RV combo is the current flagship in the Super Goldtone range; its controls and functions are similar to those of the GA-30RV illustrated on the previous two pages, but it has a 60-watt output, delivered through two 12-inch (30.5-cm) Celestion speakers, and making it (in Gibson's words), "perfect for situations where both power and portability are required."

The elegant, vinyl-covered new Super Goldtone line also includes a "half stack" amp and cabinet model (shown here). The amp head, the GA-30RVH, is rated at 30 watts; like its combo cousin, the 30RV, it has two preamps (with – appropriately – "retro"-styled, gold-colored knobs), an optional footswitch controller, a reverb, and an effects loop for external pedals or other devices. It matching cab, the SGT, contains

Gibson Super Goldtone GA-60RV combo, 2001. (Both photos courtesy Gibson Guitar Corporation)

an impressive complement of Celestion drivers: two 10-inch (25.4-cm) and two 12-inch (30.5-cm) cones, with the smaller units left open-backed, and the 12-inch (30.5-cm) speakers sealed to maximize their bass response. The SGT can be connected to one or more amps in mono or stereo (in stereo mode, a 10-inch (25.4-cm) and 12-inch (30.5-cm) speaker is assigned to each channel), and is capable of handling up to 240 watts of output.

   The GA-30RVH/SGT combination has been praised by critics for its warm, rich sound and glamorous looks: one reviewer commented that it had the makings of a modern classic, and it seems more than likely to hold its own in the current, highly competitive guitar
amp marketplace.

*Gibson Super Goldtone
GA-30RVH amp and SGT
cabinet, 2001.
(Both photos courtesy
Gibson Guitar Corporation)*

THE ORANGE AD30R AND AD15

The gaudy colors of Orange equipment have always stood out from other manufacturers' more drab looking designs; the company's products, adorned with their distinctive "Voice of the World" crest, are instantly recognizable, whether onstage or in a music store. Still run by its founder, Clifford Cooper, an Englishman with an engineering background, Orange went into business in 1968. Its first amps were sold in Cooper's central London instrument shop, and their classic tube-driven sound (as well as their orange vinyl finish)

soon endeared them to discerning customers on both sides of the Atlantic; early purchasers included Fleetwood Mac and Stevie Wonder.

After a hugely successful period in the 1970s, Orange fell on harder times in the following decade, but the revival of interest in guitar-driven rock during the 90s saw the

Orange AD15 combo, 2001. (Both photos courtesy John Henry's, London)

Orange AD30R combo, 2000.
(Both photos courtesy John Henry's, London)

firm's fortunes revive. Today, it produces a small, but impressive range of tube-powered guitar and bass amplification (an example of the latter can be seen on pages 364–365), as well as a solid-state budget range – the "Orange Crush" series!

The two Orange guitar combos illustrated here are both professional, tube-based units. The AD30R, introduced in 1998, is a single channel model with a spring reverb; boasting a 30-watt output and a 12-inch (30.5-cm) speaker, it has sold well in Europe and America, and is one of the company's most popular amps.

The Orange AD15 is smaller, but no less impressive. Orange's publicity states that "when [it] was reviewed in the States, they rated it well above their home-grown brands of similar design. [Reviewers in the UK] liked it so much, they went and bought one. We have even heard of music shop staff [choosing] to go without pay just to get one of their own… it looks like we got it right with the AD15." Rated at 15 watts, the amp sounds subjectively much louder due to its efficient, Class A tube circuitry, and is a formidable performer in any musical environment.

MESA/BOOGIE

MESA, one of the USA's most highly regarded amp-makers, has its origins in a small operation run, during the late 1960s, from a workshop in a shack at Lagunitas, near San Fransicso. There, musician and engineer Randall Smith constructed his first prototype amps, whose hot-rodded circuitry was concealed within the casings of small, bought-in Fender Princeton combos. As Smith comments on the company's website, "The trick was to get all the high power electronics, big transformers and a JBL 12" [speaker] reliably built inside a package that was intended to house a 10-inch speaker and produce 12 watts!"

MESA/Boogie Single Rectifier Solo 50-watt amp head, 2000. (Both photos courtesy John Henry's, London)

The results met with the approval of leading Bay Area players, including ace guitarist Carlos Santana, who gave Smith's amps their "Boogie" name. Growing demand eventually led to expansion and the setting-up of today's MESA/Boogie company. Smith and his colleagues are currently based in the Northern Californian city of Petaluma, and their many years of success have made them all the more committed to excellence and innovation; Smith describes the attitude of his staff as one of "fanatical devotion to performance and quality."

Two of MESA/Boogie's current products are shown here. Their strikingly finished Single Rectifier amp head delivers 50 watts of output, and has twin channels, offering five "modes" of operation: these provide "clean" or "pushed" sounds (from Channel 1); or "raw," vintage high gain" and "modern high gain" via Channel 2. It has comprehensive gain and tone controls, and an effects loop with a "mix" feature that allows sounds from external pedals and other devices to be blended with the amp's own signal.

The Nomad 45 stack in our other picture is also available in combo form; it provides no less than three channels, giving the user even more tonal options, and is fitted with a spring reverb and outputs for headphones and recording. It delivers 45 watts to its matching speaker cabinet, which contains two 12-inch (30.5-cm) Celestion drivers.

MESA Nomad 45 amp and cab, 2000.
(Both photos courtesy John Henry's, London)

THE MESA HEARTBREAKER AND ROCKET 44

The MESA/Boogie Mark I, introduced in the 1970s and based on Randall Smith's early experiments in his "Dog House" workshop in Lagunitas, California, brought the fledgling company widespread acclaim and attention. It had two channels (clean and "high gain") and a distinctive sound that found its way onto many classic records of the time. Twenty-five years after its launch, MESA decided to commemorate this seminal amp (described by Smith as an "evolutionary milestone") by producing a "tribute" model with similar specifications, but a highly individual appearance. Christened the Heartbreaker, it is a 100-watt combo with two 12-inch (30.5-cm) speakers, and is designed (in MESA's words) as a celebration of "the stylistic yin and yang" of the period that saw the birth of the Mark I.

MESA Heartbreaker, 2001. (Courtesy John Henry's, London)

MESA Rocket 44
combo, 1990s.
(Courtesy John
Henry's, London)

The names MESA has given to some of the Heartbreaker's features and functions
have abandoned technical terminology for something more sensual. Instead of clean
and high gain, its two channels are labelled "love" and "lust." There is a
"bold/curvaceous" switch, a "Tweed" selector that compresses the combo's output
power to mimic the sound of 1950s-vintage, tweed-covered Fender amps, and the
Heartbreaker's front panel is decorated with a striking, blood-red "chained heart"
tattoo. The amp's looks are quite unique – and its cosmetic refinement is more than
matched by its impressive performance.

The other MESA amp shown here, the Rocket 44 combo, may seem a little more
prosaic than the Heartbreaker, but it still packs a powerful punch of its own. Its
single channel offers three "modes" ("lead," "rhythm," and "contour"), and, like
most of its MESA stablemates, it boasts refinements like analog reverb, an effects
loop, and a "silent recording" switch, which mutes the unit's 10-inch (25.4-cm)
speaker when its output is not required.

TRACE ELLIOT'S "TRAMP" SERIES

Trace Elliot went into business in the late 1970s, producing high quality, handmade bass amplification. From its headquarters in the English county of Essex, east of London, the firm's fame spread rapidly; it later diversified into designing and building sound equipment for electric keyboard and guitar players, and is especially noted for its high quality amps for acoustic instruments (see pages 368–369 for examples). The company is now owned by Gibson, but retains its Essex base, where all its equipment is manufactured.

The two Trace Elliot amps on these pages are part of the firm's "Tramp" range of guitar rigs. The Quad Chorus combo is a stereo unit, delivering 2 x 65 watts into two Celestion 12-inch (30.5-cm) speakers. In common with all the Tramp models, it has a tube preamp and a transistorized power amplifier stage; there are three channels, providing "clean," "vintage gain," and "high gain" sounds, and the amp includes EQ, a three-spring reverb, and the onboard chorus effect that gives it its name. This "Quad chorus" consists of two chorus "sweeps," running simultaneously at different rates, which are then combined as a stereo chorus circuit. Trace Elliot claims that "the overall effect that this produces is richer sound with less of the periodic 'cycling' typical of cheaper chorus effects."

Trace Elliot Super Tramp Quad Chorus combo, 2001.
(Courtesy Trace Elliot)

The H100 mono 100-watt amp head is seen here with two 412 cabinets, each containing four 12-inch (30.5-cm) Celestion drivers. Like the Quad Chorus, it has three preamp channels with a "boost" facility, selectable from the unit's front panel or via a footswitch. Amp and cabs are built for heavy duty; they have a black vinyl finish, protective steel corners, and a "kickproof" steel grille covering the speakers.

Trace Elliot Super Tramp H100 amp and 412 cabs, 2001.
(Courtesy Trace Elliot)

TRACE ELLIOT'S "SPEED TWINS"

Trace Elliot describes its all-tube "Speed Twin" range of electric guitar amps as "[treading] a fine line between classic styling and tone and today's needs for flexibility – [they are] modern, professional units designed to cope with the most demanding conditions and deliver unrivalled tone every time," The two "flagship" Speed Twins, the H100 and the C100, are shown here; they share a number of advanced features, some of which are only rarely encountered in guitar amplification.

Both the C100 combo and the H100 (an amp head designed to be used with Trace Elliot's GSC412 flat-or angled-fronted speaker cabs) are rated at 100 watts, and have two channels (clean and overdriven). More unusual is the preamp "style" switch fitted to both units. Its "normal" position gives low to medium gain sounds via four of the amps' tube

Trace Elliot Speed Twin C100 combo, 2001.
(Both photos courtesy Trace Elliot)

stages; but when moved to "alternative" mode, the switch triggers extra power by adding an extra (fifth) tube stage and boosting the gain of one of those already in use.

This dual mode of operation is selectable from the amp itself, or with a pedal. However, it is also possible to toggle the preamp "style," as well as the units' reverb and effects loops, using a Musical Instrument Digital Interface (MIDI) controller (this could be an MIDI-equipped effects box, a synthesizer guitar, or similar external device) plugged into a socket at the back of the unit. The Speed Twin line also features smaller, 50- and 30-watt combos, and a "piggyback" 50-watt amp and cab – although these models do not provide MIDI as standard (it is offered as an optional extra).

Like the Tramp models, the Speed Twins use Celestion speakers: a single 12-inch (30.5-cm) cone in the lower-power combos, two 12-inch (30.5-cm) drivers in the C100, and four of them in each GSC412 cabinet.

Trace Elliot Speed Twin H100 amp and two GSC412 cabinets, 2001. (Both photos courtesy Trace Elliot)

LINE 6's DIGITAL MODELLING COMBOS

Line 6, based in Thousand Oaks, Southern California, is one of the fastest growing companies in today's music industry. Its amps and effects units (which include the Pod, one of the most widely used guitar "tone shapers") are based around "digital modelling" technology similar to that used by Vox in its Valvetronix units (see pages 332–333). Line 6 was, in fact, responsible for the first-ever amp of this kind, the AxSys 212, which appeared in 1996; and its current top-of-the-line digital modelling combo, the AX2-212, takes the concept to remarkable new levels.

Line 6 AX2-212 digital modelling combo, 2001. (Both photos courtesy John Henry's, London)

The AX2-212 is capable of recreating the sound of 28 different amps. Its "TubeTone" circuitry accurately imitates the characteristics of various familiar tube- and transistor-driven models (there are also some more "off-the-wall" simulations), and allows the player to combine them with a comprehensive range of onboard effects. The results are fed to the AX2-212's stereo, 100-watt power amp stage, and delivered through its two 12-inch (30.5-cm) speakers; there are also headphone and direct recording outputs. With so many variable parameters, the number of possible sounds the amp can provide is almost infinite; 128 factory presets deliver popular combinations of tones and effects, and players can also create and save their own customized settings in one of the unit's 128 programable channels. This data can be stored via MIDI, which may also be used to control the amp. Line 6 claim, with some justification, that "if [a sound's] in your head, you can find it in the AX2," and several leading guitarists are now using these almost overwhelmingly versatile amps.

Line 6's Flextone II also relies on the company's digital modelling circuitry. It offers no less than 32 amp models (such as "Brit Classic," "Modern Class A," and "Rectified"), 16 effects, and a "ToneTransfer" capability that allows users to move sound settings to and from their Pod units, or add new "tones" from software or the company's online library. The Flextone II puts out 60 watts into its single 12-inch (30.5-cm) speaker, and weighs in at 47lb (21.3kg) – 16lb (7.2kg) less than the AX2.

Line 6 Flextone II digital modelling combo, 2001. (Both photos courtesy John Henry's, London)

THE CRATE "BLUE VOODOO" AND "VINTAGE CLUB" SERIES

Crate Amplifiers, of St. Louis, Missouri, has been making award-winning combos and stacks (as well as mixers, PA gear, effects units, and accessories) since 1979, and prides itself on its "young, powerful, aggressive, and successful" image. This feisty company profile is certainly reflected in Crate's impressive line of professional audio products, including the "Blue Voodoo" and "Vintage Club" amps shown here.

The "Blue Voodoo" (BV) range, aimed at gigging musicians, is built to withstand the rigors of the road while delivering reliable, powerful performance night after night. The model shown here is the BV-120H, a tube-driven amp head rated at 120 watts; there are low and high gain channels, and the unit is designed to be operated with one or

Crate BV-120H amp head and BV412 cab, 2001. (Courtesy John Henry's, London)

Crate VC 50 combo, mid-1990s.
(Courtesy John Henry's, London)

two of Crate's matching speaker enclosures, the BV412s. As their name suggests, each of these is fitted with four 12-inch (30.5-cm) drivers, and is capable of handling up to 200 watts – more than enough for the "big, bad… soul-shaking" sound promised in the firm's publicity! (A 50-watt BV amp is also available.)

For guitarists looking for something a little more compact, Crate offers its Vintage Club combos, which are used by leading players such as Bo Diddley and Joe Walsh. The mid-1990s Vintage Club 50 shown in our photo incorporates two channels, a reverb unit, and two Celestion 12-inch (30.5-cm) speakers. It has recently been discontinued, and the current VC range comprises three newer models, all with similar, tube-powered designs: the VC508 (a small unit with a 5-watt output and an 8-inch (20.3-cm) speaker), and the 30- and 50-watt VC3112B and VC5212B.

COMBOS BY PEAVEY AND YAMAHA

Peavey DeltaBlues 210 combo, 2001. (Both photos courtesy John Henry's, London)

Meridian, Mississippi, is the headquarters of the largest amplifier and sound equipment manufacturer in the USA, Peavey Electronics. Its founder, Hartley Peavey, was born in Meridian, and has lived there all his life. A skilled engineer and woodworker as well as a gifted entrepreneur, he made his first amplifiers as a teenager, and formed the company that bears his name in 1965, with $8,000 borrowed from his father. From its beginnings in a single-room workshop, Peavey Electronics has grown steadily over the last three decades, developing and producing highly successful lines of solid-state and tube-driven amplification, as well as guitars, basses, drums, and keyboards, and realizing Hartley's long-held vision of "building quality equipment at fair and reasonable prices." The DeltaBlues 210 shown here is one of Peavey's bestselling guitar combos. It is an all-tube design with a two-channel preamp, three-band EQ, built-in tremolo and reverb, and a 30-watt output. The unit contains two 10-inch (25.4-cm) speakers, and can be connected to additional drivers (as well as external effects) via sockets on its back panel.

Yamaha is another, even larger and longer established corporate music business giant. It had its origins in a small reed-organ manufacturing operation started by Torakusu Yamaha in Japan in 1887. Ten years later, this became the Nippon Gakki company, which made its early reputation as a piano-maker, and later diversified into motorcycles and electronics. It launched its first range of guitars in the mid-1960s, and has since become a dominant international force in instrument- and amp-design. Among Yamaha's current guitar combos is the all-transistor DG80-212, a MIDI-equipped unit with extensive tone modelling features (providing various flavors of "lead," "drive," and "crunch") and comprehensive digital signal processing, including three types of digital reverb, and a "tape echo" delay effect. It delivers a powerful 80 watts into its single, British-made Celestion 12-inch (30.5-cm) speaker.

Yamaha DG80-112 combo, 2001. (Both photos courtesy John Henry's, London)

353

THE POLYTONE MINI-BRUTE AND THE ELECTRO-HARMONIX FREEDOM

The size and weight of some guitar amps can cause serious problems for players – especially those without trucks to transport them and roadies to set them up! There is a growing demand for lighter, more compact combos, not just for practice use, but also for serious professional work onstage and in the studio; and several ingenious designs currently on the market manage to combine portability with uncompromised power and tone.

Perhaps the most remarkable of these is the Polytone Mini-Brute, made by a company in Hollywood, and part of a range of top-quality solid state units that includes the 8lb (3.6kg), 100-watt Mega Brain amp head, as well as keyboard and bass combos. The Mini-Brute shown here puts out 110 watts and has a 12-inch (30.5-cm) speaker – but is easy to

Polytone Mini-Brute combo.
(Courtesy John Henry's, London)

carry, and measures only 15½ by 14 inches (39.4 by 35.5cm). Fitted with dual channels, reverb, EQ, an effects loop, and a jack to plug in an extra speaker (if one is needed!), it offers all the facilities most players require. Unsurprisingly, many musicians become devoted to their Brutes and Brains. Veteran jazz guitarist Phil Upchurch was recently quoted as saying "I love every Polytone I've ever used," adding that in 30 years of use, his amps had broken down only twice.

The other miniature combo shown here, the Electro-Harmonix Freedom, is a much cheaper, smaller device than the Polytone, but it boasts some innovative features of its own. Its rechargeable battery can operate away from the mains for up to six hours, and its hardwood casing conceals a surprisingly powerful 15-watt amplifier (with volume, tone and "bite" controls) and 8-inch (20.3-cm) speaker. Electro-Harmonix, responsible for the first-ever battery-powered amp back in the early 1970s, claims that the unit is "not a practice amp, not a toy," and that its low noise circuitry and preamp output socket make it suitable for recording as well as impromptu performances on the street or the beach.

Electro-Harmonix Freedom portable amp. (Courtesy Electro-Harmonix)

JIMMY BRUNO'S AMP SET-UP AND THE BURNS ORBIT

Jimmy Bruno, one of today's top jazz guitarists, has discerning tastes in instruments and amplification. A long-time user of handmade seven-string guitars by luthier Robert Benedetto, his onstage set-up also comprises a Walter Woods amp and a "Raezer's Edge" speaker cabinet. These are seen in our photo, together with Bruno's only effects box, a digital reverb unit by Alesis.

Walter Woods, based in Van Nuys, California, builds custom, lightweight amps that are favored by numerous jazzmen – including vibraphonists and bassists as well as guitar players. Woods amps are invariably transistor designs (with various esoteric refinements) encased in small red aluminum boxes, but their specifications and facilities vary widely; Jimmy Bruno's amp has two preamp channels and a bare minimum of controls. Its 75-watt output is fed to his Raezer's Edge Stealth 12 cabinet – designed by Rich Raezer of Swarthmore, Pennsylvania, whose products Bruno has endorsed for several years. A ported reflex design loaded with a single 12-inch (30.5-cm) driver (the twin ports can be seen below the speaker grille), it provides a focused, powerful sound, and can handle peaks of up to 300 watts.

By contrast, the other amp shown here is an unusual British model – a reissue of the transistorized Orbit combo developed in the 60s by the Burns

Woods custom amplifier, Raezer's Edge Stealth 12 cab, and Alesis Nanoverb, 1997. (Courtesy Jimmy Bruno/Rich Raezer/Robert Benedetto)

company. Its founder, Jim Burns (1925–99), was a highly talented luthier and designer, whose amps and guitars were used by many distinguished players, including jazzman Ike Issacs, and Hank Marvin of The Shadows; his Tri-Sonic pickups were also fitted to the famous Red Special guitar hand-built by Queen's Brian May. Sadly, Burns' technical skills were not matched by his business acumen, and his career was plagued by financial and other difficulties. Forced to sell his original firm in 1965, he made two unsuccessful comebacks in the 1970s, but lived to see the revival of some of his designs (including the Bison guitar and bass, and the Orbit combo) by a new firm, Burns London, to which he was a consultant. This company continues to market these and other designs, which are selling steadily.

Burns Orbit combo, 1990s. (Both photos courtesy Acoustic Centre, London)

BASS AMPS 1 –
THE TRACE ELLIOT V8

So far, we have focused on amplification for standard electric guitars, but over the next few pages we turn our attention to a cross-section of recent bass guitar rigs. The featured models use a variety of technologies, but most are physically large units, with the high wattages and massive speaker sizes needed to produce floor-shaking low frequencies for contemporary rock, reggae, and other popular music styles. Such sounds involve formidable amounts of electronic and acoustic energy, and put heavy demands on any amp and cabinet; as a result, rugged construction, as well as ample reserve power, is essential. Flimsily built or inadequately specified gear will simply be unable to withstand the pounding most bassists are likely to inflict on it night after night.

However, one glance at the Trace Elliot V8 seems to confirm that it is more than equal to such onstage rigors. Its black buffalo covering, the metal mesh screening off its 16 pre- and

power-amp tubes, and the stainless steel corners protecting the edges of its head and cab, all exude solidity; and the amp's 400-watt output (incorporating a switchable gain boost that adds in two extra tube stages) should be sufficient in almost any imaginable circumstances. The V8 also has an onboard compressor, with a slow attack and release. Trace Elliot explain that this, rather than limiting the bassist's signal, "is designed to maintain warmth and a usable dynamic range, [making the V8] perfect for aggressive funk and rock playing." Other features include a three-band EQ, a direct inject (DI) output for recording or PA feed, and an effects loop.

The V8 is seen here with Trace Elliot's 1084 cabinet, which contains no less than eight 10-inch (25.4-cm) drivers, and can handle up to 640 watts. Alternative cabs are available with 12-inch (30.5-cm) or 15-inch (38-cm) speaker cones.

Trace Elliot V8 bass amp and 1084 cabinet, 2001.
(Courtesy John Henry's, London)

BASS AMPS 2 – THE TRACE ELLIOT V4 AND COMMANDO 10

Some of the Trace Elliot V8's features are also available on other, smaller-sized V-series bass amps. These include the V4-210H combo, which shares its big brother's tube compressor circuitry, but turns in a more modest (though still impressive) 200-watt output, delivering what the company describe as a "smooth, expansive" sound through its twin 10-inch (25.4-cm) speakers.

Trace Elliot's "Commando" amps are even more compact; the range comprises three bass combos, the 15, the 12, and the Commando 10 seen in our photo. These units are named for their speaker sizes, and combine uncompromising performance with a remarkable degree of portability; the 10 tips the scales at only 37.5lb (17kg), and its dimensions are a manageable 19 x 16 inches (48 x 41cm). It achieves some of this reduced weight and size by using solid-state circuitry instead of the tubes used on the V8 and V4. The Commando's field effect transistor (FET) input stage provides, in Trace Elliot's words, "a valve-like warmth… [and] can produce a soft overdrive effect akin to a mildly overdriven

Trace Elliot Commando 10 bass combo, 2001. (Courtesy Trace Elliot)

Trace Elliot V4 bass combo, 2001.
(Courtesy Trace Elliot)

[tube] amplifier." It has a three-band EQ, plus an additional "mid-shift" control that, when activated, can reduce lower-mid frequencies, while providing a corresponding boost to the upper-midrange. The combo, rated at 65 watts, is able to play "clean" or "dirty," depending on the musician's preference. Trace Elliot comments that "[its] power output stage has been designed to 'soft clip'… with no damage resulting to the amplifier or loudspeaker. This will increase the overall subjective volume, if you are prepared to use a 'grungy' bass sound!" Bassists wishing to experiment with soft clipping may choose to avoid the wrath of their neighbors by plugging in a pair of headphones – a socket for them is fitted to the Commando 10's front panel.

BASS AMPS 3 – TRACE ELLIOT'S 712 AND 1210H COMBOS

Trace Elliot's comprehensive line of bass guitar amplification includes two ranges of models with (respectively) seven- and 12-band onboard graphic equalization. Unlike conventional treble, middle, and bass knobs, which provide broad overall control, graphic EQ allows players to target specific bands of frequencies for boost or attenuation; this can be especially useful when solving feedback problems, as well as for precise tone shaping.

On the Trace Elliot 712 combo (as on other models in the "seven-band" series) the graphic EQ is built into a high-performance preamp, the GP7, which also supplies a balanced "direct inject" signal to a mixing desk or other external device. For maximum flexibility, EQ settings can be switched in or out of the feed to this DI output. The preamp also features a "mid pre-shape" circuit for extra punch, and a dual

band compressor, placed after the "shape" and "graphic" sections in the signal chain. The 712 has a 65-watt power amp stage, which drives a single 12-inch (30.5-cm) speaker.

The 300-watt 1210H combo incorporates the

Trace Elliot 712 bass combo, 2001. (Courtesy Trace Elliot)

*Trace Elliot 1210H bass combo, 2001.
(Courtesy Trace Elliot)*

GP12X preamp, which boasts a 12-band graphic giving close control over frequencies from 30Hz (the bass guitar's bottom "E" string vibrates at 41.2Hz, but lower-pitched resonances are sometimes encountered) to 15kHz. In addition to its "pre-shape" and compression controls, which are similar to those on the GP7, the GP12 also offers "harmonic emphasis" – a switchable circuit that adds brightness to the player's sound by synthesising new harmonics from its signal; Trace Elliot describes the effect as akin to fitting a new set of guitar strings. Other preamp facilities include an overdrivable "valve stage" providing increasing levels of warm, tube-generated distortion, and noise reduction. The combo has four 10-inch (25.4-cm) speakers, plus a horn driver to handle higher frequencies, and can also be connected to external cabs.

Trace Elliot's seven- and 12-band amps share a pleasing cosmetic touch: their green, adjustable-brightness electroluminiscent front panels enable the controls to be seen in the dark!

BASS AMPS 4 – AMPEG AND ORANGE

Now part of the same St. Louis Music group as Crate (see pages 350–351), Ampeg was founded in the 1940s by musician Everette Hull, the inventor of a pickup, known as an "Amplified Peg," designed to be fitted to a string bass. The company subsequently became involved in amplifier development (they are believed to be the first firm to install a reverb unit to a guitar amp), and are especially renowned for bass rigs such as the Pro Series SVT-2 (the initials stand for Ampeg's patented "Super Valve Technology") shown here.

The SVT-2PRO delivers 300 watts; surprisingly, it is the smallest amp in the Pro Series, which also includes 450- and 1600-watt models (the latter is the biggest amp of its kind currently

available anywhere). Its front panel has "ultralow," "bright," and "ultrahigh" switches, bass and treble controls plus a "tunable" midrange knob giving cut or boost at five selectable frequencies, and a nine-band graphic equalizer. It appears here with Ampeg's PR-410HLF cabinet, incorporating four 10-inch (25.4-cm) speakers and an additional horn driver. As well as handling peak levels of up to 1200 watts, the PR-410HLF is strong enough to withstand even the roughest treatment when in transit between gigs; it is built from 13-ply Baltic birchwood, and the edges and corners are PVC-protected.

Ampeg SVT-2PRO head and PR-410HLF cabinet, 2001. (Courtesy John Henry's, London)

Two British-made Orange guitar amps were featured on pages 338–339. The Orange bass stack in the photo opposite is powered by the company's AD140B head – a modified version of their AD140 guitar amp, which has won many plaudits from players, and was voted "the best amplifier in the world" by Guitarist magazine. Both guitar and bass versions of the AD140 boast a 140-watt output, and the model can be used with one of two Orange cabs: the 1X15, containing a single, 15-inch (38-cm), 400-watt rated driver; or the 4X10, loaded with a quartet of 10-inch (25.4-cm) units and a high frequency horn.

Orange AD140B head and matching cab, 2001. (Courtesy John Henry's, London)

BASS AMPS 5 – ASHDOWN AND SWR

Ashdown Engineering, which has its home near Colchester in Essex, England, was founded in 1997 by ex-Trace Elliot Managing Director Mark Gooday. The company's products combine stylish design with majestic levels of performance; the ABM900 Bass Magnifier amp in our picture is a stereo model, delivering 2 x 575 watts to its matching ABM-1510 cab. All Bass Magnifiers share the same preamp specifications: standard bass, middle, and treble controls are supplemented by graphic EQ-style sliders (visible between the tone knobs on the unit's front panel) giving 15dB cut and boost at 180Hz, 340Hz, 1.3kHz, and 2.6kHz. There are also connections for Direct Inject output and effects, as well as a stereo input, designed for use with a sampler or other external sound source. Another feature of the Bass Magnifiers is their "sub-harmonizer," which delivers an extra dose of low frequency energy; this device is switchable from the amp or via a pedal. The Ashdown 1510 cab contains one 15-inch (38-cm) and two 10-inch (25.4-cm) speakers and a horn; it is rated at 600 watts for continuous power handling, and can accommodate even higher peak program levels.

Ashdown ABM900 amp and AMB-1510 cab, 2001. (Both photos courtesy John Henry's, London)

The second bass rig on these pages was created by the SWR Sound Corporation, of Sun Valley, California. SWR was started by Steve W. Rabe in 1984, and its high-end amps and speakers are used by many star names, including former Led Zeppelin bassist John Paul Jones, Phil Lesh of the Grateful Dead, and Marcus Miller. The amp head in our photo is the company's top-of-the-range SM-900, which can be used in stereo (2 x 350 watts) or mono (800 watts), and incorporates EQ, limiter, effects loops, and a DI output. With it is "Big Bertha," a 2 x 15-inch (38-cm)-loaded enclosure, weighing almost 100lb (45.4kg), that delivers what the firm's publicity describes as "classic, thundering tone." Other cabs in the SWR stable have equally colorful names, such as "Son of Bertha," "Big Ben," "Goliath" (Senior and Junior models), and "Henry the 8 x 8" (there are no prizes for guessing the number of speakers it contains, or their size!). More SWR amplification can be seen on pages 372–373.

SWR SM-900 amp and "Big Bertha." (Both photos courtesy John Henry's, London)

ACOUSTIC GUITAR AMPS BY TRACE ELLIOT

Acoustic guitarists nearly always need to amplify their instruments onstage. Some of them prefer to use microphones and in-house PAs, but the risk of feedback and the problems of relying on unfamiliar sound systems (sometimes controlled by less-than-sympathetic engineers) have led many modern players to opt for "electro-acoustic" guitar/amp setups. These involve the use of guitars fitted with piezo transducers or other types of onboard "bugs," whose output is fed to specially designed, high quality combos. Such units may look superficially similar to standard electric guitar rigs, but have lower distortion and coloration, and are built to handle the broader frequency spectrum and greater dynamic range generated by many acoustic instruments.

Trace Elliot is recognized as one of the leaders in this rapidly growing area of amplification, and two of its acoustic guitar amps, the TA100R and TA200S, are shown on these pages. The 100R is a 100-watt model, containing four 5-inch (12.7-cm) speakers; it provides low level, high level and balanced inputs, digital reverb and delay, and – crucially – a five-band graphic equalizer and "notch" filter. The latter is intended to attenuate

Trace Elliot TA200S acoustic combo, 2001.
(Courtesy Trace Elliot)

Trace Elliot TA100R acoustic combo, 2000.s
(Courtesy Acoustic Centre, London)

frequencies that may be causing feedback, and can be applied anywhere between 60 and 720Hz. The combo also makes use of Trace Elliot's "Dynamic Correction" circuitry. This, in the company's words, "monitors the signal at the input stage and that being presented to the speakers, [and corrects] any anomaly between the two to guarantee an accurate reproduction of the original."

The TA200S is a slightly larger, stereo acoustic combo with eight internal speakers, a 2 x 100-watt output ,and four channels. It can be configured in various ways to allow the player to utilize stereo instruments and/or effects, and two 100Rs may also be wired up to work as "satellites" to a TA200, providing more power and a wider stereo spread.

ACOUSTIC GUITAR AMPS BY AER

AER stands for Audio Electric Research. However, despite its name, the company is a German one, set up in 1992 by Susanne Janz-Eisenmann, Michael Eisenmann, and Udo Rösner, who had previously worked together in various other European music and electronics ventures. They specialize in the design and manufacture of high quality acoustic instrument amplification, and among their many distinguished customers are ex-Focus guitarist Jan Akkerman, US resonator virtuoso Bob Brozman, and British jazzman Martin Taylor.

Both the AER combos seen here pack extraordinary amounts of technology and performance into very small units, and are capable of generating surprisingly high, distortion-free sound levels. The Acousticube IIa measures just

13 by 13 inches (33 by 33cm) and weighs under 30lb (13.6kg), but incorporates a 120-watt solid state amplifier and a two-way, 8-inch (20.3-cm) speaker. It has two channels with a comprehensive range of inputs, extensive EQ, and a "colour" switch on channel 1, intended for use with fingerstyle guitars, and giving a combination of midrange cut and treble boost. There is also a 100-preset onboard digital effects unit, providing various types of reverb, delay and other treatments, separately and in combination.

*AER Acousticube IIa
combo, 2001.
(Both photos courtesy John
Henry's, London)*

AER Compact 60 combo, 2001.
(Both photos courtesy John Henry's, London)

The AER Compact 60, shown in our other photograph, is even lighter and tinier, and puts out 60 watts. Like the Acousticube, it accepts almost any type of incoming signal, and can even serve as a small PA system, with a microphone and instrument being run simultaneously into each of its input channels. There is a three-band EQ, and built-in effects include digital reverb and delay, as well as a "color" circuit identical to the Acousticube's. Both AER units offer outputs for external mixing desks and tape recorders.

Among AER's other innovative products are the "Active System 812" (a miniature 1000-watt PA!), and its Basic Performer, Basscube, Domino, and battery-powered Tramp combos.

ACOUSTIC AMPS BY FENDER AND SWR

Fender's recently introduced Acoustasonic combos are suitable not only for acoustic guitarists, but also mandolinists, fiddlers, and any other instrumentalists and singers seeking clear, powerful amplification. The flagship Acoustasonic SFX combo, shown here, incorporates the company's "stereo field expansion" technology, which uses a soon-to-be-patented onboard matrix system to process the output from the player's instrument through one of 32 stereo digital effect presets. The signal is then sent to the unit's speakers, and radiates throughout the performance space with what Fender claim to be up to 300 degrees of stereo sound imaging. The Acoustasonic SFX has two input channels, a total output of 160 watts, and 10-inch (25.4-cm) and 8-inch (20.3-cm) speakers, plus a piezo horn. Other Acoustasonic combos (not currently fitted with the SFX system) include the 30 (a mono, 30-watt combo); the 2 x 40-watt Junior (especially designed for acoustic-electric guitars); and the Pro, with extensive onboard effects and the same power rating as the SFX.

Fender Acoustasonic SFX combo, 2001.
(Courtesy Fender Musical Instruments Corp.)

As well as its mammoth bass rigs (seen on pages 366–367), Californian amp designers SWR also produce the Acoustic Series, a line of handmade, solid state devices used by (among others) Davey Johnstone from the Elton John band, Lindsay Buckingham (Fleetwood Mac), and UK folk guitarist Martin Simpson. SWR's publicity states that these striking-looking combos have "the warmth and ability to reproduce the natural tones and characteristics of electric/acoustic instruments." There are three currently available units: the 80-watt "Strawberry Blonde" and "Blonde On Blonde" models, and the larger "California Blonde" seen in our picture. This is a 100-watt combo with a 12-inch (30.5-cm) speaker complemented by a high-fidelity "tweeter" (treble driver). There are two channels with mono, stereo, and separate mic inputs, plus active bass, midrange, and treble controls, spring reverb, and comprehensive connections for effects, headphones, and recording machines.

SWR "California Blonde" combo, 2000. (Courtesy Acoustic Centre, London)

GUITAR EFFECTS 1

Effects are irresistible to many guitarists as they offer the prospect of sonic transformation at the click of a switch. With a touch of wah-wah, some delay, or a spot of distortion, even the most indifferent player can seem more polished and professional; while more accomplished musicians use pedals and similar devices as tools to create fresh, exciting textures from their axes and amps. The next few pages feature a range of guitar and bass effects, including standard, familiar types as well as original creations by companies such as Electro-Harmonix, DigiTech, and Yamaha.

The **Reverb** *unit (far left) creates an electronic simulation of traditional spring reverb. This pedal allows high frequencies, which can provide unpleasant "twanging" sounds when passed through the effect, to be attenuated.*

Slap Echo *provides a quick repeat of the original signal, similar to the tape delays on rockabilly and other vintage records.*

Vox Wah-Wah pedal.
(Courtesy Korg UK Ltd.)

Tremolo *is a volume modulation effect, breaking the guitar's signal into repeated "shudders" whose speed and depth can be controlled from the pedal.*

Chorus *pedals produce small delays in the guitar signal, and combine these with the instrument's direct sound to create spacious doubling effects.*

Flanging *is similar to chorusing, producing distinctive, shifting boosts and reductions in various audio frequencies.*

Phasing *involves the use of an oscillator to create "notches" across the frequency range of the incoming signal. Their speed is adjustable from the pedal.*

All distortion effects involve the deliberate roughening of the guitar's signal by introducing square wave harmonic distortion into it. The Danelectro "Grilled Cheese" unit gives control over the level and "resonance" of the effect.

The "T-Bone" pedal offers another flavor of distortion.

Danelectro's "Pastrami" overdrive incorporates a preamp that gives a powerful boost to the incoming signal, making it likely to distort when sent on to the amplifier.

Compressors *"level off" the dynamic range of incoming signals, creating an effect that can vary from a subtle, "glassy" sound to powerful punchiness.*

Also illustrated is a Vox Wah-Wah: pressing the pedal down gives a sweeping boost to a succession of frequencies, creating the distinctive "wah" effect used on countless records since the 1960s.

Danelectro effects pedals.
(Photo courtesy John Henry's, London)

GUITAR EFFECTS 2

New York-based effects manufacturer Electro-Harmonix is one of the most innovative and highest-profile creators of pedals for guitars and other instruments. Founded in 1968 by Mike Matthews, the company was immensely successful throughout the 1970s, but suffered harder times in the following decade, and was eventually sold. However, Matthews (who is also behind Sovtek, a US-based supplier of Russian-made tubes and other components) subsequently regained ownership of the Electro-Harmonix trademark, and is once again producing an extensive line of effects and accessories. These include both new models and reissues of longtime favorites such as the Micro Synthesizer (see photo), a device enabling guitarists to generate Moog-style textures. The Micro Synth is controlled by 10 sliders, which combine the incoming instrument with octave, sub-octave, and square wave signals, and filter the ensuing mixture to produce, in E-H's words, "a virtually limitless array of analog synthesizer sounds." Also shown here is an Electro-Harmonix Small Clone pedal, a rich-sounding, battery- or mains-driven "full chorus" unit with a rotary "rate" adjuster and switchable "depth" control.

Electro-Harmonix Small Clone Chorus, 2001. (Courtesy Electro-Harmonix)

Electro-Harmonix Micro Synthesizer, 2001. (Courtesy Electro-Harmonix)

DigiTech 2120 Valve Guitar System, 2001.
(Courtesy DigiTech)

Players seeking a wide range of sounds from a single, rackmountable device will want to investigate DigiTech's 2120 Valve Guitar System, which, as the firm's publicity puts it, "combines guitar tones and digital effects to produce [results] that will satisfy even the most discriminating player." It offers numerous tube- and solid state-style amp emulations (from "warm clean" and "blues tube" to "heavy sustain" and "grunge") as well as wah, delay, and other signal treatments, and has extensive preset and programmable memories for specific settings.

Most competent guitarists have little difficulty in tuning their instruments by ear; but in noisy onstage conditions, this may be tricky, and devices like the Danelectro Tuner pedal (also seen here), which provide a visual indication of whether each guitar string is sharp or flat, can be useful. On some amps, tuners like this one can be patched into the signal path to allow "silent" retuning, with the loudspeakers muted.

Danelectro Tuner pedal, 2001.
(Courtesy John Henry's, London)

GUITAR EFFECTS 3

Part of the same product line as its DG80-112 combo (featured on pages 352–353), Yamaha's "DG Stomp," seen here, offers a similar set of digital amp simulations and effects (including Compression, Modulation, Delay, Reverb, Wah, and speaker cabinet colorations) in pedal form. Designed to be equally at home onstage or in the studio, the DG Stomp has 180 "patches" (combinations of various parameters), as well as a built-in tuner and a digital audio output. In common with several similar models, it gives an almost limitless variety of sounds in a single, relatively compact box, reducing the need for guitarists to invest in multiple devices that must then be interconnected and powered.

Yamaha DG Stomp, 2001. (Courtesy John Henry's, London)

Our next two pictures show more of the Electro-Harmonix guitar pedal range. The Stereo Polychorus provides a comprehensive selection of chorus, flanging, and double-tracking treatments; to take full advantage of it, a stereo guitar amp or a pair of mono amps and speakers will be needed. Like many of E-H's effects units, the Polychorus is supplied with a leaflet giving sample control settings for widely used effects; by following the manufacturer's instructions, new users will soon be able to enjoy the pedal's "rotary speaker," "twelve string guitar," "chime," "vibrato," and other sounds.

The Electro-Harmonix Small Stone is a mono phase shifter whose "rate" and "color" controls interact to create an impressive series of sounds – from what E-H describe as "pronounced shifting effects... [as] fundamentals and harmonics glide in and out [of phase]," to gentler, slower sweeps.

Electro-Harmonic Stereo Polychorus, 2001. (Courtesy Electro-Harmonix)

Electro-Harmonic Small Stone phaser, 2001. (Courtesy Electro-Harmonix)

The final pedal featured on these pages is Danelectro's "Fish 'n' Chips" EQ. We have already encountered graphic equalizers on several of the amplifiers seen earlier; like them, this pedal offers boost and cut at various audio frequencies, acting like a advanced tone control.

Danelectro "Fish 'n' Chips" EQ pedal, 2001. (Courtesy John Henry's, London)

GUITAR EFFECTS 4

For many electric guitar players, distortion is an essential element. Much of the appeal of vintage tube amps lies in their ability to overload in a warm, "musical" way that cannot be matched by solid state models (unless they have ingenious, often digital assistance). There are technical reasons why tubes and transistors sound as they do: the distortion that comes from tube circuits tends to contain even order harmonics, which are subjectively more pleasing to the ear; while solid state amps generate less agreeable sounding odd order harmonics. These facts seem to suggest that using some type of tube-driven distortion unit is the surest way to achieve the best overdriven tone; and Electro-Harmonix's "Hot Tubes," seen here, is one of the very few pedals actually to incorporate tubes in its circuitry.

E-H has a long history of providing exceptional distortion devices. In the early 1970s, one of company founder Mike Matthews' most popular designs was the Big Muff Pi, known by some as the "king of fuzz boxes," and used by Carlos Santana, David Gilmour, and other top guitarists. According to E-H, the Hot Tubes can mimic the "classic sweet sustain" of the Big Muff, but can also be precisely adjusted to produce a wide range of other sounds, including its trademark "searing, tube-driven screams."

The pedal is mains-powered, and has master output level, gain, drive, and treble and bass controls.

Electro-Harmonix Hot Tubes, 2001.
(Courtesy Electro-Harmonix)

Danelectro Bacon 'n' Eggs Distortion, 2001.

*Danelectro Black Coffee
Metal Distortion, 2001.*

*Danelectro French Toast
Octave Distortion, 2001.
(All Danelectro pedals
courtesy John Henry's, London)*

The other three pedals on these pages, all manufactured by Danelectro, are transistor-based, but deliver their own distinctive brands of distortion. The "Bacon 'n' Eggs" model is both a fuzz and a miniature amp/speaker, while the "French Toast" unit can create a doubled signal an octave above the notes fed to it by the guitar, as well as distorting and providing basic EQ. The Black Coffee Metal Distortion pedal offers a more extreme performance, and is suitable for would-be headbangers everywhere!

GUITAR EFFECTS 5

Danelectro's "Chicken Salad" vibrato pedal is designed to simulate the sound made by the rotating Leslie speakers often used to amplify Hammond organs, and sometimes favored by guitarists. Plugging the pedal in between instrument and amp is certainly less time-consuming than rigging a Leslie, and there are just two control knobs, which set the speed and intensity of the effect.

Most of the Electro-Harmonix units seen so far have been reissues of the company's classic 70s and 80s designs – but its Q-Tron Envelope Controlled Filter (and its little brother, the Mini Q-Tron) are new products, stemming from a collaboration between E-H founder Mike Matthews and designer Mike Beigel. In 1972, Beigel was responsible for the Mutron III envelope controlled filter, which provided "automatic wah-wah," and was widely used in rock and funk. The Q-Tron is an update of the Mutron, with superior frequency response and lower noise. Its filter can be set to sweep up (giving a "wah") or down (for an "ow" effect), and the "range" control determines whether the Q-Tron produces

Danelectro "Chicken Salad" vibrato, 2001. (Courtesy John Henry's, London)

Electro-Harmonix Q-Tron, 2001. (Courtesy Electro-Harmonix)

Electro-Harmonix Mini Q-Tron, 2001.
(Courtesy Electro-Harmonix)

a preponderance of vowel-like sounds or overtones. The Mini Q-Tron offers similar performance in a smaller package.

The last item here, DigiTech's extraordinarily comprehensive GNX1 "guitar system," is part of its series of GeNetX processors. This device goes a step beyond standard amp modelling by allowing guitarists to tailor their own ideal sound using combinations of simulated amps and speaker cabinets. This can be done quickly and intuitively by selecting two existing "amp models" on the GNX1's "green amp" and "red amp" channels, and then turning its "Warp" control to experiment with various blends of the two "virtual" amps. The result, termed a HyperModel, may then be saved and played through (in conjunction with the unit's other facilities and effects), and can also form the basis for further experimentation, giving the musician (in DigiTech's words) "the ability to create a limitless library of tones."

DigiTech GNX1, 2001. (Courtesy DigiTech)

GUITAR EFFECTS 6

Danelectro "Chili Dog" octave pedal, 2001. (Courtesy John Henry's, London)

The Danelectro "Chili Dog" seen here is an "octave" pedal, which generates doubling effects one and/or two octaves below the pitch of the notes it receives from the guitar. When combined with the original signal, these extra tones can fill out the player's sound impressively – though there are sometimes inevitable delays and glitches in their production.

Built like a tank, and incorporating valve-driven circuitry like its "Hot Tubes" cousin (featured on pages 380–381), Electro-Harmonix's "Tube Zipper" is, according to company founder Mike Matthews, "the greatest product we've introduced in over 20 years." A distortion box combined with an envelope filter that can be used in "TRON" mode for treatments similar to those provided by the E-H Q-Tron (see previous pages), or switched to "TRILL" to add modulation to the envelope of the input signal, making it seem that the guitar's notes are being trilled, the Tube Zipper has the capabilty to generate what E-H describe as "entirely unique new wild effects." Current users include George Clinton, Adrian Belew of King Crimson, and Sheryl Crow's guitarist Peter Stroud.

Electro-Harmonix Tube Zipper, 2001. (Courtesy Electro-Harmonix)

Electro-Harmonix Frequency
Anaylzer, 2001.
(Courtesy Electro-Harmonix)

DigiTech Whammy, 2001.
(Courtesy DigiTech)

Electro-Harmonix's "Frequency Analyzer," also illustrated opposite, is another highly unusual piece of gear. It is a ring modulator, which takes each note supplied by a guitar or other instrument and generates two additional tones from it. The device allows the creation of "instant" moving harmonies, as well as weirder, more dissonant sounds, and works best with single-note solos – the multiple signals produced by inputting chords can rapidly get out of control! It is possible to adjust the level of the original guitar/instrument relative to the generated tones (or completely remove it), and other subtle modifications are possible.

Many contemporary guitarists make use of "whammy bar" effects, but the latest version of DigiTech's Whammy pedal makes it possible to create "dive bombing," smooth pitch bends and similar vibrato arm-type techniques entirely electronically. No strings need to be stretched (or broken!); the unit's microchips will simulate even the most extreme Van Halen or Vai-style detuning, and it can also be controlled via MIDI.

GUITAR EFFECTS 7

DigiTech's GeNetX range of "hypermodelling" guitar effects boxes includes the GNX1seen on pages 382–383, two other floor-standing units (the GNX2 and 3), and the Genesis 3 (illustrated here), a desktop device aimed primarily at the home or professional studio user.

The Genesis 3 has connections for guitar and CD (making it possible to play along with existing recordings), a MIDI interface, and analog and digital audio outputs for mixing desks and recording machines; it can also be linked to an optional foot controller. In "performance mode," its amp and speaker cabinet simulations, containing programs that mimic Vox, Marshall, MESA/Boogie, Fender, and other classic models, and its digital effects section (including wah-wah, compression, chorus, phasing, and some "digital whammy bar" programs similar to those on DigiTech's Whammy pedal) are all easily accessible to the player. Like the GNXs, the Genesis has rotary knobs for most of its key functions; and there is even a facility for setting the speed of repeat echoes on a digital delay by tapping the required tempo into the machine via a button on the front panel. This is a welcome alternative to the usual method of calculating the delay in milliseconds and programming in the figures!

DigiTech Genesis 3, 2001.
(Courtesy DigiTech)

The unit offers 48 user and 48 factory presets, and it is possible to store up to nine new "hypermodels." which are created by blending combinations of the supplied amp/speaker settings. Most of the machine's individual effect parameters can be modified when the Genesis is in "edit mode" (though some can only be changed using DigiTech's proprietary GenEdit computer software), and all presets and customized settings can be backed up via MIDI. And should the choice of sounds and effects temporarily overwhelm the user, there is a "Dry Track" feature that allows a "clean" (unprocessed) guitar signal to be sent straight from the Genesis to (say) a multitrack recorder. This can subsequently be routed back into the device during mixdown, giving more time for experimentation and adjustment.

GUITAR EFFECTS 8

The DigiTech GeNetX/Genesis units are top-of-the-range products, but the company also makes innovative gear at lower prices. Their RP series of "modeling guitar processors" starts at a modest $129.95 for the RP100. Though little larger than some single effect boxes, this unit provides a variety of favorite "virtual" amps and effects, plus refinements such as simulated speaker cabinets with different microphone placements for subtle but effective tonal variations. It also incorporates a "Rhythm Trainer" (a selection of pre-programmed drum loops that could be useful while practising or recording demos) and a digital tuner, and has stereo line out and headphone sockets, plus an input for an optional expression pedal. Guitar Player magazine described the RP100 as "a no brainer for entry-level players who want an all-in-one effects/modeling box," and its size, versatility, and price have already made it a bestseller.

*DigiTech RP100, 2001.
(Both photos courtesy
DigiTech)*

Two other RPs are also available, and here we show the most advanced of them, the RP300. It boasts a built-in pedal that gives control of some of its performance parameters in real time, two extra effects (bringing the total to 30, up to 12 of which can be used simultaneously), and several additional features and refinements. Among these is DigiTech's "Learn-A-Lick," a built-in device that can sample a phrase from a CD or tape, save it, and replay it at one quarter of its original speed without changing its pitch; this permits even the fastest, most elaborate solos to be studied and learned note-for-note. Like the company's other modelling processors, the RP300 is fitted with knobs for easy, intuitive adjustment, and can be connected to mixing desks or tape recorders as well as amps. It retails at $249.95.

DigiTech RP300, 2001. (Both photos courtesy DigiTech)

BASS EFFECTS 1

*Electro-Harmonix Bass
Microsynthesizer, 2001.
(Courtesy Electro-Harmonix)*

Bass players have never been as well provided with effects as guitarists – but in the past few years, more and more manufacturers have been turning their attention to expanding the instrument's capabilities, and now, at last, a wider selection of bass-oriented "stomp boxes" and other devices has begun to emerge. Among the leaders in this expanding market is Electro-Harmonix, which has recently reissued its classic 1970s Bass Microsynthesizer, designed (like its guitar counterpart, seen on pages 376–377) to generate powerful Moog-style sounds. The two Microsynths have similar specifications, including the same complement of voices and filters, though the sweep range on the bass unit has been modified to handle the instrument's lower frequencies. According to Electro-Harmonix, the Microsynth, relaunched in 1999, is capable of producing "everything from percussive [noises] to backward sounding bowed sounds," and many contemporary bass players, especially those working in the areas of funk and dance music, will relish the expanded tonal palette it provides.

DigiTech is also making impressive new tools for the bassist, such as the BP8 "Paradigm Bass Effect Pedal" – the first-ever processor the firm has designed for the instrument. Unlike its guitar modelling devices, which are entirely transistorized, the BP8 incorporates a tube preamp, and offers a variety of preset tube- and solid state-style "voicings," a huge range of adjustable effects (like delay, reverb, compression, chorus, envelope filter, and pitch shift), a four-band EQ section, and a notch filter to "dial out" unwanted frequencies. There is also an expression pedal and an onboard tuner, as well as standard stereo and split low/high frequency outputs (the latter are used when the driving a "bi-amped" rig, in which the deep bass and higher frequency signals are sent to separate amplifiers). The BP8's rugged build, versatility, and ease of use make it a useful addition to any bassist's arsenal, and it is equally at home on the road or in the studio.

DigiTech BP8 vacuum tube bass preamp/processor, 2001. (Courtesy DigiTech)

BASS EFFECTS 2

Electro-Harmonix's punningly named "Bassballs" pedal is described by the company as "the first and only envelope follower of its kind." Its twin sweeping filters are designed to increase the bass's presence and impact, generating shifting peaks and notches in its frequency response to produce what E-H call "vowel-like overtones". The filters' range is boosted by turning up the unit's sensitivity control and playing more vigorously, and the pedal also includes a switchable fuzz effect. "Bassballs" is available in two forms: the original, New York-made version (as seen here); and a darker-colored unit, built in Russia, and costing $20 less. Both models are electronically identical.

The DigiTech BP200 is a bass version of the RP guitar modelling devices seen on pages 388–389. Like those boxes, it derives its formidable power from the firm's proprietary AudioDNA microchip, introduced in early 2001, and recently described by Rob Urry, President of DigiTech's parent, Harman Music Group, as "the "Intel Inside" of guitar products… [which will establish] a new era in audio processing and will redefine performance, value and consumer expectations for musicians." The BP200's capabilities are as impressive as those of its guitar-based cousins; it contains 16 amp models and 22 onboard effects, which can be adjusted and combined to create distinctive new sounds; and its useful practice facilities include Jam-A-Long and Rhythm Trainer.

Electro-Harmonix Bassballs, 2001.
(Courtesy Electro-Harmonix)

DigiTech BP200, 2001. (Courtesy DigiTech)

No area of the music industry has developed as quickly and dramatically as effects design and manufacture. Thanks to current technology, sounds that, a few decades ago, were either unrealizable, or only accessible via sophisticated studio set-ups, are now almost commonplace. However, it is significant that so much of the hi-tech gear featured in the previous few pages strives not to invent wholly new effects, but to mimic or clone the characteristics of vintage equipment from the 1950s and 60s. Although frequently accused of chasing fads and novelties, the music industry and its customers often seem surprisingly sentimental – even, perhaps, conservative – in their preferences for the reassuringly familiar sounds of classic gear.

SYNTH ACCESS GUITARS 1

When the late Jerry Garcia first had the opportunity to use a guitar capable of controlling a synthesiser, he commented that it allowed him to realize one of his musical dreams, and become a horn player without needing to learn the sax or the trumpet. Modern synths and samplers give artists easy access to the sounds of these and many other instruments, and over the last 20 years countless pop and rock keyboardists have taken advantage of this powerful technology. However, surprisingly few guitarists have followed Garcia's lead and adopted MIDI-enabled axes – perhaps because of difficulties in interfacing synths and guitars that have only recently been resolved.

Piano-type MIDI keyboards are like multiple switches; pressing and releasing their keys generates the "note on/off" (and other) data required to operate synths and similar sound sources. But on guitars, notes and chords are started by striking strings; and a guitar-to-MIDI pickup has to convert these complex vibrations into note data, send a "stop" message when the strings cease sounding, deal with players' tendency to bend notes (this can confuse some MIDI systems), and filter out extraneous finger and plectrum noises that could create spurious "note on" messages.

Unsurprisingly, the earliest guitar/MIDI device, which appeared in the 1980s, were error-prone and often slow to respond. Over the last few years, though, interfacing has improved considerably, and one Canadian guitar manufacturer, Godin, has received widespread acclaim for its elegant range of "synth access" instruments. A pair of their Multiac models are shown here: each is fitted with a special RMC Poly-Drive pickup that uses individual under-string transducers to provide not only a standard analog output, but the separate "hexophonic" signals need to drive various widely used synth modules. The guitars have separate onboard volume controls for each of their two "voices," plus three-way EQ for the analog sound; and their unusual two-chamber body construction provides maximum acoustic resonance while also inhibiting feedback.

*Godin Multiac steel-strung SA
synth access guitar, 2001.
(Courtesy Godin Guitars)*

*Godin Multiac nylon-strung SA
synth access guitar, 2001.
(Courtesy Godin Guitars)*

Godin LGX-SA synth access guitar, 2001.
(Courtesy Godin Guitars)

SYNTH ACCESS GUITARS 2

Godin Guitars' founder and owner, Robert Godin, recently commented that "guitar synth triggering has become a passion" around his company's design shop; and the firm has been highly successful in producing attractive, fast tracking synth access guitars that also work well in regular, analog mode. Its LGX-SA and LGXT solid-bodies, illustrated here, offer possibly the last word in guitar/synth versatility, with Seymour Duncan humbucking pickups for regular electric sound, and custom-made, bridge-mounted L.R. Baggs transducers supplying both acoustic-type tones and synth control output.

Robert Godin describes the LGX-SA as setting "a new standard in user friendliness and performance," and contrasts its simplicity of operation with the difficulties presented by earlier guitar synth systems, which were, in his words, "technically complicated and required radical changes in playing technique." On both the LGXs, the synth interface is remarkably unobtrusive; it is controlled by two miniature knobs positioned beneath the regular volume and tone controls, and its 13-pin output connector is mounted next to the humbucker and transducer sockets on the instrument's bottom edge. The LGXT even incorporates a vibrato arm – a device which would have wreaked havoc on the performance of most previous MIDI-equipped guitars! The remainder of its specification and design are similar to the SA's, though it has different magnetic pickups – a "Jazz II" Seymour Duncan unit in the neck (front) position, and a bridge humbucker specially developed by Mr. Duncan for Godin.

Godin synth access models are designed to work in conjunction with the Axon AX100 guitar-to-MIDI converter, a rack-mountable box that can be connected to any MIDI-equipped sound device. The instruments are also compatible with Roland GR-series modules, such as the floor-standing GR30, which has its own onboard library of sounds, and a wide range of effects and features.

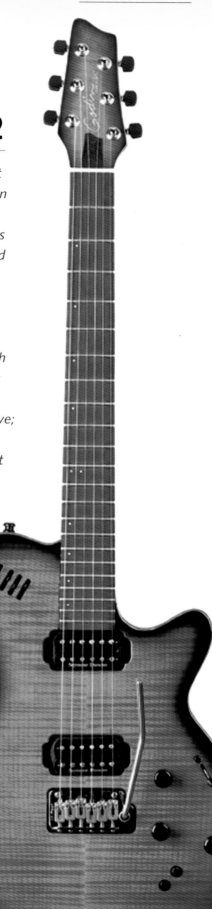

*Godin LGXT synth access guitar, 2001.
(Courtesy Godin Guitars)*

AND FINALLY...

The Pignose is a little amp with a long and impressive pedigree. The company that created it, Pignose Industries, was formed by Terry Kath, guitarist with the band Chicago, in the early 1970s, and ever since the device made its debut in 1973, it has inspired affection and loyalty in tens of thousands of users, including major names from Jeff Beck to Frank Zappa. Designed as a practice amp, it has a 3-watt output, and can run off six AA batteries. However, it has always punched above its (5lb) weight, finding its way into countless recording sessions, and even featuring in some performers' onstage set-ups! Its warm, easily distorted tones have made it a long-standing favorite among harmonica players as well as guitarists, and nearly 30 years after its first appearance, it is still selling as well as ever.

Pignose portable amp, 1990s.
(Courtesy Pignose)

Marshall's Lead 12 head and cab, a solid state, 12-watt rig whose sonic power belies its size, is the perfect solution for the stack lover with space problems. The model, whose speaker cabinet contains a single 10-inch (25.4-cm) Celestion driver, dates from the 1980s, and is, sadly, long out of production – although in 1999, the company revived the "micro-stack" concept with the visually similar Lead 15. This baby has most of the sockets and knobs found on its bigger brothers (high and low sensitivity inputs, plus gain, volume, treble, middle and bass controls), and is now a sought-after second-hand item. Some dedicated owners have even experimented (apparently successfully) with feeding the amp into a full-size, 4 x 12-inch (10.2 x 30.5-cm) cabinet!

Marshall Lead 12 micro-stack, 1980s. (Courtesy John Henry's, London)

HOW TO PLAY

If you're a non-player, but have been stimulated and excited by reading about the artists and gear featured on the previous pages, then why not take up the guitar yourself? With good quality instruments and amps readily available at reasonable prices, there's never been a better time to start learning, and this section of the book contains all the information you need to choose a guitar and begin making music for yourself – including chord charts, diagrams and pictures to guide you, familiar songs that you'll soon be able to master, and loads of practical advice. Turn the page and let's get started....

1 CLASSIC

Many budding players start out with a classical or "Spanish" guitar. Inexpensive instruments (mainly imported from the Far East) are readily available, a number of manufacturers make reduced-size models for younger students, and the classic's wide fretboard and nylon strings are easy on learners' fingers.

But unless you hope to become a Julian Bream or a Paco de Lucía, the classic has several distinct disadvantages. It's designed to be picked with the fingernails (flatpicks or fingerpicks are never used), and until you master this technique, you'll be limited to playing with your bare fingertips, which tends to produce a dull, colorless sound, even on good instruments. Compared to its steel-strung counterparts, the classic is a relatively soft-toned guitar, and attempts to boost its volume by over-vigorous plucking and strumming are not very effective. You can't amplify it with a standard pickup, as the nylon strings have no magnetic properties (though you can use a piezo transducer, and some more expensive models have one already installed). And even after you've succeeded in plugging it in, it will never make a good rock 'n' roll axe; any attempt to crank up your amplifier when it's attached to a classic will probably result in a barrage of feedback, and the guitar itself is totally unsuitable for loud, raucous playing.

However, if you're looking for a subtle folk, jazz, or Latin sound, this type of instrument can be highly effective – and if you're a beginner practising at home, you (and your family!) may welcome its quiet, gentle tone. The fingering used to form chords and scales is identical on nylon- and steel-strung guitars, so if you start out with a classic and then graduate to a flat-top or electric, everything you've already learned can immediately be applied to your new model. And if you aren't quite sure whether guitar playing is for you, buying a cheap classic (a very basic one can cost less than $50) will allow you to experiment without risking too much of your hard-earned cash.

PROS

Inexpensive

No extras needed

Easy to play

CONS

Quiet sound

Unsuitable for rock playing

Mastering classical or flamenco technique requires considerable dedication

RIGHT: *Romanillos "La Toriba" classic.*
(Courtesy Mitch Dalton)

2 FLAT-TOP ACOUSTIC

Superficially, the flat-top guitar resembles its classical cousin, but the two designs have major differences – though some of these are invisible from the outside. The flat-top needs special internal bracing and other reinforcements (including a metal bar, known as a truss-rod, inside its neck) to help it withstand the tension of its steel strings. This adds to the instrument's weight, and many flat-top models (especially the "jumbo" or "dreadnought" types) are also considerably larger than typical classics – though small size instruments are also available. Flat-tops of all types produce a bright, powerful tone with a warm, "singing" quality which suits many different musical styles, but is especially favored by folk and country artists. They can be played with picks, nails, or bare fingers, and amplified either with a magnetic pickup (several manufacturers produce units that mount inside the sound-hole, requiring no modifications to the guitar) or a piezo transducer.

A huge range of flat-tops is currently available, from imported beginners' instruments to handmade models costing thousands of dollars. Cheaper examples tend to be built from laminated timbers, and while these can often sound reasonable, guitars made with solid wood (usually spruce or cedar for the top, and rosewood for the back and sides, though there are many variations) have a superior tone, which will grow gradually richer as the instrument "mellows" with time. A number of companies are now making excellent solid-wood flat-tops at under the $500 mark.

Even a plywood flat-top is likely to cost more than a basic classic, and if you've never played guitar before, its steel strings will be hard on your fingertips, while its relatively narrow fretboard may initially feel cramped. But unlike the classic, the flat-top is part of mainstream American and British popular music tradition, and it's one of the most versatile of all guitars – equally suitable for singer-songwriter style strumming, intricate solo work, or solid rhythm playing. Its rich tone will make your early efforts sound good, and continue to inspire and excite you for years to come.

PROS

The most widely used acoustic guitar in pop, rock, folk, and country

Powerful, ringing sound

Available in a range of sizes, with or without built-in pickups

CONS

More expensive than a classic

Steel strings take a little getting used to

Poorly made or badly set-up models can be hard to play

LEFT: *Lowden O25 flat-top.*
(Courtesy Acoustic Centre, London)

3 ARCH-TOP ACOUSTIC

The most familiar style of arch-top guitar, with its large body, violin-like f-holes, and distinctively incisive tone, was developed by Gibson in the 1920s as a substitute for the banjo in jazz and swing bands (it's sometimes called an "orchestral" guitar for this reason). In those pre-electric days, rhythm guitarists needed powerful-sounding instruments, fitted with thick strings and played vigorously with a flat-pick, to make themselves heard against their fellow musicians' horns and drums, and manufacturers like Epiphone and Stromberg were soon vying with Gibson to produce bigger, louder arch-top models. With the arrival of amplification, there was less need for these impressive, often glamorous-looking guitars. Many companies used them as the basis for their new electric designs, and although arch-top acoustics remained in production, their popularity gradually declined over the following decades as more and more non-electric players switched to flat-tops.

More recently, the acoustic arch-top has made something of a comeback, and there are some superb models currently available. However, these are usually very expensive, handmade instruments, and anyone looking for a cut-price arch-top is likely to be disappointed. Many older American examples are now collectors' items (with price tags to match), while cheaper 1950s and 60s European imports are frequently dull-toned and difficult to play.

Nevertheless, you may get lucky (or know someone who's willing to loan you a vintage Gibson or Epiphone), and if you can find an acoustic arch-top that suits you, you could well be captivated by its unique qualities. To experience what it can do, listen to recordings by 1920s and 30s greats such as Eddie Lang – whose duets with fellow guitarist Lonnie Johnson and violinist Joe Venuti helped put the guitar on the map as a jazz instrument. The arch-top was also used by one of country music's most influential instrumentalists, Maybelle Carter, and its gutsy sound makes it ideal for bluegrass and other acoustic genres. If you choose to play one, you can be sure that its tone quality and looks will make a striking visual and aural impact.

PROS

Impressive, cutting tone

Authentic rhythm instrument for jazz and big band playing

Elegant, distinctive appearance

CONS

Playable examples may be costly and hard to find

Older instruments may need extensive repairs/set-up to make them usable

Often fitted with medium or heavy gauge strings – these can be hard on the fingers!

RIGHT: *1936 Gibson/Francis, Day & Hunter arch-top. (Courtesy Mitch Dalton)*

4 SEMI-ACOUSTIC/THINLINE ELECTRIC

The earliest "semis" were simply arch-top acoustics with added magnetic pickups, but as onstage sound-levels rose, these instruments tended to suffer from feedback, while their bulky bodies sometimes made them hard to handle – especially for players who wanted to stand up and move around while performing. The solution to such problems was the "thinline;" an instrument that retained the traditional arched top and f-holes, but boasted a slimmer body, with considerably reduced internal cavities. Such a guitar was no longer much use as an acoustic, but could deliver a rich, feedback-free electric sound, and its hollow construction gave it a somewhat mellower, warmer sound than a solid-bodied axe.

Ingenious variations to this basic design soon emerged – including the Gibson ES-335 (see pages 26–29) with its hollow sides and solid center, and instruments by Gretsch with sealed tops and fake, painted-on f-holes – and by the late 1950s, thinlines and semi-acoustics were in use by many different types of players. Increasingly fitted with humbucking pickups, they were capable of wide tonal variations – from the warm, mellifluous sounds favored by many jazzmen, to the wild, cranked-up timbre heard on countless rock 'n' roll and rockabilly numbers.

Today, while true, full-body semi-acoustics seem to be slightly less popular (at least among rock players), the thinline is as ubiquitous as ever. Classic designs like the Gibson 335 are available both from their original manufacturers, or in cheaper copy versions that may lack some sonic and visual refinement, but are still usable and affordable. Semis and thinlines make fine beginners' instruments: they are suitable for most popular music styles, comfortable to hold and play, and have a pleasing, if slightly conservative appearance.

However, this type of electric was never designed for the extremes of hard rock and heavy metal. Its vibrato unit, if one is fitted at all, will typically be a simple model, incapable of wide pitch-bends or other violent effects (any attempt at these will probably send the guitar out of tune), and its pickups are unlikely to be the super-high-output types preferred by some contemporary players.

PROS

Rich timbre, especially if fitted with humbucking pickups

Practical and versatile

Some semis have sufficient acoustic sound for "unplugged" practice/tuning

CONS

Too bulky for some players

Sound may be too mellifluous for your music

Unsuitable for extreme hard rock/heavy metal playing techniques

RIGHT: *Gibson L4 semi-acoustic.*
(Courtesy Mitch Dalton)

5 SOLID ELECTRIC

The solid-body is the purest, most streamlined form of electric guitar. Semis and thinlines resemble the acoustic models they're descended from, but solids are radically different; they have no resonating cavities or f-holes, only a dense, usually wooden body with magnetic pickups and a neck and strings attached. However, it's far from correct to call the solid "just a plank," as some early detractors did. While it isn't built to reflect and radiate sound, the design of its body has a crucial effect on the instrument's overall tone, and especially on its ability to sustain – something a good solid generally does better than its semi-acoustic cousins.

Ultimately, though, it is the solid's pickups – its "voice" – that are its most important components. They fall into two basic categories: single-coils, like those used on Fender Telecasters and Stratocasters, with their piercing, gutsy tone; and humbuckers (fitted to Gibson Les Pauls and many other guitars), whose double electro-magnetic coils create a warmer, throatier sound. Cheaper solids are invariably fitted with single-coil units, but you shouldn't have to pay too much more for an instrument with humbuckers, and some axes (like the modified Stratocaster in our picture) now have both types, or include coil-tap switches that convert humbuckers to single-coil operation.

Most guitar stores have a bewildering variety of solids on sale at every price range, and you can get a reasonable one (imported from the Far East or Mexico) for remarkably little money. Cheaper, factory-produced guitars like these are often highly inconsistent, with different examples of the same model varying considerably in feel, sound, and playability, so it's always worth trying out more than one if you can. Also ensure that knobs and switches work as they should, and that there is no excessive buzzing or interference when the instrument is plugged in. One final word of warning: when choosing your solid guitar, its sound and feel will be your primary concerns – but you'll also want it to look good, and may be tempted by some of the more outlandishly-shaped axes that are currently available. These can sometimes be difficult (or impossible) to play while sitting down – so check your preferred instrument for comfort, balance, and weight before purchase!

PROS

Great guitars for rock (and many other genres)

Cool appearance

Relatively easy to customize with extra hardware (special pickups, whammy bars, etc)

CONS

Useless without an amplifier

Can be heavy

More outlandish body designs may be uncomfortable

LEFT: *Fender Stratocaster (with added humbucking pickup). (Courtesy Mitch Dalton).*

6 ELECTRIC BASS

By a quirk of musical evolution, the "stand-up" double bass used in orchestras and jazz groups is tuned to the same notes (EADG) as the guitar's bottom four strings – although the bass plays an octave lower. It was Leo Fender, inventor of the Telecaster, who first designed and manufactured an electric bass guitar, with thick strings and an extra long neck to allow it to reach the same deep notes as the double bass. Leo's instrument, launched in 1951, was named the "Precision," as its fretted neck ensured that even beginners could play it in tune (accurate pitching is a constant problem for inexperienced double bassists, who have no frets or markers to guide their fingers).

Fender's bass was relatively easy for guitarists to master, and its emergence also prompted many string bassists to trade in their unwieldy stand-up instruments for the compact Precision, or the rival models later introduced by Gibson, Rickenbacker, and other companies. The electric bass soon became ubiquitous in pop, rock 'n' roll, and blues, and it is almost impossible to imagine today's music scene without it.

Bass and guitar technique have some significant differences, although the left-hand fingering is the same for both instruments. The bass's bulkier strings and the wider distances between its frets may pose a challenge for some guitarists, who also have to learn how to create harmonically correct, musically interesting bass lines (chords are rarely used). Basses can be picked with a plectrum, but most experienced performers use bare fingers and thumb, as well as slapping and other specialized playing methods.

Many bassists start out on the standard guitar and then switch over – and it can be very useful for the budding bass player to possess some rudimentary guitar skills. But if you want to commit to the bass immediately, you should be able to find a reasonable beginners' model for $300 or less – though you will have to budget for an amp (probably a small combo) as well. Don't try and economize by making do with a unit designed for normal guitars: the bass's low frequencies need more power and a larger loudspeaker; some professionals use cones of up to 15 inches (38cm).

PROS

Much easier to play and transport than a string bass

Can be played by any competent guitarist

Versatile

CONS

Useless without an amp

Thick strings, long neck, and greater distance between frets than on a standard guitar

Unsuitable for very young beginners, who should consider learning six-string guitar first

RIGHT: *Rickenbacker 4000 Series bass. (Courtesy Acoustic Centre, London)*

HOLDING THE GUITAR

BEFORE YOU start playing, it's important to make sure you feel comfortable.

When standing you should not be labouring to support the main body of the guitar, and the strap should not be tugging at your neck.

With the strap resting on your shoulder, remove your hands from the guitar. There should be an equal balance of weight, with no great pressure on any part of your body.

The guitar is a heavy instrument, but if you distribute the weight sensibly it will cause little discomfort. If Angus Young or Susanna Hoffs can career around the stage whilst playing, so can you.

WHETHER YOU sit or stand probably depends on the type of guitar and style of music you play.

If you've got an electric guitar, shorten the strap until the guitar hangs as comfortably as if you were standing.

If you're using an acoustic model, there are several ways of holding it.

Some acoustic players cross their legs – right over left – and rest the guitar just above their right knee.

Others plant both feet on the floor and rest the body across their thighs. Others use a foot stool to raise one leg and rest the guitar there.

WHICHEVER METHOD you choose, if you can remove your hands from the guitar without dropping it on the floor, you're in business.

The important thing to remember is that the arms should never take the weight of the guitar. You need them to play it, not carry it.

When standing, make sure the weight of your guitar is spread evenly.

TUNING THE GUITAR

METHOD 1: Tuning to a piano. If you have a keyboard instrument, or some other instrument with fixed notes, you can tune up to it.

On your piano, play an **E** note – it's the 12th white note below middle **C**. That's the note you want on your sixth (bottom **E**) string.

Leave the sixth string 'open' by taking your left hand off the fretboard. Now gently strike the string with your right thumb, and keep thumbing it whilst gradually turning the sixth string tuning peg with your left hand.

When the guitar note matches the piano note, it's in tune.

You can now repeat the action for each string, matching it to the appropriate keyboard note – **E, A, D, G, B, E** – moving to your right along the keyboard each time.

HOW TO TUNE YOUR GUITAR TO A PIANO

E   A   D   G   B   *   E

BOTTOM E STRING (6) | A STRING (5) | D STRING (4) | G STRING (3) | B STRING (2) | TOP E STRING (1)

* = MIDDLE C

METHOD 2: Tuning the guitar to itself – perhaps the most common method, and the one you'll need when no other instrument is at hand.

Tune the sixth (bottom **E**) string as accurately as you can. Chances are that it's in tune anyway – being the thickest string, it's less likely to detune itself than the others.

Listen to the sound of your bottom **E**. It should be a deep, full note. As we move through the strings the notes will get progressively higher, until we reach top **E** which will give a light, ringing note.

Now to tune the fifth (**A**) string. Place the first finger of your left hand just behind the fifth fret of the bottom **E** string. That's an **A** note.

Keep your finger on the fret. Now thumb the fifth and sixth strings in turn, gently turning the fifth string tuning peg until the two notes are the same.

That's got your fifth string in tune.

Put your finger just behind the fifth fret, fifth (**A**) string. That's a **D** note. Tune your fourth (**D**) string to it.

Put your finger just behind the fifth fret, fourth (**D**) string. That's a **G** note. Tune your third (**G**) string to it.

Put your finger just behind the fourth fret, third (**G**) string. That's a **B** note. Tune your second (**B**) string to it.

Finally put your finger just behind the fifth

fret, second (**B**) string. That's an **E** note. Tune your top (**E**) string to that.

To put it briefly, tuning from the bottom string up, the frets to use are 5, 5, 5, 4 and 5.

If you've done it right, your top **E** and bottom **E** strings should give the same note. The only difference is the pitch – one high pitched, one low.

METHOD 3: Buy yourself a set of plastic or metal pitch pipes – they cost next to nothing and they're designed for guitarists.

The six notes on the pipe correspond with the notes on the six guitar strings. Just blow and tune, leaving all the strings 'open'.

When sitting, a strap can still help an electric guitar to hang steady.

The most common way of holding an acoustic guitar is to steady it across one thigh.

Unlike a piano, which can stay more or less in tune for years, a guitar can go out of tune at any minute. The heat, the cold, the way you hit the strings . . . there are a thousand ways your instrument can become literally tuneless. So it's important that you learn to tune your guitar quickly and efficiently.

NUMBERING THE FINGERS

WE CANNOT pretend that our fingering system is particularly innovative, but it's simple and as long as you can count to four you'll probably get the hang of it.

Here's how the fingers of your left hand will be numbered throughout the book: (1) is the first finger, (2) is the second, (3) is the third, and (4) is the fourth or little finger.

Although the four fingers are used prodigiously, the left thumb rarely comes into play. It's mainly there to keep the guitar neck steady and help you press down firmly with your fingers.

You are advised to keep fingernails trim on both hands. Long nails make chord formation almost impossible, as the fleshy part of the fingertip struggles in vain to meet the fretboard.

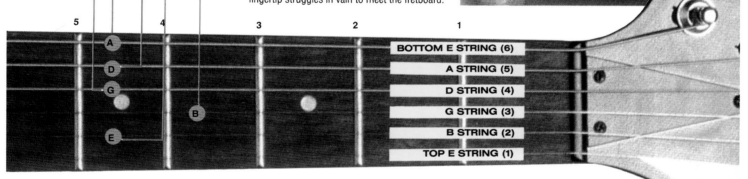

5		4	3	2	1

G NOTE
A NOTE
D NOTE
TOP E NOTE
B NOTE

A
D
G
B
E

BOTTOM E STRING (6)
A STRING (5)
D STRING (4)
G STRING (3)
B STRING (2)
TOP E STRING (1)

HOLDING THE PLECTRUM

THE FINAL piece in the guitar set-up is the plectrum, or guitar pick. Later we'll get into different ways of using a plectrum, and playing with the fingers of your right hand.

To get you off on the right track here, pick up the plectrum between the first and second fingers of the right hand, and form the hand into a 'semi-fist'.

You'll find it best to use a fairly large, flexible plectrum in these early learning days. It will be easier to manipulate, and whilst volume tends to suffer, technique doesn't.

Your local guitar store will carry mountains of these plastic triangles.

CHORDS

YOU ARE now ready to learn your first chord. A chord is a combination of notes which sound good together. In musical terms, they harmonise.

The following pages will quickly get you on the right road for chord formation, and you need know absolutely nothing about musical theory to begin practising.

As we go along we will cover the basic elements of music. But right now we just want your guitar, your hands, a little common sense and a lot of determination.

Dozens of notable guitarists have made their way with little or no musical theory. Legendary blues master Albert King plays the guitar upside down, with the strings the wrong way round. Enough said?

For now, just concentrate on getting your fingers in the right place. The rest will follow.

Being left-handed didn't stop Albert King cutting blues classics like 'Crosscut Saw' and 'Born Under A Bad Sign'. He just turned his guitar back-to-front! His thinnest (top E) string is literally at the top.

GET TOUGH

THESE FIRST few weeks are going to be rough on your fingers, as they struggle to assume a series of unnatural positions. There's not much you can do except persevere. You'll be amazed how even the strangest chord shape will eventually become second nature.

The fingertips of your left hand will suffer most, as they press down on the strings. Regular practice will soon toughen them up. You'll sense the turning point when your finger prints start to disappear.

The first time you try it, you'll find it hard to get your fingers in place, let alone press down. You might find it helps to physically grab each finger with your right hand and force it into position.

Don't worry, Eric Clapton probably had to do that when he played his first **C** chord.

CHORD OF C MAJOR

THE CHORD we've selected to start you on is **C** major, generally known as just **C**. This chord relates to many others that you will learn later.

The blue dots in the diagram indicate the position for each finger. Take your finger and place it *just behind* the fret indicated. If necessary, use your right hand to put your left-hand fingers in place.

THE **C** CHORD is formed like this:
First finger (1) just behind the first fret (the one nearest the nut) on the second (**B**) string.
Second finger (2) just behind the second fret on the fourth (**D**) string.
Third finger (3) behind the third fret on the sixth (bottom **E**) string.
Little finger (4) just behind the third fret on the fifth (**A**) string.

NOTE THAT the third finger is pushed further across the neck than the little finger. Because they are both pressing down behind the same fret, the third finger will have to sit midway between the second and third frets.

CHORD OF C MAJOR

The **C** major chord, first step in our three chord trick. Note the arched fingers, tips just behind frets.

CHORD OF C MAJOR FRONT VIEW

CHORD OF C MAJOR AS YOU SEE IT

The thumb sits behind the guitar neck, enabling the palm to support it comfortably.

NOTES ON THE TOP E STRING

As the notes go up the first (top **E**) string, the sharps fall on alternate frets—except between **B** and **C**, and between the open **E** and **F**. The 12 notes follow one another in the same order whatever the string.

NOTES ON A PIANO KEYBOARD

It's easier to pick out sharps and flats on a keyboard – they're the black notes. But the 12 notes still run in the same order as on a guitar: **E F F# G G# A A# B C C# D D# E.**

AS YOU probably know, musical notes take their names from the letters of the alphabet, from **A** to **G**.

However, they aren't the only musical notes. There are also notes called sharps or flats, and they fall between the 'main' notes.

Why are they called sharps and flats? Simple: because the sharp *is* 'sharp', in that it's pitched one note above the main note, whilst the flat note is literally 'flattened' down one note.

Here's the confusing bit. Sharps and flats are in fact the same note. The note between **A** and **B**, for instance, can be called either **A** sharp (**A#**) or **B** flat (**B♭**).

There are two places where there is no sharp note between two 'main' notes – between **E** and **F**, and between **B** and **C**. You can see this clearly on a keyboard, where the sharp notes are black.

THE CHORD of **F** major is one of the trickiest to learn at first, but once you've cracked it you'll progress faster. Like **C** it's usually known as just **F**. Here's how it's formed:

First finger (1) laying just behind the first fret across both the first (top **E**) string *and* the second (**B**) string.

Second finger just behind the second fret on the third (**G**) string.

Third finger (3) just behind the third fret on the fifth (**A**) string.

Little finger (4) just behind the third fret on the fourth (**D**) string.

NOTE THAT the bottom string is the only one that's 'open' (unfretted). It's not part of the chord – unlike the open strings in the **C** chord. Don't play the bottom **E** string.

The fifth (**A**) string can also be left out, giving a four-string chord. You can use your third finger (3) to fret the fourth (**D**) string, and give your little finger a rest

CHORD OF F MAJOR

X Not played

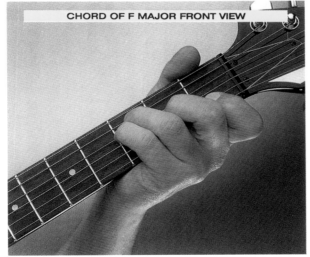

This chord will be difficult at first, with the first finger holding down two strings at once. It might help to practise that finger on its own.

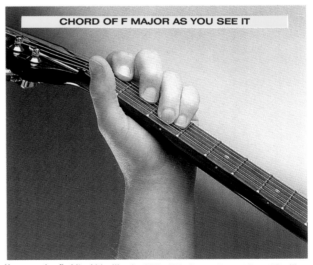

You may also find it odd 'pulling back' the little finger. Keep at it, and it will become second nature.

MAJOR KEYS

BY NOW you may be wondering if your fingers will ever toughen up enough to master that **F** chord. Don't worry, they will.

You may also be wondering why we've chucked you in at the deep end like this – surely there are easier chords to play?

Well, yes, there are. But few are as important as **C**, **F** and **G**. Together they make up the 'three-chord trick'. Once you know these three chords, you can play a wealth of rock music.

THE CHORDS of **C**, **F** and **G** did not combine by some magical force. There is a precise science to it all.

When you play these three chords, you are playing in the key of **C** major.

It's important to know about keys, especially when playing with other musicians. Before you start a song, you need to know

1	2	3	4	5	6	7	8	9	10	11	12	13	
C		D		E	F		G		A		B	C	B STRING

NOTES IN THE SCALE OF C MAJOR

*These are the notes which 'work' in the key of **C** major. A song in **C** should stick to these notes.*

what key it's in, because that tells you which notes and chords you can use.

WE'VE SEEN how music consists of 12 notes: **A A# B C C# D D# E F F# G G#**. **A#** is also known as **B♭**, **C#** is also known as **D♭**, and so on. The note after **G#** is **A**, and the whole thing starts over again.

There is a major key based on each of the 12 musical notes – **A** major, **B♭** major, and so on.

For each major key there is an eight-note 'scale' – you probably learned it at school as doh, re, mi, fah, soh, la, ti, doh.

Try playing the scale of **C** major, starting on the first fret of your second (**B**) string. The notes in the scale are **C, D, E, F, G, A, B** and **C**.

These are the notes which 'work' in the key of **C** major – and any chord which uses a combination of these notes will also 'work' in the key of **C** major.

CHORD OF G MAJOR

THE THIRD chord we've chosen is **G** – and you'll probably find it somewhat easier. Put it together with **C** and **F**, and you've got what's known as the three-chord trick, **CFG**. These three chords have combined to form countless songs.

The **G** chord has a different look to the **C** and **F** chords, because it's formed 'in reverse', with the first and second fingers going across the neck, and the third finger held back.

Here's how you do it:

First finger (1) just behind the second fret on the fifth (**A**) string.

Second finger (2) just behind the third fret on the sixth (bottom **E**) string.

Third finger (3) just behind the third fret on the first (top **E**) string.

NOTE HOW the first and second fingers arch over to come down on the strings from above, to avoid brushing against adjacent strings.

CHORD OF G MAJOR

X Not played

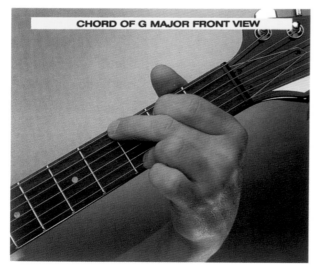

CHORD OF G MAJOR FRONT VIEW

CHORD OF G MAJOR AS YOU SEE IT

A real finger twister, the G major chord has a 'reverse' position which is shared by few other chords.

Note how the fingers come down on the strings from above so that the 'open' strings ring loud and clear.

| G | C | E | G | C | E |

NOTES IN THE CHORD OF C MAJOR

The chord of **C** major works in the key of **C** major because it uses the notes **G**, **C** and **E**. These three notes are all in the scale of **C** major.

| X | C | F | A | C | F |

NOTES IN THE CHORD OF F MAJOR

The chord of **F** major works in the key of **C** major because it uses the notes **F**, **A** and **C**. These three notes are all in the scale of **C** major.

| G | B | D | G | B | G |

NOTES IN THE CHORD OF G MAJOR

The chord of **G** major works in the key of **C** major because it uses the notes **G**, **B** and **D**. These three notes are all in the scale of **C** major.

CHORD OF D MAJOR

THE CHORD OF **D** major has an interesting set-up. In previous chords you've been getting used to pushing the second finger across the neck beyond the first finger. Now that's reversed.

D major is a four-note chord in this basic form. In other words, you only play four strings. The strings you leave out are the bottom **E** and **A** strings.

THE SHAPE OF THE **D** major chord may look a little intricate, but it's quite simple really. Here's how it's formed:

First finger (1) just behind the second fret on the third (**G**) string.

Second finger (2) just behind the second fret on the top **E** string.

Third finger (3) just behind the third fret on the second (**B**) string.

The fourth (**D**) string is played open. The sixth (**E**) and fifth (**A**) strings are not played.

THERE IS an alternative way of fretting the **D** major chord – shown on the right, below.

CHORD OF D MAJOR

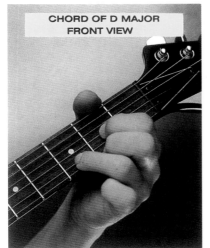

CHORD OF D MAJOR FRONT VIEW

The first and third finger must avoid touching and B string, in order for the chord to ring out loud and, more importantly, clear.

CHORD OF D MAJOR AS YOU SEE IT

Keep the little finger away from the action when forming the **D** chord, as it has a tendency to clutter the hand position.

CHORD OF D MAJOR (ALTERNATIVE FINGERING)

Place your first finger across the E, B and G strings, just behind the second fret. The second finger falls in place just behind the third fret on the second (**B**) string.

THE GUITAR

INSTRUCTION MANUAL

PLECTRUM TECHNIQUE

ORIGINALLY MADE from bone and tortoise-shell, most plectrums are now moulded in plastic.

They vary considerably in size and flexibility. There's no hard and fast rule regarding which type to use for which style of playing.

Initially, a large, flexible plectrum is likely to be more suitable. The sound will be slightly muted, but there won't be too much resistance against the strings, so you should quickly gain the confidence to move to a smaller, stiffer type.

You'll probably find a small, stiff plectrum is better suited to lead playing. Some guitarists even play with a coin, to give a really hard attack on the strings and for scratching effects.

Certainly a smaller plectrum can be more useful for more controlled work. On some stringed instruments, the strings are so close together that only a small plectrum will do.

Whatever style you choose to play, most guitar tutors suggest holding the plectrum between your thumb and the first joint of your first finger.

Fine. But this again is very much a matter of personal choice.

Some very talented musicians play with the plectrum between thumb and second finger. It may look awkward, but if it feels right, alright.

The rule of, er, thumb is that as long as the plectrum is at the correct angle when striking the strings, you're OK.

HOLD THE plectrum as shown, but not too tightly. No white knuckles please.

Keep the plectrum steady—there should be a minimum of movement when it strikes the strings. But don't hold your wrist stiff or clench your fist, as it will make for less fluidity and speed.

The plectrum should be at ninety degrees to the strings as you play—so if the guitar is vertical, the plectrum should be horizontal.

Aim to get a sharp, clear sound. Stick with it, because it's easy to become satisfied as soon as you begin to make any sort of coherent sound from the guitar. As many guitarists have learnt to their cost, it's easy to ignore your right hand as you learn more chord shapes with your left.

Keep working on your plectrum technique, or you run the risk of becoming 'one-handed'.

To sum up: clear tone, flexible wrist, but a firm grip. And relax.

'THAT'LL BE THE DAY'

'THAT'LL BE The Day' is a simple yet timeless rock number built around the three major chords of **C**, **F** and **G**.

It's a little unusual in its structure, because it starts with the chorus, before reverting to the traditional verse/chorus pattern.

At first, we'll play the song entirely with downward strokes. Just take it slowly, and the rhythm will come naturally.

HOW TO USE THE GRID

Chords: Chords are represented by letters. Each chord change is highlighted by a change in colour.

A coloured box with no chord marked in it means that you should simply let the previous chord ring out without striking a new chord.

Rhythm: Each coloured box represents one beat. Tap your foot steadily, playing one strum for each beat. There are four beats to each bar.

Where a box is split in two, there is a chord change after half a beat. This may sound tricky, but if you follow the lyrics you'll find it quite straightforward.

KEY TO SYMBOLS AND COLOURS

⊓ One downward stroke
☐ **C** major
☐ **G** major
☐ **F** major
☐ **D** major

TITLE	KEY	TEMPO
'THAT'LL BE THE DAY' (CHORUS)	C MAJOR	MEDIUM

1	2	3	4	1	2	3	4
F	F	F	F	F	F	F	F
⊓	⊓	⊓	⊓	⊓	⊓	⊓	⊓
That'll	be	the	day,	when you	say	good-bye.	Yes.

1	2	3	4	1	2	3	4
C	C	C	C	C	C	C	C
⊓	⊓	⊓	⊓	⊓	⊓	⊓	⊓
That'll	be	the	day,	when you	make me	cry.	You

1	2	3	4	1	2	3	4
F	F	F	F	F	F	F	F
⊓	⊓	⊓	⊓	⊓	⊓	⊓	⊓
Say you're	gon -na	leave	me,	you know	it's a	lie,	'cause

1	2	3	4	1	2	3	4
C					G	C	
					⊓	⊓	
That'll	be	the	da- a-	ay	when I	die.	Well you

TITLE	KEY	TEMPO
'THAT'LL BE THE DAY' (VERSE)	C MAJOR	MEDIUM

1	2	3	4	1	2	3	4
F	F	F	F	C	C	C	C
⊓	⊓	⊓	⊓	⊓	⊓	⊓	⊓
Give	me all	your lov-	ing and	your	tur- tle	dov- ing.	

1	2	3	4	1	2	3	4
F	F	F	F	C	C	C	C
⊓	⊓	⊓	⊓	⊓	⊓	⊓	⊓
All	your hugs	and kiss-	es and	your	mon- ey	too.	Well.

1	2	3	4	1	2	3	4
F	F	F	F	C	C	C	C
⊓	⊓	⊓	⊓	⊓	⊓	⊓	⊓
You know	you love	me ba-	by,	un- til	you	tell me	may- be

1	2	3	4	1	2	3	4
D	D	D	D	G	G	G	G
⊓	⊓	⊓	⊓	⊓	⊓	⊓	⊓
That	some	day	well	I'll	be	through.	Well.

420

The relaxed wrist position, just prior to striking the strings.

The plectrum is swept across the strings at 90 degrees.

Striking the strings: keep the hand firm, but flexible.

LYRICS

CHORUS
That'll be the day, when you say goodbye. Yeah,
That'll be the day, when you make me cry. You
Say you're gonna leave, you know it's a lie. 'Cause
That'll be the da-a-ay when I die.

VERSE 1
(Well you)
Give me all your loving and your turtle doving,
All your hugs and kisses and your money too, well,
You know you love me baby, until you tell me maybe,
That someday well I'll be through. Well,

CHORUS
That'll be the day, when you say goodbye. Yeah,
That'll be the day, when you make me cry. You
Say you're gonna leave, you know it's a lie, 'cause
That'll be the da-a-ay when I die.

VERSE 2
(When)
Cupid shot his dart, he shot it at your heart, so
If we ever part and I leave you, well,
You say you told me and you, you told me boldly,
That someday, well, I'll be through. Well,

'THAT'LL BE The Day' was one of the key songs in rock and roll history. Released in summer 1957, it launched Buddy Holly on a meteoric career that was cut short by his death in an air crash in February 1959.

Inspired by the urgent rhythms of Bo Diddley and Elvis Presley, Holly added a fresh, melodic simplicity that was quite unique. The songs poured out: 'Peggy Sue', 'Rave On', 'Oh Boy', 'Not Fade Away', 'Everyday', 'Words Of Love', 'Brown Eyed Handsome Man', 'Heartbeat', 'Raining In My Heart', 'It Doesn't Matter Anymore' . . . every one a classic.

Artists influenced by Holly include The Hollies (who took his name), Elvis Costello and Marshall Crenshaw (who both copied his looks and much of his musical style), Don McLean (whose 'American Pie' was about him), The Beatles (who recorded 'Words Of Love'), The Rolling Stones ('Not Fade Away').

Released under the group name of The Crickets, 'That'll Be The Day' was written by Holly with his drummer Jerry Allison and producer Norman Petty, who guided Holly's brief, brilliant career. It reached No.3 in the States and No.1 in the UK.

The song has since been recorded by at last 45 different artists, and gave its name to one of the best '70s rock movies.

The legendary Buddy Holly – left, with drummer and co-writer Jerry Allison, and right, in action on his Fender Stratocaster.

TONES AND SEMITONES

ON PAGE 18 we looked at the key of **C** major.

The scale of **C** major consists of the notes **C, D, E, F, G, A, B**. These are the notes which work in the key of **C** major.

The chords of **G** major and **F** major use notes from this scale, which is why they work in the key of **C** major.

NOW LET'S look at another key: **G** major. It too has a scale. The notes in the scale of **G** major are **G, A, B, C, D, E** and **F#**.

Compare this scale to the scale of **C** major. Although they start on different notes, and the **G** scale includes a sharp note, there is one very important factor the two scales have in common.

The spaces between notes on each scale are the same.

Each of these scales climbs the fret-

**NOTES IN THE SCALE OF C MAJOR
(ON THE B STRING)
AND NOTES IN THE SCALE OF G MAJOR
(ON THE G STRING)**

board in gaps of **2, 2, 1, 2, 2, 2, 1** frets.

This is true for any major scale.

THERE IS a technical term for the gap from one fret, or note, to the next. It's called a semitone. And a space of two semitones is called a tone.

So from **C** to **C#** is one semitone, and from **C** to **D** is one tone.

Using these terms, your major scale – 2, 2, 1, 2, 2, 2, 1 – goes up by jumps of *tone, tone, semitone, tone, tone, tone, semitone*.

You can use this formula to work out the notes in any major scale.

'THAT'LL BE THE DAY'

NOW THAT you've worked out on a simplified version of 'That'll Be The Day', you might like to try it with a slightly more developed rhythm.

Instead of simple downward strokes, this time you should try a downstroke followed by an upstroke, so that you play each chord twice in each beat.

At first this may seem difficult, so just concentrate on getting the rhythm right and don't let the chord changes distract you.

Don't worry if it sounds a little stilted. Find your own pace, and the rhythm will follow naturally.

THERE'S ANOTHER interesting rhythmic twist. The last line of the verse consists of one bar of downstrokes only, followed by a bar of triplets.

A triplet is three notes played in the space of a single beat. All you do is add an extra stroke into each beat. Check this bit out first by tapping it out with your middle three fingers: rat-tat-tat, rat-tat-tat, rat-tat-tat, rat-tat-tat.

This gives a strong percussive effect which you can hear on a lot of 'oldies'. Songs from the '50s often used a 'triplet' rhythm – James Brown's 'I'll Go Crazy' was a prime example, and Madonna's '50s pastiche 'True Blue' deliberately revived it. It's also to be found on modern hits such as Tears For Fears' 'Everybody Wants To Rule The World'.

KEY TO SYMBOLS AND COLOURS

⊓ One downward stroke
V One upward stroke
☐ **C** major
☐ **G** major
☐ **F** major
☐ **D** major

TITLE		KEY	TEMPO
'THAT'LL BE THE DAY' (CHORUS)		C MAJOR	MEDIUM

1	2	3	4	1	2	3	4
F	F	F	F	F	F	F	F
⊓ V	⊓ V	⊓ V	⊓ V	⊓ V	⊓ V	⊓ V	⊓ V

That'll · be · the · day, · when · you · say · good-bye. · Yes,

1	2	3	4	1	2	3	4
C	C	C	C	C	C	C	C
⊓ V	⊓ V	⊓ V	⊓ V	⊓ V	⊓ V	⊓ V	⊓ V

That'll · be · the · day, · when · you · make · me · cry. · You

1	2	3	4	1	2	3	4
F	F	F	F	F	F	F	F
⊓ V	⊓ V	⊓ V	⊓ V	⊓ V	⊓ V	⊓ V	⊓ V

Say · you're · gon -na · leave · me, · you · know · it's · a · lie, · cause

1	2	3	4	1	2	3	4
C					G	C	
⊓					⊓ V	⊓	

That'll · be · the · da- · a- · ay · when · I · die. · Well you

TITLE		KEY	TEMPO
'THAT'LL BE THE DAY' (VERSE)		C MAJOR	MEDIUM

1	2	3	4	1	2	3	4
F	F	F	F	C	C	C	C
⊓ V	⊓ V	⊓ V	⊓ V	⊓ V	⊓ V	⊓ V	⊓ V

Give · me · all · your · lov- · ing · and · your · tur- tle · dov- ing,

1	2	3	4	1	2	3	4
F	F	F	F	C	C	C	C
⊓ V	⊓ V	⊓ V	⊓ V	⊓ V	⊓ V	⊓ V	⊓ V

All · your · hugs · and · kiss- · es · and · your · mon- ey · too. · Well,

1	2	3	4	1	2	3	4
F	F	F	F	C	C	C	C
⊓ V	⊓ V	⊓ V	⊓ V	⊓ V	⊓ V	⊓ V	⊓ V

You · know · you · love · me · ba- · by, · un- til · you · tell · me · may- be

1	2	3	4	1	2	3	4
D	D	D	D	G	G	G	G
⊓	⊓	⊓	⊓	⊓ V ⊓	V ⊓ V	⊓ V ⊓	V ⊓ V

That · some · day · well · I'll · be · through. · Well,

THE NOTES in a scale are known not just by their names – C, D, E, etc – but also by numbers.

The first note in the scale – the one on which the scale is based – is called the first or root note. So the root note of the scale of C major is C.

After that, they're known simply by their numbers. So B is the second note in the scale of C major. The second note in the scale of G major is A.

This is useful when talking about chord structure.

ALL MAJOR chords are constructed from the root, third and fifth notes of their major scale.

So the chord of C major consists of the notes C, E and G – the root, third and fifth notes of the C major scale.

And the chord of G major consists of the notes G, B and D – the root, third and fifth notes in the scale of G major.

The technical name for this group of three notes is a triad.

So you now know how to work out the notes in any major scale, and from that you can work out the notes of any major chord.

NUMBERS OF THE NOTES IN THE SCALE OF C MAJOR						
C	D	E	F	G	A	B
Root	2nd	3rd	4th	5th	6th	7th

NUMBERS OF THE NOTES IN THE SCALE OF G MAJOR						
G	A	B	C	D	E	F#
Root	2nd	3rd	4th	5th	6th	7th

CHORD STRUCTURE

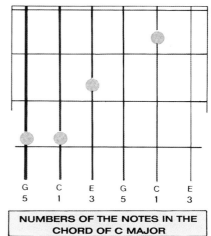

G	C	E	G	C	E
5	1	3	5	1	3

NUMBERS OF THE NOTES IN THE CHORD OF C MAJOR

CHORD OF E MAJOR

E MAJOR is a favourite chord of heavy metal and R&B guitarists. Its simple, full sound has inspired a thousand thumping guitar riffs.

Bearing in mind the musical alphabet, where E is the note before F, it follows that the E chord is one note or fret below the F chord. The shape is similar, but the way you form the chord with your fingers is not.

There are just three strings to be held down – the G, D and A strings. Here's how the E major chord is formed:

First finger (1) just behind the first fret on the third (G) string.

Second finger (2) just behind the second fret on the fifth (A) string.

Third finger (3) just behind the second fret on the fourth (D) string.

E major is a dramatic chord, as the open top E and bottom E strings provide the governing notes of the chord, and they sound out first, last and longest.

Combined with A major and D major, it forms the same three-chord trick in the key of A major as C, F and G in the key of C major.

CHORD OF E MAJOR

A relatively simple position, with three fingers in use, and three strings left open. The thumb should feel nice and relaxed.

CHORD OF E MAJOR FRONT VIEW

CHORD OF E MAJOR AS YOU SEE IT

If the fingers do not maintain good contact with the strings, you may hear some fret 'buzz'. Relax, and arch that wrist for the best position.

THE KEY OF A MAJOR

OUR SECOND set of chords – **A**, **D** and **E** –form a three-chord trick in the key of **A** major.

The scale of **A** major follows the same pattern as the scale of **C** major: tone, tone, semitone, tone, tone, tone, semitone.

In other words, you can play the scale on your **A** string (the fifth), starting with the open string and sliding up the neck in gaps of 2, 2, 1, 2, 2, 2, 1 frets.

The chords of **A**,**D** and **E** all use notes in this scale. This means you can use them in a song in the key of **A** major.

KEY OF A MAJOR	
NOTES IN THE SCALE	A B C# D E F# G#
NOTES IN CHORD OF A MAJOR	A C# E
NOTES IN CHORD OF D MAJOR	D F# A
NOTES IN CHORD OF E MAJOR	E G# B

PLAYING SCALES

UP TO now we've been content to confine ourselves to chord work. Chords are the basis of nearly all guitar styles, and it makes sense to lay that firm foundation.

But as a rock guitarist, you will eventually need to play single notes. And with that in mind, it won't do any harm to begin practising scales now.

Please don't be put off by the thought of playing scales. The phrase may have associations with dull classical music lessons, but in fact almost every major guitarist is an adept scales player. Scales are the lead guitarist's map of the fretboard.

You'll be lost without them . . .

FOR OUR first scale, we're going to show you the scale of **G** major – twice. First in a simplified format, and then in its more usual form.

Try the easy one first, using downward strokes of the plectrum.

You begin by playing your open third (**G**) string, then work your way up the strings, placing each finger where indicated. Note that the sixth note in the scale is the open **E** string.

When you get to top **G** (third fret, top **E** string), work your way back down again.

YOU SHOULD aim to move from bottom to top and back down again in one smooth, flowing motion, playing each note for an equal length of time. You may find it sounds better if you only play the top note once before starting back down again.

CHORD OF A MAJOR

WHEN WE were planning *Play Rock Guitar,* a colleague observed that "If you can conquer the **A** chord, you can conquer Everest."

It really hadn't occurred to us that **A** major was any more complicated to learn than any other chord. However it does have one confusing aspect, because it can be fingered in three different ways.

TRADITIONALISTS would point to the formation in picture 1:

First finger (1) holding down the third (**G**) string behind the second fret.

Second finger (2) just behind the second fret on the fourth (**D**) string.

Third finger (3) just behind the second fret on the second (**B**) string.

IN OTHER words, all three fingers are pressing down behind the second fret. This is the reason for alternative fingerings. It can get mighty cramped whichever way you play the **A** chord, and you have to find the variation that suits you best.

CHORD OF A MAJOR (1)

CHORD OF A MAJOR FRONT VIEW (1)

The 'D' style variation for the A chord gives your fingers the most room, as long as the first finger can fret the G string cleanly.

CHORD OF A MAJOR AS YOU SEE IT (1)

Although it looks a little awkward, there are advantages using this position particularly when moving to 'sympathetic' chords like **E**.

When you can do that, try out the 'real' scale of **G** major – the second shown here, which begins on the third fret, bottom **E** string.

This scale takes you right through two octaves, from bottom **G** to top **G**. The notes in between are **A**, **B**, **C**, **D**, **E** and **F#**. See if you can identify them as you play them. Once you know them, name each note in your head as you play it.

You'll notice there are no open strings in this scale. This gives you more control over each note: you can kill it or let it ring out, depending on how quickly you raise your finger off the string.

AFTER YOU'VE played this scale a few times using downward strokes of the plectrum, try another variation: down, up, down, up, down, up, etc.

Try not to take your fingers too far off the fretboard – it will slow you down.

The important thing when playing a scale is to get a smooth flow. That can only come through being relaxed – and that, in turn, can only come through practice.

So from now on, run through these scales every day before you begin your chord practice. It's all good preparation for your future career as a soloist!

SCALE OF G MAJOR

SCALE OF G MAJOR

CHORD OF A MAJOR

PERSONALLY, I prefer the arrangement shown in picture 2 for playing **A** major:

First finger (1) behind the second fret on the fourth (**D**) string.

Second finger (2) behind the second fret on the third (**G**) string.

Third finger (3) behind the second fret on the second (**B**) string.

THAT IS the most comfortable position, as least as far as my fingers are concerned. But there's a further alternative, shown in picture 3, with the second, third and little fingers in the same sequence.

The advantage of this third alternative will become apparent when we get onto new chords which use the basic **A** major position, with added notes to be played by the first finger (1).

The essential thing with any chord is to get it ringing out loud and clear. Play each string separately. If there's a buzzing noise, that means the string isn't playing cleanly—one of your fingers is brushing up against it. As usual practice will eliminate this problem.

CHORD OF A MAJOR (2)

CHORD OF A MAJOR FRONT VIEW (2)

The second variation of the A shape, with the first, second and third fingers nicely in a row on the second fret.

CHORD OF A MAJOR AS YOU SEE IT (2)

Keep the little finger airborne when forming this A shape, as there is a tendency for it to drop onto the E string.

CHORD OF A MAJOR (3)

This position can be adapted for other chords, as you'll discover later. The second, third and fourth fingers line up just behind the second fret.

BARRE CHORDS

A BARRE CHORD is one where the first finger holds down all six strings.

It may sound easy, but it's not. Try holding down six strings with one finger yourself, and you'll soon see why to some players the barre position is as hard to tame as Rambo.

But although barre chords are difficult, they are also extremely useful. Indeed, there are several good reasons for playing a barre.

For a start, it's a way of bringing more strings into play. Take the chord of F major. Up to now we've played it as a five-string chord, leaving the open bottom E string unplayed.

Using a barre, with the first finger pushed right across the neck, we can play an F note on that bottom E string, and so bring it into the chord.

CHORD OF F MAJOR (NOT BARRED)

BARRE CHORD OF F MAJOR

You needn't try this now—you'll get the chance to practise the chord on page 28. But the point to understand is why we use the barre: to bring all six strings into play.

THE SECOND important use of the barre is to help you play different chords using just one chord shape.

By keeping your fingers in the F shape,

and moving up two frets, you automatically have a barred G major chord.

If you move up two frets again, you have a barred A major chord. You don't have to change the hand position at all, other than to move it along the neck.

THE THIRD important use of the barre chord is to enable you to change chords

CHORD OF B MAJOR

AS YOU can see, the chord of **B** major is closely related to the chord of **A** major. In the same way that the note of **B** is two frets above the note of **A**, so the chord of **B** major is two frets above **A** major.

B major is an important chord. Along with **A**, it completes the three-chord trick in the key of **E** major: **E**, **A**, **B**.

But it's not an easy chord. In its simplest position, shown here, it is a four-note chord. In other words, the bottom two strings must not be played.

HERE'S HOW the basic **B** major is formed:

First finger (1) just behind the second fret on the first (top **E**) string.

Second finger (2) just behind the fourth fret on the fourth (**D**) string.

Third finger (3) just behind the fourth fret on the third (**G**) string.

Little finger (4) just behind the fourth fret on the second (**B**) string.

The bottom two strings (**A** and **E**) are not played.

CHORD OF B MAJOR

X Not played

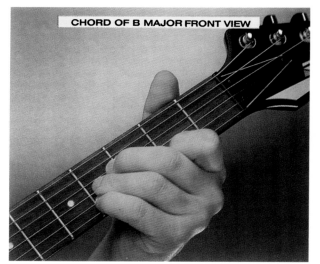

CHORD OF B MAJOR FRONT VIEW

Our most difficult chord to date, with a stretch of two frets. Establish the first and second fingers, then let the others drop into place.

CHORD OF B MAJOR AS YOU SEE IT

If you feel pressure on your thumb, don't hold the chord too long. Try to pack the second, third and fourth fingers tight.

However, the two most used barre shapes are the ones in our **G** major and **C** major example. These two shapes are in fact derived from **E** major and **A** major.

Let's look at the **E** major shape. First, form a chord of **E** major using your second, third and fourth fingers (second finger, first fret **G** string; third finger, second fret **A** string; fourth finger, second fret **D** string).

This leaves the first finger 'free' to barre any fret. If it barres the third fret, that gives us our **G** chord.

Now let's look at the **A** major shape. Again, form an **A** major shape using the second, third and fourth fingers (all behind the second fret, **B**, **G** and **D** strings).

Again, the first finger is free to barre any fret. Move this chord shape along the neck to barre third fret, and you have the **C** major chord from our example.

more quickly.

Take for instance a **G** major barre chord, formed on the third fret. Without moving your first finger, you can shift smoothly to a **C** major barre chord.

There are other barre chords you could form on the same fret—minor chords, seventh chords—which we'll come to later.

THE CHORD of **B** major is one that benefits immensely from the barre shape. Instead of the four-string chord opposite, we can bring all six strings into play.

Place your first finger right across all six strings on the second fret. The other four fingers line up in the same way as the unbarred chord:

First finger (1) barres all six strings just behind the second fret.

Second finger (2) just behind the fourth fret on the fourth (**D**) string.

Third finger (3) just behind the fourth fret on the third (**G**) string.

Little finger (4) just behind the fourth fret on the second (**B**) string.

AT FIRST you'll find barre chords almost impossible. Don't worry, it's the same for everyone.

Just keep practising—in time you'll find yourself using them as easily and naturally as any other chord.

BARRE CHORD OF B MAJOR

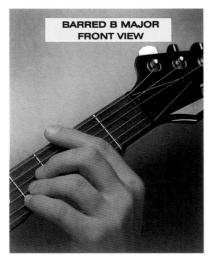

This shape is even more difficult, but it's far more useful. If you can take the strain, you'll make a fine guitarist.

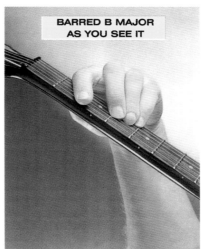

Note that the barring finger isn't straight. As long as all the notes play clearly, that's OK.

IF WE move the barred **B** major shape up one fret we get **C** major. This is a useful variation on the 'open' **C** you already know.

BARRE CHORDS

THE BIG problem with barre chords is actually playing them. Holding down all six strings with one finger can be brutal. A simple exercise will soon get you into the 'feel' of the barre shape, and the more you do it, the more natural it will become.

Try this: without forming a chord shape, simply barre all six strings with your first finger and play through the strings. If you have six clear notes, with no buzzes, you're winning.

If this is too much of a strain, you can enlist the second finger to support the first.

If you can discipline yourself to repeat this arrangement for, say, five minutes a day, you'll get your reward.

A helpful exercise for barre chords: the first finger barring first fret.

If the going gets tough for the first finger on its own, bring in the second finger to help.

BARRED F MAJOR CHORD

This is just about the most useful chord you'll every learn. Using this chord shape you can play every single major chord without changing your hand position—all you do is move the hand along the neck.

Here's how it's formed for its lowest version—the one nearest the headstock—F major:

First finger (1) barres all six strings just behind the first fret.

Second finger (2) just behind the second fret on the third (G) string.

Third finger (3) just behind the third fret on the fifth (A) string.

Little finger (4) just behind the third fret on the fourth (D) string.

BARRE CHORD OF F MAJOR

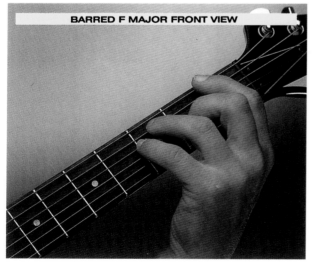

BARRED F MAJOR FRONT VIEW

The barre position adds an extra note to the F chord, giving you a full six-string shape. Make sure the first finger covers all frets.

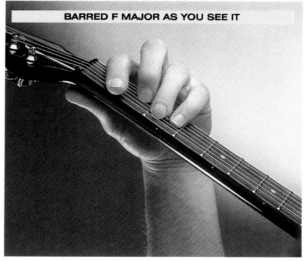

BARRED F MAJOR AS YOU SEE IT

It's difficult to keep the first finger straight, with the other fingers pulling it towards them. As long as the notes are clear, it doesn't matter.

USING BARRE chords, you can now work out different ways of playing all the major chords you've learnt so far.

To take one example: on page 25 you learned an open **D** major chord, comprising just four strings. Using a barre, you can now play two six-string chords of **D** major as well.

D major can be found as an 'A' style barre chord on the fifth fret, and as an 'E' type barre chord on the tenth fret.

ONE LAST point on barre chords. Some people complete a chord of this nature not by barring to cover the sixth string, but by hooking their thumb round the neck.

Generally this is frowned on by guitar teachers, but if it's good enough for Prince and Springsteen, who are we to tell you not to do it?

BARRE CHORDS

OPEN CHORD OF D MAJOR

BARRE CHORD OF D MAJOR ('A' SHAPE)

BARRE CHORD OF D MAJOR ('E' SHAPE)

BARRE CHORD OF G MAJOR

BARRED G MAJOR FRONT VIEW

BARRED G MAJOR AS YOU SEE IT

The barred **G** chord is exactly the same as **F**, two frets up. The first finger should feel a little easier away from the nut on the neck of the guitar.

BARRE CHORD OF A MAJOR

BARRED A MAJOR FRONT VIEW

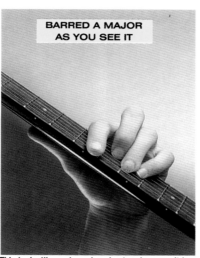

BARRED A MAJOR AS YOU SEE IT

This looks like a nice relaxed set-up because it is. Don't fear the barre chord: it could be your best friend.

BARRED F CHORD SHAPE

THIS SHAPE is known as either the 'E' or 'F' shape. If you move it a couple of frets up the neck, you can form **G** major:

First finger (1) barring all strings just behind the third fret.

Second finger (2) just behind the fourth fret on the third (**G**) string.

Third finger (3) just behind the fifth fret on the fifth (**A**) string.

Little finger (4) just behind the fifth fret on the fourth (**D**) string.

TO FORM the barre chord of **A** major, we simply move two frets along. Because we barre this chord on the fifth fret, we sometimes refer to it as **A** played at the fifth fret.

First finger (1) barres all six strings just behind the fifth fret.

Second finger (2) just behind the sixth fret on the third (**G**) string.

Third finger (3) just behind the seventh fret on the fifth (**A**) string.

Little finger (4) just behind the seventh fret on the fourth (**D**) string.

MINOR KEYS

SO FAR, everything we've dealt with has been 'major'—major keys, such as the key of **A** major; major scales, such as the scale of **A** major; and major chords, such as the chord of **A** major.

As you know, there are 12 notes in music—**C, D, E, F, G, A, B**, plus the five sharp/flat notes **C#/D♭, D#/E♭, F#/G♭, G#/A♭** and **A#/B♭**.

Each of these 12 notes has a major key based on its own major scale. And each note has its own major chord.

Now we come on to something new. For each 'major' there is a partner, known as a 'minor'.

Each of the 12 notes has a minor key based on its own minor scale. And each note has its own minor chord.

So you've got a total of 24 musical keys that you can work in—12 majors and 12 minors. And you've got 12 major chords and 12 minor chords which you can use—these are known as the primary chords.

THE TOP sections of the next six pages concentrate on minor keys, while the lower section shows you the most important minor chord shapes.

Once you understand how the major and minor scales and chords are constructed, and how they relate to one another, you could say that you basically understand music.

You can, if you wish, skip over this section and simply concentrate on learning to play the chords shown at the bottom of each page. But if you want to learn the complex language of music, we've done our best to give a simple explanation.

So let's get started . . .

MINOR SCALES

DO YOU remember how a major scale was made up? If you check back to page 18, you'll see how we played the scale of **C** major on our **B** string, with gaps of 2, 2, 1, 2, 2, 2, 1 frets—or tone, tone, semitone, tone, tone, tone, semitone.

The notes in the scale of **C** major were **C, D, E, F, G, A, B, C**.

To get the scale of **C** minor, we take the major scale and flatten the third, sixth and seventh notes by one semitone each.

So the notes in the scale of **C** minor are **C, D, E♭, F, G, A♭, B♭**.

The gaps between the notes in a minor scale are 2, 1, 2, 2, 1, 2, 2—or tone, semitone, tone, tone, semitone, tone, tone. (Technically, this is known as the Aeolian minor scale.)

CHORD OF E MINOR

OUR FIRST departure from the major chords is a simple and logical step, providing us with a necessary option in song structure.

The minor chords are often called the 'mood' chords, because they carry a sad, resonant sound, as opposed to the bright or forceful sound of a major chord. Yet you'll notice something familiar about them.

As you play the minor chord you'll recognise the root note and sound of its major counterpart—for example **A** minor will sound similar to **A** major, but will have a more mournful or soulful sound.

OUR STARTING point will be **E** minor (or **Em** for short). Just two fingers—the first and second—are required here:

First finger (1) just behind the second fret on the fifth (**A**) string.

Second finger (2) just behind the second fret on the fourth (**D**) string.

Strum this chord and hear the slightly sombre effect, in direct contrast to the dynamic **E** major chord.

CHORD OF E MINOR

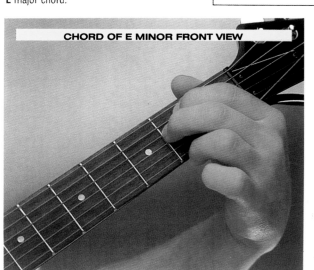

E minor is a simple two-finger chord. Note how the third finger stays well clear of the strings.

The thumb curls round the neck of the guitar, with the palm supporting the instrument's neck.

TAKE A LOOK at the scales of **C** major, **C** minor, **A** major and **A** minor. They are the notes you can use in the keys of **C** major, **C** minor, **A** major and **A** minor, whether playing single notes or chords.

You'll notice there's quite a difference between the notes in the scales of **C** major and **C** minor. But look at the scales of **C** major and **A** minor. One starts on **C**, the other on **A**— but the notes are exactly the same: C, D, E, F, G, A, B.

This is because **A** minor is the 'relative minor' of **C** major.

This means that any chord or note which

can be used in the key of **C** major can also be used in the key of **A** minor.

It also means that the chords of **C** major and **A** minor are related—play them and you'll hear why. It's strange, but true, that you will often use **C** major and **A** minor together—but you'll almost never use **C** major with **C** minor. They just don't go.

The same goes for all major/minor chord pairs. Every major chord has its relative minor, with which it works well—for **C** major it's **A** minor, for **A** major it happens to be **F#** minor.

If you look at the table on the left, you'll see that **A** is the sixth note in the scale of **C** major, and **F#** is the sixth note in the scale of **A** major.

Armed with this knowledge, see if you can work out the relative minor for **G** major. The answer's on the next page.

HOW MAJOR AND MINOR SCALES RELATE

SCALE OF C MAJOR	C	D	E	F	G	A	B	C
SCALE OF C MINOR	C	D	E♭	F	G	A♭	B♭	C
SCALE OF A MAJOR	A	B	C#	D	E	F#	G#	A
SCALE OF A MINOR	A	B	C	D	E	F	G	A

The scale of **A** minor has more in common with the scale of **C** major than with **A** major. In fact they share the same notes, because **A** minor is the relative minor of **C** major.

THE NEXT minor chord position involves the use of three fingers, to form **A** minor (**Am**).

Place your first finger (1) on the first fret of the second (**B**) string.

Second finger (2) just behind the second fret on the fourth (**D**) string.

Third finger (3) just behind the second fret on the third (**G**) string.

TRY PLAYING an **A** minor chord, then an **E** minor and a **C** major.

You'll notice that your second finger remains on the second fret of the fourth (**D**) string, playing the **E** note which links the three chords together.

Practise changing between the three chords, bring in **G** major as well—you'll soon hear some interesting chord patterns.

CHORD OF A MINOR

Like **E** minor, **A** minor is a resonant 'open' chord requiring accurate fingering for a full, clean sound.

A minor and **E** minor sound really good together. Practise moving smoothly from one to the other.

RELATIVE MINORS

YOU CAN now add a relative minor chord to each of the three-chord tricks you already know, to make what we might call four-chord tricks.

So **C**, **F**, **G**, **A** minor (or **Am** for short) is the four-chord trick in the key of **C** major.

These four chords all work in the key of **C** major because they use notes which are in the scale of **C** major (the notes in the scale being **C**, **D**, **E**, **F**, **G**, **A**, **B**).

The chord of **C** major uses notes **C**, **E**, **G**.
The chord of **F** major uses **F**, **A**, **C**.
The chord of **G** major uses **G**, **B**, **D**.
The chord of **A** minor uses **A**, **C**, **E**.

IT'S ESSENTIAL to know the relative minor for each major chord, because the two go hand in hand.

The table below gives the relative minor for every major key or chord.

MINOR CHORD STRUCTURE

MINOR CHORDS are made up in exactly the same way as major chords: from the first, third and fifth notes of their scale.

The scale of **A** minor is **A**, **B**, **C**, **D**, **E**, **F**, **G**. Therefore the notes in the chord of **A** minor are **A**, **C** and **E**.

MAJOR KEYS AND THEIR RELATIVE MINORS												
MAJOR KEY	C	Db	D	Eb	E	F	F#	G	Ab	A	Bb	B
RELATIVE MINOR KEY	A	Bb	B	C	C#	D	D#	E	F	F#	G	G#

There is a logical way to work out which major key or chord relates to which minor key or chord. The relative minor is always three frets—three semitones—down from the major. From **C**, count down three semitones and you get **A**. Therefore **A** minor is the relative minor of **C** major.

NOTES IN THE CHORD OF E MINOR

CHORD OF D MINOR

THE **Dm** CHORD is perhaps the trickiest of the basic minor chords to form. Here it is:

First finger (1) just behind the first fret on the first (top **E**) string.

Second finger (2) just behind the second fret on the third (**G**) string.

Third finger (3) just behind the third fret on the second (**B**) string.

The fourth (**D**) string is played open. The bottom two strings are not played.

NOW YOU'VE got a three-chord trick of minor chords, consisting of **Am**, **Dm** and **Em**. These chords work together in the key of **A** minor.

Try different sequences of the three: together they combine to give a powerful, mournful effect.

And you can put them together with your original three-chord trick—**C** major, **F** major and **G** major—to form one giant six-chord trick to be used in the keys of **C** major or **A** minor. In other words, **C** or **Am** is your logical starting point—but it's you making the music, so suit yourself.

CHORD OF D MINOR

X Not played

CHORD OF D MINOR FRONT VIEW

Your fingers should take on a 'spidery' look when forming **Dm**, with the first joints at the knuckle nicely bent.

CHORD OF D MINOR AS YOU SEE IT

Your little finger may want to 'pop back' onto the strings, so remember to keep it tucked into the palm of your hand.

NOTES IN THE CHORD OF A MINOR

NOTES IN THE CHORD OF D MINOR

LET'S TAKE another look at some major chords and their relative minors. As we know, the major chords of **C**, **F** and **G** go together to form a three-chord trick in the key of **C** major.

Well, here's another useful fact: if you can use a major chord in a certain key, you can also use its relative minor chord.

So if we can use **C**, **F** and **G** in the key of **C** major, we can also use their relative minor chords—**Am**, **Dm** and **Em**.

These are the six primary chords that work in **C** major. They also work in the key of **A** minor.

ANOTHER WAY of putting it is to say that in every key there are six primary chords we can use. These six chords are based on six of the seven notes in the scale.

To take **C** major as our example, here's

HOW CHORDS WORK TOGETHER

the scale, along with the chords that work in the key of **C** major:

Root note: **C**.   Chord: **C** major.
2nd note: **D**.   Chord: **D** minor.
3rd note: **E**.   Chord: **E** minor.
4th note: **F**.   Chord: **F** major.
5th note: **G**.   Chord: **G** major.
6th note: **A**.   Chord: **A** minor.
7th note: **B**.   Chord: none.

In a minor scale, the only note which doesn't give us a chord to use is the second. Let's take the scale of **A** minor:

Root note: **A**.   Chord: **A** minor.
2nd note: **B**.   Chord: none.
3rd note: **C**.   Chord: **C** major.
4th note: **D**.   Chord: **D** minor.
5th note: **E**.   Chord: **E** minor.
6th note: **F**.   Chord: **F** major.
7th note: **G**.   Chord: **G** major.

This formula can be applied to any major ▶

CHORD OF B MINOR

THE CHORDS of **B** minor and **C** minor take the **A** minor chord shape and move it along the fretboard.

The first—and most useful—of these two very similar chords is **B** minor. Unfortunately, in its easier unbarred form **B** minor is just a four-note chord. Here's how it's formed:

First finger (1) just behind the second fret on the first (top **E**) string.

Second finger (2) just behind the third fret on the second (**B**) string.

Third finger (3) just behind the fourth fret on the fourth (**D**) string.

Little finger (4) just behind the fourth fret on the third (**G**) string.

The bottom two strings are not played.

THE CHORD of **B** minor is useful because it's the relative minor of **D** major, and can be used in the same keys as its major relative.

So you can use it in the keys of **B** minor, **D** major, **G** major, **E** minor, **A** major and **F#** minor—and all bar **F#** minor are common keys.

X Not played

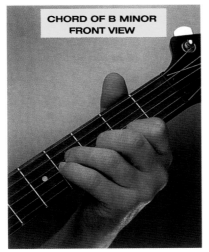

With the third and fourth fingers close together, there's a tendency to touch adjacent strings. Keep them well spaced if you can.

The thumb will fall back when forming **Bm**. Don't force it into an unnatural position. The left hand should always feel comfortable.

The chord of **C** minor is formed by moving the **B** minor fingering one fret up the neck. Again, the bottom two strings aren't played.

SHARPS OR FLATS?

AS WE know, a sharp/flat note can be called either sharp or flat—so how do we decide which it should be?

The simple explanation is that the note name changes according to what key you're using it in.

Here's how it works. You can't have two notes with similar names in the same key. So for instance you can't have **G** and **G♭**, or **G** and **G#**, **G♭** and **G#**. So if there's a **G** in the scale, the note **G♭/F#** will be called **F#**.

On top of that, you can't have both sharps and flats in the same key—a key may include up to six sharp notes (the key of **F#** major) or five flat notes (the key of **D♭** major). But never both.

For this reason, keys with sharps are sometimes known as sharp keys, and keys with flats are sometimes known as flat keys.

One final point. In the table opposite, you may notice that in the keys of **F#** major and **D#** minor there's a note called **E#**. This is the note we usually call **F**, but because there's already an **F**-note (**F#**) in the key, it's called **E#**. This is the only time this occurs.

DON'T WORRY about what you call sharps or flats—if you refer to a note as **D#** when you should be calling it **E♭**, any musician will know what you mean.

But for any reader who wants to know how the system works, hopefully this has answered your questions.

or minor scale, to give you the primary chords that sound good in any key.

This doesn't mean these are the *only* chords you can use—there are lots of chords called sevenths, ninths, diminished and so on which we'll meet later.

It also doesn't mean you can't use other primary chords if you're writing a song—after all, rules are there to be broken. But these are the primary chords which use notes from each scale: the ones it's most natural to use.

THE TABLE opposite sets out all the major and minor scales, and all the chords that 'work' in every single key. You don't need to try to take it in all at once. Even the most experienced of musicians occasionally stumble over their scales. But as a reference table you'll find it invaluable.

CHORD OF F MINOR

LIKE ITS big brother **F** major, **F#** minor is formed around the first fret of the guitar. The first finger assumes a 'half-barre' position across the first three strings, because in effect you're just moving the **E** minor chord up one fret. Here's how it's formed:

First finger (1) barring just behind the first fret across the first, second and third (top **E**, **B** and **G**) strings.

Third finger (3) just behind the third fret on the fifth (**A**) string.

Little finger (**D**) just behind the third fret on the fourth (**A**) string.

The bottom **E** string is not played.

AS WITH the **F** major chord, this can be played as a four-string chord with the third finger fretting the fourth string and the bottom two strings unplayed.

CHORD OF F MINOR

X Not played

CHORD OF F MINOR FRONT VIEW

The first finger has a tough job holding down three strings here. Don't despair if the chord sounds fuzzy at first.

CHORD OF F MINOR AS YOU SEE IT

Try to help the first finger by using the second as support. The other two fingers will feel easier this way.

TABLE OF SCALES AND CHORDS

	NOTE IN SCALE	PRIMARY TRIAD CHORD	SCALE (READ DOWN FROM ROOT NOTE)										
MAJOR KEY	Root	Root major chord	C	D♭	D	E♭	E	F	F#	G	A♭	A	B♭	B
	Second	Minor chord	D	E♭	E	F	F#	G	G#	A	B♭	B	C	C#
	Third	Minor chord	E	F	F#	G	G#	A	A#	B	C	C#	D	D#
	Fourth	Major chord	F	G♭	G	A♭	A	B♭	B	C	D♭	D	E♭	E
	Fifth	Major chord	G	A♭	A	B♭	B	C	C#	D	E♭	E	F	F#
	Sixth	Relative minor chord	A	B♭	B	C	C#	D	D#	E	F	F#	G	G#
	Seventh	– – – –	B	C	C#	D	D#	E	E#	F#	G	G#	A	A#

	NOTE IN SCALE	PRIMARY TRIAD CHORD	SCALE (READ DOWN FROM ROOT NOTE)										
MINOR KEY	Root	Root minor chord	A	B♭	B	C	C#	D	D#	E	F	F#	G	G#
	Second	– – – –	B	C	C#	D	D#	E	E#	F#	G	G#	A	A#
	Third	Relative major chord	C	D♭	D	E♭	E	F	F#	G	A♭	A	B♭	B
	Fourth	Minor chord	D	E♭	E	F	F#	G	G#	A	B♭	B	C	C#
	Fifth	Minor chord	E	F	F#	G	G#	A	A#	B	C	C#	D	D#
	Sixth	Major chord	F	G♭	G	A♭	A	B♭	B	C	D♭	D	E♭	E
	Seventh	Major chord	G	A♭	A	B♭	B	C	C#	D	E♭	E	F	F#

CHORD OF F# MINOR

LIKE THE **F** major chord, the **F** minor chord shape slides easily along the neck to give other five-string minor chords. If you slide one fret, you have **F#** minor—a useful chord, because it works in the keys of **A** major, **D** major, **E** major, **B** minor and **C#** minor. It's the relative minor of **A** major, and sounds great played between **A** major and **E** major.

One fret further gives you **G** minor, and on the fifth fret you can play an alternative version of **A** minor to the one you already know.

Don't forget, though, that the open bottom **E** string is not played.

CHORD OF F# MINOR

X Not played

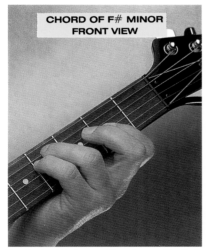

CHORD OF F# MINOR FRONT VIEW

The chords of **F** minor and **F#** minor are identical, but one fret apart. This chord sounds good with **A**, **D** or **E** major.

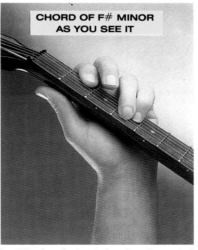

CHORD OF F# MINOR AS YOU SEE IT

Try sliding from **F** minor to **F#** minor, then on to **G** minor. You'll soon get to know your way around the fretboard.

CHORD OF G MINOR

The chord of **G** minor is essentially the same as the chords of **F** minor and **F#** minor. You just play it on the third fret. The bottom **E** string is not played.

435

FINGER STYLE

A TRUCKLOAD of the most sophisticated equipment in the world can't disguise a weak right hand. Some guitarists work so hard on getting their chord shapes correct with their left hand, they forget about the right.

We've already looked at how to use a plectrum for rhythm work, and how to play the scale of **G** major with a plectrum. We'll be taking that further later, when we begin playing single-note solos, riffs and more scales.

But there's more to the right hand than just wielding a plectrum. Assuming you have the full set – four fingers and a thumb – it's purely a matter of practice before your right hand can perform tricks of its own.

The use of the fingers to pluck the strings is known as finger picking, or finger style.

These diagrams show the different strings that may be played with each finger (and thumb) of your right hand.

Generally, it's associated more with folk than rock guitar, but it's more common in rock than is generally recognised: you can hear right-hand fingering skills in the work of guitarists as varied as Mark Knopfler, Steve Howe and Jeff Beck.

THE QUICKEST way to utilise the fingers as 'fleshy plectrums' is to consider them playing the strings in sequence, from bottom to top **E**. The thumb will strike downwards on the bottom **E** string, the fifth (**A**) string, and occasionally the fourth (**D**) string. The fingers will 'pick' upwards from the **D** string through to the top **E** string.

There is no set rule for which finger plays which string, but the three diagrams above show possible combinations.

BARRED MINOR CHORDS

AS WE explained on page 26, barre chords simplify the work of the left hand, enabling you to use familiar chord shapes anywhere on the guitar.

There are two important minor chord shapes – **Em** and **Am** – which can be barred to provide a simple set of chords using the same shape.

Barring **Em** on the first fret gives us **Fm**. The set-up is:

First finger (and second, if you like) across all strings, just behind the first fret.

Third finger just behind the third fret on the fifth (**A**) string.

Little finger just behind the third fret on the fourth (**D**) string.

Move the whole thing two frets further, and you've got **Gm**.

BARRE CHORD OF F MINOR

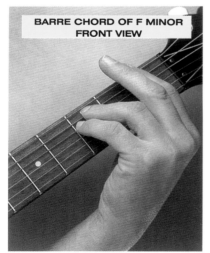

BARRE CHORD OF F MINOR FRONT VIEW

This is a fairly difficult barre chord to form, as it falls on the first fret where the strings are less forgiving.

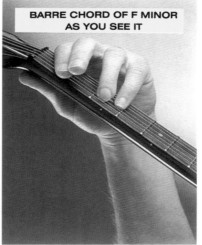

BARRE CHORD OF F MINOR AS YOU SEE IT

When forming a barre chord such as **F** minor, remember to use your second finger to support the first, if that helps.

BARRE CHORD OF G MINOR

You can identify any of the **Em** style chords by their position in relation to the **E** strings. **Gm** falls on the third fret, which is the **G** note on the **E** strings.

LET'S TRY working out with the right hand on just one chord – an open **G** major.

First, form the chord with your left hand, then strike the bottom string a couple of times with your thumb. You will immediately notice the mellow tone it produces.

Now pluck the top string with your third finger, by pulling it upwards. Alternate these two notes until you feel relaxed and comfortable.

The note you're playing is of course the same on both strings, **G**.

Now here comes the tricky bit. Using the thumb only, strike the bottom **E** string and then the fifth (**A**) string. Forget about the other fingers for the moment; just concentrate on getting the thumb working on those bottom two strings.

The **A** string is being held down on the second fret, giving a **B** note.

Practise this until you're completely happy with your performance. Don't try and race ahead here. Whilst the sounds you are making may seem repetitive and dull, it's the right hand which is benefiting. You're only shortchanging yourself if you adopt a 'nuts to this bit' attitude.

IF WE are still on speaking terms, and you are happy to proceed, we will now make full use of the right hand in conjunction with the **G** chord.

The first finger will pluck the **G** string, the second finger the **B** string, and the third finger the top **E** string. Ignoring the thumb, pull these three strings together. A little fuzzy, eh?

Looking at the picture here, note the position of the fingers in relation to the strings. For maximum clarity of tone, pull

*Finger picking stance, thumb poised over bottom **E**.*

the strings from a point just below the tip.

The next move is to bring in the thumb. Try this: strike the bottom **E** string with the thumb, then pull the top three strings.

BARRING THE **A** minor shape on the second fret gives us **B** minor – the relative minor to **D** major, and an important link in a chord chain that includes **D**, **G** and **A**.

B minor is formed as follows:

First finger holds down all the strings on the second fret.

Second finger just behind the third fret on the second (**B**) string.

Third finger just behind the fourth fret on the fourth (**D**) string.

Little finger just behind the fourth fret on the third (**G**) string.

AS WITH all barre chords, this shape can be used at any point on the neck. Form this shape at the fifth fret, and you have **Dm**. You also have a convenient place to change either to **Em** (by sliding up to the seventh fret) or to **Am** (by holding the barre on the fifth fret, but adjusting the other fingers into the **Fm** shape).

BARRE CHORD OF B MINOR

BARRE CHORD OF B MINOR FRONT VIEW

Bm is an important chord, as it is the relative minor to **D** major, and will therefore appear frequently in songs written in **D**, a common key.

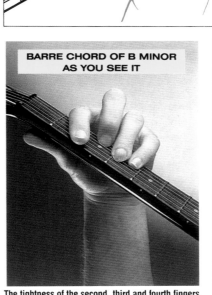

BARRE CHORD OF B MINOR AS YOU SEE IT

The tightness of the second, third and fourth fingers takes some getting used to when forming these **Am** style chords in their barre positions.

BARRE CHORD OF C MINOR

This is **Cm**, which surprisingly is not used as much as **C#m** (one fret along) because **C#m** is the relative minor of **E** major. You can use this shape to form any minor chord.

INSTRUCTION MANUAL

▶ Repeat these moves alternately until it feels comfortable.

YOU MIGHT describe the sound you are now making as *dum-ching, dum-ching*. Silly, I know, but it helps us get the message across.

To broaden the scope of the thumb, let's bring in the fifth (**A**) string. Alternate it with the bottom **E** string to give this effect:

Dum (bottom **E**) *ching* (top three strings).
Dum (**A** string) *ching* (top three strings).
Dum (bottom **E**) *ching* (top three strings).
And so on.

Don't worry too much about your *ching* at this point. Just work on that thumb.

You should try to get it moving almost independently, so that while it plods along giving a regular bassline, the fingers play the tricky bits.

FINALLY, WE need to incorporate the **D** string. Working on the *dum-ching* principle, first strike the bottom **E** string with your thumb, then pluck the top three strings, as above. Now add the **A** string (thumb), followed by the *ching* effect. And then the new bit: strike the **D** string with the thumb, followed by the *ching*.

Incidentally, you can take each *dum-ching* as one beat. If you add a fourth *dum-ching* based on the **A** string, that will neatly complete one four-beat bar, and you can start at the **E** string again.

AND THAT, in its most basic form, is finger style. Once you've conquered the **G** chord in this style, you can apply the technique to other chords, and begin to work up chord changes.

Generally, it sounds best if the root note of each chord is played by the thumb on the first beat of the bar. So if you are playing open chords, these are the strings to play first with the thumb:

E or **Em**: Sixth (bottom **E**) string;
A or **Am**: Fifth (**A**) string;
D or **Dm**: Fourth (**D**) string;
G: Sixth (bottom **E**) string;
C: Fifth (**A**) string;
F or **Fm**: Fourth (**D**) string.

Bearing that in mind, try these chord sequences:
C Am F G
Am Em
G D C G
Am G F E.

As always, take it slowly at first.

ON PAGE 40 we look at a few different fingerpicking patterns.

NOW THAT we've looked at the minor chords, here's a song which employs an interesting selection of major and minor chords – 'The Boys Are Back In Town' by Thin Lizzy.

For our purposes here, we've modified the song a little. Later on you'll get the chance to play it in its full glory, complete with seventh and minor seventh chords – and in a different key. But for now, let's try it in the key of **C**, and with a simplified rhythm and chords.

You've already encountered most of the chords you'll need. Our version has seven: the original three-chord trick of **C**, **F** and **G**, along with their relative minors **Am**, **Dm** and **Em**, plus one new chord, **A♭**, which we'll show you along with the complete song on page 40.

THE RHYTHM is a regular four beats to the bar (**4/4** in musical terms), but you have a choice of two ways to play it, shown on the two grids here.

The easiest way (top grid) is simply to play one downstroke for each beat. That's not much like Thin Lizzy played it. but it will make sense, and it will certainly help at first while you're working out the chord sequence.

Once you're familiar with the chords, try adding the slightly more difficult rhythm element marked on the lower grid. It entails both down and up strokes, but not in a straightforward down-up-down-up pattern.

Tap your foot steadily, quite slowly, counting out 1-2-3-4. The rhythm pattern is down, down-up . . . down. Repeat it over and over, and should find the emphasis changing to DOWN, down-UP. . . down, DOWN, down-UP. . . down, DOWN, down-UP. . . down.

If you can't get the hang of this, don't worry. Just concentrate on playing downstrokes, but every now and then slip in an upstroke so that you gradually add a bit of swing to it.

When you feel you're ready, go on to page 40, where the whole song is laid out.

⊓ Downward stroke   V Upward stroke

☐ **C** major   ☐ **E** minor   ☐ **G** major
☐ **F** major   ☐ **A** minor

TITLE	KEY	TEMPO
'THE BOYS ARE BACK IN TOWN' (OPENING LINES)	C MAJOR	MEDIUM SLOW

1	2	3	4	1	2	3	4
C	C	C	C	Em	Em	Em	Em
⊓	⊓	⊓	⊓	⊓	⊓	⊓	⊓
Guess who		just	got	back	today,		them

1	2	3	4	1	2	3	4
F	F	F	F	Am	Am	Am	Am
⊓	⊓	⊓	⊓	⊓	⊓	⊓	⊓
Wild-eyed		boys	that had	been away			

1	2	3	4	1	2	3	4
Em	Em	Em	Em	Am	Am	Am	Am
⊓	⊓	⊓	⊓	⊓	⊓	⊓	⊓
Haven't changed,			hadn't	much	to	say,	but

1	2	3	4	1	2	3	4
F	F	F	F	G	G	G	G
⊓	⊓	⊓	⊓	⊓	⊓	⊓	⊓
Man	I	still	think them	cats	are	crazy	

Above: This is how to play the song using all downward strokes: one stroke for each beat, regular as clockwork. If you want, you can play it all the way through like this.

1	2	3	4	1	2	3	4
C	C		C	Em	Em		Em
⊓	⊓ V		⊓	⊓	⊓ V		⊓
Guess	who just		got	back	to day,		them

1	2	3	4	1	2	3	4
F	F		F	Am	Am		Am
⊓	⊓ V		⊓	⊓	⊓ V		⊓
Wild-eyed	boys		that had	been	away		

1	2	3	4	1	2	3	4
Em	Em		Em	Am	Am		Am
⊓	⊓ V		⊓	⊓	⊓ V		⊓
Haven't	changed,		hadn't	much	to say,		but

1	2	3	4	1	2	3	4
F	F		F	G	G		G
⊓	⊓ V		⊓	⊓	⊓ V		⊓
Man,	I still	think	them	cats	are crazy		

Above: This is the rhythm we suggest you use. It can be applied to the whole of the grid on page 40. You don't play a chord on the third beat of the bar, but just let your previous chord ring out.

Four expert fingerpickers, from left: Mark Knopfler fingerpicks while smoking a cigarette; Albert Collins fingerpicks with a capo on his guitar neck; George Thorogood fingerpicks whilst playing bottleneck; Jeff Beck fingerpicks and palms his tremolo arm at the same time.

'THE BOYS ARE BACK IN TOWN'

'THE BOYS Are Back In Town' was the high point in the saga of Thin Lizzy – a tale of a black Irish bass player, a drummer and about a dozen guitarists.

The bass player was Phil Lynott; the drummer, also from Dublin, was Brian Downey. From 1970 to 1983, they accompanied some of the finest hard rock guitar players in the world – Brian Robertson, Scott Gorham, Gary Moore, Snowy White, John Sykes, Eric Bell and even Midge Ure.

All these guitarists were great technicians. Each of them could have adorned any heavy metal band. But it was Lynott who elevated Lizzy above heavy metal, with his wit, charm and imaginative songwriting. His subjects ranged from rock and roll to blood and thunder, from cowboys to warriors. The common factor was romance, enhanced by the melodic double guitar sound.

Released in 1976, 'The Boys Are Back In Town' was taken from the 'Jailbreak' album, which sent Thin Lizzy high into the charts in both the US and UK. Other hits included 'Whiskey In the Jar', 'Dancin' In The Moonlight' and 'Don't Believe A Word', but Thin Lizzy will always be remembered for "them wild-eyed boys"

Sadly, Phil Lynott died in January 1986, but his songs remain as a testament to a great talent. 'The Boys Are Back' is typical of the freshness he managed to bring to fairly standard chord progressions, and the Thin Lizzy songbook is well worth picking up as an object lesson in how to write great guitar songs.

Right: Thin Lizzy leader Phil Lynott with three of his guitarists (from left: Brian Robertson and Scott Gorham, who played together on 'The Boys Are Back In Town', and Gary Moore).

FINGER STYLE PATTERNS

ONCE YOU'VE got your *dum-ching* working, you should try to use individual fingers to pluck individual strings, rather than all three at once.

Here are some possible finger picking patterns which you can apply to almost any chord. We've marked the thumb (**T**) as striking the bottom **E** string, but it could equally well play the fifth (**A**) string, depending on the chord.

Usually the thumb will play the root bass note—bottom **E** string for **E** major and **G** major, the fifth string for **A** major and **C** major, and so on.

You don't read these charts like chord diagrams, which is why the strings are open-ended. Just move from left to right, as if reading a book. Follow the blue ball.

So in the first chart, you play the sixth string with your thumb, then the top **E** string with your third finger, then the **B** string with your second finger, then the **G** string with your first finger.

In each pattern, when you reach the end you simply start at the beginning again.

When working on a new pattern, try it at first with just one chord, repeating it until you get it right. Then try changing chords, taking care to strike the correct bass note at the start of each bar.

SIX RIGHT HAND PATTERNS FOR FINGER STYLE PLAY

'THE BOYS ARE BACK IN TOWN'

HERE IT is, then – your biggest test to date: the long, complex chord sequence of 'The Boys Are Back In Town'.

It has a 12-bar intro (four bars repeated three times). Then there's a 16-bar verse and 12-bar chorus. And for good measure, there's an eight-bar 'bridge' to take you from the chorus back to the verse. This bridge is where the famous twin guitar riff occurs.

Looking at the running order opposite, you'll notice there's also a second bridge (Bridge 2), which isn't shown on the grid here. We'll include that later, when we develop the song – you can get along without it for now.

AS EVER, take this nice and slowly at first. Try to master each section on its own before stringing them all together.

Don't worry too much about the rhythm – as long as you've got something that sounds good to you, you can work your way through the song, practising the different chord changes.

The most unusual chord is **A♭** major, which you won't often find it in a song in **C** major. Phil Lynott uses it to break up the pattern and make a contrast. The 'natural' chord to put there would be **Am** (try it yourself).

Apart from that 'unnatural' **A♭**, this song is a classic illustration of the six chords which 'work' in a key – those chords, in the case of **C** major, being **C**, **Dm**, **Em**, **F**, **G** and **Am**.

AS WE said, the **A♭** chord is introduced to add contrast between the first and second parts of the verse. You can emphasize that contrast. For the first ten bars of the verse, use open chords near the nut of your guitar. But after you hit that **A♭** on the fourth fret, try playing an F-shape **G** (third fret), an Fm-shape **Am** (fifth fret), a Bm-shape **Dm** (fifth fret), and finally an F-shape **G** again. These can all be played either as barre chords or as four-string chords.

KEY TO SYMBOLS AND COLOURS

⊓ Downward stroke   ∨ Upward stroke
☐ C major ▨ E minor ☐ G major
☐ F major ▨ A minor ▨ D minor
☐ A♭ major

CHORD OF A♭ MAJOR

As this chord falls between **F** and **G** in the song, we suggest that you play it as an F-shape chord on the fourth fret.

HOW TO PLAY

SCALE OF C MINOR

IF YOU'RE still practising the scale of **G** major, which we showed you on page 25, you should be fairly fluent by now. You could also probably do with a change – and now that we've looked at the minor chords, this is a good time to try a minor scale: **C** minor.

As before, there's an easy version and a 'proper' version. The simpler one takes you through a one-octave scale, from **C** to **C**.

The longer version is two octaves.

Try the shorter one first, starting on the fifth fret of your third (**G**) string. For the last note, slide your little finger from the sixth fret, top **E** string, to the eighth.

The notes in the scale of **C** minor are **C**, **D**, **E♭**, **F**, **G**, **A♭** and **B♭**. Try to identify each note as you play it.

You'll notice that there are no open strings in this scale. This means that you can move the whole exercise up and down the fretboard.

Move it all up two frets, and you've got the scale of **D** minor.

Bearing this in mind, you can return to the scale of **G** major – the second version, with no open strings – and try that scale in different parts of the fretboard.

Move it two frets up, and you'll be playing the scale of **A** major.

SCALE OF C MINOR

SCALE OF C MINOR

'THE BOYS ARE BACK IN TOWN'

LYRICS AND RUNNING ORDER

INTRO (Three times)

VERSE 1
Guess who just got back today,
Them wild-eyed boys that had been away.
Haven't changed, hadn't much to say,
But man, I still think them cats are crazy.
They were asking if you were around,
How you was, where you could be found.
Told them you were living downtown,
Driving all the old men crazy.

CHORUS
The boys are back in town . . .
(Eight times)

BRIDGE 1 (Twice)
VERSE 2
You know that chick that used to dance a lot,
Every night she'd be on the floor shaking what she'd
  got,
Man, when I tell you she was cool, she was red hot,
I mean she was steaming.
And that time over at Johnny's place,
Well this chick got up and she slapped Johnny's face,
Man, we just fell about the place,
If that chick don't wanna know, forget her.

CHORUS
BRIDGE 1 (Twice)
BRIDGE 2
Spread the word around,
Guess who's back in town.
Just spread the word around.

VERSE 3
Friday night they'll be dressed to kill,
Down at Dino's bar and grill.
The drink will flow and blood will spill,
And if the boys wanna fight you better let 'em.
That jukebox in the corner blasting out my favourite
  song,
The nights are getting warmer, it won't be long,
Won't be long till summer comes,
Now that the boys are here again.

CHORUS/BRIDGE 1/FADE

1	2	3	4	1	2	3	4
G	G		G	Am	Am		Am
⊓	⊓ V		⊓	⊓	⊓ V		⊓
Told	them	you	were	living		down	town,

1	2	3	4	1	2	3	4
Dm	Dm		Dm	G	G		G
⊓	⊓ V		⊓	⊓	⊓ V		⊓
	Driving	all	the	old		men	crazy.	The

CHORUS

1	2	3	4	1	2	3	4
C	C		C	C	C		C
⊓	⊓ V		⊓	⊓	⊓ V		⊓
Boys	are	back	in	town,	the	boys	are	back	in	town.

1	2	3	4	1	2	3	4
Dm	Dm		Dm	F	F		F
⊓	⊓ V		⊓	⊓	⊓ V		⊓
						I	said	the

1	2	3	4	1	2	3	4
C	C		C	C	C		C
⊓	⊓ V		⊓	⊓	⊓ V		⊓
Boys	are	back	in	to-	o-	o-	own.	The

1	2	3	4	1	2	3	4
Dm	Dm		Dm	F	F		F
⊓	⊓ V		⊓	⊓	⊓ V		⊓
Boys	are	back	in	town.				The

1	2	3	4	1	2	3	4
C	C		C	C	C		C
⊓	⊓ V		⊓	⊓	⊓ V		⊓
Boys	are	back	in	town,	the	boys	are	back	in	town,	the

1	2	3	4	1	2	3	4
Dm	Dm		Dm	F	F		F
⊓	⊓ V		⊓	⊓	⊓ V		⊓
Boys	are	back	in	town,	the	boys	are	back	in	town.

BRIDGE 1

1	2	3	4	1	2	3	4
C	C		C	F	F		F
⊓	⊓ V		⊓	⊓	⊓ V		⊓

1	2	3	4	1	2	3	4
C	C		C	G	G		G
⊓	⊓ V		⊓	⊓	⊓ V		⊓

SEVENTH CHORDS

THE CHORDS we've covered to date are all known as primary chords.

C major is the primary chord in the key of **C** major. **A** minor is the primary chord in the key of **A** minor.

Each primary chord is made up from the first, third and fifth notes of the scale.

So the chord of **C** major consists of the first, third and fifth notes in the scale of **C** major—**C**, **E** and **G**. And the chord of **A** minor consists of the first, third and fifth notes in the scale of **A** minor—**A**, **C** and **E**.

Primary chords are the most important chords you'll ever learn. But there are vast numbers of other chords waiting to be played—most of them with weird names like augmented, diminished, sevenths, ninths and thirteenths.

You shouldn't feel intimidated by these strange names. Often you find the simplest chord imaginable hiding behind some long name—for instance, **E** minor seventh sounds complex, but it's the easiest chord ever invented.

Anyway, having introduced you to the primary chords, it's time to branch out—and by far the most common chords outside of primary chords are seventh chords.

THERE ARE three main kinds of seventh chord: major sevenths, minor sevenths and dominant sevenths.

Of these, the chord most used by guitarists is the dominant seventh. In fact, when guitar players talk about **A** seventh, or **A7**, they mean **A** dominant seventh.

As the name implies, seventh chords are all wrapped up with the seventh note of the scale. The way they're made up is very simple.

For each key, we start with the triad of notes that make up the primary chord—the first, third and fifth.

If you take a major triad and add the seventh note of the major scale, you have a major seventh chord.

If you take a minor triad and add the seventh note of the minor scale, you have a minor seventh chord.

Here's the tricky bit. If you take a major triad and add the seventh note in the *minor* scale, you have a dominant seventh chord.

And that, in a nutshell, is seventh chords.

THERE IS of course a little more to it than that. For one thing, guitar chords don't always include all the notes that make up a particular chord—take a look at **C7**, opposite. But any seventh chord *will* have the appropriate seventh note.

CHORD OF C SEVENTH

FOR A GUITARIST, the most common variation on the major chord is the dominant seventh chord. Generally known as just the seventh, it's written in musical shorthand with a figure **7**, as in **C7**. Along with minor chords, sevenths serve to break the mood of the straight major chord sequence.

Let's start with our old three-chord trick, **C**, **F** and **G**. **C7** is a tough, bluesy chord, and a favourite of guitar players brought up on a diet of Muddy Waters, Buddy Guy and BB King.

Here's how it's formed:

First finger (1) just behind the first fret on the second (**B**) string.

Second finger (2) just behind the second fret on the fourth (**D**) string.

Third finger (3) just behind the third fret on the fifth (**A**) string.

Little finger (4) pulls back to the third fret on the third (**G**) string.

The bottom **E** string is usually left unplayed, while the top **E** string is played 'open'.

C7 is the dominant seventh chord in the key of **F** major, and sounds good followed by **F**.

CHORD OF C SEVENTH

X Not played

CHORD OF C SEVENTH FRONT VIEW

This **C7** set-up looks more difficult than it is, although the little finger may want to wander the first few times.

CHORD OF C SEVENTH AS YOU SEE IT

The thumb falls between the first and second fingers behind the neck. Try to avoid pressure on the fleshy part of the thumb.

SCALE OF C MAJOR	C	D	E	F	G	A	B

SCALE OF C MINOR	C	D	E♭	F	G	A♭	B♭

G C E G B E — **NOTES IN THE CHORD OF C MAJOR 7**

G C G B♭ E♭ G — **NOTES IN THE CHORD OF C MINOR 7**

C E B♭ C E — **NOTES IN THE CHORD OF C DOMINANT 7**

The chord of **C** major 7 (**Cmaj7**) has the notes **C, E, G, B** (first, third, fifth and seventh notes in the scale of **C** major).

The chord of **C** minor 7 (**Cm7**) has the notes **C, E♭, G, B♭** (first, third, fifth and seventh notes in the scale of **C** minor).

The chord of **C** dominant 7 (**C7**) has the notes **C, E, B♭** (first and third notes in the major scale, plus the seventh note in the minor scale).

G7 IS a full six-note chord, with just three strings held down. Here's how it's formed:

First finger (1) just behind the first fret on the first (top **E**) string.

Second finger (2) just behind the second fret on the fifth (**A**) string.

Third finger (3) just behind the third fret on the sixth (bottom **E**) string.

Your pinkie can wander to its heart's content, but remember to arch your other fingers, or you run the risk of touching adjacent strings and muting the sound of the open notes.

G7 sounds good followed by **C** major, because it's the dominant seventh chord in the key of **C**.

CHORD OF G SEVENTH

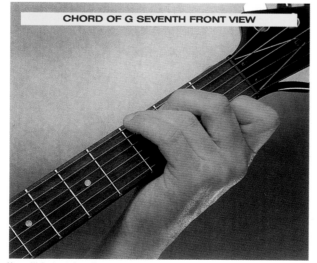

You will feel a twinge in your third finger as you stretch to make this **G7** chord. Pull the little finger back as far as you can.

G7 is one of the most used seventh chords, as it is found in many blues songs in the key of **C**.

DOMINANT SEVENTH CHORDS

THERE IS of course a good reason why we call it the *dominant* seventh.

When you play with other musicians you may hear them refer to 'sub-dominant' and 'dominant'. These are simply musical terms for the fourth and fifth notes of a scale.

So if you're playing in **C** major, the sub-dominant is **F** and the dominant is **G** . . . **CFG**, our first three-chord trick.

As you know, the reason these three chords work in **C** major is because they all consist of notes found in the scale of **C** major. The same goes for their three relative minor chords, **Am**, **Dm** and **Em**.

The same also applies to most of the major seventh and minor seventh chords. The odd one out is **G** major **7**, because it has the notes GBDF#, and F# is not in the scale of **C** major.

This is where the dominant seventh chord comes in. In **G7** the **F#** is replaced by **F**, so that you can use it in the key of **C**.

THE DOMINANT seventh chord is almost always followed by the root chord of the major key it's related to.

Try playing **G7** followed by **C**, or **D7** followed by **G**—you'll soon recognise it as one of the most used and most satisfying chord changes in rock.

STRING NUMBER	6	5	4	3	2	1
NOTES IN THE CHORD OF C MAJOR 7	G	C	E	G	B	E
NOTES IN THE CHORD OF F MAJOR 7		C	F	A	C	E
NOTES IN THE CHORD OF A MINOR 7	E	A	E	G	C	E
NOTES IN THE CHORD OF D MINOR 7		A	D	A	C	F
NOTES IN THE CHORD OF E MINOR 7	E	B	D	G	B	E
NOTES IN THE CHORD OF G MAJOR 7			G	B	D	F#
NOTES IN THE CHORD OF G DOMINANT 7	G	B	D	G	B	F

All these seventh chords work in the key of **C** major, except for **G** major 7. So in the key of **C**, we use **G** dominant 7 (**G7**) instead.

MAJOR KEY	C	Db	D	Eb	E	F	F#	G	Ab	A	Bb	B
DOMINANT SEVENTH CHORD	G7	Ab7	A7	Bb7	B	C7	C#7	D7	Eb7	E7	F7	F#7

CHORD OF F SEVENTH

A FOUR-STRING chord, **F7** uses a half-barre with the first finger (1) placed across the first four strings just behind the first fret. The second finger (2) then holds down the third (**G**) string just behind the second fret.

If you are still practising our barre chord exercise, you may find it more comfortable to use both your first and second fingers to barre the four strings, whilst using the third finger (3) to hold down the **G** string.

You may not use **F7** very often—it's the dominant seventh chord in the key of **B** major—but this is a useful chord, because you can slide it up and down the fretboard.

If you move two frets along, to the third fret, you've got **G7**. Take it to the fifth fret, and you've got **A7**. These are alternatives to the versions of **G7** and **A7** shown here in their own right.

CHORD OF F SEVENTH

X Not played

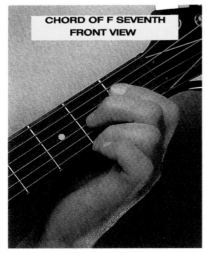

F7 looks simple, but you don't have the support of the second finger in this semi-barre position. It's got its own job to do.

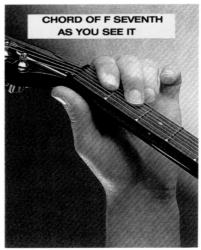

Try holding down the first four strings with the first finger a few times before adding the second finger to this **F7** chord shape.

CHORD OF A SEVENTH

Like F7, A7 involves a half-barre. The first finger (1) barres the first four strings just behind the second fret. The second finger (2) holds down the first (top E) string on the third fret.

THE THREE DIFFERENT types of seventh chord—major sevenths, minor sevenths and dominant sevenths—all have very different qualities.

We'll talk about how to use minor seventh chords and major seventh chords in a few pages time.

The one thing they share with their dominant seventh counterparts is an air of being 'unfinished', as if they need to be followed by another chord.

This is particularly true of dominant seventh chords, where the chord that follows is almost always the root chord of the key.

Dominant sevenths are especially popular in blues and rhythm 'n' blues. They have a tough, hardhitting sound, with the 'unfinished' quality giving either an urgent edge (when a seventh chord is used as the leading chord in a song or part of a song), or a pleasing inevitability when used before the root chord.

THE MOST common use of dominant seventh chords is in a 12-bar blues. Almost every old blues song by Muddy Waters, BB King or Howlin' Wolf, and most '50s rock and roll songs by the likes of Buddy Holly and Chuck Berry used the 12-bar blues form. Many modern rock songs such as ZZ Top's 'Legs' fit the 12-bar format.

A 12-bar blues consists of three lines of four bars each. A typical 12-bar will go:

C F C C/
F F C C/
G F C G7.

Count four beats for each chord. You can use **G** instead of **G7**, but you'll notice at once that it doesn't have the same effect.

E7 IS a simple two-fingered chord. The first finger (1) is placed just behind the first fret on the third (**G**) string, and the second finger (2) goes just behind the second fret on the fifth (**A**) string.

You'll notice the obvious similarity to the **E** major chord—we've simply removed the third finger from the fretboard.

E7 sounds good followed by **A** major, because it's the dominant seventh chord in the key of **A** major.

CHORD OF E SEVENTH

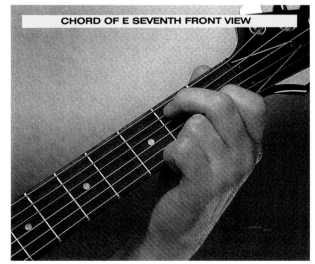

Do they come any simpler? The point here is to get a clear sound from the open strings, so maintain good position with the first and second fingers.

A real blues chord, which will only work if the open strings are kept clear. Keep that third finger tucked away from the top **E** string.

TREMOLO ARM

IT DON'T mean a thang if it ain't got that twang – or to put it another way, welcome to our brief rundown on tremolo.

The tremolo arm was probably most used in the early '60s, by twang merchants such as Duane Eddy and Hank Marvin of The Shadows.

With the notable exceptions of Jimi Hendrix and Jeff Beck, later guitarists tended to ignore it, but it has enjoyed a renaissance in the '80s, particularly among heavy rock players. Current exponents include Gary Moore, Steve Vai and Stevie Ray Vaughan.

Right: two members of the tremolo club, at opposite ends of the musical spectrum – Hank of the Shads and Richie Sambora of Bon Jovi

CHORD OF D SEVENTH

D7 IS relatively simple, and has a nice earthy sound. Here's how it goes:

First finger (1) just behind the first fret on the second (**B**) string.

Second finger (2) just behind the second fret on the third (**G**) string.

Third finger (3) just behind the second fret on the first (top **E**) string.

The fourth (**D**) string is played open.

The fifth (**A**) and sixth (bottom **E**) strings are not played.

D7 is the dominant seventh chord in the key of **G** major, and sounds most natural when followed by a chord of **G** major.

B7 IS probably the most awkward chord to date: it's shown in the diagram on the right (below).

If you feel that your fingers are leaving your hand in protest, don't panic. This is a difficult chord shape even for an experienced player, but it will come with practice.

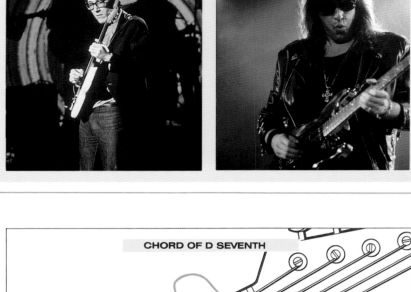

CHORD OF D SEVENTH

X Not played

CHORD OF D SEVENTH FRONT VIEW

A four-string chord, where the third finger is 'pulled back' to the top E string. Keep the second finger nice and arched.

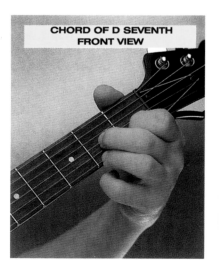

CHORD OF D SEVENTH AS YOU SEE IT

A common set-up, which is used for a variety of chords. Keep the hand looking like a werewolf's claw, and you're in business.

CHORD OF B SEVENTH

B7 is an awkward you-know-what because once learnt, it is not a position that is repeated anywhere else on the fretboard. But it is good discipline, so press on.

THE TREMOLO arm is a device for raising or lowering the pitch of a note, giving a slurring sound. Combined with different pedals and tone controls, it can produce a range of effects from screeching feedback to a sleepy twang.

Sometimes known as a vibrato system or 'magic wand', the tremolo arm is linked to the bridge of the electric guitar.

As you push or pull the tremolo arm, the bridge pivots, causing the strings to go slack or taut.

With old tremolo systems, this often put your guitar out of tune, but that no longer happens with modern tremolos such as the one on the Yamaha RGX 211 featured in this book.

While playing, you can either bounce the whole hand against the tremolo arm to give a quick, not too tremulous effect, or you can link your little finger round the arm in order to depress it when the time is right. But be warned: over-use will probably depress the audience.

Pulling a tremolo arm can help you get feedback. Used with an overdriven amplifier, it can give you extra noise, distortion, whirring sounds and other interesting things.

BY NOW, your fingers should be almost 'thinking' for themselves in constructing chords, particularly those using a barre.

There are two main seventh chord shapes which can be turned into barre chords: the **E7** and **A7** shapes.

The barred **F7** shown here is a derivation of the open **E7** shape, raised one note.

Place your first finger across all six strings on the first fret, with the second finger just behind the second fret on the third (**G**) string, and the third finger just behind the third fret on the fifth (**A**) string.

As we've explained previously, by raising or lowering a barre position, you can go through the entire scale with one chord shape.

In the case of **F7**, by raising the position two frets we form **G7**, two more is **A7**, and so on.

Don't be confused by variations in chord shapes. On page 44, we showed you a half-barre **F7** – a four-string chord. Using the full barre gives you a six-string chord. Neither is necessarily better: they are just different options. The barre chord gives a fuller sound.

BARRE CHORD OF F DOMINANT SEVENTH

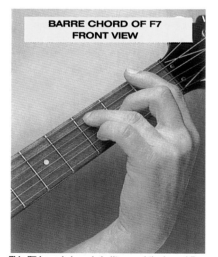

BARRE CHORD OF F7
FRONT VIEW

This **F7** barred shape is built around the barred **F** major. You just take your little finger off the **D** string.

BARRE CHORD OF F7
AS YOU SEE IT

One advantage of barre chords is extra control. Unlike open chords you can stop the sound instantly just by raising your hand.

BARRE CHORD OF B7

Perhaps the most popular of all barred seventh shapes is this **A7** derivative. You may find it more comfortable to support the first finger with the second.

447

MINOR SEVENTH CHORDS

MINOR SEVENTH chords are interesting, because they emphasize the relationship between relative major chords and minor chords.

Take a look at **E** minor 7 and its relative major, **G**:

Starting from the bottom E string, open **G** has the notes G B D G B G.

Em has the notes E B E G B E
Em7 has the notes E B D G B E.

As you can see, **Em7** is almost an exact cross between **G** and **Em**.

The same is true for other minor sevenths—in fact, by a strange coincidence, you can go from each of the three major chords in our **CFG** three-chord trick to its relative minor seventh simply by lifting two fingers off the fretboard (that is, from **C** to **Am7**, from **F** to **Dm7**, and from **G** to **Em7**).

Because of this close relationship, a minor seventh chord has many subtle uses, as it gives strong overtones of both the minor chord and its relative major.

| G | B | D | G | B | G |

NOTES IN THE CHORD OF G MAJOR

| E | B | E | G | B | E |

NOTES IN THE CHORD OF E MINOR

| E | B | D | G | B | E |

NOTES IN THE CHORD OF E MINOR SEVENTH

MINOR SEVENTH CHORDS

MINOR SEVENTH chords can be used in a variety of situations. If a major or minor primary chord sounds too definite or forceful, try slipping in a minor seventh.

You can use a minor seventh instead of the minor chord it's formed from, or instead of its relative major. So if you're looking for a substitute for **F** minor, try **Fm7**. But if you want a substitute for **F** major, try **Dm7**. It may not turn out to be what you want, but it's worth a try.

PROBABLY THE most used minor seventh chord is **Am7**, which sounds great either as a barre chord (see above), or as the open chord shown here. It is mostly used in conjunction with its relative major, **C**.

Am7 is formed with just two fingers: the first just behind the first fret on the second (**B**) string, and the second just behind the second fret on the fourth (**D**) string. In other words, it's **Am** with one finger removed.

CHORD OF A MINOR SEVENTH

CHORD OF A MINOR SEVENTH AS YOU SEE IT

Like many minor seventh chords, **Am7** has a nice, spacious sound and feel.

CHORD OF F MINOR SEVENTH

What could be simpler? A half-barre position, with the first finger doing all the work. This **Fm7** shape can be moved along to form any minor seventh chord—four strings only.

CHORD OF G MINOR SEVENTH

In both the **Fm7** and **Gm7** positions, remember to use the second finger to support the first if it feels more comfortable. Here's where our barre exercise comes into its own.

IT IS of course possible to barre a minor seventh chord – and it's often preferable, too, because the barre brings in the bass notes which give these chords their rich sound.

As you can see below, many of the 'open' minor seventh chords have bass strings which are not played.

There are two minor seventh shapes which readily lend themselves to being barred – the **Fm7** and **Bm7** shapes. The **Fm7** shape in particular is much improved when barred. Ironically, it's the easiest barre chord in the book.

As with many of the other barre chord shapes we've encountered, the fifth fret is where much of the action goes on, because you can form a closed **Am7** on the fifth fret using the **Fm7** shape, and a closed **Dm7** using the **Bm7** shape.

BARRED MINOR 7 CHORDS

BARRED F MINOR 7

BARRED A MINOR 7

BARRED B MINOR 7

BARRED D MINOR 7

MINOR SEVENTH CHORDS

CHORD OF E MINOR SEVENTH

Em7 is a simple chord, with the second finger placed just behind the second fret on your fifth (A) string and the remaining strings played open.

CHORD OF E MINOR SEVENTH AS YOU SEE IT

Probably the easiest chord in the book, Em7 is more like a tuning exercise than a chord shape!

CHORD OF B MINOR SEVENTH

Note the relationship between Bm7 and its relative major chord, D. The difference is just one extra finger. The bottom two strings are not played.

CHORD OF D MINOR SEVENTH

Dm7 is a four-note chord with the bottom two strings left unplayed. The first finger holds down the B and top E strings on the first fret, with second finger on second fret, G string.

CHORD OF D MINOR SEVENTH AS YOU SEE IT

Note the relationship between this Dm7 chord and its relative major, F – they're very similar.

CHORD OF C MINOR SEVENTH

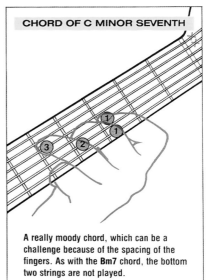

A really moody chord, which can be a challenge because of the spacing of the fingers. As with the Bm7 chord, the bottom two strings are not played.

INSTRUCTION MANUAL

MAJOR SEVENTH CHORDS

MAJOR SEVENTH chords are easy to define: you simply take the major triad (root/third/fifth) and add the seventh note in the major scale.

So C major 7 will have the notes CEGB, and G major 7 will have the notes GBDF#.

What is less easy to define is their sound, their appeal and their uses. This is because they vary so. They also employ some very flexible chord shapes: move them along the neck, and you find you've got something completely different.

Take our three-fingered version of A major 7 – the one with the top E string left open. Try playing that chord, then moving your hand shape up one fret – but leaving the E and A strings open. You are now playing a chord of D minor ninth.

Move the chord shape up again, five frets from its original position – keeping those E and A strings open – and you've got what sounds like an alternative version of A major 7. In fact it's an A major sixth chord. (We explain sixths and ninths on page 66.)

There is, however, a genuine alternative A major 7 in close proximity.

Form an open A minor shape (as shown on page 31), and move it five frets along the neck – and hey presto, another A major 7, with those E and A strings ringing out the same as before.

NOW TAKE a look at F major 7. You can play it as a straightforward four-string chord, or you can try a nifty alternative by adding the fifth string, third fret as in a conventional F major – and then hooking your thumb round the neck to fret the bottom E string on the first fret.

That way you get the best of both worlds:

a solid root note F on the bottom string, with a nice twangy seventh note (E) on the top string.

Now move this chord two frets up the neck, to the G position – still leaving that top E open. You are now playing a G sixth chord.

Now move the chord on again, up to the fifth fret – still with the top E string open. There's another fine chord: A major with an extra E note.

THESE ARE just a few ideas for ways you can play around with chords – major sevenths are particularly adaptable. Make the most of them, because they're the last new chords you'll meet before the Chord Directory (pages 67–80), where you can investigate sixth, ninth, thirteenth, augmented and diminished chords. You'll

MAJOR SEVENTH CHORDS

CHORD OF A MAJOR 7

A major 7 is formed from A major – the first finger holding down the D, G and B strings on the second fret, with the little finger or third finger stretched to the fourth fret, top E string. The A string is played open. The bottom E string is optional.

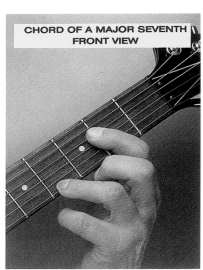

CHORD OF A MAJOR SEVENTH FRONT VIEW

A short stretch for the third finger here – note the slight change from A7 to A major 7.

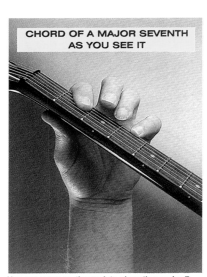

CHORD OF A MAJOR SEVENTH AS YOU SEE IT

You can move up the neck to play other major 7 chords, but it then becomes a four-string chord.

CHORD OF D MAJOR 7

D major 7 requires just the first finger, which holds down the G, B and top E strings on the second fret. The D string is played open. The bottom two strings should not be played, but it won't hurt if the open A string creeps in accidentally.

CHORD OF D MAJOR SEVENTH AS YOU SEE IT

A simple chord, halfway between D major and D7 – and an interesting sound too.

CHORD OF F MAJOR 7

F major 7 is a nice natural hand spread, with the first finger placed on the first fret, B string, the second finger on the second fret, G string and the third finger on the third fret, D string. The top E string is left open. The bottom two strings are not played.

also find lots of different ways of playing the chords you've already learnt.

If you can't wait till page 67, by all means jump ahead and try out some of the chords on display. Your fretboard is waiting to be explored – and the Chord Directory is your map.

Get as much out of it as you can. Don't just use the Chord Directory as a reference; use it for inspiration as well as information.

And keep trying new tricks. Now that we've shown you the basic chords, don't just fall back on them time after time. Forge ahead, and forge your own style.

Meanwhile, if you've taken in the majors, minors, sevenths and so on – the essentials of rhythm guitar – then you should be ready for the next step . . . how to play rock lead guitar.

MAJOR SEVENTH CHORDS

CHORD OF A MAJOR 7

CHORDS OF D MINOR 9 AND A MAJOR 6

CHORD OF F MAJOR 7

CHORDS OF G MAJOR 6 AND A MAJOR

MAJOR SEVENTH CHORDS

CHORD OF B MAJOR 7

B major 7 requires a barre across the second fret, with the second finger placed on the third fret, G string, the third finger holding down the fourth fret, D string and the fourth finger on the fourth fret, B string. The bottom E string is not played.

CHORD OF B MAJOR SEVENTH AS YOU SEE IT

B major 7 is nearly a full barre chord, and so can be used to form different major seventh chords.

CHORD OF E MAJOR 7

E major 7 has a tricky little set-up on the first fret, where the first finger is placed on the **D** string, and the second finger holds down the **G** string. The third finger is pushed across to the second fret, **A** string. The bottom and top **E** strings and **B** string are played open.

CHORD OF G MAJOR 7

G major 7 is the same chord as F major 7, but 'up' the fretboard two notes. The first finger holds down the second fret, top E string, second finger on the third fret, B string, third finger fourth fret, G string, whilst the little finger holds down the fifth fret, D string.

CHORD OF G MAJOR SEVENTH AS YOU SEE IT

You can slide this chord up the neck to form other major 7 chords.

CHORD OF C MAJOR 7

C major 7 is a five-note chord, with the second finger holding down the second fret, **D** string and the third finger on the third fret, **A** string. The G, B and top E strings are played open. You can, for a variation, play the bottom **E** string open, or fretted at the third fret.

451

TRANSPOSING KEYS

TO 'TRANSPOSE' is the technical term for moving a piece of music from one key into another.

A song doesn't have to be played in the key it was written in. You can take a song in

the key of **G** major, for instance, and change the chords so that it can be played in **C**. This is called transposing the key.

But why should you want to do this?

When the song was originally written or

recorded, it was set in a key that suited that particular band or singer's style. If you are straining to sing the chorus, or find it difficult to finger a certain chord, you can transpose the key to suit yourself.

CAPO

THIS WEIRD looking device is called a capo, and it makes transposing keys easy. For example, if the capo is clamped on the first fret, all your standard chords such as **E, C** and **Am** are raised one note. So in the picture we have a chord of **B♭** minor, played like **Am**.

Suppose you need to play a song in **E♭** – three semitones up from **C**. By clamping the capo on the third fret, you can play it as if the song was in **C**.

THERE ARE two methods of transposing. Both of them are quite easy.

Let's say you want to transpose to a key fairly close to your original key – for instance from **C** to **D**. You simply check how far apart the root notes are (from **C** to **D** is two semitones), and then move all the chords in the song the same distance. So if your original chords were **C, Am, F** and **G**, you add two semitones to each, giving **D, Bm, G, A**.

THAT METHOD is fine if the two keys are close together. But if you want to transpose

'THE BOYS ARE BACK IN TOWN'

TRANSPOSING THE SONG

AS PROMISED, here is our new, improved version of 'The Boys Are Back In Town', incorporating some of the seventh chords we've been looking at.

What's more, in the light of the information above about transposing keys, we've decided to transpose it. On page 40 we learned how to play it in **C** major. Now we're going to play it in the key of **G** major.

So let's just take a look back at the grid on page 40. The chords used were **C, Dm, Em, F, G, Am** and **A♭**. Of these, the only chord which doesn't fit naturally into the key of **C** is **A♭**. All the others can be tranposed easily using the table on page 35.

We've reproduced the relevant section of that table at the top of the page opposite, and we've marked the original key, **C** major, and the new key of **G** major. Just check across the columns:

C is replaced by **G**;
Dm is replaced by **Am**;
Em is replaced by **Bm**;
F is replaced by **C**;
G is replaced by **D**;
Am is replaced by **Em**.

As for our **A♭**, if **A** is replaced by **E** then it should be obvious that we replace **A♭** with **E♭**.

SEVENTH CHORDS

IF YOU compare this grid with the one on page 40/41, you'll see that those transpositions have been made. But you'll also see that we've replaced some straightforward major and minor chords with the sevenths and minor sevenths which Thin Lizzy used in the original.

In the fourth line of the verse, in the key of **C** we had **F** and **G**. If we transpose those chords, it should give us the chords of **C** and **D**. Instead, we'll be using **Am7** and **D7**.

That **D7** is repeated in the last bar of the verse, and the last bar of Bridge 1. Note that each time it's used, it leads to the root chord, **G**.

Notice also the second bar in Bridge 1. In the key of **C**, that was an **Am** chord. Directly transposed it would give **Em**. Instead, there's that simplest of chords, **Em7**.

TITLE	KEY	TEMPO
'THE BOYS ARE BACK IN TOWN'	G MAJOR	QUITE FAST

VERSE

G	G	G	G	Bm	Bm	Bm	Bm
C	C	C	C	Em	Em	Em	Em
Bm	Bm	Bm	Bm	Em	Em	Em	Em
Am7	Am7	Am7	Am7	D7	D7	D7	D7
G	G	G	G	Bm	Bm	Bm	Bm
C	C	C	C	E♭	E♭	E♭	E♭
D	D	D	D	Em	Em	Em	Em
Am	Am	Am	Am	D7	D7	D7	D7

CHORUS

G	G	G	G	G	G	G	G
Am	Am	Am	Am	C	C	C	C
G	G	G	G	G	G	G	G
Am	Am	Am	Am	C	C	C	C

LYRICS

The words fall in the same place as on page 40/41. We haven't included the intro as it's just the chorus without words.

CHORD OF G/B

In Bridge 1 there's a chord marked **G/B**. It means **G** major with a **B** bass note. Play an open **G** but miss the bottom **E** string.

from, say, **C** to **G**, it's not that easy. So here's another method.

As you know, the notes in a scale can be numbered from root note to seventh note (or, in Roman numerals, from **I** to **VII**).

All you have to do is number the chords of the song in its original key, then put in the appropriately numbered chords from the new key.

The easiest way to do this is by using our indispensable scales and chords table from page 35.

You can just read straight across from one key to another.

ANY SONG can be transposed. Obviously, if a song is in a major key it can only be transposed *to* a major key. A minor key song can only be transposed to another minor key.

The table below highlights how to transpose from **C** major to **G** major.

	NOTE IN SCALE		PRIMARY TRIAD CHORD	SCALE (READ DOWN FROM ROOT NOTE)											
MAJOR KEY	Root	(I)	Root major chord	C	D♭	D	E♭	E	F	F#	G	A♭	A	B♭	B
	Second	(II)	Minor chord	D	E♭	E	F	F#	G	G#	A	B♭	B	C	C#
	Third	(III)	Minor chord	E	F	F#	G	G#	A	A#	B	C	C#	D	D#
	Fourth	(IV)	Major chord	F	G♭	G	A♭	A	B♭	B	C	D♭	D	E♭	E
	Fifth	(V)	Major chord	G	A♭	A	B♭	B	C	C#	D	E♭	E	F	F#
	Sixth	(VI)	Relative minor chord	A	B♭	B	C	C#	D	D#	E	F	F#	G	G#
	Seventh	(VII)	– – – –	B	C	C#	D	D#	E	E#	F#	G	G#	A	A#

It's easy to transpose keys using this table – you just read across from one scale to another. You can transpose minor keys too, by checking the table on page 35.

RHYTHM

YOU'LL SEE that we've left out the DOWN, down-UP. . . down rhythm we used on pages 40/41. As we said then, it was a simplified rhythm to help you through the song.

The fact is, there isn't a consistent rhythm guitar part on the record. Instead, guitarists Scott Gorham and Brian Robertson sketch in the bare bones, leaving plenty of holes for vocals, bass and lead guitars.

The one consistent rhythmic pattern they use is to hit the first beat of each bar with a resounding chord, and if you were playing this with a band that would be the essential element of the rhythm guitar part.

The other important facet of Thin Lizzy's rhythmic approach to this song is the way the guitarists hit a lot of their chords slightly 'early' – half a beat before the start of the bar.

This is generally known as 'pushing' the beat. It's very tricky to get right, and we're not expecting you to manage it just yet. If you want to try it out, you can. But if you want to stick to a regular rhythm pattern, you can do that too.

BRIDGE 2

YOU'LL NOTICE that we've added the final part of the grid: Bridge 2. Refer to page 41 to see where it occurs in the running order.

Perhaps now you can see why we've held it back – the section is full of triplets.

If you cast your mind back to 'That'll Be The Day', you may remember that a triplet is where three notes are played in the space of one beat: da-da-da, da-da-da, da-da-da, da-da-da. On record, these triplets are played as single notes hammered out by the lead guitarist, but if you want to try it with the chords, be our guest. Otherwise, stick to your regular rhythm.

CHORD OF E♭ MAJOR

You'll need this chord – it takes the place of the A♭ we used when we played this song in **C**.

KEY TO SYMBOLS AND COLOURS

⊓ Downward stroke   ∨ Upward stroke

☐ G major   ☐ A minor
☐ B minor   ▣ D major/D7
☐ C major/A minor 7   ☐ F major
☐ E minor/E minor 7   ☐ E♭ major

LEAD GUITAR

WE HAVE now explored the world of basic guitar chords pretty thoroughly. We've looked at major chords, minor chords and three different types of seventh chord – how they are constructed, how to play them, and how they work together.

In other words, you have the essential ingredients of rhythm guitar. Later, we'll return to the subject, with more unusual chords such as sixths, ninths and thirteenths. But right now it's time for something completely different: lead guitar.

THE TWO terms, lead guitar and rhythm guitar, tend to conjure up very different images. Lead guitar equals glamour; rhythm guitar means drudgery.

As with all stereotyped images, this isn't strictly true. Some of the world's greatest guitarists are rhythm specialists – for in-stance Nile Rodgers, whose rhythm guitar was the force behind a whole musical movement. His work with Chic had far-reaching effects, and some would claim that he was the most influential guitarist of the '80s.

More to the point, few major guitarists play only lead or only rhythm. The two go hand in hand, and ideally you should have a good grasp of both.

THERE ARE, of course, almost as many definitions of lead guitar as there are lead guitarists. If we say that lead guitar entails playing single notes, then there are numerous different ways in which single notes can be used within a song.

Most common is the guitar riff – the repeated pattern of notes which holds a song together. Riffs are most used in heavy metal: two of the more famous examples would be Led Zeppelin's 'Whole Lotta Love' and Deep Purple's 'Smoke On The Water'.

Other uses for single note playing include 'fills' and embellishments – either planned or spontaneous little additions which enhance the song rather than being central to it in the way a riff usually is.

'The Boys Are Back In Town' provides good examples of this. Having two guitars gives one of them the luxury to 'sit back' and choose his moments while the other provides the central backbone (the same can equally be true if you have a keyboard player).

If, on the other hand you haven't got another guitarist or keyboard player to share the role of giving melodic meat to a song, you may want to develop a style that

BLUES RHYTHM GUITAR

THE BLUES is the main foundation of rock music today. Rock developed directly out of the blues, and there has probably never been a major rock guitarist who was not influenced to some extent by blues players or blues music.

So let's look first at blues rhythm guitar.

In our section on sevenths, we briefly mentioned 12-bar blues. No doubt it's a term you already know. What you may not realise is that, with what you've learnt to date, you can now play a 12-bar blues in just about any key.

All '12-bars' are based on our original three-chord trick – which in the key of **C** would be **C, F, G.**

If you check the chart on page 35, you'll see that they are the chords formed from the first, fourth and fifth notes of the scale – which we can refer to in Roman numerals as **I, IV** and **V.**

These are the three chords used in a basic 12-bar blues. The song grid shows how it goes.

Here are the chords **I, IV** and **V** in some popular keys for blues. You can use any of these three-chord tricks with our 12-bar grid:

CHORD I	C	D	E	G	A
CHORD IV	F	G	A	C	D
CHORD V	G	A	B	D	E

TWELVE BAR BLUES

BAR 1	BAR 2	BAR 3	BAR 4
I	I	I	I

BAR 5	BAR 6	BAR 7	BAR 8
IV	IV	I	I

BAR 9	BAR 10	BAR 11	BAR 12
V	IV	I	I

KEY TO COLOURS □ CHORD I   □ CHORD IV   □ CHORD V

Most 12-bar blues are in 4/4 time (four beats to the bar), and this one is no exception. Try it out in different keys – you'll soon realise that it's just about the most natural 'rock' chord progression there is. You can make a number of variations to this basic 12-bar. Here are some you may care to try:
Bar 2 Chord IV. Bar 4 Chord I7 (in C, this would be C7). Bar 6 Chord IV7. Bar 8 Chord I7. Bar 9 Chord V7. Bar 12 Chord V or V7.

Muddy Waters' best-known 12-bar was 'I Got My Mojo Workin''.

Status Quo paid tribute to the 12-bar with their 'Twelve Gold Bars' album.

mixes straight rhythm with riffs and 'fills'.

Perhaps the purest form of single note playing is the solo – the guitar break, usually in the middle of a song, where the spotlight shifts from the singer to the guitarist, and you get a chance to express yourself for the duration.

For our purposes, we'll assume that this is your goal as a lead guitarist. If it's not, and you just want sufficient skill and technique to play riffs and embellishments, you'll be able to get what you need from this section anyway. So let's look at soloing.

TO MOST beginners, and indeed to many people who've played guitar for years, guitar solos are one of the mysteries of life. Hopefully, this section can dissolve some of that mystery for you.

The content of a solo is, by definition, in the hands of the player. Some solos are improvised; some follow a set pattern; but all solos work within the context of the player's own style and skill – and that comes from a combination of experience, practice, instinct and knowledge. We can supply the last bit; the rest you'll have to develop for yourself.

You may not realise it, but if you've been practising the scales we showed you earlier – for **G** major and **C** minor – then you've already started that process.

Nearly all lead guitar styles are based on scales and a knowledge of chord structure, so you've already got a lot of the basics. This section aims to give you a context for them – plus, inevitably, a lot more hard work for you to do.

Our starting point, perhaps surprisingly, will be blues rhythm guitar.

LEAD GUITAR

Foreigner lead guitarist Mick Jones has a distinctive and influential hard rock style.

BLUES RHYTHM GUITAR

THE 12-BAR blues is where barre chords really come into their own. Try playing a 12-bar in the key of **A**, using all barre chords.
Chord **I**: **A**. An **F**-shape barre chord, fifth fret.
Chord **IV**: **D**. An **F**-shape barre chord, 10th fret.
Chord **V**: **E**. An **F**-shape barre chord, 12th fret.

AN AMAZING number of rock songs are played like this, from early Beatles to ZZ Top. And many of them employ the following variation, shown below as Riff 1:

Instead of **A** major, form a barred **A7** at the fifth fret. On each alternate beat, bring your little finger down on the ninth fret, fifth (**A**) string – in other words, two frets beyond your third finger. Keep your other fingers where they are.

Repeat the process at the 10th and 12th frets with **D7** and **E7**.

THERE ARE other variations on this theme which you can use when laying down a basic blues rhythm. Try Riff 2, below, again keeping your hand in the barred **A7** position, and concentrating on your bottom three strings:

Beat **1**: Barred **A7** (emphasize bottom **E** string).
Beat **2**: Little finger ninth fret, bottom **E** string.
Beat **3**: Barred **A7** (emphasizing **A** string).
Beat **4**: Little finger ninth fret, **A** string.
Beat **1**: Barred **A** major (emphasizing **D** string: flatten your third finger to get this effect).
Beat **2**: Little finger ninth fret, **A** string.
Beat **3**: Barred **A7** (emphasizing **A** string).
Beat **4**: Little finger ninth fret, **E** string.

THESE BLUES rhythm parts can be played fast or slow. Try not to speed up or slow down.

BARRE CHORD OF A MAJOR

BARRE CHORD OF A7 (RIFF 1)
* POSITION FOR LITTLE FINGER (ALTERNATE BEATS)

BARRE CHORD OF A7 (RIFF 2)
* POSITIONS FOR LITTLE FINGER

Eric Clapton was raised on 12-bar blues such as 'Crossroads'.

Dave Edmunds' biggest hit 'I Hear You Knocking' was a 12-bar blues.

Many ZZ Top hits such as 'Rough Boy' stick close to the 12-bar format.

INSTRUCTION MANUAL

LEAD BLUES SCALES

THE BEST way to begin playing lead guitar, and then to improve your lead playing, is to practise scales.

There are numerous different kinds of musical scales, and each offers some unique run or combination of notes which can contribute in some way to your repertoire.

You already know two basic scales – one for a major key, which appeared on page 25, and one for a minor key (page 41). We happened to show the scales of G major and C minor, but in fact they can be used in any major or minor key simply by moving them up or down the fretboard.

What makes those two scales so useful is the fact that they include all the notes pertaining to their particular keys, and no notes from outside the key. So if you are playing a song in the key of G, the scale of

G major gives you a fingertip map of the notes which will work in that song.

Other scales have different qualities. Some include notes from outside the key. Some leave notes out. The more scales you know, and the more contexts you try them out in, the greater your lead guitar armoury.

AMONG THE most useful are the three 'blues scales' shown on this page. These scales happen to be in A, but you can of course move them up or down the fretboard for use in any key.

Technically speaking, the blues scale is a kind of minor scale, but it is mainly used in its major key. If you look at the table here you'll see the relationship between our blues scales in A, and the normal scale of A major.

Our blues scales contain three additional notes – C, D# and G. These are in fact the flattened third, flattened fifth and flattened seventh notes in the A major scale.

SCALE OF A MAJOR AND BLUES SCALES IN A												
SCALE OF A MAJOR	A B	C#D	E F#	G#A B	C#D	E F#	G#A					
BLUES SCALE IN A (1)	G A	C	D	E	G	A	C	D	E	G	A	
BLUES SCALE IN A (2)	A	C	DD#E	G	A	C	D	E F#G	A B C			
BLUES SCALE IN A (3)		C	D	E	G	A	C	DD#E	G	A	C D	

BLUES SCALES IN A

HERE ARE three blues scales to practise. They're all in the key of **A** and they are designed for use with a 12-bar blues sequence.

The best way to practise them is by playing them over a blues rhythm track supplied either by a friend or by recording yourself. But whether you practise your blues scales over a 12-bar or on their own, the same basic rules apply as for the other scales you've learnt.

Take them slowly at first, using all downward strokes. Then play alternate down and up strokes. Keep the left hand close to the fretboard, and aim for a crisp, clean, regular run through the scale, from bottom to top and back down again.

Once you're on top of them, try to play them less regularly, putting a firmer emphasis on certain notes, missing notes out, playing faster here, slower there, and so on.

In short, give them expression. This is the essence of successful lead playing, and as you practise you will gradually formulate your own approach and your own style.

LINK RUNS

YOU'LL NOTICE that each of our three scales is based around a couple of frets, in a particular part of the fretboard.

Scale 1 is the lowest, based around the second, third and fifth frets. Scale 2 centres on the fifth, seventh and eighth frets. And Scale 3 takes in the seventh, eighth and tenth frets.

You'll notice also that some notes appear in both Scale 1 and Scale 2, while others appear in both Scale 2 and Scale 3. It therefore stands to reason that the three scales can be linked together.

Our two link runs show you how to do this, but these are only our suggestions. Obviously, you can go from one scale into another at any point where they overlap – and as they're all blues scales in **A**, they fit together naturally.

In fact, as you'll soon realise, they are basically the same scale played in different parts of the fretboard.

Practise linking scales together, and before you know it you'll have the freedom of the fretboard.

BLUES SCALE IN A (1)

BLUES SCALE IN A (2)

BLUES SCALE IN A (3)

LINK RUN BETWEEN SCALES 1 AND 2

Slide between the second and fifth frets, D string

LINK RUN BETWEEN SCALES 2 AND 3

Slide between the fifth and seventh frets, G string

You'll also notice that the blues scales miss out one note from the major scale – G#, the seventh note.

The overall effect is to create a less rounded, more 'bluesy' selection of notes which sound good in a guitar solo.

INCIDENTALLY, ALTHOUGH we haven't included them, the open E, G, D and A strings can also be incorporated into a solo based on the blues scale of A.

This won't necessarily be the case if you transpose these scales to another key – which, as we said before, can be done simply by moving the whole thing up or down the fretboard.

The most popular keys for blues are A major, E major, C major and G major. The blues scale of A is shown here – we'll leave you to work out E, C and G.

ONE FINAL point. We said that this blues scale is a kind of minor scale. Used in a bluesy context such as heavy metal, R&B, soul or blues, it works in its major *or* minor key. So the blues scale of A works in both A major and A minor.

But it does have other uses, of a less bluesy nature, and on occasion it can be used in its relative major key, C.

Bear in mind, though, that it contains notes that are not related to that key, and which could sound discordant.

Remember, at the end of the day, scales are only a guide. They should not be taken as a hard and fast rule.

With the knowledge they give you, you can work out your own riffs and runs. Don't be afraid to take risks, cut corners and break the rules—it's essential to create your own style.

HAMMER-ON AND PULL-OFF

AS YOU struggle to pick your way through all these scales, you may be wondering how your favourite guitarists manage to play so fast.

Naturally, the main factor is practice, practice and more practice. However, there are a couple of techniques you can use to increase your speed: hammer-on and pull-off.

Here is a simple hammer-on. Put your first finger on the fifth fret, top E string. Play this note and then hammer-on your third finger onto the seventh fret – but don't play this second note with your right hand.

This technique is always easier with a distortion or sustain pedal, but you should be able to get a good sound from the second note without the help of effects. The secret is in really pressing your third finger down *hard*.

NOW LET'S return to blues scale 2. Try playing it from the bottom E string to the top, but only picking with your plectrum on the red notes. A letter H means hammer-on.

When you do pick, use down strokes to start with. You'll find it harder to hammer-on with your little finger at first, because it's not as strong. After a bit of practice it becomes easier.

Once you can hammer-on with scale 2, try it on the other scales. You'll soon find it enables you to play them a lot faster. It also gives you more scope for phrasing your melody lines.

THE NEXT technique to try is pull-off. Put your third finger on the seventh fret, top E string, and your first finger on the fifth fret at the same time. Pick whilst your third finger is down, but as soon as the note has sounded, pull your third finger away from the fingerboard. Leave your first finger on, but don't play the string again.

You will find that the note at the fifth fret will sound as you lift your third finger.

ONCE AGAIN, let's put this to use on our second blues scale in A. This time, play the scale from the top string to the bottom, and only pick on the red notes. There is a P on the diagram at the points where you should pull-off.

BLUES SCALE IN A (2) WITH HAMMER-ON

BLUES SCALE IN A (2) WITH PULL-OFF

USING PULL-OFF

TRY THIS embellishment which lead guitarists add to their solos using the pull-off technique.

Put your first finger across the top two strings on the fifth fret. Pick only on the red notes, starting at the eighth fret, top E string, then going to the second string.

After playing the second string, go back to the first. Repeat this several times. It will sound very impressive when you can play it fast.

BB King demonstrates pull-off.

OPEN TUNINGS

LIKE SEAN Connery and James Bond, open tunings and bottleneck guitar are synonymous.

The idea of an open tuning is to create a chord without holding any strings down. This is achieved by re-tuning selected strings on the guitar.

The easiest open tuning is **E**. You simply tune your third, fourth and fifth strings up to give the notes **G#**, **E** and **B**. Instead of the usual **EBGDAE**, your open strings now play the notes **EBG#EBE**.

If you play right across the strings with your left hand off the neck, you'll recognise that this is the chord of **E** major.

It follows that if you barre all the strings on any fret, you'll have another major chord—**A** major at the fifth fret, **B** major at the seventh, and so on.

The interesting thing is that you can now barre a chord with anything that comes to hand—and create all kinds of different effects.

THIS IS where the bottleneck comes in. First lay your hands on a small bottle, then barre the strings with the bottle, and strum. You'll hear a whining noise that you should recognise, because you are now playing a rudimentary form of bottleneck or slide guitar—as practised by blues guitarists for over fifty years.

The style was popularised by country blues guitarists such as Robert Johnson and Son House. It was taken into the electric age by the likes of Muddy Waters and Elmore James, and has been refined in a rock context by Ry Cooder, Duane Allman, Johnny Winter and Ron Wood.

It's called bottleneck because one popular way of playing this style was to take the neck off a bottle and thread it over the little finger.

A good alternative is a length of steel or copper pipe—you can make one yourself or buy them in guitar shops. Less regular slide players use all kinds of things from bottles to cigarette lighters held in the left hand.

It's worth pointing out that you don't *have* to re-tune to use a slide—but of course you can't play slide guitar chords without an open tuning.

Whatever style of music you play, it's useful to know about open tunings and bottleneck guitar. Like fingerpicking, it's another string to your bow.

Like many techniques, it was developed by blues guitarists—but any imaginative player should be able to find a use for it.

OPEN TUNINGS

OPEN TUNING TO A CHORD OF E MAJOR

| E |
| B |
| G# |
| E |
| B |
| E |

Notes on the open strings. The third, fourth and fifth strings are tuned higher than normal.

● Check your tuning at these frets. Seventh fret, bottom E string will give you the **B** note you need for your fifth string.

OPEN TUNING TO A CHORD OF G MAJOR

| D |
| B |
| G |
| D |
| G |
| D |

Notes on the open strings. The top, fifth and bottom strings are tuned lower than normal.

● Check your tuning at these frets. Fifth fret, bottom string will give you the **G** note you need for your fifth string.

THE MOST popular open tunings are **D**, **E**, **G** and **A**. Here you can see how to tune your guitar to open **E** and **G**.

To get an open **D** tuning, take the **E** tuning and tune all the strings down two semitones. To get an open **A** tuning, take the **G** tuning and tune all strings *up* two semitones.

The higher tunings in each case (**E** and **A**) are more suited to rock guitarists with light guage strings. Blues players often use heavier strings, and so prefer the **D** and **G** versions.

If you experiment with the two tunings shown here—**E** and **G**—you'll begin to notice that they have different characters.

The **E** tuning gives a harder attack. It was the one used by that fierce Mississippi bluesman Robert Johnson, and for the blues power chords of Elmore James. It's the one favoured by most rock players.

The **G** tuning is more of a country tuning. Used by Son House, Bukka White and Muddy Waters, it gives the mournful sound favoured by Ry Cooder on his film soundtracks.

George Thorogood carries on the Elmore James tradition at Live Aid, Philadelphia, 1985.

BOTTLENECK GUITAR

FOR AN elementary R&B slide lick, tune to open **A** then try this, using whatever you've found for a bottleneck:

Open **E** (one four-beat bar);
Slide to fifth fret (**A**) for one bar;
Slide to seventh fret (**B**) for one bar;
Back to open **A**.

Having done that, you'll probably wonder what all the fuss is about. Well, here's the secret: the key to successful bottleneck guitar lies not in the slide, but in the expression you give it.

If you listen to Muddy Waters playing bottleneck, you can actually hear the bottleneck rattling against the guitar—this is beause he's trembling his hand furiously. That's how the slide guitarist achieves the different nuances in sound—not just by sliding, but by trembling!

ANOTHER CLUE to good bottleneck is where on the neck you play it. Generally, the higher the better. Elmore James, arguably the greatest bottleneck player of all, concentrated nearly all his famous riffs and phrases on the 12th fret.

The triplet riff he used on countless songs such as 'Dust My Broom'—dah-dah-dah, dah-dah-dah, dah-dah-dah, dah-dah-dah, DOW-dum—was achieved by sliding up to the 12th fret at the start of each triplet, playing just the first two strings. The DOW-dum was also played at the 12th fret, on the third and fourth strings respectively.

TABLATURE IS a method of reading music designed specifically for guitar. It's especially useful for showing solos, and there are many books available which feature famous solos transcribed note for note into tablature—it's usually written above the conventional music. These are the basics of tablature:

STAVE: Tablature is written on a 'stave' of six horizontal lines which represent the six guitar strings, from top **E** string (top line) to bottom **E** string (bottom line).

The tablature stave usually has the word **TAB** at the beginning. There are vertical 'bar lines' to indicate the end of each bar.

TIME SIGNATURE: Most rock is in **4/4** time, meaning four beats per bar.

NOTES: On page 56 we showed the blues scale in **A** (1). The first two bars above show the 12 notes of that scale.

Each note is represented by a fret number, written on the string played. So our first note is third fret, bottom **E** string. Fingers to use are numbered below the stave. Down/up symbols are above it.

In the first bar, the notes are played one per beat. The second bar shows the next eight notes played *two* notes per beat.

CHORDS: The same rules apply, except that all the strings played have fret numbers, all stacked above each other.

The third bar of tablature above shows two chords. First comes an open **E** major. The figure **0** indicates an open string.

Next there's a **D** major chord, with only four strings played. No number on the stave line means don't play that string.

LEAD TECHNIQUES

STRING BENDING

BLUES PLAYERS use notes called blue notes. These are created by bending strings so that their pitch is raised slightly. Put three fingers down and push the top **E** string towards the **B** string and back again. Alternatively, play a note on the **G** string and either pull it towards the **B** string or push towards the **D** string.

LEAD CHORDS

WHILE PLAYING a solo or a scale it's sometimes effective to drop in a chord. To save you having to form a full chord, there are some 'half-chords' which work just as well.

The three trebly chords shown here are often used by lead guitar players to break up their solos or to accentuate the rhythm guitarist's chords. We've shown them in **A**, but you can use them in any key by changing frets.

Use in the key of **A** major over Chord **I**

Use in the key of **A** major over Chord **IV**

Use in the key of **A** major over Chord **V**

VIBRATO

VIBRATO IS one of the techniques lead guitarists use to give notes expression—the thing that makes each player unique.

Vibrato was developed by blues players such as BB King, to give certain notes in a solo more depth. It's achieved by the rapid sideways movement of the string—in short, the string vibrates.

Practising vibrato can be a little strange to start with, as the finger tends to slip off the string.

You only need your left hand to try it out. Place your first finger just behind the seventh fret, top **E** string. Move the string ever so slightly towards you, then allow it to return to its starting position. Now pull the string away from you, and ease it back again.

Vibrato is a combination of these two movements, but at quick-fire pace.

The next move is to play a string, then vibrate. Work up speed as you go along, but don't expect miracles overnight. In the course of time, as a lead guitarist, you'll find it takes its place automatically in your box of tricks.

Vibrato and string bending require strong fingers. Angus Young of AC/DC employs both techniques, making up for the lack of a tremolo arm on his Gibson SG by moving the strings physically.

ROBERT CRAY

AS AN example of lead guitar for you to play, we've selected a song by one of the world's most exciting guitarists, Robert Cray. Along with Stevie Ray Vaughan, he has put the blues back on the map and high in the charts.

Cray is a spare, unflashy player. His band has the tautness of Booker T And The MGs, with Cray's guitar as sharp as Steve Cropper on the rhythm, and as attacking as Buddy Guy on the solos.

'Phone Booth' is the best-known track on Cray's 1984 breakthrough album, 'Bad Influence'. Written by Cray with bassist Richard Cousins, sax player Mike Vannice and producer Dennis Walker, it's a 12-bar blues with some unconventional chords.

It gives you a new angle on the 12-bar blues, and a chance to use your blues scale in **A** in a solo.

In the spotlight: Robert Cray turns up the heat on his Stratocaster.

WHEN WE first played 'The Boys Are Back In Town', we used major and minor chords instead of the more complex seventh chords of the original. Robert Cray's 'Phone Booth' fits into the same pattern.

In essence it's a minor key 12-bar blues, with some neat little variations. Our diagrams on the right show the conventional major and seventh chords Cray could have used; instead, he makes it more interesting by introducing minor sixth and augmented seventh chords.

These chords aren't difficult, but if you do find them tricky, you can easily substitute the chords shown. Use **E** or **E7** instead of **E7+** (E augmented seventh). Use **F** or **F7** instead of **Cm6**. Use **G** or **G7** for **Dm6**.

Incidentally, Cray's use of **E7** in the key of **A** minor is an old blues trick—'House Of The Rising Sun' is a classic example.

'PHONE BOOTH' (CHORDS)

BEFORE YOU attempt the solo for 'Phone Booth', here are the chords and words. The chord names may be unfamiliar, but don't let that put you off. They're all fairly simple shapes which can be played near the nut of the guitar.

There are three new chords here: **E7+**, **Cm7** and **Dm7**. If you want, you can substitute more familiar chords—see above page 61.

If you need to remind yourself of the shapes for **Am7** and **Dm7**, see page 48.

RHYTHM

LIKE NEARLY all blues songs, 'Phone Booth' is in **4/4** time—four beats to the bar. The Robert Cray Band play it at quite a lick, with a heavy emphasis on every beat.

Cray uses a tricky 'shuffle' guitar rhythm, but it will sound fine if you just play a firm rhythm right on the beat, using sharp downstrokes.

As ever, take this song slowly at first. Once

you've got it working with open chords, you might find it effective to use the barre chords of **Am**, **Am7** and **Dm7** which you can play at the fifth fret.

If you can, record yourself playing the chord sequence over and over, so that you can practise soloing to your own accompaniment. Don't forget that you may struggle with the solo at first, so don't play too fast on the backing track!

TITLE	KEY	TEMPO
'PHONE BOOTH' (CHORDS)	A MINOR	QUITE FAST

BAR 1 — Am / Am7 | **BAR 2** — E7+ | **BAR 3** — Am / Am7 | **BAR 4**

Phone booth baby,   number's scratched   on the wall.   I'm in a

BAR 5 — Dm7 | **BAR 6** | **BAR 7** — Am / Am7 | **BAR 8**

Phone booth baby,   number's scratched   on the wall.   I'm

BAR 9 — Cm6 | **BAR 10** — Dm6 / E7+ | **BAR 11** — Am / Am7 | **BAR 12**

New in Chicago,   got no one else to call.

KEY TO COLOURS

☐ A minor   ☐ A minor 7   ☐ E7 augmented   ☐ D minor 7   ☐ C minor 6   ☐ D minor 6

LYRICS

I'm in a phone booth baby, number's scratched on the wall.
I'm in a phone booth baby, number's scratched on the wall.
I'm new in Chicago, got no one else to call.

Been walking all day, old friends I can't find.
Heart's so cold, had to buy me some wine.
Calling you baby took my very last dime.

SOLO

I'm in a phone booth baby, number's scratched upon the wall.
I'm in a phone booth baby, number's scratched on the wall
I'm new in Chicago, got no one else to call.

Said "Call me—Dorita—any time day or night".
You know I'm broke and I'm cold baby, and I hope you'll treat me right.
I'm in a phone booth baby, with the cold wind right outside.

SOLO (FADE)

CHORD OF E MAJOR

CHORD OF E7

CHORD OF E AUGMENTED 7

CHORDS OF F AND G MAJOR

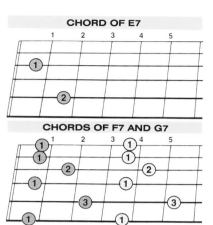

CHORDS OF F7 AND G7

CHORDS OF Cm6 AND Dm6

X Not played

OUR SOLO is based very loosely on Robert Cray's—and they're both based on the blues scale in **A** which we covered in page 56.

Learning a solo pattern is tough. Play the notes slowly until they fit together, then start putting your own rhythmic expression into it.

Obviously, this is just one possible solo that you could play over this chord sequence. Once you've tried ours, have a go at one of your own, using the blues scale as your basis.

HOW TO READ THE SOLO

WE'VE WRITTEN this solo out in tablature. Each line of tablature corresponds exactly to the grid of chords above it. We showed the basic rules of tablature on page 59, but there are a couple of new things here.

In Bar 3 you'll see three notes joined together in one beat. That's our old friend the triplet. Both here and in Bar 10, **H** means hammer on.

At the end Bar 3 there's a note with a tail, followed by a squiggle—that's a note lasting half a beat, followed by a half-beat rest or silence. In other words, if you're tapping your foot there's a gap as you bring the foot up.

A note followed by an arrow should be sustained or held for the length of the arrow. If there's no note on a beat, just hold your fire. Tablature is broken up by vertical bar lines. We've added faint lines separating each beat.

TITLE	KEY	TEMPO
'PHONE BOOTH' (SOLO)	A MINOR	QUITE FAST

BAR 1   Am   Am7   BAR 2   E7+   BAR 3   Am   Am7   BAR 4

BAR 5   Dm7   BAR 6   BAR 7   Am   Am7   BAR 8

BAR 9   Cm6   BAR 10   Dm6   E7+   BAR 11   Am   BAR 12   Am7

BASS GUITAR

WE'VE LOOKED fairly thoroughly at both ways of playing an ordinary six-string guitar—lead and rhythm. Briefly, for anyone interested, here's a basic rundown on playing bass guitar.

The transition from guitar to bass isn't as difficult as you might suppose, and it's possible to make your initial foray in bass technique on any six-string guitar.

The bass guitar has four strings, tuned in the same way as the bottom four strings of a guitar—G, D, A, E—but one octave lower.

So the riffs below can be practised using either a bass or a six-string.

YOU'LL SOON realise that a lot of what we said about lead guitar scales and techniques such as hammer-on can be applied to the bass.

Traditionally, while the lead guitarist is given free rein, the bass player 'chug-a-lugs' along in the background. This doesn't mean that the bass player's role is any less important.

The bass is a vital element of any song, giving it both a rhythm and a melodic guide. When playing bass you should always put your rhythm function first.

If you break up the rhythm, it must be for a reason. Our bassline for 'Phone Booth' illustrates this, setting a firm rhythm but deliberately changing it from time to time, to highlight certain bars.

Harmonically, you should follow the chord sequence. Some bass patterns have relatively few notes; others may be quite complex; but the one thing they usually have in common is that the root note of each chord is played on the first beat of the bar. Above all, keep it simple!

The best known bass player? Paul McCartney in days of yore with rhythm guitarist John Lennon.

BASS GUITAR

HERE ARE some possible basslines for a chord sequence of **C/F/G/C**.

In the first grid you simply finger the notes of **C**, **F** and **G** four beats at a time – 1, 2, 3, 4 (**C**), 1, 2, 3, 4 (**F**), 1, 2, 3, 4 (**G**) back to 1, 2, 3, 4 (**C**). Count each note as you play it.

WHILST THIS simple set-up is musically correct, and often used, it's hardly going to stretch your imagination. So let's introduce a four-note pattern for each four-beat bar.

In the second diagram we start on the **C** note, and add three other notes sympathetic to the **C** chord, **E**, **F** and **G**. For our first shot at this, we'll play all four notes on the **A** string.

You can repeat this exact same order on the string above **A**, the **D** string, although this time you will be playing notes sympathetic to the **F** chord. And you can use exactly the same line of notes for **G**, played on the **A** string. Revert back to the **C** sequence for the final chord.

FINALLY, INSTEAD of sliding along one string at a time, keep it nice and tight by following the third grid—it stays within one hand's span on the fretboard.

BASSLINES

C A3 (2)	**C** A3 (2)	**C** A3 (2)	**C** A3 (2)	**F** D3 (2)	**F** D3 (2)	**F** D3 (2)	**F** D3 (2)
G D5 (3)	**G** D5 (3)	**G** D5 (3)	**G** D5 (3)	**C** A3 (2)	**C** A3 (2)	**C** A3 (2)	**C** A3 (2)
C A3 (1)	**E** A7 (1)	**F** A8 (2)	**G** A10 (3)	**F** D3 (1)	**A** D7 (1)	**B**♭ D8 (2)	**C** D10 (3)
G E3 (1)	**B** E7 (1)	**C** E8 (2)	**D** E10 (3)	**C** A3 (1)	**E** A7 (1)	**F** A8 (2)	**G** A10 (3)
C A3 (2)	**E** D2 (1)	**F** D3 (2)	**G** D5 (3)	**F** D3 (2)	**A** G2 (1)	**B**♭ G3 (2)	**C** G5 (3)
G E3 (2)	**B** A2 (1)	**C** A3 (2)	**D** A5 (3)	**C** A3 (2)	**E** D2 (1)	**F** D3 (2)	**G** D5 (3)

KEY TO GRID

C	Note played
A3	String and fret played
(2)	Finger used

KEY TO COLOURS

☐ Played under a chord of **C major**

☐ Played under a chord of **F major**

☐ Played under a chord of **G major**

There are three distinctive methods for using your right hand while playing bass guitar. In the first picture, the first two fingers of the right hand pluck the strings, in an area just above the pick-up. The second illustration shows the relatively new 'slapping technique', when the thumb 'bounces' off the strings. In the final photograph, the right hand strikes the strings with a plectrum.

The best known bass stance? Bill Wyman holding his bass guitar like a portable double bass.

The best bass player in America? Jazz funk maestro Jaco Pastorius plucks his Fender Jazz bass.

'PHONE BOOTH' (BASS)

KEY TO GRID

F	Note played
D3	String and fret played
(2)	Finger used

0 = Open string

NOW THAT you've tried some simple bass guitar exercises, let's put that to use in the context of a song you should know well by now—'Phone Booth' by Robert Cray.

This is a nice, stripped down bassline which follows two rhythmic patterns. For some bars, you play on the first, third and fourth beats. In others, you play on beats 1, 2½ and 3. This simple device stops the song becoming boring, and gives a different feel to different chords.

If you have recorded a rhythm track in order to practise the solo, you can put it to use again now, by playing bass to it. Better still, once you've mastered the bass part, record that onto your rhythm track and give yourself a really strong backing track for solo practice.

TITLE	KEY	TEMPO
'PHONE BOOTH' (BASS)	A MINOR	QUITE FAST

BAR 1 | | **BAR 2** | | | | **BAR 3** | | | | **BAR 4** | |
A A A | | E | E E | | | A | | C E | A | | C E
A A A | | E | E E | | | A | | A3 D2 | A | | A3 D2
0 0 0 | | 0 | 0 0 | | | 0 | | (2) (1) | 0 | | (2) (1)

Phone booth baby, number's scratched on the wall. I'm in a

BAR 5 | | **BAR 6** | | | | **BAR 7** | | | | **BAR 8** | |
D F A | | D | F A | | | A | | C E | A | | C E
D D3 G2 | | D | D3 G2 | | | A | | A3 D2 | A | | A3 D2
0 (2) (1) | | 0 | (2) (1) | | | 0 | | (2) (1) | 0 | | (2) (1)

Phone booth baby, number's scratched on the wall. I'm

BAR 9 | | **BAR 10** | | | | **BAR 11** | | | | **BAR 12** | |
C C G | | D | E G | | | A | | C E | A | | C E
A3 A3 G3 | | A5 | E E3 | | | A | | A3 D2 | A | | A3 D2
(2) (2) (2) | | (3) | 0 (2) | | | 0 | | (2) (1) | 0 | | (2) (1)

New in Chicago. got no one else to call.

KEY TO COLOURS

☐ Played under a chord of **A minor**
☐ Played under a chord of **A minor 7**
☐ Played under a chord of **E augmented 7**
☐ Played under a chord of **D minor 7**
☐ Played under a chord of **C minor 6**
☐ Played under a chord of **D minor 6**

HOPEFULLY, THIS brief crash course in bass playing will have given you some understanding of what it's all about. We should point out, however, that although you can mess about on the bass strings of a six-string guitar, you won't really know whether it's right for you until you try out a real bass with four heavy strings.

As ever, if you do want to play bass, the bottom line is practice, practice and more practice. The only way to conquer any instrument is to *keep practising!*

463

INSTRUCTION MANUAL

HOW TO READ MUSIC

HERE AS promised is our crash course in reading music the traditional way. Please note, these are only the basics—a detailed study would fill many more pages.

An ability to read music is useful but by no means essential. Many rock musicians survive perfectly well without it.

Having said that, you will definitely need to read music if you hope to become a session musician, and it's useful if you want to send your songs to a publisher, or get other musicians to play them.

For most people, however, the crunch comes when they want to play other people's songs, because all sheet music uses traditional musical notation.

Chords are usually named on sheet music, but for the riffs, melody and bassline you'll need to read music. What follows should help you to do that.

NOTES ON THE GUITAR AT POSITION I

NOTES ON THE GUITAR AT POSITION V

NOTES

WE HAVE divided reading music into two parts: notes (this page) and rhythm (opposite). This page tells you whether a note is **C** or **C#**, etc. The opposite page tells you how long it lasts.

When discussing lengths of notes, we show them in relation to our song grid. Please note that each grid is one bar in length. The divisions and the numbers **1, 2, 3, 4** show the beats.

MUSICAL STAVES

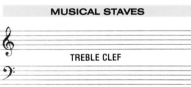

TREBLE CLEF

BASS CLEF

Here are two musical 'staves'. A stave consists of five horizontal lines, and is the traditional equivalent of our music grid.

The two staves are marked with 'clefs'. The treble clef is roughly equivalent to lead/rhythm guitar; the bass clef usually shows the bass guitar part. We won't be paying much more attention to the bass clef—but you read it in the same way as the treble clef.

NOTES ON A STAVE

Musical notes can appear either on or between the notes on a stave. An easy way to remember the notes in the spaces is that, reading upwards, they spell **FACE**. As for the notes on the lines, they stand for that well-known phrase Every Good Boy Deserves Fun.

You'll notice that we have two **E**'s and two **F**'s on our stave. That's because those at the top of the stave are an octave above those at the bottom. In other words, this isn't any old **E** or **F**—they do in fact relate directly to precise notes on the guitar.

The diagram at the top of page 65 shows these notes on the guitar.

HIGHER AND LOWER NOTES

Obviously there are higher and lower notes than we can show on the stave. Lower notes are shown below the stave with short 'ledger' lines through or below them as necessary; higher notes are shown above the stave.

SHARP AND FLAT NOTES

By now you've probably noticed that there are no sharp or flat notes on any of the staves we've looked at. Sharps or flats are signposted by the sharp/flat symbols at the beginning of the stave. A sharp symbol on the top line of the stave means **F** is replaced by **F#**. A flat symbol on the bottom line means **E** is replaced by **E** , and so on.

KEY SIGNATURES

C MAJOR	G MAJOR	D MAJOR	A MAJOR	E MAJOR	F MAJOR
A MINOR	E MINOR	B MINOR	F# MINOR	C# MINOR	D MINOR

The sharp/flat symbols at the start of a stave are known as the key signature, since the presence of certain sharp/flat notes tells you what key you're in.

If there are no sharp/flat notes, the music must be in the keys of **C** major or **A** minor, as they are the only keys with no sharps or flats. If there's one flat symbol on the middle line of the

stave, it means **B** is replaced by **Bb**—and that should tell you that the piece of music is in the key of **F** major or **D** minor, as they are the only keys with that one flat note.

Here (above) are the most common key signatures. If you have trouble working others out, refer to the chart on page 35, which shows which keys have which sharp/flat notes.

UNRELATED NOTES

D SHARP	D FLAT	D NATURAL

When a note unrelated to the key appears—for instance in a dominant seventh chord—the note is preceded by a sharp, flat or 'natural' sign.

CHORDS

C MAJOR	C MAJOR 7	C 7

A chord is shown by stacking all the notes on top of each other, because they are played together.

NOTES ON THE GUITAR

RIGHT AT the start of the Instruction Manual, we showed the 12 musical notes as laid out on one guitar string.

That's not how a guitarist would usually picture them. In the guitarist's eye, the notes form a cluster around each fret, so they can all be played within a short distance of one another.

THE DIAGRAMS on the left show how the notes lie around the first fret and fifth fret—known as Position **I** and Position **V**. Try and work them out on the seventh and tenth frets for yourself later.

THE DIAGRAMS on the right show where you can locate the notes on a music stave on the neck of your guitar.

HOW THE NOTES ON A STAVE RELATE TO POSITION I

Open top **E** string	(E)	(F)	1st fret top **E** string
1st fret **B** string	(C)	(D)	3rd fret **B** string
2nd fret **G** string	(A)	(B)	Open **B** string
3rd fret **D** string	(F)	(G)	Open **G** string
		(E)	2nd fret **D** string

HOW THE NOTES ON A STAVE RELATE TO POSITION V

5th fret **B** string	(E)	(F)	6th fret **B** string
5th fret **G** string	(C)	(D)	7th fret **G** string
7th fret **D** string	(A)	(B)	4th fret **G** string
8th fret **A** string	(F)	(G)	5th fret **D** string
		(E)	7th fret **A** string

BARS

Music staves are divided into bars by regular vertical lines.

LENGTHS OF NOTES

SEMIBREVE (Whole note, lasting full four-beat bar)
(Below: as seen on the music grid)

MINIM (Half note: two minims in a semibreve)
(Below: as seen on the music grid)

CROTCHET (Quarter note, one beat of four-beat bar)
(Below: as seen on the music grid)

QUAVER (Eighth note: eight to a semibreve)
(Below: as seen on the music grid)

SEMIQUAVER (Sixteenth note, a quarter of a beat)
(Below: as seen on the music grid)

These (above) are the different note lengths, in relation to our music grid, and the names given to them.

TIME SIGNATURES

$\frac{4}{4}$ $\frac{3}{4}$ $\frac{2}{4}$

These are the most common time signatures. The top number is beats per bar. The number below describes the beat—4 means it's a 'quarter note' beat. Most rock songs are in **4/4**.

SILENCES OR RESTS

SEMIBREVE REST
(Below: as seen on the music grid)

MINIM REST
(Below: as seen on the music grid)

CROTCHET REST
(Below: as seen on the music grid)

QUAVER REST
(Below: as seen on the music grid)

SEMIQUAVER REST
(Below: as seen on the music grid)

The symbols above represent 'rests' or silences. They also show how notes of different lengths can be used in one bar.

DOTTED AND TIED NOTES

When a note is 'dotted', it lasts for its normal length plus half its length again.

	BAR **1**
	BAR **2**

When two notes of the same pitch are 'tied' (linked by a curved line), the note is held for the total length of both notes. The note is not played twice, it is just sustained.

1 BEAT 1 BEAT 1 BEAT 1 BEAT

When more than one quaver or semiquaver occur on the same beat, unless there is a rest between them they are linked together. Unless they are 'tied' by a curved line, they are played separately.

Notes above the middle line of a stave usually have stems pointing downwards. Notes on the middle line can have either up or down stems.

SIXTHS, NINTHS, THIRTEENTHS

IN THE Chord Directory which begins opposite, there are three types of chord we haven't met before: sixths, ninths and thirteenths. These chords may sound complicated, but they are often remarkably easy to play. You can create added interest in a song by replacing some of the primary chords you already know with these 'jazz' chords. The trick is knowing when to use them.

Here are some basic substitution rules, to show which chords can replace which. And while we're on the subject, we might as well chuck in some ways of using major sevenths, minor sevenths and diminished chords too . . .

TO START with, experiment with each 'rule' by itself. Choose a song which has simple chords, and gradually substitute more difficult ones. You'll be surprised by the way these new chords give a song a much jazzier feel.

First, you need to work out what key the song is in. Then you should work out where each chord stands in relation to the root major chord, and number them like this: Root chord = Chord I. Chord derived from second note = Chord II. Chord derived from third note = Chord III. And so on, remembering that in Roman numerals V is five, VI is six, and VII is seven.

Rule 1. A major chord can be replaced by a major seventh chord or a sixth chord. So C can be replaced by C maj 7 or C6.

Rule 2. Chord I can be replaced by III minor 7 or IV minor 7 (which is of course the relative minor 7).

So in the key of C, C major can be replaced by Em7 or Am7. And in the key of G, G major can be replaced by Bm7 or Em7.

Combining these first two rules together, in the key of C, C major can be replaced by C maj 7, C6, Em7 or Am7.

Rule 3. Chord V is usually the dominant seventh chord. In jazzier pieces, it can be replaced by the ninth or thirteenth chords.

So in the key of C, the dominant seventh G7 can be replaced by G9 or G13.

Rule 4. Chord VI is usually the relative minor. It can be replaced by a relative minor seventh, or by III♭ diminished, or by I major 6.

So in the key of C, Am can be replaced by Am7, E♭ diminished or C6.

SIXTHS, NINTHS, THIRTEENTHS

SIXTH CHORDS

A SIXTH chord is formed by taking the major triad – the first, third and fifth notes in the major scale – and adding the sixth note.

In the key of C major, you take the triad (CEG) and add the sixth note, A. So C6 has the notes CEGA.

In the key of G major, you take the triad (GBD) and add the sixth note, E. So G6 has the notes GBDE.

NINTH CHORDS

A NINTH chord is a little harder to explain. It is in fact an extension of a dominant seventh chord.

As you know, a dominant seventh chord consists of the major triad, plus the seventh note in the minor scale.

So C7 has the notes CEGB♭. And G7 has the notes GBDF.

To form a ninth chord, we add in the ninth note of the major scale – that is, the second note from the next octave.

So C9 has the notes CEGB♭D. And G9 has the notes GBDFA.

If you look at some of the ninth chords in the Chord Directory, you'll notice that they don't all have all five of the required notes. But whatever notes may be missing from the chord, you'll always find the ninth note present.

THIRTEENTH CHORDS

A THIRTEENTH chord is formed in a similar way to a ninth. Again, we take the dominant seventh chord. But this time we add the thirteenth note in the major scale – that is, the sixth note from the next octave.

So C13 has the notes GEGB♭A. And G13 has the notes GBDFE.

CHORD OF C SIXTH

C6 – or C major sixth, to give it its full title – is like A minor with the little finger added in a C position.

CHORD OF D SIXTH

Try this interesting sequence D, D major 7, D7 and D6. Like the others, D6 is a four or five-string chord.

CHORD OF A NINTH

A major ninth is in fact A dominant seventh with the ninth note B added on the third string. The bottom two strings are optional.

CHORD OF E THIRTEENTH

E major 13 is similar to E7. The thirteenth note C# is added on the second string. Play all six strings.

CHORD DIRECTORY

This 13-page Chord Directory shows you how to play most of the chords you are ever likely to need.

Each of the first 12 pages is devoted to one key. For each key, we show nine different chords: major, minor, seventh, major seventh, minor seventh, sixth, ninth and thirteenth.

Each chord is shown in three different formations, giving you the same chord in different parts of the fretboard. The three versions of a chord are displayed on one guitar neck, in different colour dots.

Dots of the same colour comprise one chord shape.

A coloured cross means *do not play* that string when forming the chord using dots of that colour.

A string with no dots or crosses of a certain colour is *played open*.

Finger numbers are marked in black on each coloured dot.

And that's it: a simple system giving over 300 chord shapes.

As you know, the chord referred to in the Chord Directory as the seventh is also known as the dominant seventh.

Finally, there's a page devoted to diminished and augmented chords.

CONTENTS

KEY OF C

KEY OF D

470

471

KEY OF E

CHORD DIRECTORY

KEY OF F# (Gb)

475

KEY OF Bb (A#)

DIMINISHED AND AUGMENTED CHORDS

DIMINISHED CHORDS

IN THIS 'Strange But True' episode, we show the unusual situation of *one* chord shape with four different names. Believe it or not, there are only four diminished chords – so each has to serve for four of the 12 keys.

Here's how it works. Diminished chords are derived from the diminished scale. The diminished scale is a four-note scale which divides the 12 notes precisely in three.

Each scale gives us one chord, consisting of the four notes in that scale. And that chord can be named after any of those four notes.

So the first scale in our diagram gives us a chord which can be called **C** diminished or **D#/E♭** diminished or **F#/G♭** diminished or **A** diminished.

A DIMINISHED CHORD is normally used in a key for which it is the seventh note/chord. For instance, the seventh note in the scale of **C** is **B**. So **Bdim** is the diminished chord used in the key of **C**, even though it contains a **G#** note which is not in the key of **C**.

Try them out for yourself on a few chord sequences – for instance:

    Bdim C Edim F
    Bdim Am7 F#dim G.

You'll notice how, like dominant sevenths, they have an 'unfinished' quality. For this reason, they make good stepping stones between more important chords – try for instance **Gm7** to **G#dim** to **Am7**.

DIMINISHED SCALES			
C	D#	F#	A
C#	E	G	B♭
D	F	G#	B

CHORD OF D DIMINISHED OR F DIMINISHED OR G#/A♭ DIMINISHED OR B DIMINISHED

CHORD OF C DIMINISHED OR F#/G♭ DIMINISHED OR A DIMINISHED OR D#/E♭ DIMINISHED

CHORD OF E DIMINISHED OR G DIMINISHED OR A#/B♭ DIMINISHED OR C#/D♭ DIMINISHED

Each of these diminished chords is a four-note chord. The bottom two strings are not played.

AUGMENTED CHORDS

AUGMENTED CHORDS are the partners in crime to diminished chords. While the diminished scale cuts the 12 notes into quarters, the augmented scale chops them in six. This means that there are just two six-note augmented scales.

As with diminished chords, an augmented chord can have several names and work in several keys.

The augmented chord is a triad – first, third and fifth in the scale. But you'll notice that whether you start on **C**, **E** or **G#**, the first/third/fifth triad is always the same: **CEG#**.

This chord is known as either **C** augmented (**C+**) or **E** augmented (**E+**) or **G#/A♭** augmented (**G#+/A♭+**).

From which you may deduce that just four augmented chord shapes are required to cover all 12 keys.

Like diminished chords, augmented chords make good 'passing' chords between more important chords.

CHORD OF C AUGMENTED OR E AUGMENTED OR G#/A♭ AUGMENTED

AUGMENTED SCALES							
C	D	E	F#	G#	B♭	C	
C#	D#	F	G	A	B	C#	

CHORD OF C#/D♭ AUGMENTED OR F AUGMENTED OR A AUGMENTED

CHORD OF D AUGMENTED OR F#/G♭ AUGMENTED OR A#/B♭ AUGMENTED

CHORD OF D#/E♭ AUGMENTED OR G AUGMENTED OR B AUGMENTED

Each of these augmented chords is a four-note chord. The bottom two strings are not played.

Glossary

action: Height of strings above the guitar's fingerboard. A low action makes it easy for a player to form notes and chords with his/her fretting hand, but may compromise the instrument's tone and cause string buzzing. High action often improves and boosts the sound, but can lead to playing difficulties.

active: Guitars with active circuitry have volume and tone controls that offer an electronic boost *(gain)* to the signals they process. Standard, passive guitar controls can provide only attenuation.

Alnico: Type of magnet widely used in pickup manufacture. The name is derived from the magnet's constituent materials: aluminum, nickel and cobalt.

archtop: Guitar with top carved or pressed into an arched shape (cf *flat-top*).

back pickup: Pickup mounted closest to the *bridge*, providing a cutting, treble-rich tone often favored for solo passages.

binding, purfling: Strip(s) of wood, plastic or other material decorating the edges of a guitar's body.

bout: Most guitars have bodies shaped like a figure-of-eight; the wider sections above and below their waists are referred to as upper and lower bouts. *Archtops* and *flat-tops* are frequently categorized by the maximum width of their lower bouts (17 inches/43.2 cm, 18 inches/45.7 cm, etc.)

bridge: Unit mounted on the lower part of a guitar's *top*, and fitted with one or more *saddles* of metal, wood or other materials. It sets the end of the strings' vibrating length (which begins at the *nut*), and can usually be adjusted to affect their height and intonation.

burl: Naturally-occurring knot in a piece of wood.

carved top: Arched guitar top shaped by hand or machine carving (cf *pressed top*)

classical guitar: Instrument modelled on the designs of Spanish guitar-maker Antonio de Torres (1817-1892) and his successors, with six gut (later nylon) strings. It is played *fingerstyle* with the nails or (very occasionally) fingertips.

CNC: Computer Numeric Control. A method of controlling high precision machine tools with computers during guitar manufacture.

coil-tap: Circuit that converts a *humbucking pickup* to *single-coil* operation.

combo, combo amp: Amplifier and loudspeaker(s) combined in a single, portable unit.

course: Pairs of strings tuned in unison or in octaves, and fretted and struck simultaneously.

cutaway: Incision in the upper part of the guitar body adjacent to the neck, allowing the player's fretting hand to reach the highest positions more easily. See *Florentine cutaway*, *Venetian cutaway*

decal: Name tag or other symbol/trademark applied to an instrument via a transfer or similar means. Most often seen on guitar *headstocks*.

digital modelling: Simulation of the tonal characteristics of amplifiers, speakers and associated analog devices, created with microprocessors or other computer-derived technology.

Dreadnought: Large-bodied *flat-top* acoustic guitar design first introduced by the Martin company in the early 1930s, and named after a famous class of battleship. The Dreadnought style has been widely emulated by other guitar makers. See *Jumbo*

drone string: Unfretted string, tuned to a preset pitch, fitted to harp- and sitar-guitars.

Electric Spanish: Term used by Gibson (and some other manufacturers) for electric guitars designed to be played in the "traditional" position (i.e. held in the arms). The name (and the Gibson catalog prefix ES) differentiates these instruments from electric *Hawaiian guitars* (given the EH prefix by Gibson), which are placed horizontally on the performer's lap and fretted with a steel bar.

feedback: Howling or squealing effect caused when an electric guitar picks up its own amplified sound from a nearby loudspeaker. Some rock players deliberately induce feedback and use it as a musical tool.

fingerpicks: Plastic, metal or tortoiseshell attachments, worn on the fingers and/or thumb of a steel-strung guitarist's striking hand, and used to increase the power and clarity of *fingerstyle* playing.

fingerstyle: Term applied to various methods of striking the strings with fingers and thumb rather than a *plectrum*. Classical guitarists normally pick with the nails of their thumb, index, middle and ring fingers. Players of steel-strung guitars deploy a wider range of fingerstyle techniques, and often use *fingerpicks*.

flat-top guitar: Steel-strung guitar with a flat (i.e. not arched) top.

floating pickup: Pickup that makes no contact with a guitar's top, thereby preserving the instrument's acoustic integrity. (Pickups mounted directly onto the top tend to deaden its vibrations, compromising the acoustic sound.)

Florentine cutaway: Term used by Gibson to describe the sharp-horned *cutaway* seen on guitars such as the ES-175 (see pages 12-13). cf *Venetian cutaway*

front pickup: Pickup mounted closest to the neck, providing a warm, rounded tone often favored for chordal and rhythm playing.

full-body, full-depth: Hollow body electric guitar with a depth (typically c.3"/7.62cm) equivalent to that found on acoustic models.

gain: Boost provided to an electronic signal by an amplifying circuit.

Harp guitar: Guitar with additional unfretted bass strings providing extended range. Developed by a number of late-19th/early 20th century luthiers, and recently revived, in a radically altered solid-body form, by Californian luthier Steve Klein (see pages 122-123).

Hawaiian guitar: Guitar designed to be played in a horizontal position on the performer's lap. Notes and chords are formed using a metal bar instead of the fingers of the fretting hand, permitting the characteristic glissandi associated with Hawaiian guitar styles. The instrument's *action* is higher than a standard guitar's, and its neck profile is frequently square. Hawaiian guitars are also known as *lap steels*.

headstock: Section of guitar neck above the nut. The *machine heads* are mounted on it.

humbucker, humbucking pickup: Twin-coil electro-magnetic pickup invented by Gibson engineer Seth Lover (1910-1997). Like the *single-coil pickup* from which it was developed, the unit is mounted under a guitar's strings. As these are struck, they create variations in the pickup's magnetic field and generate electrical currents in its double coils; the resultant signal is amplified and fed to loudspeakers. One of the humbucking pickup's coils is wired out-of-phase with the other; this has the effect of cancelling or helping to suppress ("buck") hum and noise.

jack socket: Insertion point for the jack plug that connects an electric guitar to an amplifier via a lead.

Jumbo: Large-bodied, *flat-top* acoustic guitar design first introduced by Gibson in 1934 as a competitor to Martin's *Dreadnought*. Jumbo-style instruments have subsequently been produced by many other *luthiers*.

laminate: Material made by bonding together two or more thin sheets of different woods or other constituents.

lap steel: Synonym for *Hawaiian guitar*.

locking nut: Type of *nut* often fitted to guitars with advanced *vibrato units*. It features bolts or other devices to prevent strings going out of tune when the vibrato is used.

lutherie: The practice of making guitars and other stringed instruments.

luthier: Maker of stringed musical instruments, including guitars, violins and lutes (the term is derived from the French word 'luth').

Lyrachord: Carbon-fiber material developed and used by the Kamen company for the backs of their Ovation guitars.

machine head: Geared string tuning mechanism mounted in the guitar's *headstock*.

Masonite: Type of hardboard used in the construction of Danelectro guitars (see pages 90-91) and their replicas.

MIDI: Musical Instrument Digital Interface - standard protocol for the exchange of performance data between synthesisers, sequencers and other digitally controlled devices. Some specially equipped guitars can send and receive MIDI information.

monitor: Small onstage loudspeaker allowing a musician to hear all or part of the sound being fed to a *PA system*.

neck-through-body: Method of guitar construction in which a single piece of wood is used for the neck and the center section of the instrument's body.

nut: Block of bone, ivory, ebony, metal or synthetic material mounted at the *headstock* end of the neck. It sets the height and position of the strings as they pass through the grooved slots cut into it, and also defines the start of the vibrating length of each open string (see *bridge*).

PA system: PA stands for 'public address', and refers to the system of amplifiers and loudspeakers used at live performances to boost signals from onstage microphones and other sound sources.

parallel; Pickup coils are normally wired in "series" (i.e. with the same current flowing in turn through each of them). Some guitar makers equip their instruments with a switch to convert the pickups to "parallel", an electrical mode in which the same voltage is applied to each coil. This creates a thinner sound, somewhat similar to the effect of using a *coil-tap*, but with the advantage that a parallel-switched humbucking pickup retains its noise-reducing capacity, as both its coils are still in circuit.

passive: Standard guitar volume and tone controls are passive (i.e. without *gain* circuitry). They can reduce output level and attenuate higher frequencies, but are unable to boost signals from the instrument's pickups.

phase: The electrical polarity of one pickup or coil relative to another. Pickups on some guitars can be switched out-of-phase, creating a distinctive, slightly hollow-sounding tone.

pick: See *plectrum*.

pickguard: See *scratchplate*.

piezo-electric pickup: A transducer that converts vibrations from a guitar body or bridge into electrical currents which can then be amplified and fed to loudspeakers. Piezo-electric pickups provide a cleaner, more uncolored sound than electro-magnetic pickups (see *humbucker, single-coil pickup*).

plectrum, pick: Thin, pointed piece of plastic, tortoiseshell or other material, held between the thumb and forefinger of a guitarist's striking hand and used to pick or strum the instrument's strings.

pressed top: Arched guitar top pressed into shape (using heat or other means) instead of being carved out. (cf *carved top*)

purfling: See *binding*

resonator guitar: Guitar originally developed by John Dopyera (1893-1988), fitted with one or more metal resonator assemblies. These instruments were manufactured by the National and Dobro companies, which merged in 1935.

reverse body: Design where the instrument's treble wing or "horn" is larger/higher than the one on its opposite (bass) side.

saddle: Platform made from wood, metal or other material, mounted on (or forming part of) the *bridge* of the guitar at the point where the strings pass across it. Many electric guitar bridges feature individually adjustable saddles for each string.

scratchplate, pickguard: Protective plate of plastic, tortoiseshell or other material, suspended (just below string height) above a guitar's *top*, or screwed/glued directly onto its body. It is designed to protect the instrument's finish from damage by stray *plectrum* strokes.

semi-acoustic guitar: A guitar fitted with one or more electro-magnetic pickups, but also featuring a hollow body and some degree of acoustic sound.

semi-solid guitar: Guitar combining solid construction (usually at its with hollow body cavities. The most famous example is probably the Gibson ES-335 (see pages 26-29).

series: See *parallel*

single-coil pickup: Electro-magnetic pickup fitted with a single coil (as opposed to the *humbucker's* twin coils) and mounted beneath a guitar's strings. Their vibrations create variations in the pickup's magnetic field and generate electrical currents in the coil; these are amplified and fed to loudspeakers.

solid, solid body: Electric guitar with no resonating cavities, constructed from a solid slab (or glued-together pieces) of wood.

soundhole(s): Hole(s), normally round, oval, or f-shaped, cut into a guitar's *top*. Their original purpose was to project the instrument's acoustic sound, but on many electric instruments, their function is chiefly or exclusively decorative.

stop tailpiece, stud tailpiece: Metal block-type *tailpiece* found on many *solid* and *semi-solid* electrics. Unlike the more traditional hinged trapeze tailpiece, the "stud" or "stop" unit is attached to the body only a little way below the bridge.

tailpiece: Metal or wooden fitting, installed below a guitar's bridge, and acting as an anchor for its string ends. Traditional *archtop* guitar-style tailpieces (also seen on some *solid-body* instruments), are often hinged and in a trapeze shape. Later, units such as the *stop* or *stud tailpiece* (qv) became popular with many makers and players.

thinline: Archtop electric guitar with reduced depth (typically c.1 3/4"/4.4cm) compared with its acoustic counterparts.

top: The "face" of the guitar; its uppermost body surface, with pickups, *bridge* etc. mounted on it. The tops of *semi-acoustic* and many *semi-solid* instruments feature *soundholes* and bracing on their undersides.

tremolo arm, tremolo unit, "trem": See *vibrato unit*

truss-rod: Metal bar inserted into a guitar neck to improve its strength and rigidity. Most steel-strung acoustic and electric guitars have adjustable truss-rods whose tension can be changed to correct bowing or warping in the neck.

Truss-rods are not normally fitted to classical guitars.

Venetian cutaway: Term used by Gibson to describe the rounded-horn *cutaway* seen on guitars such as the ES-5 (pages 14-15). cf *Florentine cutaway*

vibrato unit, vibrato arm: Mechanical device, usually attached to or built into a guitar's *tailpiece*, which allows the player to create pitch bends by loosening the instrument's strings with a lever or arm. *Vibrato* is the musical term for rapid pitch fluctuation, while *tremolo* is the effect produced by a series of fast repetitions of the same note. Therefore, "vibrato unit" is the correct name for pitch-bending devices of this kind, although many manufacturers and players refer to them as "tremolos" or "trems".

whammy bar: Nickname (used by rock and especially heavy metal guitarists) for a *vibrato* or *tremolo* arm.

Wildwood: Type of dyed wood produced in Scandinavia and used by Fender on some of its instruments (see pages 40-41).

X-bracing: Method of strengthening the tops of guitars and controlling/modifying their tonal characteristics by using struts crossed in an "X" pattern. It was first popularized by C.F. Martin (1786-1873), and has become a standard method of bracing for *flat-top* and some *archtop* designs.

Resources

Contact details for most of the luthiers and manufacturers featured in this book are listed here. Company websites (where these are provided) are usually the best places to seek information about current models, specifications etc.

AER

Christine-Englerth-Straße 30
45665 Recklinghausen
Germany
www.aer-amps.de

ALEMBIC

3005 Wiljan Court
Santa Rosa
CA 95407
www.alembic.com

AMPEG

St. Louis Music, Inc.
1400 Ferguson Avenue
St. Louis
MO 63133
www.ampeg.com

TOM ANFIELD

c/o Ritz Music
3a Lacy Road
London SW15 1NH, UK
www.guitar-centre.com
/mainpages/about_ta.htm

ASHDOWN

c/o Positive Impact Marketing
Box 167
Winsted CT 06098
www.ashdownmusic.co.uk

ROBERT BENEDETTO

www.benedetto-guitars.com
See Fender website for
Guild/Benedettos

BREEDLOVE GUITAR COMPANY

19885 8th Street
Tumalo
OR 97701
www.breedloveguitars.com

JOHN BUSCARINO

2348 Wide Horizon Drive
Franklin
NC 28734
www.buscarino.com

MARK CAMPELLONE

5 Mapleville Road
Smithfield
RI 02828
www.mcampellone.com/Guitar/index.htm

CHAPMAN STICK

6011 Woodlake Avenue
Woodland Hills
CA 91367-3238
www.stick.com

COLLINGS

11025 Signal Hill Drive
Austin
TX 78737
www.collingsguitars.com

CRATE

St. Louis Music, Inc.
1400 Ferguson Avenue
St. Louis
MO 63133
www.crateamps.com

0DIGITECH

8760 South Sandy Parkway
Sandy
UT 84070
www.digitech.com

PATRICK EGGLE GUITARS

Queen's Chamber
Old Snow Hill
Birmingham B4 6HW
United Kingdom
(no website)

ELECTRO-HARMONIX

20 Cooper Square
New York
NY 10003
www.ehx.com

FENDER

www.fender.com

FYLDE

Hartness Road
Gilwilly Industrial Estate
Penrith
Cumbria CA11 9BD
United Kingdom
www.fyldeguitars.com

G&L

2548 Fender Avenue
Fullerton
CA 92631
www.glguitars.com

GIBSON

www.gibson.com

GODIN

19420 Avenue Clark-Graham

Baie D'Urfé

Québec

Canada H9X JR8

www.godinguitars.com

JAMES GOODALL GUITARS

PO Box 3542

Kailua-Kona

HI 96745-3542

www.goodallguitars.com

GRETSCH

PO Box 2468

Savannah

GA 31402

www.gretsch.com

GUILD

www.guildguitars.com

or see Fender website

HERITAGE GUITARS

225 Parsons St.

Kalamazoo

MI 49007

www.heritageguitar.com

THOMAS HUMPHREY GUITARS

1167 Bruynswick Road

Gardiner

NY 12525

www.thomashumphrey.com

JACKSON GUITAR COMPANY

PO Box 961077

Fort Worth

TX 76161-0077

www.jacksonguitars.com

JERRY JONES GUITARS

www.jerryjonesguitars.com

KLEIN GUITARS

521 Broadway

Sonoma

CA 95476

www.kleinguitars.com

JEAN LARRIVÉE GUITARS

780 E. Cordova Street

Vancouver, BC

Canada V6A 1M3

www.larrivee.com

LASKIN

26 Noble Street

No. 12, Toronto

Ontario

Canada M6K 2C9

www.williamlaskin.com

LINE 6

www.Line6.com

LOWDEN (USA)

14950 F.A.A. Boulevard

Fort Worth

TX 76155

www.lowdenguitars.com

HUGH MANSON

www.mansons.co.uk/manson_guitars/hand
-made-guitars.html

LINDA MANZER

www.manzer.com

MARSHALL (USA)

316 South Service Road

Melville

New York

NY 11747-3201

www.marshallamps.com

MARTIN GUITAR COMPANY

513 Sycamore Street

Nazareth

PA 18064

www.martinguitars.com

MESA ENGINEERING

1317 Ross Street

Petaluma

CA 94954

www.mesaboogie.com

JOHN MONTELEONE

P.O. Box 52

Islip

NY 11751

www.monteleone.net

NATIONAL RESO-PHONIC GUITARS, INC.

871 Via Esteban #C

San Luis Obispo

CA 93401

www.nationalguitars.com

ORANGE MUSIC ELECTRONIC COMPANY (USA)

P.O. Box 421849

Atlanta

GA 30342

www.orange-amps.com

OVATION

Kaman Music Corporation
P.O. Box 507
Bloomfield
CT 06002-0507
www.ovationguitars.com

PARKER GUITARS

P.O. Box 388
Wilmington
MA 01887
www.parkerguitars.com

PEAVEY

www.peavey.com

PENSA GUITARS

169 West 48th Street
New York
NY 10036
www.rudysmusic.com

PIGNOSE INDUSTRIES

3430 Precision Drive
N. Las Vegas
NV 89030
www.pignoseamps.com

POLYTONE

www.murchmusic.com/polytone.htm

PRS GUITARS

380 Log Canoe Circle
Stevensville
MD 21666
www.prsguitars.com

RAEZER'S EDGE

726 Girard Avenue
Swarthmore
PA 19081
www.raezers-edge.com

RICKENBACKER INTERNATIONAL CORPORATION

3895 South Main Street
Santa Ana
CA 92707
www.rickenbacker.com

ROSENDEAN FINE GUITARS

6 Lime Grove
Woking
Surrey GU22 9PW
United Kingdom
www.rosendean.com

SANTA CRUZ GUITAR COMPANY

151 Harvey West Boulevard Suite C.
Santa Cruz
CA 95060 USA
www.santacruzguitar.com

ERIC SCHOENBERG

106 Main Street
Tiburon
CA 94920
www.om28.com/es/

GARY SOUTHWELL

Chaucer Court Workshop
Chaucer Street
Nottingham NG1 5LP
United Kingdom

TAYLOR GUITARS

1940 Gillespie Way
El Cajon
CA 92020 USA
www.taylorguitars.com

ALAN TIMMINS

F1 Resophonic Instruments
42 Owen Avenue
Long Eaton
Nottingham NG10 2FS
United Kingdom

TRACE ELLIOT (USA)

1150 Bowers Road
Elgin
IL 60123
www.trace-elliot.com

RICK TURNER

815 Almar Avenue
Santa Cruz
CA 95060
www.renaissanceguitars.com

MIKE VANDEN

www.vanden.co.uk

VOX (USA)

316 South Service Road
Melville
NY 11747-3201
www.voxamps.co.uk

YAMAHA (USA)

6600 Orangethorpe Avenue
Buena Park
CA 90620
www.yamaha.com

Index

Page numbers in *italic* refer to illustrations

Picture Credits